Performing Music History

John C. Tibbetts · Michael Saffle
William A. Everett

Performing Music History

Musicians Speak First-Hand about Music
History and Performance

To Du——uane!
My Starbucks coffee
buddy!
Best!
John Tibbetts
K.C. 15 Jan '19

Forewords by Emanuel Ax and Lawrence Kramer

palgrave
macmillan

John C. Tibbetts
Department of Film and Media Studies
  University of Kansas
  Lawrence, KS, USA

William A. Everett
Conservatory of Music and Dance
  University of Missouri-Kansas City
  Kansas City, MO, USA

Michael Saffle
Department of Religion and Culture
  Virginia Tech
  Blacksburg, VA, USA

ISBN 978-3-319-92470-0 ISBN 978-3-319-92471-7 (eBook)
https://doi.org/10.1007/978-3-319-92471-7

Library of Congress Control Number: 2018951048

Cover credit: Painting by John C. Tibbetts, after the series of images by J. J. Grandville, et al, collectively entitled "Concert a mittraile," ("Concert of Gunfire"), 1845–46
Cover design by Ran Shauli

This Palgrave Macmillan imprint is published by the registered company Springer Nature Switzerland AG
The registered company address is: Gewerbestrasse 11, 6330 Cham, Switzerland

Epigraph

I drink to those artists whom nothing can debase or dishearten, the true, the valiant, and the strong. Let us band together and be patient, energetic, and proud. Let us prove to the peoples distracted by so many grave concerns that if we are the last born of civilization's children and have only for a moment enjoyed its deepest affection, we were worthy of it. Possibly they will then understand how much art would suffer if we were to perish.

Hector Berlioz, *Evenings with the Orchestra*

Foreword I

Speaking of Musicians

We musicians love to talk about our work. Not content with mere music performance, we often enjoy opportunities to comment on what we are up and what we
know about the history of the music we play.

There are so many sides to talking about music and music history. There's the
music, which is endless. There's each musician's approach. And there are the traditions surrounding those performers we heard as kids. It's not so different from
any other subject you're interested in. I happen to be a huge fan of sports. I watch
football games and I watch tennis matches, my two favorite sports. And I welcome
any chance to hear a great quarterback talk about what's happening on the field.
That's instructive on many levels, and I can appreciate what's going on all the
more.

It's true we have already lots of books filled with memoirs, essays, and conversations with musicians. Some of my favorites include books about cellist Gregor
Piatogorsky, pianists Claudio Arrau and Glenn Gould (the latter one of my very
favorite books), and, more recently, scholar artists like Charles Rosen and Alfred
Brendel. I particularly enjoy André Previn's memoirs about Hollywood. They're
wonderful and we couldn't do without them. But there's something especially
wonderful about hearing the *performer's actual voice* in all its inflections and timbres and intonations—something as nuanced in its own way as the touch on the
keyboard. So many of us are so accustomed to performance that it's wonderful to
have opportunities like this to talk about this crazy profession of ours. I hope that
if people enjoy our work, they won't mind listening to us talk about it and maybe
learn something more about it—and us—in the process. You may find, moreover,
that informal conversations like these can go off in freer, more unexpected directions than what you would find on the written page.

A few years ago I had a wonderful experience sitting down with my colleagues
and friends at the Library of Congress to talk about piano performance and traditions. The late Eugene Istomin presided over our group, which included Charles

Fig. 1 Emanuel Ax

Rosen, Leon Fleisher, and Yefim Bronfman. These conversations, which are now available on video through the Library of Congress Website, were a rare opportunity for all of us to get together and just let the topics carry us where they will.[1] And at this writing I'm planning a series for the CBC about ten selected piano

---

[1] For more information about this and other issues, see "For additional investigation" at the end of the present volume.

concertos, talking about them as well as playing them. It's the world we live in. Pianists like us are seen and heard in so many different ways via so many different media. We find ourselves talking from the stage, too, which didn't use to be very acceptable. I find myself speaking more and more during recitals. It makes me relax and makes me feel that I'm communicating more with individuals. I'm even happy if they respond to me. Why not? All this sort of thing should be part of the awareness and training of young pianists today as they enter the profession.

But ultimately there's always the music. The music. On some level you enjoy it without referring to words at all. It's a mistake to feel that you need education before you listen. The best education is to just listen. And maybe then there will be a time when you will want to know about it. That's the way I am with sports. To me it's the exact same analogy. I knew nothing about football when I arrived in this country. And after a time I became fascinated by it. And now I'm to the point where I understand the referees' signs. I'm up to date on all of that. It's very exciting. It makes me a kind of participant in a sense. Now, maybe the readers of *Performing Music History* can also join in on the fun.

As for me, I'd love to be a coach for the New York Giants!

New York, USA,   Emanuel Ax
                                                                                           The Juilliard School

Emanuel Ax began his studies in Warsaw, where his family settled when he was seven years old, then at The Juilliard School in New York City. Today he is a member of Juilliard's piano faculty. Ax has twice won Grammeys, on both occasions (1995 and 2004) for his recordings of the piano sonatas of Franz Joseph Haydn (1732–1809). In 2007 he became a Fellow of the American Academy of Arts and Sciences.

Foreword II

Score, Performance, History

Any performing musician is also a historian. No matter what genre or tradition a singer or instrumentalist embraces, there is a genre, there is a tradition, to contend with. [Friedrich] Nietzsche [1844–1900] once said that the best way to honor one's teacher is to break with the teaching. He might have added that it takes considerable learning to do that. For some musicians, the past stretches back years or decades or perhaps a century. For others, in particular for classical musicians like those whose words compose most of this volume, it may stretch back many centuries. Classical musicians serve competing imperatives. Their performances must speak to the present day and at the same time speak for the past, sometimes the distant past. To link the past and the present, the performers need reliable materials to work with and a credible sense of how what they play may have sounded under different historical circumstances. Only then can they know what to do with the peculiar form of writing from which they must make music: the score.

The rise of interest over the past half century in historically informed performances and in scores stripped of editorial barnacles has unquestionably broadened our auditory horizons but it has not been without controversy. The search for "authenticity" inspired some musicians and exasperated others. A classic case in point is an essay that Richard Taruskin published in the journal *Early Music* in 1984. At the time, the aim of fully recapturing the auditory past had caught the imagination of many performers intent on reviving early music. Taruskin vigorously opposed the "purism" and "positivism" that he believed had ensued, reminding those involved that the auditory past can never be recaptured, only reconstructed. The reconstruction is necessarily imperfect and depends on latter-day choices and attitudes:

> Everyone by now agrees (if only for the sake of argument) that we will never really know "what was." But that is not what we want to find out, anyway. We want to find out what

Fig. 2 Lawrence Kramer

was, or rather, *is* good for the music—and for ourselves. And of course by that I mean ourselves in the actual here and now, not some projection of ourselves into an imaginary past.[2]

Although present-day attitudes have become more nuanced than those Taruskin was denouncing, the reminder is still resonant, especially when we realize that

---

[2] Richard Taruskin, "'The Authenticity Movement Can Become a Positivistic Purgatory, Literalistic and Dehumanizing,'" *Early Music* 12 (1984): 3–12, at 10.

the demand for creative reconstruction, well informed but independent minded, applies not just to early music but to *all* fully scored music, from the most canonical repertoire pieces to the newest compositions and those still in the making. The most accurate notes and the fullest historical knowledge are only the beginning, and sometimes barely that.

The musicians who speak for themselves in these pages take up varying positions on the question of authenticity, which is a perennial one. That is part of what makes what they have to say absorbing. But all of the classical musicians, and some others, too, all in their individual ways, wrestle with the equally perennial question that shapes the everyday life of classical music. What do you do with the score?

The score has had a hard time of it in recent years. Written music, music imbued with a cultural preference for literacy, plays a dark role in Taruskin's massive *Oxford History of Western Music*.[3] Scores have become suspect as sources of unwarranted or excessive authority, as incarnations of an oppressive reverence for the finished musical work (which does not exist), as symbols of the lost cultural supremacy of classical music, as editorial versions masquerading as original texts, and as carriers of an imperfect notation that has to be overcome as often as it is followed if one is to produce a compelling musical performance. Nicholas Cook, whose book *Beyond the Score* goes deeply into these questions, has proposed regarding the score not as a fixed template for the music it supposedly inscribes but as a script in the dramatic or cinematic sense, a guideline to be modified in production and performance.[4]

The trouble with these views, which certainly have some validity to them, is that they do not seem to reflect the day-to-day activity of music-making by classical performers and composers. In my experience, anyway, the performers do not treat their scores as objects of reverence but as tools of the trade that can and should be marked up, cut, pasted, and scribbled on at need. This is especially true when the score involved is not a full score but a performance part. At the same time, as a composer I labor hard over my scores (which music notation software happily makes easy), but I have never expected them to be "followed" in some literal way that I would be hard put to define. What I most want from a performance is to hear, not what I have done in the score, but what the performers can do *with* it. I want to learn something, to hear something new or unexpected.

Besides, both performers and composers have surely always assumed that the notes on the page are approximations at best. Whoever supposed that playing the notes is playing the music? The rare exceptions prove the rule. I have even been told (by the performer involved) of one "complexist" composer who became upset when a soloist actually managed to execute all the multilayered rhythmic

---

[3] Taruskin, *The Oxford History of Western Music*, 5 vols. (Oxford and New York: Oxford University Press, 2009).

[4] Nicholas Cook, *Beyond the Score: Music as Performance* (New York: Oxford University Press, 2013), 260.

and metric relationships in his score, which he then vowed to rewrite so that such "fidelity" would be (even more) impossible.

Nonetheless, fidelity of *some* sort remains the norm in classical music performance. It is not easy to answer the question "fidelity to what?" but whatever the answer, a performance generally preserves the object of this fidelity more strictly than a film or play production preserves the letter of its script. A score is not a lead sheet. There is no reason to abandon the script metaphor, but it does need to be made one among others. Because music cannot simply "exist" like a statue or a painting, or even like a text, we need multiple metaphors for its mode of existence. Or rather for its modes of existence, because a classical composition does not exist in the same way as a popular song or folk song or jazz improvisation—the list goes on. So the question before us is limited to musical compositions: fully scored "works" (whether we believe in the reality of works or not).

In this context it may be helpful to compare the performance of a score to a translation, in the special sense of Walter Benjamin (1892–1940), whose counter-intuitive remark in his 1923 essay "The Task of the Translator" states that translations of classic texts are not addressed to readers unable to read the original language. Translation, Benjamin explains, is a medium of the life of the original, a life that he insists is to be understood non-metaphorically. "The life of the original," he writes, "attains in [translation] to its ever-renewed latest and most abundant flowering." This life, moreover, is not self-contained, but purposive: "In translation the original rises into a higher and purer linguistic air, as it were…. It points the way to … the predestined, previously inaccessible realm of reconciliation and fulfillment of languages."[5] This realm, which Benjamin admits is not "total," can be understood as an idealized, utopian representation of the process of continuous translation that takes place *within* languages as well as between them. The impulse behind this utopianism is the positive side of modernist doubt about the stability of language; the same impulse played a substantial role in the flowering of poststructuralist theory in the later twentieth century. But neither idealism nor skepticism is anything more than a symptom. Translation, and in this it remains a model for the performance of the score, does not make the original intelligible but, instead, gives the prior intelligibility of the original an extended life by changing the terms on which the original survives. In a sense, that means that after a certain point there is no original, but saying so is a little too glib. The translation, the performance, the reading preserves the original in the past tense, something that "is" only by approximation and detour.

What implications does this model of translation have for performing fully scored music? It would certainly require that the study of a score include consideration of the different possibilities of getting from one point to another, the availability of alternative routes through the maze of notation. Doing so does not require, although it may obviously include, consulting the history of

---

[5] Walter Benjamin, *Illuminations*, trans. Harry Zohn (New York: Schocken, 1969), 75.

performances, because each actual performance must find its own way among multiple possible routes. Historical information settles very little; at its best, it bequeaths the performer a set of choices. Possibility is the *sine qua non* of musical performance, even if what may be done is always influenced in some way by what has been done. We would not hear a period-instrument performance of a Haydn symphony as we now do if the era of big symphonic performances had never taken place. What we hear in such a performance, however, is not what Haydn's audiences would have heard, even if the sounds could somehow be made identical. Too much technology, too much history, too much change in the auditory environment has intervened. It may well take musical anachronisms to be responsive to the conception we divine in a score. To realize that conception—which, it cannot be overstated, is as much the performer's as it is the score's—it is first necessary to search out the places where the score seems to plead for interpretation, where it demands that the performer make a choice.

At the inevitable risk of arbitrariness, I will turn to a single example, [Franz Peter] Schubert [1797–1828]'s famous song *Der Erlkönig* to illustrate the forking path between the score and its audible translation. The example will not be comprehensive. It will concentrate on just a few revealing details to exemplify the larger question of what it takes to translate printed marks into living music. But it should help to show what the musicians whose words compose this volume confront when they thoughtfully and tirelessly seek to do right by the music they love: the fact that, no matter how hard one tries to recover authentic, original performance materials, no matter how much one learns about context and performance practice, even the most successful recovery is a gathering of question marks.

The last few measures of Schubert's *Erlkönig* ask a great deal of both the singer and the pianist. The ballad by [Johann Wolfgang von] Goethe [1749–1832] that the song recounts describes a desperate night ride on which a father fails to save the life of his feverish son, who repeatedly hears the ghostly *Erlkönig* (roughly: elf king) lure him with promises of happiness. The poem's narrative divides among four voices, those of the father, the son, the *Erlkönig*, and a narrator. Schubert's setting is celebrated for the precision with which it discriminates among both the voices and their accompaniments: frantic for the boy, blandly reassuring for the father, seductive for the Erlkönig, frantic again for the narrator, who is also the boy's advocate.

This last detail marks a sharp difference between the poem and the song. In keeping with the conventions of the poetic ballad, Goethe's narrator is a neutral reporter. His language (or hers; the narrator has no gender identity, a point we will come back to) is plain almost to the point of indifference, especially in its delivery of the final line: *In seinem Armen das Kind war todt* [in his arms the child was dead]. Schubert demurs. He makes the narrator empathetic throughout, and, in the enunciation of the final line, tragic. The score spells out the tragic tone unambiguously. It instructs the line to be sung in recitative, marking the utterance off from the rest of the song and inviting the voice to use the inflections of expressive speech; it shadows the word "*Kind*" with an isolated diminished-seventh chord on the piano; it introduces a pregnant pause before the concluding *war todt*; and it ends with an abrupt *forte* cadence on the heels of the *pianissimo* recitative, which may or may not rise to *piano* after the pause.

But what does the score at this point *not* tell us? What does it leave us to think about all the more inquiringly *because* it does not tell us? The answers to these questions are particularly suggestive because Schubert wrote three versions of the song prior to the one he eventually published, and each version scores the closing measures differently. We can accordingly say with some confidence that the question of just what to "say" by the scoring of this passage was a problem that gave its composer some trouble. Of course it would be standard scholarly procedure, or would have been once, to examine the sequence of scores as a record of Schubert's efforts to bring the music to its definitive form. But we should at least consider the possibility that such linear narratives idealize too much and fix too much. The four scores may be more tellingly thought of as defining a field of possibilities that is oriented but not exhausted by the final version. The successive versions show the score in use as an instrument of discovery. The considerations that seem to have led to the writing and rewriting of this passage do not disappear with the end product. They leave traces through which the end product may appear more fully.

In the first three versions, the word *Kind* coincides with the piano's diminished-seventh chord. The rest before *war todt* is measured in the first and third versions, but prolonged by a fermata in the second. The final version is very different. It shifts the diminished seventh off the beat, so that the chord cuts across the enunciation of *Kind*, and it restores the fermata to the rest before *war* while also introducing the soft/loud split (not found in the earlier versions) between the recitative and the cadence. This scoring throws harmony, tempo, rhythm, and dynamics all off center in a few harsh strokes.

Even for performers with no knowledge of the earlier versions, the close of the published score is unusually heavy in its interpretive demands: how long to hold the fermatas; how speech-like to make the recitative, and with what inflections; how strongly to raise the voice (if at all) in response to a shift in the accompaniment from *pianissimo* to *piano*; how heavily to attack the cadential chords. The score is unambiguous in its notation, but it is unambiguous to excess. It exposes its own inability to say just how this conclusion should be delivered. It indicates by its surplus of notation that the score cannot merely be read or followed or realized. The score must be felt.

Schubert's revisions, in effect if not in intention, work toward an ending that the score can only fail to inscribe. The music needs that failure so as to release the meaning that only the performers can provide, which is just what the score instructs them to do. In particular, the performers must decide whether the voice should pass with restraint between the two halves of its final phrase or, in response to the rise from *pianissimo* to *piano* introduced by the diminished-seventh chord, should heighten its intensity and allow a tone of anguish or protest to creep in. In the first case the piano's closing chords would contradict the voice and accuse it of understating the tragedy. In the second case the piano would supplement with outrage the voice's expression of pity. Schubert adds a visual nuance to this dilemma, which neither answer solves, by rescoring the first measure of recitative so that the opening phrase appears over empty space in the piano part—a void.

The situation is further complicated by the sex of the singer. The narrator has no identity and therefore no sex, but the singer of course has both, and the singer's sex, or rather the gender roles it invokes, cannot help but inflect the way the narrative voice sounds to a listener. (The first singer of *Erlkönig* was a woman, albeit a purely fictional one, the protagonist of a musical play entitled *Die Fischerein* [The Fisher Maid].) The song, depicting the failure of the father to safeguard his son, forms an exemplary "paternity case" or "paternity suit" in which the father-son bond as a cultural ideal is subjected to sharp scrutiny and critique. Sung by a woman, the song is both a lament and an accusation. It relentlessly exposes the father's failure—the failure of traditional paternity—to nurture, to sympathize, to question assumed certainties. In this context the cries of the boy also express the helplessness of a mother notably excluded from the dramatic situation. When the boy's voice is heard, it sounds in the register a boy would share with a woman, not in the masculine register the boy will not live to acquire.

This critique is present as a subtext when a man sings the song, but in that case the singing voice may suggest a fraternal solidarity that to some extent excuses the father's failure by rewriting it as a tragedy. For a tenor, the problem posed by the last few measures of the score may be the need to project compassion without making excuses. Or so the score communicates, if it does, by *not* telling us.

These comments are hardly the last word on their subject. Many questions remain unanswered, even unasked. How, for example, should we assess the differences between the scores of art songs and those of instrumental works, between solo works and ensemble works, between all of these and the scores of operas, or, further afield, of film scores or transcriptions of jazz recordings? Nonetheless, enough has been said perhaps to establish that the score is neither script nor scripture. It is simply inscription: a means of preserving music, because we know how to perform it, and a means of changing music, because each performance is a creative as well as a recreative act. As I have put it elsewhere: "Scores are visual maps of acoustic possibility. The performer neither humbly "follows" the score nor proudly appropriates it. The performer *imagines* the score. What makes this different from any other act of imaginative response is its medium. The performer imagines the score in sound."[6]

As that last sentence implies, musical performance involves more than doing things with voices or instruments. It is an imaginary as much as an acoustic phenomenon. Recognizing that double character is the basis of the interviews in this volume. The underlying principle is that what performers say about their playing is no less historically revealing than the playing itself. Or, more exactly, it can become so if we listen carefully to what the performers say and are willing to

---

[6] Lawrence Kramer, *The Thought of Music* (Berkeley and London: University of California Press, 2016), 176.

interpret, not just to repeat, what they tell us. The telling is part of what endows the playing with meaning. Like the act of performance itself, reflection on performance is a creative intervention, not a passive act of reporting. The value of the interviews collected in this volume is not merely anecdotal; it is historical. The interviews invite us to imagine along with the performers what they ask of the music in their care and what the music they care for asks of them.

New York, USA   Lawrence Kramer
                                                                                       Fordham University

Lawrence Kramer Distinguished Professor of English and Music at Fordham University, Lawrence Kramer studied at the University of Pennsylvania and Yale; since 1993 he has edited *nineteenth-century Music*, an important musicological publication. Among his books are *Musical Meaning: Toward a Critical History*; *Opera and Modern Culture: Wagner and Strauss*; *Why Classical Music Still Matters*. His trilogy of books, *Expression and Truth, Interpreting Music*, and *The Thought of Music*, has won the 2017 ASCAP Virgil Thomson Award. He is also a composer whose works have been performed across the USA and Europe.

Contents

List of Figures

Introduction

"Welcome to the Banquet!"

The name and the example of the great French composer Hector Berlioz (1803–1869), whose incendiary image adorns the cover of *Performing Music History*, frequently came to mind during the preparation of this volume of interviews.[1] The assembled musicians and composers who speak out here hold a colloquy, of a kind, not altogether dissimilar from the chorus of voices found in Berlioz's wry and witty *Evenings with the Orchestra* (1852) and its sequel, *The Musical Madhouse* (1859).[2] Berlioz collected conversations, arguments, and declamations voiced among imaginary, bored pit orchestra musicians taking a break during their performances. One musician recalls an anecdote about Franz Liszt [1811–1886]: During a concert the great virtuoso impulsively stepped away from the piano and addressed his listeners: "I would make so bold as to ask whether you will kindly come and take supper with me!"[3] (Fig. 1).

And so, on behalf of my colleagues, Professors Michael Saffle and William Everett, I step forward and address the Gentle Readers of this book: "*Welcome to the banquet!*"

What can be said of the musicians and composers speaking out in these pages? Berlioz might have been taking their measure, with not a little irony, when he describes the conditions and consequences of celebrity:

---

[1]We refer to our cover illustration, J. J. Grandville's cartoon, *Concert a mittaille* (1846).

[2]This loosely translates Berlioz's original title, *Les Grotesques de la musique*. The appearance of Berlioz's company of musicians roughly parallels other contemporaneous associations of artists, fictive and real, who speak out about their musical lives in Carl Maria von Weber's *Harmonische Verein*, E. T. A. Hoffmann's *The Serapion Brotherhood*, and Robert Schumann's *Davidsbund*.

[3]Hector Berlioz, *Evenings with the Orchestra*, ed. and trans Jacques Barzun (New York: Alfred A. Knopf, 1956), 45.

© The Author(s) 2018
J. C. Tibbetts et al. (eds.), *Performing Music History*,
https://doi.org/10.1007/978-3-319-92471-7_1

Fig. 1 "The Concert of Gunfire" (1846), painting by John C. Tibbetts after the engraving by Granville

You have reached the summit. Frantic applause will be yours and likewise endless engagements. Authors will pay court to you; managers will no longer keep you waiting in their anterooms, and if you ever write to them, they will answer you.... Flowers and sonnets will be heaped around your feet.... You have now been promoted deity; try to remain a good fellow none the less—and don't look down on people who offer you good advice. [Berlioz, *Evenings*, 66–67]

Speaking personally, my own experiences with musicians who welcomed me to the "banquet" of their performing world has turned topsy-turvy any presuppositions I had about their status and fame. Not the "deities" Berlioz warned against, but the "good fellows" he praised, they freely engaged with my questions, no matter how amateurish the questions might be. For example, a defining moment during my career as a broadcaster and educator came during an interview in 1983 in Kansas City with pianist Emanuel Ax. He had just finished rehearsing the [Frédéric] Chopin [1809–1849] Second Piano Concerto with the Kansas City Symphony. By pre-arrangement, and on assignment from a local classical radio station, I met him on stage where, to my delight, he remained seated at the piano while literally accompanying his remarks with musical demonstrations.

That a musician of his stature would freely do this with an inexperienced journalist was astonishing (see his preface to this volume). Since then, his example has proven not the exception, but the rule, of many, many subsequent interviews granted this writer. *Performing Music History* is the proof of Berlioz's example—although, happily, each of the personages here is no figment of the imagination, but very real indeed.

Once inside these exchanges, I am now outside them. As G. K. Chesterton (1874–1936) rightly observed, "The next best thing to being really inside a thing is to be really outside it."[4] Taken together, they provide an oral commentary on the history of music, from medieval chant to the American Song Book. Some of these musicians look back on their careers from the long view of history: Rudolf Firkušný (1912–1994) recollects his youthful tutelage and friendship with composers Leoš Janáček (1854–1928) and Bohuslav Martinů (1890–1959); György Sándor reveals his personal and professional association with Béla Bartók (1881–1945); and Maureen Forrester remembers her early training under Bruno Walter in performing Gustav Mahler [1860–1911]. Others are speaking *in the moment*, reacting to their current career trajectories. At the time of our 1988 interview, dancer and singer Tommy Tune was preparing his landmark musical *Will Rogers Follies*. In 2017 Jennifer Higdon reveals her new interests in opera with *Cold Mountain*; John Kander discloses his new Broadway musical show projects, subsequent to the death of his longtime collaborator, Fred Ebb; and Steven Isserlis continues his musical collaborations with contemporary composer György Kurtág.

How I wish these pages could somehow convey the *sound* of their voices—the street-smart-smart vernacular of Jay McShann (1917–2006) on Kansas City jazz, the gentle musings of John Cage [1912–1992] on aleatoric composition, and the melodiously poised Emma Kirkby on the songs of Henry Purcell [c. 1659–1695]. And how I wish they could convey the *performances* that freely punctuate many of the interviews, such as Samuel Baron's examples on the flute of Baroque practices; Leif Ove Andsnes's piano simulations of the Norwegian hardanger fiddle; Malcom Bilson's demonstrations of the unique fortepiano sound; and McShann's boogie-woogie inflection to the jazz standard, *Moten Swing*.

Interviews, or conversations? Yes. The soul of both is sympathy. The condition of both is intimacy. Either way, some of the two-way exchanges found here encourage and relish the relative ease, give-and-take, and informality of a *conversation*. Others display the more formal interrogation of an *interview*. If pressed to the wall, I would cite as examples of the more conversational style John Cage's citation of Henry David Thoreau [1817–1862]'s sensitivity to the *sounds* of nature as a primary inspiration; George Shearing [1919–2011]'s sly blending of piano jazz with classical counterpoint; William Bolcom's and Joan Morris's irreverent quotations of ragtime song lyrics; John McGlinn [1953–2009]'s headlong urgency regarding the restoration of *Show Boat*; Carlisle Floyd's amusing anecdotes

---

[4]G. K. Chesterton, *The Everlasting Man* (New York: Dodd, Mead & Company, 1925), xii.

about the staging of his seminal American opera *Susannah*; Barry Tuckwell's hair-raising accounts of the hazards of playing the horn; and Christopher Parkening's impassioned revelations of the spiritual wellsprings fueling his guitar performances.

As for the more rigorous interview mode, Benjamin Bagby plucks the epic string of medieval Anglo-Saxon and Germanic oral traditions in his interpretations of *Beowolf* and the music of Boethius (c. 477–524) and Hildegard of Bingen (1098–1179), also known as St. Hildegard; William P. Mahrt examines the formation of medieval chant practices; Brian Newbould and Paul Badura-Skoda relate in considerable detail their Schubertian researches into historical keyboards and manuscripts; Anne-Sophie Mutter comments on the niceties of bowing, finger vibrato, and the physical postures of violin playing; Thomas Hampson reconstructs the original conception of [Robert] Schumann [1810–1856]'s song cycle *Dichterliebe*; Rosalyn Tureck devotes her long life to bringing the music of Johann Sebastian Bach (1685–1750) to today's audiences; Mark Markham disputes traditional considerations of just what "impressionist" music is; Russell Sherman analyzes with sober precision the proto-modernism of Franz Liszt; while Chen Yi and Zhou Long cross-pollinate their American works with the traditions and practices of their Chinese heritage.

Several musicians wear seven-league boots, as it were. Julian Bream takes Elizabethan music on tour with his Julian Bream Consort. Samuel Baron brings Bach to far flung audiences with his Bach Aria Group. Max Morath proclaims that he's "Livin' the Ragtime Life" with his one-man stage shows. And finally, the irrepressible Peter ("P.D.Q. Bach") Schickele rope-swings his way into the hearts of audiences everywhere as he deconstructs/"decomposes" the cherished traditions of Baroque music.

Inevitably, differences of opinion abound. They reflect private reservations and differing professional viewpoints on a variety of topics, such as John Eliot Gardiner and Simon Preston on, respectively, "George Frideric Handel" (also Georg Friedrich Händel, 1785–1759) and "Freddie" Handel; Garrick Ohlsson and Charles Rosen on the validity of Schumann's coded musical texts; Claude Frank and Richard Goode on their respective traversals of the complete piano sonatas of Ludwig van Beethoven (1770–1827); or Carl Davis and Philip Glass on the various functions of "film music." One way or another, the participants all enjoy their opportunities to have their say.

How apt is William Hazlitt [1778–1830]'s commentary on the art of conversation: "The subjects are more at liberty to say what they think, to put the subject in different and opposite points of view … to obviate misconception, to state difficulties on their own side of the argument, and answer them as well as they can."[5]

The conversations and interviews span the years 1983 to the present. Some transpired on the road—backstage, in hotels, private homes, music festivals,

---

[5]William Hazlitt's, "On the Conversation of Authors" was first published in the *London Magazine*, September 1820.

including the Bard College summer weekends festivals; the Schumann Festivals in Düsseldorf, Germany; Liszt Conferences in Hamilton, Ontario, and Stockholm, Sweden; and the International Arts Festivals in Bergen, Norway. Many others transpired in my home base in Kansas City, Missouri, which, through world-class presenters like the Harriman-Jewell Series, the Friends of Chamber Music, The Art Institute of Kansas City, the Folly Theater Jazz Series, and the Performing Arts Series of Johnson County Community College, have brought for decades a remarkable roster of performing artists. To Tim Ackerman, Clark Morris, and the late Richard Harriman of the Jewell Series; Cynthia Siebert of the Friends; and Emily Behrman of JCCC go my special thanks for their assistance in arranging contacts and access with performers.

Excerpts from a number of these conversations were originally broadcast on KXTR, formerly the classical FM station of Kansas City, where I worked for many years as the Arts and Entertainment Editor. The encouragement and support of Mr. Robert P. Ingram and his wife, Beth Ingram, made possible remarkable opportunities for contacts and broadcast outlets. I also want to thank Steve Robinson, former Vice President of WFMT, for his continuing support in my broadcast career. None of these interviews, in their original states, has appeared in print before.

My thanks go to those members and friends of the Academy who have generously encouraged and assisted in my endeavors over many years: Professors Lawrence Kramer (who wrote the Introduction to this book) of Fordham University; Alan Walker, formerly of McMaster University, Ontario; Leon Plantinga of Yale University; Michael Beckerman of New York University; Elliott Antokoltez of the University of Texas, Austin; Rufus Hallmark of Rutgers University, Arbie Orenstein of the Aaron Copland School of Music, Queens College; David Ferris of Rice University, Houston; D. Kern Holoman of the University of California, Davis; Erik Battaglia of the Conservatory of Turin; David Beveridge, formerly of New Orleans University; and Caroline Jewers, Jack Winerock, and Richard Angeletti of the University of Kansas.

I am deeply in the debt of many scholars who have passed on, including Professors Jacques Barzun of Columbia University, J. Bunker Clark and Dick Wright of the University of Kansas; and independent scholars Nancy B. Reich, Eric Sams, and Peter Ostwald. Likewise, my colleague William Everett wishes to recognize Professors Ed Williams, formerly of Pennsylvania State University and the University of Kansas; Carol Reynolds, formerly of Southern Methodist University, Dallas; and the late Herbert Turrentine, also of SMU. Michael Saffle recognizes James Deaville of Carleton University, Ottawa, Canada, Cornelia Szabó-Knotik of the Universität der Musik und darstellende Kunst, Vienna; Hon-Lun Yang of Hong Kong Baptist University; and Robert Groves of the North Dakota State University, Fargo. Finally, all three editors wish to thank their respective department chairs, with Michael Saffle singling out Brian Britt, whose term ends just as this volume is going to press. And a personal thanks to thank Ms. Mary Lou Pagano—math teacher, opera singer, equestrienne—who throughout the preparation of this book has been a constant and supporting partner and muse.

Final acknowledgments go to the musicians and composers in this book. *Performing Music History* in its own modest way respectfully attempts to address their professional concerns, accurately transcribe their words, and faithfully evoke the spirit and devotion with which they serve music and us, the listeners.

And so, the discourse of this book beckons you to a "banquet" of voices and music. Tilt your ear close to these pages. You will "hear" amidst the various accents, rhetoric, and jargon the *lingua franca* of music itself.

A word to our readers: Footnotes appear sparingly throughout the pages that follow. Individual terms are footnoted only once, the first time they appear in the volume, although in a few cases the same term is footnoted twice to clarify its historical significance. With few exceptions the names of individual composers appear only in the text, although first names and dates (for those composers who have died) are often added in square brackets. So are observations about behavior during interviews: laughter, instrumental illustrations, and so on. Dates, however, are not provided for performers mentioned in passing by individual interviewees. Finally, secondary sources are not footnoted; instead, we supply a list of important titles "for additional investigation."

John C. Tibbetts
Kansas City, Missouri, 25 August 2018

Medieval and Early Modern Music

Introduction

Music from the medieval[1] and early modern periods[2] encompasses a dizzying array of musical styles, genres, and purposes. Much of the music that survives from these times was intended for either the church or the aristocratic court. Music was considered in many ways a cultivated art form, the domain of the religious or political elite. Nevertheless, "popular" music flourished, although we know comparatively little about it today. In the interview that follows, Benjamin Bagby examines the origins of "bardic" music, often associated with the so-called Dark Ages. That music remains obscure, but a few examples survive and can be performed today.

When it comes to discussing music and musical practices in Western Europe, a great deal of this early repertory resided in some sort of oral or aural tradition, even after musical notation began to emerge (around 800 C.E.) and the four-line staff was established (around 1000 C.E.). Sacred music was notated first, since it was the monks and clergy who were educated in this practice.

Monophonic (single line) chant traditions continued to be practiced long after notated polyphonic traditions (more than one musical line occurring simultaneously) began in the twelfth and thirteenth centuries. We must not forget that unaccompanied chant is still sung today, as William Mahrt informs us—as do all of our authors—in his interview. The best known of the early polyphonic, chant-based works are those of Léonin (c. 1150–1201) and Perotin (died 1205 or 1225). Among the most popular later polyphonic genres was the motet, in which each

---

[1]Approximately 300–1400 C.E. Unless otherwise indicated, all subsequent dates are "Common Era" dates.

[2]Defined by historians as c. 1400–1789, the year of the French Revolution.

J. C. Tibbetts et al. (eds.), *Performing Music History*,
https://doi.org/10.1007/978-3-319-92471-7_2

voice (usually three) sang its own melody and text. One voice typically sang a chant melody, while the other two intoned new material.

A thriving secular music scene also existed. Various noble songwriters, such as the troubadours and trouvères in France, created songs of courtly love in which a knight extols the virtues of an idealized lady. Instrumental performers crossed paths with monks, pilgrims, and other travelers, and musical exchanges were commonplace.

The transition in musical style from the medieval period into the Renaissance (to use our modern terms for these historical eras) took place over a relatively long period of time. The formidable linear complexities of late medieval music gave way to a new style rooted in complementary musical lines that emphasized vertical sonorities. Polyphonic vocal writing shifted from works in which each voice sang its own text to ones in which all the voices sang the same words at basically the same time. Four distinct parts (rather than three) became the norm as this new style strengthened its grip on the musical world. Furthermore, individual parts were no longer as interchangeable as they had been in the past. Range was now a conscious factor in creating polyphonic music. Our now-familiar names for the four parts—soprano, alto, tenor, and bass—began to be used, and textures based on shared musical material became common.

Soon, the euphonious purity of a style rooted in imitative and non-imitative polyphony became the norm and the so-called Renaissance period in music (c. 1450–c. 1600) was in full flower. Composers such as Josquin des Prez (c. 1450–1521) became international figures who gained fame for their works in both sacred and secular circles. In addition to crafting masses and motets (polyphonic settings of non-liturgical Latin sacred texts), composers also created madrigals, settings of secular poetry, which became extremely popular in Italy and England. Some English madrigals also took on new lives as lute songs when performed by solo voice and lute, rather than by a vocal ensemble.

Emma Kirkby and Julian Bream explain some of these developments, and Kirkby also discusses Renaissance and early Baroque dance. Instrumental music began to flourish as well, with ensembles performing dances, transcriptions of vocal pieces, and various original works. At the same time, Protestant musicians such as Martin Luther (1483–1546) began composing chorales: sacred hymns for congregations rather than priests to sing during church services. Later, Protestant composers wrote polyphonic motets and even masses as well as musical stories of Jesus' suffering and death called Passions. Among these late seventeenth-century composers were Heinrich Schütz (1585–1672) and Dietrich Buxtehude (c. 1636–1709).

In the early 1600s, a new style emerged, and musical practitioners were quick to acknowledge and embrace this development. In 1602, for example, the singer-composer Giulio Caccini [1551–1618] entitled his latest collection of songs *Le nuove musiche* [The New Musics]. In his preface to the volume Caccini told performers that these pieces, scored for solo voice and basso continuo,[3] were created in a new and distinctive style. The tonal harmonic system we practice today, where certain chords lead functionally to other chords, became established during the seventeenth century. Renaissance polyphony, with its equality among parts, was giving way to a modern approach that privileged the upper and lower parts. This monodic style emphasized clear declamation of text over an instrumental complement, which was purposefully crafted to accompany the melodic line. With these developments in how the voice was being treated, new genres were ripe for development. Soon to emerge were operas and cantatas, genres that featured the voice in prominent ways and needed intelligible texts for the audience. Judith Malafronte discusses not early opera as well as the early music movement and its concern with performances practices.

As the Baroque era (to use the musical term, roughly 1600–1750) continued, notions of virtuosity developed. Performers moved to the forefront of new means of musical expression, whether it was singers improvising striking passages in opera, keyboard players adding ornamentation to ordinary melodic lines, or organists creating expansive spontaneous works based on hymn tunes.

The dialectic between fantasy and intellect is another hallmark of music from this time. Keyboard fantasias, which are intended to evoke a sense of improvisation, rest comfortably alongside the fugue, perhaps the most scientific and rule-ridden musical utterance of the time, where nearly every parameter of each part's imitative utterance is carefully controlled. Composers as well as performers proved themselves to be virtuosi in creating works that demanded a strict adherence to regulations while at the same time infusing them with a sense of impassioned humanity.

Michael Saffle and William Everett

Benjamin Bagby: "We're Making these Songs Heard Again for the First Time in a Thousand Years!"

John C. Tibbetts
17–18 November 2016, Kansas City, MO

For more than thirty years vocalist, harper, and scholar Benjamin Bagby has specialized in performing medieval Anglo-Saxon and Germanic oral poetry. His reconstruction and performances of the Old English epic poem *Beowulf* are celebrated around the world. In 1977 he and the late Barbara Thornton founded Sequentia, an early music group dedicated to researching,

---

[3]The basso continuo consists of a harmony-providing instrument, such as a harpsichord, guitar, or lute; and an instrument that plays a bass line, such as a viola da gamba, 'cello, or bassoon.

Fig. 1 Benjamin Bagby

performing, and recording pre-1300 Western European music, including the music of Hildegard of Bingen and a variety of oral traditions (Fig. 1).

    The following interview took place during Bagby's recent visit to Kansas City, Missouri, where he performed with the group Sequentia.

JOHN C. TIBBETTS: You're a scholar, performer, and a showman. Do you privilege one over the other?
BENJAMIN BAGBY: I think by the time I'm on stage the scholar part is way behind me. I'm not by any means interested in showing off the scholarship on stage. Showman? Yes, there's an element of that, because I am trying to adapt a very archaic story to a modern performance setting. The medieval singer of tales did not have a battery of lights and a lighting designer and a stage with an audience sitting in rows reading a projection of the titles on a screen behind him. That's all show.

Have you ever performed in a mead hall of some sort, a setting more appropriate to what you do?
Of course! Once in Canada I performed in a tribal hut in an area near Vancouver Island.

What is a tribal hut?
It's actually a wooden house, a long type of building very similar to a building in old Germanic Europe with a fireplace for a fire in the center, a hole in the roof, and benches around the outside.

Was there a scholar or, better yet, a scholar-musician who, somewhere along the line, became an important mentor or precedent for you?
There was a very important scholar of oral poetry at the University of Missouri-Columbia named John Miles Foley. He set up a center for oral literature and oral poetry, with an online journal. He was my mentor for the work I have done on *Beowulf.* I worked with him a lot about ten to fifteen years ago. There was another mentor in the Anglo-Saxon language who was a professor at the University of Texas at Austin named Thomas Cable. He helped me a lot in the beginning when I had no idea about metrics and pronunciation and all of the things about the language that one needs to know.

Where does research in music of the period come in?
They weren't particularly interested in music or able to help me much with it. That was something I more or less worked out on my own during the many years I spent involved with medieval music.

I may be over-romanticizing this, but as a little boy did you hear someone telling you a story that struck some kind of chord in you?
I don't come from a particularly story-reading family, nothing like that. I wish I could say I had a grandfather who read to me, but I didn't. I was in the seventh

grade when I first came across the story of Beowulf in a modern English translation. And that really struck my fancy. I was also given Dante[1265–1321]'s
Inferno by my English teacher at the time.[4] A big sensation to me. If you remember back in the 1960s, we weren't allowed to say certain words, and one of those
words was "hell"! And Dante's *Inferno* was all about hell, and it gave me an
excuse to say this word and not get in trouble!

Nevertheless, the sound *of the human voice and the* text *of a story are combined in
your work.*
They kind of came together later in my career. I was conservatory trained and
always interested in early music, from Bach to German *Lieder*, which was my
focus in my late teens and early twenties. More to the point, when I was sixteen,
I went to a performance by the New York Pro Musica of medieval music, thir-
teenth- and fourteenth-century music. It just blew me away. I was completely captivated by the sounds. This was just after the death of Noah Greenberg. John White
was the director at that time. That set me onto a path from which I have not yet
emerged.

So when you say "early" music, you're not fooling around!
I mean the earliest European music, Western European. Getting into Greek music
involves other modes, other tunings, other instruments, and certainly another language. If I were a young man now, knowing what I know, I would be very interested in starting to think about the Homeric epics and how they were listened to.[5]

*Has it struck you with the particular irony that audiences today, used to the raz-
zle-dazzle of rock concerts, are flocking to sold out houses of your performances of*
Beowulf *and other things? What's going on?*
I think everybody likes the honesty of an acoustic experience and a story that is
told, and there's something about also listening to the old language that we don't
understand. Sure, people say, "Why don't you do it in modern English?" And my
answer is a simple one, "Because the old language is the music, and if I change
the language it would be different music." So that I think there's something very
appealing about plugging into some kind of ancestral sound that might have been
something our ancestors heard and knew, and the stories they heard and knew, and
it gives us a feeling of connection maybe that we have missed lately.

So, what about bards and troubadours? Are they the same thing?
I've been chastised by Irish scholars for using the word "bard" as a general
term for "storyteller" because they say, "No, no, no, the bard is a specific Irish

---

[4]Born Durante degli Alighieri and best known simply as "Dante."

[5]The legendary Greek poet Homer may have lived c. 800 B.C.E. The surviving poems attributed
to him, the *Iliad* and *Odyssey*, were performed in antiquity by bards who sang or chanted then,
possibly with instrumental accompaniment.

phenomenon and you can't apply that word to other places at other times." I understand that. There's a scholar named Albert Lord, who wrote a very important book in the 1960s about oral poetry called *The Singer of Tales*. At some point we all lived in tribes and I think even in politics today you see a lot of tribal energy at work.

You beat the drum and everybody heard it!
Yeah, and you identified with your tribe. The success of your tribe is all that matters to you at the expense of all other tribes. Every tribe has its stories and those stories belong to the tribe, and we want to hear them over and over again because they reinforce our sense of identity and who we are, where we come from, and why we're better than the others.

Would you have been comfortable as a strolling player?
No, not the strolling thing, no. The ones who knew the stories and were installed in the tribal fabric, they were highly valued by their people because they *were* the history of the people in a pre-literate society where there are no records of anything. It's all just what is remembered. The genealogies, the battle stories, the deeds of our glorious ancestors, everything we need to know about who we are and where we came from.

They wouldn't have been wandering around the country?
No, they were probably very well taken care of by their tribes.

So where do we get this notion of a strolling player?
The Victorians. They messed up the Middle Ages big time! [laughs] The reception of the Middle Ages in the Victorian era leads to things like Richard Wagner [1813–1883] and the whole idea of the knight in shining armor. That's a very late thing, fourteenth, fifteenth century. This idea of chivalry was kind of a Victorian virtue. But when you look at the ninth-century Carolingian courts,[6] you see they were obsessed with learning, obsessed with books, obsessed with study and very joyful spirit of discovering, re-discovering, all the texts which antiquity had provided them.

You're saying that in the ninth century they would be looking back at what they regarded as antiquity?
We think that's a specialty of the Renaissance, that the Renaissance re-discovered ancient Rome and Greece; but already in the ninth century there was a huge fascination with everything from antiquity, if for no other reason than wanting to learn to write and read really good Latin, like that used by the Roman poet Ovid [(43 B.C.E.–17/18 C.E.)].

---

[6]The age of Charlemagne (742–814), who became King of the Franks in 768 and Holy Roman Emperor in 800.

So, Ovid is one source for you, and Boethius is another. Now, who was Boethius?
Boethius was a late, late Roman nobleman, when the Roman Empire in the sixth century had already begun to dissolve. It was no longer the Rome of the Republic, or even the Empire. It retained some of its luster and retained its structures, but the content was long gone. Boethius held a high position as Roman consul, but he got into trouble with his local Germanic overlord and was wrongfully accused of treason against the Empire. He was executed about 536. I think he scared them. He was very political. He was also a philosopher, wrote mathematical treatises, and a book about music. It's highly theoretical. It has nothing to do with playing music or singing or anything like that. It's about music as a manifestation of number and structure.

It sounds like something out of Pythagoras!
Yes, it's based on Pythagorian theory: octaves, fifths, fourths, and so on.[7]

Do we know what the music of Boethius' day sounded like?
We have twenty-some manuscripts containing an enigmatic kind of musical notation. They're hard to decipher and the melodies have remained largely lost to us. I've worked with Milman Parry and with Sam Barrett, a musicologist at Cambridge. Unfortunately, Parry died quite young. Barrett's also interested in these very earliest songs. And he's found all the manuscripts of Boethius' lyrics that exist. He's transcribed some, but others are only semi-transcribable. I got together with him last April at Cambridge, where we sat at a table and hashed through dozens of songs and came up with very hypothetical transcriptions of a dozen of them. We're making these songs heard again for the first time in a thousand years!

I imagine you in some kind of dark archive, handling these very, very precious documents ...
Well, I wish it were that way, but it's not. We're talking about a very high-tech digitized library archive.

Is it safe to say that we now know more about this whole area of study than, say, we knew a hundred years ago?
For sure, yes. We have more of an overview of the totality of manuscript production and a much wider spectrum of manuscripts to compare. We know much more about the musical notation. We know much more about the traditions of the scriptoria or workshops where the books were made. A hundred years ago there were only a few isolated scholars here and there.

---

[7]Pythagoras (570–495 B.C.E), the near-legendary Greek philosopher, is credited with working out the mathematical intervals of the overtone series.

You described the music notation as enigmatic. Can a layperson understand what you mean?
First of all, we're talking about music-making that we've never heard! It's like we're looking at a shadow but can only guess at the face of that shadow. We don't have enough information. We don't know who came up with this idea of notating music. We do know about neumes[8] in chant, but there's no staff, no way to know the pitches. But because these pieces were very stable in tradition, coming from oral tradition, they were written down over a period of hundreds of years. By the thirteenth century you start to have staff notation and chant is being written with very clear pitches. The chant books are quite clear. And so, you can take that pitch information, refer back to the neumes, and see that that's the same melody. So, today we take these manuscripts as authentic testimonies of medieval music that were written down for the purpose of imposing authority.

What kinds of songs are we talking about?
People were singing all kinds of songs; they weren't just singing chant. Our [new] program is called *Monks Singing Pagans*, which is a way of saying that religious people also sang non-religious songs, because that was a very important part of musical life in the Christian tradition at that time. Of course, every monk and cleric was singing up to eight hours a day. Getting up at three in the morning, singing for two hours, a little break, another hour, another break, another half hour—and then there was mass! A long day of singing!

At the same time everybody knew *The Labors of Hercules*.[9] In the Middle Ages, Hercules was a metaphor for striving to improve, for rectifying injustice, for overcoming the self. This is developed later into the twelfth century in a song by a court poet named Pierre de Blois [c. 1130–c. 1211], who was working for Eleanor of Aquitaine [1122–1204] and Henry II [of England] and the Plantagenets.[10] Pierre wrote a wonderful song about Hercules where he says, "Yea, he did this and he did that, and he was very strong and he defeated this monster, and blah, blah, blah, blah ... but he had no power at all when he met a pretty girl!"

Now, when we hear these songs, what do we see *on stage, what's the stage picture, per se?*
You see the three of us in Sequentia. Only one person is singing; these are solo songs.

---

[8]Neumes are musical symbols identifying one or more notes sung to a single syllable of text. Early neumes were placed directly above words in the text rather than on a four- or five-line staff.

[9]Revered as a hero and god in ancient Greece and Rome, Hercules (in Greek, Heracles) was born to Jupiter (Zeus), king of the gods, and the moral woman Alcmene; he was celebrated for his physical strength and numerous adventures.

[10]The Plantagenet dynasty ruled England from 1154, with the accession of Henry II, until 1485, when Richard III died.

And the language we hear?
There are some pieces in Old English. There are one or two pieces in Old High German, and Old Saxon, and quite a number of pieces in Latin.

Without the subtitles, if we listen carefully for a while, would our ears begin to pick out some meanings?
Probably. But you would have to be given the broad outline of what's going on. I think with that, the mind kind of sketches in the broad meaning.

Let's talk about one of your instruments, the lyre. Is your own instrument [shown in the portrait at the beginning of the interview] based on a historical model?
Yeah. It's based on an instrument that was found in a burial site in what is now southwest Germany, the Black Forest, where a nobleman had been buried. Two harps were found in this gravesite. One of them has since disappeared; the other one survives in fragmentary form. It was broken into pieces. The archaeologists could more or less reconstruct it.

You are stroking out a pattern on the strings while you're reciting, talking, chanting. What is that pattern?
The whole thing is based on how I decide to tune the instrument. Certain elements of the tuning are predetermined. If you have strings that are made of gut in the sixth or seventh centuries, they're not going to be superfine strings; they're probably going to be a little thicker than, let's say, a lute's strings. With a thicker string, you have to tune it up till it starts to make a tone, which dictates your lowest note. You tune the thinnest string until it seems it may break; that's probably your highest note. Those two notes are roughly one octave apart. Interestingly enough, that octave corresponds to the vocal range of a medium-high male voice: G below middle C to G above middle C. The only thing to solve after that is what are the other four strings are going to be. It's six strings in all. And there are not too many alternatives available. In antique society, in Christian society, in pagan society, everybody agreed that certain intervals are consonant, like the perfect fifth, the octave, the unison, and the perfect fourth. I doubt that there was one accepted tuning that everybody used. I think that it was local and traditional and family-based or clan-based, or even piece-based.

What of your "signature" performance piece, Beowulf.[11] *You're not avoiding it after all these years; you're not tired of it?*
No, no, not at all. Every performance reveals new things to me. It's constantly surprising me how beautifully it's made and how cleverly it's put together. I read it in a translation by John Ciardi. And now we have translations by Seamus Healey

---

[11]*Beowulf* is an epic poem written in Old English, the language spoken in Anglo-Saxon England before the Norman Conquest in 1066.

and J. R. R. Tolkein [1892–1973]. But I don't really use translations much. I'm so fixed on the original that I don't read the translations anymore.

Is there an Urtext[12] *for* Beowulf, *a manuscript?*
It's not an *Urtext*, exactly. It's an oral phenomenon which is long lost. There is only one manuscript. It is faulty. It was copied obviously from something else that's lost.

You've seen it?
I've seen it, yes. It's on display in the British Library behind heavy glass, and it has a five-watt bulb nearby. You really have to squint. They keep it in a very dark place because it's quite fragile. There was a fire in the early eighteenth century [1731] and it almost burned up. They saved it by throwing it out the window, but it was badly singed and the manuscript was damaged. Luckily, it had been copied over a few times by hand in the eighteenth and nineteenth centuries.

Do we know who actually put pen to parchment?
No. Maybe a scribe somewhere in England. There's a big fight about the dating of this poem. Some people say it was created at the time the manuscript was written. Others say it dates way back to the sixth or eighth century. If I were to perform the whole text as we find it in the manuscript, it would be a five-hour performance. Mine is only a third of that.

Are people disappointed that you leave out the dragon?
Sometimes. I get asked all the time when am I going to do the next part and I indeed was planning to do that about fifteen years ago. There was a project to learn the rest of the epic or at least the next part about Grendel's mother. But I realized that the reality of concert life, festivals, and music series is that they don't know how to deal with something that long.

Do you enjoy the sounds of those words coming out of your mouth?
Like I said earlier, that's the music for me. I love performing *Beowulf*. But it's a long haul. I mean, it's a hundred minutes of non-stop singing and playing and acting. It takes over. You know, I don't have any musical notation for what I do. There's no score. My agent once said to me, "You should copyright this. You should send your score into the Library of Congress and get it copyrighted." And I said, "Score? What score? It's just some sketches".

---

[12]An original or unedited version of any work.

William P. Mahrt: "Chant Helps Lift the Heart to God"

Michael Saffle
June–July 2017

**Gregorian chant, named after Pope and Saint Gregory I, called "the Great"
540–604), remains among the oldest relics of the Western musical tradition**

Fig. 2 William Mahrt

and for more than a thousand years served as the primary form of musical expression in the Roman Catholic Church. Some chants for the Mass, such as the Introit, are sung in processions and have a practical function, while others, such as the Offertory, are intended for spiritual reflection and are characterized by a large number of melismas, where many notes are sung to one syllable. Still others, such as the Gloria and the Credo, include a great amount of text and require a syllabic performance style, where nearly every syllable of text is sung on own note. Other Catholic services, including the Hours (prayer-like services held throughout the day and, today, mostly in monasteries) also employ chant.

William P. Mahrt specializes in the performance of medieval and Renaissance music and teaches at Stanford University, where he directs the Stanford Early Music Singers, an ensemble that presents concerts of music from the late Middle Ages through the early Baroque. For nearly fifty years he has led the St. Ann Choir in Palo Alto, California, in acclaimed performances of chant and Renaissance music in liturgical chant (Fig. 2). **Mahrt is president of the Church Music Association of America and editor of its journal** *Sacred Music.*
   This interview was conducted by correspondence.

MICHAEL SAFFLE: How did you become interested in early music, especially early church music?
WILLIAM MAHRT: I grew up in a farming town in Eastern Washington, where the music at church was exclusively pious Catholic hymns sung during mass. I attended a Jesuit university, where I learned philosophy and theology but not Latin or Gregorian chant. I had a scholarship playing trombone in the band, and my teacher believed that instrumentalists should play a wide variety of instruments, so I also had lessons in flute, clarinet, oboe, violin, trumpet, etc. When I went to the University of Washington, I was drafted into a schola [choir] to sing all of the Gregorian chants for Holy Week, a daunting task. I have no idea of how it sounded, but at the end of the week, I said, "This is what I have been waiting for!" and joined the chant schola at the cathedral. When I went to Stanford I joined a choir that was just being formed at St. Ann Chapel to sing chant and Renaissance polyphony; after a year, the director left, and I took over. A Renaissance wind band was also formed at Stanford, and the director said, "Here, play this recorder," something rather simple after my lessons on the clarinet, flute, and other wind instruments. Directing the church choir meant searching for repertory, and, as a graduate student, I learned as much about early music this way as I did in my classes.

What is chant and when did it originate?
Gregorian chant is the original monophonic liturgical music of the Latin Church. It has origins in Jerusalem in the fourth century and was developed extensively in Rome through the seventh century. Transmitted to northern Europe in the eighth century, it was first written down in the ninth and tenth centuries. It spread

throughout Europe, and by the late Middle Ages [i.e., the thirteenth and fourteenth centuries] it existed in distinct traditions among various nations and religious orders. It continued to be performed alongside polyphonic and concerted church music, and remains an ideal norm for church music even today.

Is chant performed the same way today that it was in the early Middle Ages?
Chant is not even performed the same way today from place to place. The method of the monks of Solesmes in the early twentieth century prescribed a systematic way to perform chant with the purpose of unifying its performance throughout the Church. Still, national styles emerged, and even the Solesmes method itself was performed in very distinctly German, Swiss, French, and also American styles.

So, how do modern performers and scholars believe chant should *be performed?*
Based upon the study of manuscripts pioneered by the Solesmes monks, scholars have investigated the rhythmic signs of the manuscripts and developed a sophisticated rhythmic interpretation that goes under the name of semiology. This is applied in a multiplicity of ways and has produced a wide variety of performance styles, some of which can be heard on recordings, though in its most pure form, it has had limited application to liturgical performance.

Some evidence suggests that some chants were performed in proportional rhythms—longs and shorts. The rhythmic signs disappear from the manuscript tradition quite soon. It appears that there was a gradual evening out of the rhythm, so that by the twelfth century, chant could be called *cantus planus*, "plainsong," music in even note values. Over its history, the chant was gradually sung more and more slowly, so that by the seventeenth century, when organ accompaniment was added, different harmonies accompanied each chant note, making it sound something like a chorale.[13] It was in the nineteenth century that chant was "restored" according to several systems, the most notable one being that at the Abbey of Solesmes. Here the individual notes of the chant were grouped into larger units resulting in a quicker and more vital rhythm, a development that was the foundation of how the chant is performed today.

I imagine you have to work with singers—and also with university students, of course—in order to teach them how to perform chant. Is that correct?
Yes. Beginning instruction in chant is usually based upon the method of Solesmes, but more advanced singing explores more complex methods of performance. I believe that the chant is essentially liturgical music and its proper venue is the liturgy. There the chant must be considered in relation to its various functions. The method of Solesmes is such a forceful rhythmic system that it tends to iron out

---

[13]In this context, a chorale is a harmonized melody in which all voices (usually four) move at the same time. The term "chorale" is also used for early Lutheran hymns, originally sung without accompaniment.

the important stylistic differences between the liturgical genres. On its foundation, however, these differences can be developed.

And how have you performed chant throughout your career?
I studied the Solesmes method and have adapted some of its principles, but I place greater emphasis upon the text, treating as entities the syllables and words, the phrases, and likewise the neumes[14] and melismas. I seek to perform the various genres from syllabic to melismatic chant differently. Syllabic chants, with one or maybe two notes for each syllable, require greater emphasis upon the rhythm of the text. Melismatic chants, in which a single syllable may be set to many notes, require more than counting in twos and threes, as in the Solesmes method, but a wider principle of rhythm that integrates each melisma.

Moreover, each genre must be considered in relation to its purpose in the liturgy. Processional chants need to project a sense of elegant rhythmic motion that suits the procession; melismatic chants often inspire meditation, and so their performance must be elevated. I have verified the effect of melismatic chants by observing a "pin-dropping" silence in the congregation, a witness that the piece elicits a recollection that precludes distracted motion.

Furthermore, I think the object of the chant should be contrasted with the object of concert music. The object of concert music is the piece itself. With chant, the object is not the piece itself, but the more general object of the liturgy, divine worship. The chant helps lift the heart to God. I love to quote Rebecca Stewart, who describes sacred music as "always seeking," moving forward outside of itself.

We hear of "guitar masses" today, and pop music used in Catholic churches. If chant is no longer the official music of the Catholic Church, why do you still study and perform it? Isn't it "forbidden" now, at least without special permission from church officials?
Gregorian chant is still the official music of the Catholic Church. The Second Vatican Council says specifically that Gregorian chant "should be given principal place in liturgical services," and there was never any official prohibition of it. Liturgies from St. Peter's Basilica in Rome regularly incorporate Gregorian chant, and many other great churches and monasteries maintain it. Your question raises an important issue, however, because chant has generally fallen out of use liturgically, and has been replaced by music not as suitable to the sacred context. There is, however, a growing movement to revive it, and it is being performed in many more churches now. The colloquia of the Church Music Association of America, meeting for a week each summer, cultivate and exemplify its extensive use. Our study and performance is specifically intended to propagate its wider employment in the liturgy.

---

[14]In this context, part of certain systems of notating pitch. Especially associated with medieval music.

When did singing something other than monophonic (single-line) chant begin?
By the end of the ninth century, theoretical sources describe singing chants in parallel intervals—fourths, fifths, and octaves. This suggests that theorists were exam-
ining actual and perhaps considerably older practices. In fact singing in parallel
intervals is documented in many cultures of the world.

Moreover, this kind of singing can emerge spontaneously for reasons of vocal
range or acoustics. I cite two examples from my own experience. I once attended
Evensong at Grace Cathedral in San Francisco and sat next to an elderly lady
obviously very familiar with the service. When it came time for the hymn, she
sang the melody very forthrightly a fourth below the notated pitch. It was clear
that she could not reach the higher pitches, and so she gravitated to lower ones, in
spite of the fact that what she sang disagreed with some of the harmonies played
on the organ. I also visited a Baroque chapel in Freising, Bavaria, where a small
congregation was reciting the rosary. The people recited the prayers in a mono-
tone, descending somewhat at the ends of sentences. The acoustics of the chapel
reinforced their pitches, so that the voices gravitated to harmonic intervals: the
women recited a fifth higher than the men. All of this is to say that "parallel organum"[15] is likely to crop up often, based either on the limitation of voices or on
acoustic reinforcement.

Another kind of organum is singing a chant over a drone. One voice holds a single pitch, while another sings a chant melody above it. In some cases, the drone
can shift to accommodate large-scale changes in the chant melody. Other kinds
of organum involve a second voice singing harmonizing notes against the chant,
note-against-note, then more than one note against each chant note. The history of
organum documents these and other developments.

*Was the chant itself employed or even altered when extensive polyphonic music
was introduced to churches during or after the twelfth century?*
We know so little about the earliest polyphony, but it is clear that when you add a
counterpointing melody to a chant, particularly many notes-against-one note, the
rhythm of the chant is slowed down slightly and evened out. The development of
polyphony ultimately made the chant into a *cantus firmus* [literally, fixed song]—
the foundation in long notes of intricate counterpoint. And much later, this term
became the name Italians used to designate the chant itself: *canto fermo*.

Later polyphony shows two ways of employing chant. First, as a *cantus firmus*,
the chant is sung in long notes with the other parts singing elaborate counterpoint
in shorter note values. Second, in cantilena style, which usually is in three parts,
the soprano part sings the chant in a somewhat ornamented style while the two
lower parts supply supporting counterpoint: this style is sometimes called
discant-dominated style.

---

[15]Organum refers to early multi-part (polyphonic) music based on chat. In parallel organum, all
parts move in the same direction at the same time, although not on the same pitch.

In performance terms, when did the Middle Ages really end?
An important characteristic of medieval performance was singing from memory. Even though the chant melodies were written down and can be found in manuscripts and prints all over Europe, they were fundamentally sung from memory. Statutes for choirs as late as the fifteenth century prescribe that choir boys should be given a certain number of years to memorize the chants, a continuation of an essentially medieval practice. The maintenance of this singing from memory and of the extensive chant repertory suggests that the Middle Ages did not quite end for a long time. I view the Renaissance to be an overlay upon the Middle Ages; many elements of medieval music persisted, particularly in the liturgy, while many new elements were added.

Which kind of music do you most enjoy performing, and why?
I take Gregorian chant to be normative to the liturgy and its performance is a given. I would be completely satisfied if I were to perform only Gregorian chant the rest of my life. Still, polyphonic music is an extraordinarily beautiful amplification of liturgical practice. I was first attracted to polyphony in transcribing the music of Heinrich Isaac [c. 1450–1517], and experimenting with its performance, so much so that I changed my field of concentration and wrote my dissertation about him. Still, for me, the greatest Renaissance music is that of Josquin des Prez. I performed a series of concerts with the Stanford Early Music Singers and the St. Ann Choir between 1995 and 1997, including all of the clearly authentic Masses of Josquin. Settings of the Ordinary, of course, not the Propers.[16] It was one of the best things I ever did musically.

In the area of secular music, I take the late sixteenth-century Italian madrigal to be a high point of musical history, as great a high point as is the symphony of the eighteenth century or the opera of the nineteenth. Madrigals by Cipriano de Rore [c. 1515–1565], Giaches de Wert [1535–1596], Luca Marenzio [c. 1554–1599], and their contemporaries, are inspired by the intense introspection of Petrarch's[17] poetry and achieve a sublime synthesis of music and poetry. Even though the expressive character of these pieces is best sung one-to-a-part, I sing them with my Early Music Singers, more than one-to-a-part, to give the singers the experience of these extraordinary works.

Please tell us a little about the problems in performing early music today.
At one time, an ideal in the performance of early music was authenticity. This has been discounted in some circles, but unjustly. The notion is that the music should

---

[16]The Ordinary of the Mass includes those sung parts that do not change and appear in every Mass (Kyrie, Gloria, Credo, Sanctus, Agnus Dei), while the Propers of the Mass constitute those chants that vary from service to service (Introit, Gradual, Alleluia, Offertory, Communion). The Gloria is omitted during Advent and Lent, as is the Alleluia during Lent.

[17]Petrarch, born Francesco Petrarca (1304–1374), was one of the foremost Italian humanist poets. Composers in the sixteenth century frequently set his words to music.

be performed in the context of the conventions in which it was conceived. To do otherwise, however, is not wrong—it is not a moral issue, but an aesthetic one: what method of performance is the most beautiful? Take for example the accompaniment of Gregorian chant on the organ. The principal problem is that the "harmony" of Gregorian melodies is not triadic but intervallic, and when triadic harmonies are added, they distort the intrinsic harmonies of the chant melodies. We know chant was accompanied on the organ from the seventeenth century on, and method books appeared in the nineteenth and twentieth centuries. So, from a historical point of view, it might be said that there is some authenticity to it, yet the melodies are slowed down and their intrinsic harmonies obscured. It is not as beautiful.

How does combining a career as a university professor with musical performance work for you?
The work of the university provides opportunities for intellectual perspectives not easily accessible elsewhere. As an example, John Freccero, a reputed scholar of Dante, gave a year-long course in Dante's *Commedia*. I attended it with interest. We followed the *Inferno* with rapt attention to all the historical characters who landed in the underworld. But when it came to the *Purgatorio*, there were passages that mentioned liturgical chants I had frequently sung. When they came up for discussion, I constantly interrupted, "but that is because of the liturgy that piece belongs to." I subsequently wrote an essay on music in the *Commedia*. A further essay—on the *Paradiso*, drawing upon fourteenth-century music theory to illuminate its conclusion—showed why music ceases at the culmination of Dante's journey. It has been the integration of performance and scholarship that drew me to Stanford and remains a most satisfactory basis for my work.

Emma Kirkby: "The Eye, The Hand, The Word"

John Tibbetts
28 October 2009, Overland Park, Kansas

Introduced by Arabs in southern Europe during the Muslim incursion of the eighth and ninth centuries, especially Spain, the oud was a guitar-like, plucked string instrument with a deep rounded body and a fretted fingerboard. The oud was one of the European lute's ancestors, although lute-like instruments can be found in many past and present cultures.

In the words of the *Toronto Globe and Mail*, the "clear" and "agile" voice of Emma Kirkby makes hearing her "an experience not to be missed." Born in the United States, Kirkby was educated in England and has achieved much of her success with early music. A Dame of the British Empire, she was awarded

all best to John, & thanks for
a lively conversation about Dowland,
Monteverdi et al.!
                    Emma Kirkby

Fig. 3 Emma Kirkby

the Incorporated Society of Musicians' Distinguished Musician Award in 2016. Swedish lutenist Jakob Lindberg has partnered with Kirkby in many musical ventures, including programs presented in several American cities. Trained at the Royal School of Music in London, Lindberg has recorded the complete lute works of John Dowland (1563–1626) as well as a great deal of other music (Fig. 3).

This conversation with Emma Kirkby transpired before her concert at Johnson County Community College, Overland Park, Kansas.

JOHN C. TIBBETTS: There is some evidence that John Dowland is attracting today's pop artists!
EMMA KIRKBY: Sting [a popular 1980s pop singer] gave his all to his Dowland recording. I respect that absolutely. I wouldn't do it the same way myself, but I'm not him. But he has a terrific voice, and there are some very good things about it. He was approaching it as, what would you say, a highly intelligent layman. I just applaud his courage!

I'm sure the name alone made the recording possible.
Well, that's the thing. We beat away for thirty-five years on Dowland, and then Sting comes along in six months and completely changes the scene. He puts down his name on the map so we can't complain about that, we're very grateful for it, essentially.

Did you grow up with music in your home?
My dad loved music and had a fruity baritone voice, which he enjoyed to use and we sang in the car. But no, it wasn't a big deal, just something we liked. I was very lucky, because the six schools I went to were very, very musical. The very earliest reports said that I had a lovely singing voice. But I didn't know that at the time, and my parents didn't think anything of it. I just ended up going to schools where singing was a big deal. Not solo singing, though. I'm grateful for that.

A great English tradition in itself.
When I'm with my musician colleagues, I know that their grasp of music is far more sophisticated than mine. They've got all the terms for everything, and they are very, very well trained. The way I see it, they're musicians and I'm a singer. Having said that, I would like to think I'm a musical singer and who's someone a good colleague for musicians.

I've heard that your voice is sometimes described as a "light voice," or "white" voice, whatever that means.
[Giuseppe] Verdi [1813–1901] wrote some beautiful pieces *per voci bianche* or white voice. He wanted women's voices that sang straight [i.e., without vibrato]. It's a lovely effect. He prized them and wrote especially for them. But this term "white," is almost a term of abuse now. It was something Verdi wanted then, at least as a change from other things.

Why do lutenist Jakob Lindberg and you call one of your tours "Orpheus in England?"
We have these two composers, John Dowland at one end of the seventeenth century and Henry Purcell on the other. They were the only two English composers

who were honored with the title "Orpheus" in their own lifetimes.[18] Dowland travelled across Europe, to the Continent, especially to Germany. His patron, Moritz, Landgraf of Hesse, was a great supporter of the performing arts in North Germany. He called Dowland *der englische Orpheus* [the English Orpheus]. And Purcell was already dead when they put out a compilation of work in 1698 and called it *Orpheus Britannicus*. I think people really did take this title very seriously.

The myth of Orpheus is certainly central to almost any consideration of music.
Yes, indeed. And they *did* take it very seriously. And I think people have started to take it seriously again recently. In fact the lutenist Anthony Rooley, with whom I've done a lot of work, has written a book called *Revealing the Orpheus Within.*[19] He's a devotee of Orpheus. Like most musicians are, whether we admit it or not. We're following in the footsteps of someone who became a standard for what music is.

The lute is obviously very important to your performance practices, isn't it?
Hugely important to me. Absolutely. If I were Bill Gates or some similarly rich and benevolent person, I would put in every conservatory in the world six lutes, at least, with good players along with historical keyboards to supplement the hugely successful but very loud pianos that are in every room. I think young singers need the variety of experience with all these things. I wouldn't forbid them to sing with pianos, far from it. By the law of averages, though, most people are playing piano rather loudly. The piano's often too large for the room it's in and the young singer has to crowd in beside that piano just to survive! This is particularly true for the sort of voices like mine and those of young sopranos with fairly light voices. So, I would love to add this more intimate dimension to the experience of all young singers. As Anthony Rooley used to put it, you might say the lute has no dynamics, but actually, as a Yorkshireman might say, "It starts at nowt [nothing] and tapers off." Actually, it's not true to say it starts at "nowt" or *piano*, of course; the lute can carry very well, it's very clear. It draws the ear in. And it draws your attention outward to other sounds in the room. I think it *clarifies* people's listening. Generally, as you settle into an evening with the lute, people get calmer and quieter. They listen better.

Is it at all unusual then among vocalists to use the lute in recital?
It's just as much a question of finding a good instrument, isn't it?
And good players.
Good players are fairly thin on the ground. It's a big commitment to play the lute. It's not an easy instrument. On the other hand, the players will tell you that its repertoire is much, much larger than that of the guitar. The guitar is a lovely

---

[18]Born to the Muse Kalliope and the Thracian king Oeagrus, Orpheus was a legendary musician, so skilled he was able to persuade the king of Hell to release Eurydice, his dead wife.

[19]For this and many other books mentioned below, see "For additional investigation" at the end of the present volume.

instrument but some of the best players sort of get to the end of the repertoire after a few years and have to start commissioning new pieces, and so on. Whereas a lute player will always find new things because it was the queen of instruments for several hundred years. It's a very rich treasure trove of music in fact.

What of the chittarone? Is it a kind of lute?
Yes, it is. The chittarone tends to have a very large back and belly and a very long neck, so that it can play really deep bass notes. You've got the advantage of the beautiful plucking in the middle that all the lutes have but you also have these wonderful, sounds like giant belly rumbles, the rumbling fantastic deep notes of the chittarone. Any chittarone player has to stand up to tune it in order to reach its pegs at the top. It always makes the audience laugh whenever they get up and start fiddling around with the pegs at the top. It's a wonderful sound and it's quite substantial. And they loved it so much in the early Italian opera period that one visitor complained you could barely see the action on the stage because of the forest of chittarone necks coming up from the pit! Like other plucked instruments, they can support you very well and they can also just retreat and leave you to make an incredibly light nuance with no competition, so that you can really take every level of utterance and know it's going to reach the audience.

Does Mr. Lindberg also perform on that instrument?
He does indeed. But what he's got with him on this particular tour is a very special instrument, which is not a chittarone, but an instrument that has ten courses and an extra kind of rider peg. If he decides to do, for instance, Sylvius Leopold Weiss [1687–1750], a contemporary of Bach, who was a wonderful lute virtuoso—if he wants to play his music, he sets it up slightly differently. What he's got is a historical instrument. It's a beauty, bought at a Sotheby's auction fifteen years ago. The wood has been dated and it's reckoned it's from a pine tree on the higher reaches of the Alps that started growing in 1418 and was made into a lute in in the 1590s in South Germany in Augsburg. One could even speculate—not too unjustifiably—that Dowland himself might have seen this instrument. He passed through South Germany on his way to Italy in the 1590s. He wanted to go down and speak to the great composer Luca Marenzio. Dowland got as far as North Italy but didn't quite make that meeting.

Does it have its own separate seats on airplanes?
Indeed it does. Absolutely. And there is an issue with humidity. Every new venue, Jakob's got his hygrometer, and if it registers—

What is that?
—a hygrometer measures the humidity of a place. If the percentage of humidity is lower than 35, the lute does not leave its case until the humidity's been raised, because if it dries out too much, it's in danger of splitting.

How long have you been concertizing with him?
With Jakob? Well, we've known each other a very long time because we worked together in all the groups back in the 1980s and 1990. And it must be at least ten years since we first made duos together.

Will there be solos in your Dowland performances?
Absolutely. I exploit that to the hilt. I love having him play a lot and I love listening to it.

Pardon my ignorance on this, but are Dowland's galliards also to be sung?
Yes, they are. The most famous piece he ever wrote is called "Lachrimae, Flow my Tears." And the words were published in 1600. Scholars think the words probably came second, which was unusual. Most of the songs started with the text.

Was it also a tradition for a woman to sing them?
Not in public, but domestically, yes, very much so. Dowland's *First Book of Songs* in 1597 was a huge success. It went into three reprints, which was quite unusual. And he set all his songs in Book One in four parts, actually. It's very cleverly laid out. You've got two pages, and on the left page you've got the top line and the lute part. On the other pages, you've got at the same angle as the top line one of the other parts, namely the bass. Then, if you turn the thing ninety degrees, you've got the tenor. Ninety degrees again, you've got the alto. So you can lay the thing flat on the table and people sit around the table to read it.

Oh, how wonderful!
You don't always need the three extra parts sung, but they sound very nice if they are. You can just work on the left-hand page with voice and lute, or you can add the other voices. Or you can put those parts onto gambas; it's up to you. All those, I think, would have been viable options. And the women would have sung as part of the evening entertainment and evening pleasures in large families and stately households and so on. I don't know the numbers, but the sales of Book One must have been sufficient to warrant the further printings, over sixteen years in fact.

And wherever Dowland went then, they were sung by ... him?
We don't know if he sang. We definitely know that he *played*, of course! He coupled the talent of the passionate artist with the soul of the scholar and historian. I think probably his real strong suit was the playing, and he would have grabbed the nearest good singer to sing the songs. He boasted about "Flow my Tears" that it had been published in eight capitals of Europe. It was his "calling card." It is a very beautiful pavane.[20] There are also plenty of songs in the form of the galliard. The "Frog Galliard" and the "Earl of Essex" are galliards. Those are quite popular

---

[20]A slow dance in duple meter, actually little more than a stroll with a partner of the opposite sex.

now. They signified popular personalities of the time. "Captain Digorie Piper," I believe, was a real pirate! Other times we have to guess. But a lot of songs will have a story, if we could only decode it.

What do you mean?
Take the galliard, for example. It's very much a personality thing. It's the dance where the man shows off and the woman swishes her skirt and simpers and admires the man. It's not completely a lazy dance for the woman; there's a certain amount of jumping needed as well. It's just not as spectacular as the man. It was said that the queen used to dance six galliards before breakfast every day.

Did Purcell know Dowland's music?
Good question, I don't know if he knew Dowland but he certainly knew Thomas Morley [c. 1558–1602], who was a contemporary of Dowland. Morley's music was still used in Westminster Abbey when Purcell was there. And indeed for Queen Mary's funeral music they used the Morley music alongside Purcell's brand new or relatively new compositions. That church tradition lasted for sixty, seventy years.

Now, I for one find Purcell a very mysterious character.
It's true that we don't know that much about his personal life, it's true. We know he died in rather odd circumstances and there have been odd stories about that. I think the impression is of someone who was good fun, with a very genial character, and obviously someone phenomenally prolific, who worked cheerfully alongside other composers, too. In the theater, he was often collaborating with others, particularly towards the end of his life. He was extremely well taught by Matthew Locke [1621–1677] and John Blow [1649–1708]—and indeed by himself.

And he had the ear of the King apparently, Charles II?
Well, yes, I don't know that Purcell was more or less influential than anyone else, particularly. Charles was a benign and useful patron. But it was said that he really didn't like music that he couldn't tap his feet to. So I hardly think he was the connoisseur of the further reaches of things. But, yes, he was very benign and of course his whole reign was a great sunshine of an era after the Protectorate. People just couldn't believe their luck when he came on the throne and the theater started up again—and, you know, music.

What do we really know about his operas? Were the productions as scenically bizarre as we think? You know, gods and cherubs flying down from the rafters in chariots ...?
Oh, I would think so, but don't forget that even before when Inigo Jones was doing pretty amazing things in his masques for King James, and even before the

Stuart dynasty got going, amazing effects were happening on stage.[21] You know, at the end of each [masque], people would take away bits of scenery as souvenirs. Theater was the ultimate ephemeral art form! Later on, things were a bit more careful. What we do know is that some of the plays for which Purcell wrote music were incredibly grim affairs. And people joked about the English taste for entertainment—that they couldn't cope with theater unless there was music and they could manage music without words.

Do we know how the singers sounded?
Of course we can't know how they sounded. All we can do is listen to the instruments and see what kind of vocal sound might have worked with them. If you're in a duet with a beautiful instrument, or if you're singing those two and three and four part choruses or church pieces or anthems, you need those dissonances. There has to be a fairly clean attack. There has to be straight sound, otherwise, those dissonances go for nothing.

What about vibrato, or lack of it?
Yeah, a vibrato that confuses us about the pitch is going to spoil any dissonance obviously. Even [William] Shakespeare [1564–1616] has this rather beautiful metaphor about that, where Othello kisses Desdemona [in *Othello*] early on in the play and he, as they kiss, says something like, "Let this be the only discord," or something like that. He uses the metaphor of their kiss as a bit of dissonance that is going to resolve. So, the idea is that those dissonances in music, they're bittersweet.

As someone relatively unfamiliar with Monteverdi's madrigals, I wonder: was he ahead of his time, or was that merely the convention of the day?
[Claudio] Monteverdi [1567–1643] was ahead of his time in the sense that he was really good at distilling what was going on and finding the human side of things in the drama. But in terms of astonishing dissonance, you have to think of [Carlo] Gesualdo [1566–1613] as well. And even Gesualdo wasn't alone. I mean, Gesualdo came from a tradition where they were all trying to do this. And then before Gesualdo there was Pomponio Nenna [1556–1608]. They were all searching, trying to imagine what it was like in the Greek tragedies. And they were looking for what they called *pykna*, which were little points of excitement. They knew that the music in Greek tragedy must have been amazing, but they had no idea what it was like. They were attempting to use this music to express extreme human emotions, as in tragedy. And that's what they were after with polyphony, four or five part music, using those effects. At the same time, of course, single voices were starting to emerge from the texture, relegating the others more into the background. Then you get to the songs where the lute no longer plays an intricate part but a continuo, a supportive role. So, the solo voices are beginning to emerge from the murk, if you like. Though I also love the murk myself!

---

[21]Invented in Italy, the masque was a form of "masked" amateur dramatic entertainment, popular especially with English aristocrats during the sixteenth and seventeenth centuries.

That's very English, I suppose, "to love the murk"!
It is! But then, at the same time someone like Monteverdi could work wonderfully with both. I mean, he excelled in the *prima prattica* [first practice or style], the old way of doing it, which was perfectly balanced polyphony in the style of [Giovanni] Palestrina [1525–1594]. But Monteverdi also had the *seconda prattica* [second practice or style], which was taking those voices and letting them collectively express strong human emotions and gradually become more like a clutch of soloists and eventually the soloists themselves.

In explaining singing, you deploy a whole arsenal of metaphors. My favorite, which I'm asking you about now, is that the diaphragm is like a trampoline.
This was my teacher's expression; it was so useful. People put so much emphasis on the diaphragm and the abdomen and how support comes from below. Support just stays below but it doesn't start things off. Which brings us to the trampoline. The trampoline can only react to what falls onto it. And that reaction then comes into play. Therefore, it's really important how you breathe and how the air goes in through the mouth. If you breathe through the nose, it is filtered and things start getting a bit limited and sticky, if you're not careful. So I'm very open and I just take breath in through the mouth as anyone would in normal circumstances. That is *inspiration,* which also means your soul and your mind are *inspired.* It's the idea that sparks the breath. In fact, it's what you do *before* you take the breath that matters as well.

And you have this notion of performance and gesture as an "eye-line" and as a kind of "triple play"—
Yes, yes—eye, hand, word. You find your eye line, you make the gesture, and you speak or sing. But it happens incredibly fast. Don't separate them too slowly; then you lose everything. Once I did a little show with William Christie, Judy Nelson (bless her heart), and some other singers, and we went to Caen (or was it Nantes, I can't quite remember), where we had a week to work up a Monteverdi sequence with madrigals. Inside, where we were performing, was this staircase, and we were all in costume. When we were not singing, we had to stand, leaning on the staircase banister and looking down and observing and seem to be listening. And the effect on the audience was extraordinary. The organizers said they never had an audience so quiet. It was wonderful because they were being shown *how to listen.* Now, if you were in France in the seventeenth century performing for the Sun King,[22] you never took your eyes off his face. But I don't think it's necessary for us in every Baroque performance, because we haven't always got the Sun King in the middle of the front row!

---

[22]Louis XIV of France [1638–1715], a monarch who encouraged music and dancing among members of his court.

Julian Bream: "I Do Feel that My Consort Helped Get the Early Music Movement Underway"

John C. Tibbetts
8 April 1995, Kansas City, Missouri

Praised by the *New York Herald Tribune* as "an exceptional musician who is able to recreate a whole era with his playing," Julian Bream has won fame as a guitar virtuoso who also plays the lute. A child prodigy, albeit as a pianist, Bream studied piano and composition at the Royal College of Music and guitar with celebrated performer Andrés Segovia. In 1985 Bream was promoted to the rank of Commander of the British Empire. In 1988 he became an Honorary Member of the Royal Philharmonic Society. Bream's Consort has performed around the world (Fig. 4).

The following conversation took place in Kansas City, Missouri, on the occasion of Bream's recital at the Folly Theater.

Fig. 4 Julian Bream

JOHN C. TIBBETTS: Although you've probably been asked this many times, I have to wonder what physical and mental adjustments must you make from going from the lute to the guitar?

JULIAN BREAM: The tuning is different, for a start. And then you're playing on double strings instead of single strings. The lute has a lighter touch and a different right hand position. You play along the string on the lute and across it on the guitar. I never found any real difficulty in expressing music on the lute. It seemed to me much more natural to me than playing the guitar.

I suppose it goes without saying, that if you could you go back and listen to Dowland perform, you would do so unhesitatingly.

Oh yes. Absolutely.

What questions might you ask of him?

Well, I wouldn't bother. I would just *listen*.

Is he a figure of about whom we know enough or is he a mystery man?

No, we know quite a bit. Although he was born in Ireland, he became one of the greatest musicians in Queen Elizabeth's court. But he probably spent half his life outside of England. During the 1590s, he traveled widely thorough Germany, Holland, and Italy. In the Renaissance, people were travelling like mad; they were moving all over the place. Knowledge of Latin worked in a lot of countries, so there were few communication barriers. He was treated like a statesman in Denmark by King Christian [IV]. Later back in England he enjoyed the patronage and favor of many highly placed dignitaries, like the Earl of Essex, for whom he wrote one of his most famous galliards. But he seems always to have been in debt and most of his music was unpublished in his lifetime.

I can truly say that my first exposure to the works of Dowland and others from that time was through your recordings, thank you very much. But when you first heard Dowland's music, what did you think? Did you already feel special qualities about it?

What attracted me—and it is interesting that it should attract somebody in their mid-teens—was the lyricism and the melancholy of so much of his music. There's a wonderful melancholy with Dowland. Very rich and reflective and plaintive. Plangent, that's the word. I was, as it were, hooked. It was almost like a drug.

Is there an artist of Dowland's time that none of us knows about but who is a very special pleasure for you?

Well, that's very interesting. I would have thought that the most brilliant lutenist of that period was a chap called Daniel Bacheler [1572–1619], who was a fantastic player at the age of eight. He composed a lot. He was younger than Dowland, and they composed music for each other. Another musician that, I think, is one of the exquisite musicians of that period was a chap called Philip Rosseter [1568–1623]. He was a lutenist to the court of James I and wrote a couple of books of nice, beautiful songs. They're very simple but the actual proportions of everything are so sublime that it is music that really does touch the heart. He also wrote for the theater.

Tell me about your boyhood, your upbringing.
I was born in 1933 in Battersea, London, and I spent a lot of time in my grand-mother's pub, an old beer house. I loved her. My parents were very unusual, very individual. My father was a very successful commercial artist and a natural musi-cian who could not read music but could play all the pop songs of the period on the piano. I used to lie under the piano, listening in sheer ecstasy. And he had recordings of Stephane Grapelli and Django Reinhardt, which I loved. Because of Django, I was drawn to the guitar like a magnet. My mother was very beautiful, but rather distant in her way, although she was very warm to me. I didn't take up music myself until years later, but that was on the piano and 'cello, not the guitar. However, my father always had a guitar around the house, so I got rather fond of that, too. And when he saw I was interested, he gave me my first introductory lessons on it. There were no teachers around in those days, so I was largely self-taught. We played duets together. And then I heard Segovia on a recording, and that's when I knew what I wanted to do. Later I had a chance to observe what he was doing and went to as many concerts of his that I could. I had two meetings with Segovia, in 1947 or 1948, and he had me play and passed comments—not all complimentary, I must say. I didn't play very well. I was very nervous. But that year was my professional debut with the guitar.

So, when do you make the move from guitar to lute? I mean, who would have thought of such a thing, in those days especially?
Well, that's quite a point. My father did bring home, about 1949, a lute, which was a German instrument, what then was known as a guitar lute. It was a lute-shape but strung like a guitar. And they were made in Germany in the 1920s and 1930s as part of a sort of nationalism, in a way. The lute made by these music fascists was considered part of German folklore. They were factory made but very well made. My father bought it from a sailor in the streets in London. He was going on a boat and I remember it cost only five dollars! It was very cheap.

So, when you first saw this instrument...?
I thought, well how interesting. And the amusing thing was I could play it, because it was a guitar lute. And then I got my interest in early music quite by accident. We heard early music in England because the BBC [British Broadcasting Corporation] in 1946 or 1947, they started a special program for music lovers. There was quite a lot of early music being performed just then. And so, you know, I heard some of this and I loved it.

Was there a particular person there to encourage your interest in the lute?
I had a friend who was a harpsichord maker who in fact did this conversion for me, making my guitar lute into a real lute. And he encouraged me and he knew one or two musicologists at Cambridge who found a bit of music for me, things of

that nature. I had already discovered the music of Dowland through an edition by Peter Warlock [1894–1930].[23] And I fell in love with this music.

Did you ever talk to Mr. Segovia about the possibility of playing on both instruments professionally?
I didn't think he cared much for the lute. But he did eventually say—I mean it was years later— that I was the only one who could make the lute sound halfway decent, or words to that effect. So that was some sort of praise!

Did you have difficulty in persuading managers that in addition to the guitar you wanted to play the lute as well?
Well, in fact, they were rather attracted by that because the lute had a historical sort of nostalgia about it, which people loved. And also, it gave a certain anti-quated seriousness to what I did. For a lot of people, the guitar was a light music instrument, not capable of expression of any depth. And so the lute was a very good additional string to my bow, as it were. And in fact, I began, after a while, to play the lute on the radio in this serious music program I told you about earlier.

Let's talk about the Julian Bream Consort. An ensemble like that must have been unusual at the time, right?
It was a kind of "Elizabethan Dance Band" with a "rhythm section," if you will, of lute, bandora,[24] and cittern.[25] It started in the 1950s. I remember being asked to take part in a radio broadcast with musicologist and conductor Thurston Dart. I went to the studio and there were some musicians on the treble viol, the bass viol, and the bass recorder. It was quite a motley crowd. Thurston put his beat down, and away we went. It was the start of my work with a broken consort.[26] Because it was six people, there were two bowed instruments, one blown instrument, a bass flute, and three plucked instruments. It was the sort of standard band of the 1580s and 1590s, the kind of group you would have heard in the theater doing incidental music for ceremonial occasions, weddings, and so forth.

Was this music you might have heard at Shakespeare's Globe Theater?
Oh sure, absolutely. And you know, you would have heard it in many places, such as in masques for evening entertainment in these grand palaces and homes. And it was a very popular combination, you know.

---

[23]"Peter Warlock" was the pen name of Philip Arnold Heseltine. Heseltine published music as Warlock and wrote music criticism under his birth name.

[24]A large plucked string instrument popular in the late 1500s and early 1600s.

[25]A plucked string instrument from the Renaissance with a flat back, in contrast to the curved back of a lute.

[26]A broken consort consists of different kinds of instruments—perhaps several recorders, string instruments, and a keyboard instrument. A whole or closed consort consists exclusively of the same kind of instrument—perhaps string instruments only.

When did your Consort first perform professionally?
Well, by 1960 the Early Music Movement was just getting underway. I was beginning to realize that my group had the kind of professionalism that could attract a wide audience. Indeed, I do feel that my Consort helped get the Early Music Movement underway. So, there we were at the Aldeburgh Festival [in 1961], and we followed that in short order at Wigmore Hall in London.

What was an evening on stage with your Consort like? Were you dressed in an Elizabethan style?
I was against sort of dressing up and being special, because I wanted for us to look like professional musicians. No period costumes. No stuffed dummies.

Even before you made long-playing recordings with your Consort, you were with Westminster, right?
Westminster Records had just become the thing. It was a great label, very adventurous. The quality of the recordings was very high. They were made mainly in Vienna. I made my recordings in one of the loveliest halls, the Mozart Hall in Vienna. And I think that the company was largely undercapitalized. Eventually they did topple, which was a very sad day I think for the recording business. I was with them three years, around 1955–1958, I think.

Was it a natural progression from there to RCA Red Seal?
It was a different, a totally different company. RCA in the late 1950s was a very big and prestigious company. It recorded all of [violinist Jascha] Heifetz and [pianist Artur] Rubinstein. What they did was extraordinary. There was a very good producer called Peter Dellheim. And he somehow managed to convince his bosses that the sort of repertoire I wanted to do would be commercially okay. He was a great producer and a very good friend of mine. He kept me in that company.

It was a new era in my playing. In those days, the early 1960s, we recorded in New York at the RCA Studio on 22nd Street. But recording in New York turned out to be hard going—too nervous, too edgy. And the subways constantly affected our playing.

Eventually RCA let me record back in England. And that was a wonderful arrangement. I had my own producer, my own engineer, and I was living in London by that time. I could choose the venue, and I made records in the most beautiful place in the north of London called Kenwood House, a very famous house with a beautiful picture collection.

Nowadays, we find ourselves in the age of compact discs. I guess that is good news for those of us who do not have your original LPs.
Well, interestingly enough, two years ago [i.e., in 1993] for my sixtieth birthday, RCA reissued my complete catalogue on compact disc, some twenty-eight CDs. A little later they released two CDs that I made with guitarist John Williams. Then I made four records for EMI, three of which are out already and one coming

out probably in a couple of months. All in all, they are a mix of old and new repertoire.

I venture to say they now sound better than ever! Think of the quiet surface, no tape hiss, right?
Absolutely.

Judith Malafronte: "My Career has Basically Encompassed Music from Monteverdi to Bach and Handel"

Michael Saffle
July 2017

Defining "early music" depends on who provides the definition. Generally thought to encompass all European musical styles prior to 1750, the Early Music Movement (EMM) now includes works written in the 1800s. Similarly, *how* this music is performed varies greatly, and solid musicological evidence supports various interpretations and approaches. In recent decades, performances and recordings of operas from the 1600s and early 1700s have steadily increased, bringing this virtuoso art form to modern audiences. Singers who specialize in early music utilize characteristic vocal timbres and techniques, including straight tone (no vibrato), and singers must be well versed in a variety of ornamental embellishments, many of which are improvised while performing.

A former member of the Waverly Consort, mezzo-soprano Judith Malafronte has performed with opera companies, orchestras, oratorio societies, and early music groups throughout the world. She has recorded widely and her writings appear regularly in *Opera News*, *Early Music America*, and other publications. *New York Times* critic Bernard Holland observed that "she blended power and agility with great success" in her performance of the title role in Handel's *Ariodante*, an opera all but unknown for 200 years until it was "resurrected" with acclaim in 1985. Malafronte is currently on the faculty at the Yale University School of Music (Fig. 5).

This interview was conducted both by correspondence and during a face-to-face meeting at the 2017 Shenandoah, Virginia, Valley Bach Festival, where Ms. Malafronte was teaching a master class in early music performance.

MICHAEL SAFFLE: How did you acquire an interest in early vocal music? Many Americans still don't know anything about it.

JUDITH MALAFRONTE: As a young piano player I was attracted to the sonorities and textures of Bach in particular. For my senior recital in college I played

Fig. 5 Judith Malafronte

[Igor] Stravinsky [1882–1971], [Wolfgang Amadeus] Mozart [1756–1791], Bach, and Schubert. I quickly came to terms with the fact that I didn't really like music that was actually composed for the piano. My singing voice was light and clear, and I happily avoided nineteenth-century repertoire. The juries at Eastman would listen to my Monteverdi and [Olivier] Messaien [1908–1992] and cry, "Don't you sing any standard repertoire?"

One startling discovery for me was the music of [Francesco] Landini [?1335–1397], Guillaume [de] Machaut [c. 1300–1397], and [Guillaume] Dufay [c. 1397–1474], and I learned every piece in the *Historical Anthology of Music* that Harvard published years ago. I found the vocalism extremely attractive in a soloistic way, full of subtlety and expressive possibilities. At the same time, my undergrad choir performed the Monteverdi *Vespers* (this was in 1967), and I was blown away by the writing, particularly the harmonic sonorities, the vocal virtuosity, the edgy rhythms. I knew virtually nothing of sixteenth-century music, didn't listen to choral ensembles, and thought Renaissance polyphony was for amateurs. Now I adore this repertoire, but still would rather be singing Isaac and Josquin than listening to it.

Were you able to support yourself by singing sixteenth- and seventeenth-century music?
My first job was with the Waverly Consort, and I was in heaven getting paid to sing Renaissance ensemble music, with the occasional medieval pageant show. Initially the commercial aspects were a shock, after my fairly purist grad school education, but the business model was the New York Pro Musica ensemble, not treatises by [Johannes] Tinctoris [c. 1435–1511].

No one was talking about tactus or tempo proportions [the relationships indicated by various time signatures]—the director would just pick a convenient tempo. The concerts were conceived with a lot of variety, mostly upbeat music, and the funny instruments were always the focus of any audience interest.

Those "funny" instruments? Can you give us some examples?
Well, shawms[27] are still amusing, especially if played poorly! There were viols and lutes, even a theorbo, recorders and crumhorns—goodness, does anyone play the crumhorn any more? The occasional sackbut or cornetto. I think there was even a hand-pumped organetto. These were all novelties around 1980. The thing about historical instruments that is still true today, when we have much more sophisticated playing, is that the instrument itself provides an entry into the earlier style. The Baroque bow, for example, demands that you play the violin or 'cello differently. You can't make even and seamless up and down bows, which you spend years in a conservatory learning how to do. You have to play in a lighter, more nuanced way. Earlier instruments pose technical challenges that are different from their modern counterparts, and these technical differences impact the performance, whether it's tuning, phrasing, expression, articulation, or whatnot. Singers don't have this handy toggle switch when moving between historical and modern styles, so in a way the singers are dependent on the sounds and textures of the instruments, not to mention the earlier tuning systems, to inspire any adjustments to their vocal sound.

---

[27]Shawms and crumhorns are early double-reed instruments, the theorbo a type of large lute, the sackbut a predecessor of the modern trombone, and the cornetto an instrument with finger holes and a brass mouthpiece.

Can you say more about the business model? How do soloists and ensemble per-formers who work with the kinds of music you do, how do they earn a living?
Working with the Waverly Consort from 1977 to 1981 was a good start at earning a living, and I filled my income out with lots of chorus work. At that time the free-lance scene was quite robust in New York City, although old-timers complained that it had been even better twenty years earlier, with more studio and recording work. There were far more professional choruses than now, and there were lots of start-up early music groups that performed in churches and on small concert series. But by the 1990s, and still today, New York has one of the smallest early music scenes anywhere.

When was New York the center of early music? the 1960s? the 1970s? Your suc-cesses suggest that there's still an audience for Baroque opera and even for the music of fifteenth- and sixteenth-century composers like Josquin and Monteverdi.
The early music audiences today are great. They've heard all the ensembles from Europe, they have large CD collections, they have sophisticated tastes, and many are amateur players themselves. Not just in New York, Boston, San Francisco, where early music got a head start in the US, but throughout the country.

So ... tell us a bit more about what you do as a performer? What do you sing?
My career has basically encompassed music from Monteverdi to Bach and Handel. Bach has played a big part, and I've sung with many modern orchestras and festivals as well as period instrument groups. Bach can stand up to any sort of musical abuse, I think, and, when everything comes together, is absolutely sub-lime. I was part of a wonderful series that presented all three surviving Monteverdi operas in a sort of dramatic cycle that unified the characters in a revelatory man-ner. I've sung Handel operas that used period decors and costumes and Baroque stage gesture to enhance the theatrical effect.

I sang many concert performances of [Jean-Baptiste] Lully [1632–1687] operas in the 1970s and '80s, for example, but that repertoire only came to life when peo-ple began spending a lot of money on the production aspect, as is appropriate for a grand, courtly, impressive entertainment that needs fabulous sets and costumes with lots of dancing. The early Italian operas, on the other hand, don't require sce-nic splendor (and they didn't in 1650 either), just clear and beautiful singing with great attention to the declamation.

It's context that's important—is this what you're saying?
I've come to understand and value context more than ever. [Francesco] Cavalli[1602–1676]'s operas were commercial successes because they appealed to the Venetian public, with comic bits sprinkled among the serious story, and needed only a small pit band. Handel's operas were dependent on star singers, who daz-zled the public with spectacular vocalism, which is why they work fine nowadays even with singers completely unversed in Baroque style. Don't forget, the Handel revival was a branch of the [Gioachino] Rossini [1792–1868] revival, with coaches

industriously rewriting the vocal lines for gleeful singers. Many of the European countertenors today, for example, are still singing glued-on ornamentation that is only meant to stupefy. But again, it works because the music is set up to work that way.

Set up to be rewritten, or to be improvised upon?
Set up to be varied. Whether you plan your ornaments in advance or improvise them on the spot (and I think great performers do a bit of both), it should sound spontaneous and exciting, both impressive and expressive.

You mentioned context earlier. What of religious music? How do you perform in church?
I can't even use the word "perform" when thinking about this music. Gregorian chant and Renaissance polyphony make total sense to me in the context of the traditional Latin mass, especially in a one-to-a-part situation like my current church job. But …

So you sing in a Catholic church? I thought the Vatican had called for simpler music in its services?
… but! I was about to say that even Mozart's masses sound best in a church service, when the movements are separated by actions and by other sounds. It's context again.

Can you say a bit more about context?
Sure. Italian madrigals sound best in intimate and casual settings for four or five singers, not by a big choir in concert, no matter how in tune or lively the performance. Bach's cantatas are fabulous done one-to-a-part, and his Passions work fine in concert format, as do Handel's oratorios, which were written for theater audiences and have nothing to do with church. As eighteenth-century music has become mainstreamed (with standard-issue opera singers performing with early music ensembles), seventeenth-century music seems to be still under the radar for many listeners and performers. When the early music revival really got under way in the 1970s, no one knew which repertoires would catch on. Who knew that medieval music would virtually disappear in the United States until only a few years ago?

And now it's back?
There are a few groups now in the United States. But I find that current students and young professionals know little about the pioneers in our field, and they don't care to know. Festivals claim erroneously to be performing a work for the first time, as if the 1970s and 1980s never happened, because it's all about marketing and publicity. There is so much available to watch and study. Performers want to be imaginative, but they haven't read the treatises and studied the scores. Singers often can't name five dead or retired singers in their *Fach* or vocal type.

And performance practice?
The conclusions performers came to in the 1970s and '80s were different from the stylistic guidelines we use today. European ensembles have different aesthetics than U.S. based groups. Cadenzas[28] used to go a certain way, now they take a different route. Continuo groups now almost always include a guitar, whether or not it's suitable, for the rhythmic punctuation it provides. A few violinists in the orchestra at the Metropolitan Orchestra have used Baroque bows for Handel. So the field is certainly alive.

---

[28]Cadenzas are improvised or quasi-improvised ornamental interludes that show off individual performers' artistic and technical ingenuity.

Late Baroque Music

Introduction

During the first half of the eighteenth century, musical complexity reached a zenith. The intellectual rigor of fugal procedures, the virtuosic exploitation of the human voice, and the aural manifestations of emotional excess all found their way into musical works. Ornamentation became so excessive that composers tried, often without success, to reign in performers whose elaborations sometimes buried the underlying musical fabric. Two of the most accomplished musicians of this era were Johann Sebastian Bach and George Friderick Handel. Other important late Baroque composers include Antonio Vivaldi (1678–1741), who worked mostly in Venice, and Georg Philipp Telemann (1681–1767), who worked entirely in Germany, especially Hamburg. Baroque composers mentioned in previous interviews include Lully, Monteverdi—a transitional figure—and Purcell. Still others are François Couperin (1668–1733) and Jean-Philippe Rameau (1683–1764), two of Bach's French contemporaries.

Baroque composers also employed instruments that are less familiar today, including the clavichord, as well as familiar instruments such as the violin, transverse flute, and horn. For additional information, see "A Clutch of Instruments" below.

Johann Sebastian Bach resided in the northern part of Germany for his entire life. Throughout his multifaceted career, he remained a performer, whether on the violin or on various keyboard instruments. Bach held positions as an organist in Arnstadt (1704–1707) and Mühlhausen (1707–1708), organist and later director of music at the ducal court in Weimar (1708–1717), director of music at Prince Leopold's court in Cöthen (1717–1723), where he led the orchestra, and director of music for the four principal churches in Leipzig and a teacher at the school associated with the St. Thomas Church (from 1723). He wrote music according to the needs of his particular job. As such, most of his orchestral works come from

© The Author(s) 2018
J. C. Tibbetts et al. (eds.), *Performing Music History*,
https://doi.org/10.1007/978-3-319-92471-7_3

his years in Cöthen, while his great sacred works, including many of his cantatas and the massive Mass in B minor, were written in Leipzig. Bach was also involved in promoting music for the general public and led the Collegium Musicum in Leipzig, which gave concerts at a popular coffee house in the city. Rosalyn Tureck and Samuel Baron discuss the intricacies and delights of performing Bach today.

Handel, by contrast, was an international figure: one of several issues raised by John Eliot Gardiner and Simon Preston. Born in the northern part of Germany, Bach traveled to Italy, where he mastered various Italian genres, including opera seria and various types of concertos, especially the concerto grosso. *Opere serie* (the plural of *opera seria*; also known as *dramma per musica*) were large-scale works on mythological or historical themes. The productions included highly elaborate solo singing and featured castrati, who became some of the highest paid and most celebrated celebrities of the day. Concerti grossi (the plural of concerto grosso) were instrumental works that, in typical Baroque fashion, placed a small group of soloists (called the concertino and usually consisting of two violins and basso continuo) in contrast with a larger string ensemble (the *ripieno*). Opera seria and the concerto grosso were ideal genres for composers, including Handel, to explore the Baroque principle of contrast, whether in terms of tempo (speed), performing forces, style (speech-like recitative or dramatic aria in opera), or dynamics (volume).

Handel made his way to England in 1710, where he continued to compose opera seria. Since theaters did not allow performances of staged works during the penitential church season of Lent, Handel developed a new genre, English oratorio. Sharing form and style with its Italian-language cousin, Handel's oratorios, particularly *Messiah* (1741), became favorites with audiences and performers alike. He also anglicized his name (from Georg Friedrich Händel) and became a British subject.

William Everett and Michael Saffle

Rosalyn Tureck: "From Bach My Whole Art Has Grown"

John C. Tibbetts
28 May 1992, Lawrence, Kansas; 10 June 1992, New York City

Few have done more to bring Bach's keyboard music to the public than Rosalyn Tureck (1914–2003). Scholar, archivist, author, orchestra conductor, and Juilliard faculty member, her indefatigable devotion to Bach, as evidenced by her many recordings and a series of legendary annual all-Bach recitals in New York's Town Hall. Tureck loved music of all kinds, however, and frequently performed works by contemporary composers. She actually made her Carnegie Hall debut playing the theremin, an electronic invention

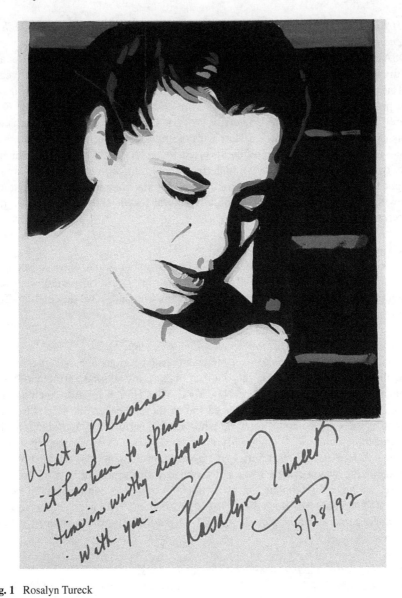

Fig. 1 Rosalyn Tureck

of Léon Theremin (1896–1993), one of her teachers. In 1952 Tureck presented the first program in the USA devoted to tape and electronic music (Fig. 1).

These conversations took place on two occasions: at the University of Kansas after her performance of the *Goldberg Variations* and at her home in New York City.

JOHN C. TIBBETTS: Why don't we begin with your connections to Bach, both as a scholar and as an artist?

ROSALYN TURECK: Well, I have worked with scholarly matters all my life; and all my scholarship is in my playing; and I have written a lot throughout the years. But now I have restructured my life so I can devote more time to the writing. As you probably know, I have a series, *An Introduction to the Performance of Bach* [1960], published by Oxford University Press. It's in three volumes, and each contains essays and music scores. I start with the tiniest pieces, like a little piece he wrote for his son, [composer] Wilhelm Friedemann [Bach (1710–1784)], which is only two lines but has Bach's own fingering. That's a fingering that pianists are not taught today. However, I believe you cannot play his contrapuntal music without knowing his own fingering. It's absolutely natural for the sort of fugal music that he wrote.

Can you give me an example?

It's a kind of an overlapping/underlapping fingering. For instance, we use consecutive fingering using the thumb. But Bach's fingering doesn't use the thumb very much, or not at all. So, you're playing 2-3-4 going up and 4-3-2 descending. That sort of thing.

Are your books too technical for the casual music enthusiast?

Not at all. Each volume advances somewhat on the previous one. A layperson can read them. Absolutely. I work very hard at making my writing very clear. A few years ago, I was giving a lecture in New York, when Harriet Johnson, then a music critic at the *New York Post*, introduced me to the audience. She said, "Rosalyn Tureck is the only author I know of who was has written an 'Introduction' that requires three volumes!" [laughs] My next series in Bach's own fingering was for my own *Tureck-Bach Urtext Series*. It's a very unusual edition. I decided to do it in a particular way, because I was not satisfied with former editions of Bach. Of course, we have for scholars the great *Bach-Gesellschaft* edition [established in the 1850s] and the *Neue Bach Ausgabe* [established in 1950], which are what I call the Old Testament and the New Testament. That constitutes the great core of Bach scholarship.

But do they satisfy the performing needs of musicians?

Let me explain. My life's work has always involved an integration of academic and performing scholarship. I've always believed in integration and not in separation. Musicians, especially performing musicians, need to have something that is based in scholarship as profound and meticulous as [the scholarly editions]. But we need to go beyond that, because these are editions which we can be sure we have some assurance about note text. But as we all know, there's more than that to performance. Performance is an art in itself. I think that actually performance as an art has been a bit neglected. It's a very profound art. As we all know, it's something much more than technique and skills. It also requires scholarship. I'm speaking in general now, not just of Bach and ancient music. As performers we must build within ourselves an edifice of scholarship, from which we fly off into the world of art.

It must be fascinating to see Bach's manuscripts.
Of course. I don't know that you'd recognize Bach's own handwriting, but I must say, it's beautiful handwriting. I'm very much interested in notation as such, because I think it's very reflective of style. The form of the notation is exactly what we know, but the beauty of it is—and I have seen this over and over again—where Bach is thinking melodically and lyrically; where you find that suddenly the beams are curved; and where it's in a fast tempo or a more aggressive kind of rhythmic figuration, those beams are absolutely straight! I have studied too many original manuscripts to doubt that feeling influences notation.

You say these are "original" manuscripts?
Let me clarify this. I study every original source that is extant, so that my text is as *"ur"* [first source] as you can get. For example, we have no original manuscript in Bach's own hand of the *Italian Concerto*. What we do have are the first two print-ings that were printed when Bach was very much alive, in 1735 and 1736. In his own copy of the first printing he added embellishments of the second movement in his own hand. That is as absolute an original as we can get. That is my *Urtext*. You have to know the age of the manuscript, the dating, the person, the ink, and all of that. Many errors cropped up in the nineteenth century when editors made changes in the *Italian Concerto's* note text in the first movement. My own edition [1983] has a facsimile of the entire work. It was necessary for me to return the text to its original, true form. I insisted that Schirmer reprint the entire version of Bach's own copy. Now we also know a different chronology of the cantatas, for instance. In many of the works that I have edited, I am finding errors that have gone on uncontested for 250 years. It's like an archaeological dig. It's marvelous.

Have you been able to visit places where Bach worked? Have any of his keyboards survived?
Oh, yes, there's a sacred feeling about it. The most direct experience of that kind was when I did a research tour of what was then East Germany. You know, Bach hardly did any travelling at all, and I visited every town in which he had lived and worked, and studied all sorts of manuscripts and went into all kinds of archives and had a wonderfully interesting time. There is an organ in Arnstadt he played, a small organ. Alas, the pipes are gone and you can't hear the sound. But the key-board is there and the bench is there and that contact gave me a deeper experience with the music.

As a performing artist, now, when did you first encounter Bach?
I began my studies in piano very early. I began to study and play by myself when I was four. I played everything I heard. And since there was a lot of music in the house, I played it all! My mother sang, my sisters were studying (they were older than I); and at eight my teacher decided to put me into a contest, the prize

of which was a proper debut in a major hall in Chicago with critics and so forth. I
won the contest and made my public debut at the age of nine. At ten, I remember
positively mooning over Bach!

*Which strikes me as an experience unfamiliar to most ten-year-old children! Did
you feel separate from many of the kids your own age?*
Not at all. It seemed to me so normal, to love Bach and to be loving music. It
never occurred to me that I was doing anything particularly unusual. When I
began studying with a Russian teacher named Sophia Brilliant-Liven, from what
used to be called Petrograd [now Leningrad] who had toured Europe with violinist
Leopold Auer, playing all the Beethoven sonatas for piano and violin, I studied
not only Johann Sebastian Bach but also Carl Philip Emanuel Bach [1714–1788],
Handel, Haydn, Mozart, and Beethoven. And there were fairly modern Russians,
composers not heard much today, like [Anton] Arensky [1861–1906], [Aleksandr]
Liapunov [1857–1918], and so forth. I knew the old Russian technique that comes
from the school of Anton Rubinstein, who created the Conservatory in Petrograd.
His brother Nikolai [Rubinstein] created the Conservatory in Moscow.

Who was the first Bach authority with whom you studied?
That was Jan Chiapuso. He was a Bach enthusiast and scholar. I didn't know that
at first. I came to him when I was not quite fourteen. I felt a most extraordinary
bond with him; he was most sympathetic. For my first lesson he assigned a prelude and fugue[1] of Bach and a Beethoven sonata and one or two other works. And
three days later I came back and handed him the Bach score. He said, "What's
this?" And I said, "Don't you want the music?" And he asked me if I had it memorized? I told him I did and played it right through. He didn't say anything. He
just assigned another prelude and fugue to me. Three or four days later I returned
for my next lesson and started with the Bach. He said, "And you have this one
memorized too?" I played it through. And that's when he broke out and said—I'll
never forget it—"Good God, girl, if you can do this, you should do special work
in Bach!" Nobody had told me that Johann Sebastian Bach was more difficult to
learn than [Felix] Mendelssohn [1809–1847]!

And all this time you were playing Bach on the piano?
As you know and as the world knows, I've been playing Bach on the piano
throughout my life. I have reasons for that. When I was seventeen, I had an
extraordinary experience that in later years I dared to call a "revelation." By the
third month of my first year at Juilliard, I was something of a veteran in Bach. I
had not only studied an enormous number of works, but I had worked with the
harpsichord, the clavichord, and the organ. And I also had made special studies in
the styles of the transcribers of the nineteenth century (something quite apart from

---

[1]A fugue is a polyphonic composition in which one motif or melody enters again and again, at
least once in a different key or beginning on a different pitch.

my studies of Bach and historical instruments). Anyway, at this time I took another prelude, the difficult one in A minor from Book I [of the *Well-tempered Clavier*]. And I started to read it, and I recognized its complexity. At that point, well, I lost consciousness. I had the feeling this lasted about twenty minutes. I can tell you that feeling of twenty minutes has stayed with me throughout my life. It wasn't a physical faint of any kind. I had a perception of the structure of Bach that I'd never been told about and had never realized before. It wasn't as though the piano was in the way, or there was a "right" or "wrong" instrument to play him on. I knew that my fingers had to operate differently. My brain had to operate differently.

By my second or third year at Juilliard, I had already learned the *Goldberg Variations* and was playing them in recital. But my teacher suggested, for my yearly examination in front of the whole board of all the teachers of the school, that I play Chopin, Liszt, and Bach and have them decide "what to do with little Rosalyn!" And so I dutifully played all kinds of virtuoso Romantic music; and then I played a few of the *Goldberg*, some fugues, and so forth. And this wonderful, distinguished group of musicians, including Carl Friedberg [1872–1955] who had studied with [Johannes] Brahms [1833–1897, pianists] Alexander Siloti, Ernest Hutcheson, Josef Lhevinne (who was one of the greatest of all pianists), and Rosina Lhevinne, was a magnificent group of people. Varied, with different backgrounds.

That's amusing, "Little Rosalyn!"
That's what everybody called her! I mean me! So, "little Rosalyn" sat there and played and when I finished the general consensus was, "Well, she can play everything so why should she specialize only in Bach?" And Josef Lhevinne said—I still hear the sound of what he said—"You have time until you are forty to play all Bach!" At that time, I guess I was eighteen. I didn't accept that.

On to Bach!
I embarked on all-Bach recitals in New York in 1937, six recitals in six weeks, and I played all 48 preludes [and fugues from Books I and II of the *Well-tempered Clavier*] and the six partitas and the *Goldberg Variations* at a time when some people were saying, "Who's Goldberg?" Everyone discouraged me from giving that series.

How unusual was that at the time to do such a thing?
It was unheard of! And everyone said I was mad! The managers said it was impossible, it can't be done. But I decided to devote myself primarily to Bach. I made this decision by myself without consulting anyone. And I didn't need to, because I had an excellent career playing other music as well. What made me sad was that even some musicians warned me that I would ruin myself; that nobody would come.

They came?

They did! It was a great success. From that point on, I played a Bach Series all over. Let me explain that I was not the first in the world to do this kind of thing with Bach. Harold Samuel had done it in England. He was *the* Bach player when I was a baby. He was playing the *Goldberg Variations* at the turn of the century when they were virtually unknown. So I don't claim to be the first to do it, but it was pretty unusual. At that time musicians as well as audiences were very much afraid of that name, Bach. We hardly had any Bach Festivals. As you can see, there's been an enormous development in interest in Bach—on whatever it's played, whether on period instruments or by modern orchestras.

When did you begin teaching?

I came on to the Juilliard faculty in my early twenties. I was so busy with my touring that I could only accept six students. I insisted that their education consist not only of piano but also of harpsichord, clavichord, and organ. I think it's equally important for a violinist to have some studies playing on the eighteenth-century strings and with the curved bow.[2] It seems to me that's just part of the ABC's of musical education. Meanwhile, I was conducting all over the world. I even had my own orchestra in England for twelve years, beginning in 1953—the Tureck-Bach Players—and we did festivals all over Great Britain. It was a very rich and rewarding experience.

When did you begin your association with political analyst William F. Buckley [1925–2008]?

That came as a result of a call from my management at Columbia Artists. They asked me if I would appear on his television show, *Firing Line*. I had heard of Buckley and knew that he had attended some of my Carnegie Hall recitals. We had a marvelous lunch. Later, I was on his television program for a full hour. I should add that we do *not* discuss politics, only music. Bill is very deeply in love with the music of Bach's time. It's real, sincere, and profound. And he has a tremendous sense of humor.

How did the idea of making recordings in his home emerge?

That was very spontaneous. Bill's birthday is in November. It was looming up. One of my annual series of Carnegie Hall concerts was also looming up. I called his wife Pat and asked if he would like to have my opening concert recorded at his Connecticut house. She arranged to have it recorded. I'm not sure if I even knew it was being recorded. We had a beautiful supper party afterwards. It was such a success, it was clear that for his next birthday I would give him another program. He then suggested another program on *my* birthday in December. All were recorded

---

[2]Early string instruments used gut strings and were tuned at a lower pitch than today's string instruments. The bow was also curved convexly (outward) rather than concavely, as it is today.

in the Stamford house in Connecticut. Bill suggested that they be released to the public. There are four in this series.

Please talk about your present writing and recording projects.
There's so much writing ahead of me! I don't look back. I've always felt that I have to go on to the next thing. I knew Arnold Schoenberg [1874–1951], and he had exactly the same thought. One is always going forward. I often feel like a tree whose branches are still emerging. There is really no end to that.

And your recordings...
I have a project of gathering all my recordings from around the world, including my settings of Bach orchestral works. In my archives are earlier recordings of more contemporary music. These are all "live" performances. Now, when I speak of "my archive," I'm referring to the Rosalyn Tureck Archive in Lincoln Center, and they have all my recordings, starting at the very beginning—hundreds of recordings of every kind of music, including works like *The Firebird* by Stravinsky and Claude Debussy [1862–1918] and the Beethoven "Emperor" and Mozart Concertos, Paganini-Liszt Etudes, and contemporary music such as David Diamond [1915–2005]'s Sonata, for which I did the world premiere. And I did the world premieres of William Schuman [1910–1992]'s Concerto and Wallingford Riegger [1885–1961]'s Concerto. Many were recorded in concert.

What do you hope people come away with, hearing recordings like these?
I haven't thought very much of that. I do have very deep feelings about my art, about its significance, and why I'm doing it. I hope this does get through to my audiences, and those listening to my recordings. I don't really regard myself as a *performer* at all. I don't walk out to *perform*, or excite my audience. All I have in mind is to reach really the deepest level of one's inner spirit in the music I'm playing. And that is the only thing on my mind. I want to reach that innermost spot of each listener, that place where everybody faces himself with truth. This is what performing means to mean, not the excitement of getting audiences to yell and scream. I value the silence almost more. In Buenos Aires I played the *Goldberg* [*Variations*] to 4000 people. Afterward I just sat there. And the whole audience sat there, too. It was utter silence. And that to me is the greatest tribute any artist can hope for. And then the applause came, slowly, and went on for nineteen minutes.

Despite your long and total devotion to Bach, is there still any mystery about him, questions that are unanswered?
Obviously, I've thought a great deal about the person and his life and his human relationships as well as his music and his thought. In all honesty, I don't feel mystery there. The real mystery, the big mystery for me, is Bach's unending genius. This is something no one can ever understand. We are all musicians and we are always discovering, seeing, perceiving new things in the music of fine composers of every period; and I regard that as normal, as a kind of thrill to see something new. But in Bach there is no end—layer upon layer, you go deeper and deeper and deeper and there is no bottom. *There* is the mystery!

Samuel Baron: "Bach's Music Is Language Itself"

John C. Tibbetts
19 March 1985, Kansas City, Missouri

Samuel Baron (1925–1997) studied the violin in childhood, then majored in flute and conducting at The Juilliard School before establishing the New York Brass Ensemble and the New York Woodwind Quintet. Baron began teaching

Fig. 2 Samuel Baron

at the State University of New York, Stony Brook in 1966, and Juilliard in 1971. He also taught at Yale (1966–1968) and the Mannes College of Music (1969–1972). In 1965 Baron joined the Bach Aria Group and in 1980 became its director (Fig. 2).

This interview took place after a concert with Baron and the Bach Aria Group at the Folly Theater, Kansas City.

JOHN C. TIBBETTS: Please tell me about the Bach Aria Group. What is the makeup of the players?
SAMUEL BARON: We have a group of nine: four singers and five instrumental-ists, the continuo ('cello and keyboard), flute, oboe, and violin. Vocalists do not usually work in a "chamber music" way. They're the soloists, they're up front, they're miked separately. Everybody else is their accompanist.

And of course your repertoire is primarily Bach.
We were set up to bring singers and players together to do Bach's repertoire, which at the time the group was formed was very, very unknown and neglected. That was the dream of William Scheide, the Group's founder and first director. It's a wonderful opportunity to have these musicians working so closely together. It's a unique form of chamber music. It makes you feel good when people tell us they're glad we came!

Did the Bach Aria Group begin the resurgence of interest in Baroque music? That took place in 1946, I believe?
You could say that or you could say that it coincided with part of a big wave, but I believe the Group deserves the credit for a heck of a lot of ear-opening in this country.

"Ear-opening." I like that! Scheide seems to have been a philanthropist who was also a music lover, someone who put his money where his mouth is.
Absolutely. Scheide's a wonderful man. He's still with us [as of 1985] and quite active, though he retired from the group. He's a musician and a scholar. Although he grew up around money in his family, he had to support himself as a college pro-fessor of music. He finally inherited a lot of money and he thought, "I want to use this for a musical purpose." He felt the best thing he could do would be to expose the works of Bach with a performing group. It is interesting in those days before Xerox, that he spent all his evenings with a very cumbersome Photostat machine, duplicating pages of full scores from the *Bach Gesellschaft* edition; and then cut-ting strips out and mounting the strips on cardboard so that he could have a flute part, an oboe part, a soprano part, etc.

That is dedication!
Yes. He mastered the repertory completely. If you went to Bill Scheide and played two chords, two certain distinctive progressions, he would say, "Oh, that's in Cantata 171, volume 24, page 37!" This, before the ease of access to long-playing

records! When the Bach Aria Group started to tour, the reviews and the reaction that followed made Scheide very happy. He was very canny in his marketing, you might say, because, as he found out after a few years, it was best to staff the group with very well-known artists. People would say, "I don't know this program but I'll certainly go hear [the late soprano] Eileen Farrell!" And later they would come away having heard Bach! Later, as LPs came out and people could hear entire cantatas with organs and harpsichords, you'd hear complaints that the Group was [only] performing excerpts and using a piano, that it should use the harpsichord instead. Scheide defended our use of the piano, saying it's the ubiquitous instrument of our time—why shouldn't we use it? A lot of people don't realize that when the Group started touring, you couldn't find a harpsichord, except maybe every 500 miles or so. Nowadays, however, you can tour and assume that there will be a harpsichord wherever you end up.

I can just see the road sign: "Next Harpsichord, 500 Miles"!
Yeah, right, right.

Meanwhile, do the rigors of touring become really tedious?
No, no, no. Being on the road is always a lot of fun. But actually, we don't tour that much these days, maybe just three weeks a year. The reason is that it's an expensive group to book. Every one of us has another life, you know, which keeps us busy in chamber music or recitals or appearances with orchestras. And so we have to plan our bookings far ahead of time.

How do you decide on which works of Bach to perform?
We divide Bach's music into the texted and the untexted music. The cantatas of course are based on text. And then you have the untexted music, the Brandenburg Concertos, sonatas, the keyboard music, and so forth. You might think that the religious music and the secular music are two different facets of Bach; but I believe that they're not. They're the same. There's a great unity in his music. His music is language itself. The text is important because it helps you to get through to his music, how he keyed certain phrases into musical symbols.

Did Bach leave performers insights into his attitudes or theories about words and music?
Well, only through the work itself. He based his work on theorists of the time. For example, his predecessor in Leipzig was a man named Johann Kuhnau [1660–1722], no slouch as a composer; and Kuhnau really wrote about how certain words could become musical motifs. He wrote what we would call today "naïve program music" based on Biblical stories, like David and Goliath. You know the story: David puts the stone in the sling, he winds up the sling, and he throws the sling, the stone hits Goliath, Goliath falls, the people rejoice. And he said the composer's job is to look for the symbol—*locus topicus*, he called it in Latin—and that symbol becomes a motif and then you build your musical composition from that motif. Bach followed that path exactly.

This sounds like the Doctrine of Affections, the Affektenlehre.[3]

He was contemporary with it. I'll give you some examples. There are some words that are obvious, like the word *eilen*—"to hurry"—when it appears in the text you get running sixteenth notes. Words like *Tränen*—"tears," or *seufzer*—to "sigh," there's always a drooping motif. Pleading, for instance the famous *erbarmedich*—"have mercy"—very often calls for an upward rising minor sixth.

Was Bach less inclined to do that sort of thing than, say, Handel?

No, I think he was more inclined. But Bach's craftsmanship, you know, his sense of building a composition, is so powerful that the pictorial element doesn't seem to dominate. It'll strike you more obviously in a work like the *St. Matthew Passion*, which is very dramatic, with a narrative and events and interruptions and interjections. It's almost operatic. But in his weekly cantatas, it's just the language that runs on below the surface. I'll tell you a funny story: In the old days of the Bach Aria Group we had a guest conductor, a well known man (I won't say his name), and he was conducting a movement from Cantata No. 3, and his tempo seemed very wrong to Bill Scheide. Bill spoke to him after the rehearsal and said, "Why in the world did you take that piece so slow?" He replied that the text talked about troubles surrounding us, so you have to use a heavy musical treatment. Well, Bill corrected him: "Why didn't you read the next line? 'I think of the Lord and I jump for joy!'"

When we talk about Bach, I suppose one thing we don't think of immediately are his contributions to flute literature. A mutual friend of ours tells me that Bach wrote a Partita for Solo Flute that is a holy terror!

Indeed yes! A terror! It's a unique work in the flute literature. It really is more closely related to the 'cello suites. It's one instrument trying to set up a network of melodies and bass notes and chords all in one. It's a beautiful work.

I'm fascinated by this whole idea of that an instrument like a flute could simulate an effective counterpoint.

There were many Baroque masters that were able to handle counterpoint on the flute very well. Bach, his son Carl Philipp Emanuel, and Telemann all wrote music for solo flute. It's a sort of a treble melody that carries it's own bass line with it. Bach flute players are very happy and lucky that Bach wrote so much for us! We start with the sonatas for flute and keyboard. They are in two groups. On the one hand, they are fully written with a two-handed keyboard part, which turns the music into a trio by texture. On the other hand, we have the flute and a bass part

---

[3]An idea, derived in part from ancient medicine and rhetoric, associated with ways of depicting individual emotions, such as joy, sadness, anger, and calm. In Baroque music this often inspired composers to devote individual movements to individual affects: thus quick, smooth music was associated with happiness; slow, harmonically complex, and ragged music with associated with melancholy; and so on.

where the right hand is just filler. These are a little flashier. And then there's the Partita for Solo Flute that you mentioned. And the flute parts in the Brandenburg Concertos and the Orchestral Suite No. 2.

To me the amazing thing is that Bach did not know the flute when he was growing up. He probably didn't hear the flute at all until he was almost 30, because it was a new instrument. See, when Bach wrote the word *Flöte*, he meant "recorder." And when he referred to the instrument that we now think of as the flute, he wrote *Querflöte* or *flute traversiere* [i.e., transverse flute]. It was a French invention. And it's interesting to speculate who the first flutist was that Bach heard. Most likely it was a Frenchman named [Pierre-Gabriel] Buffardin, who came from Paris, lived in Dresden, and was a marvelous player. Bach, Telemann, and Handel all heard Buffardin, and after hearing him they all started to write for the flute. So, he is one of our big heroes. He was a man at the right time in the right place.

John Eliot Gardiner: "Handel Had the Misfortune Never to Have Been Forgotten"

John C. Tibbetts
23 February 1989, Kansas City, Missouri

Sir John Eliot Gardiner is among the most significant advocates of the historically informed performance movement and the use of period instruments. From early studies with Thurston Dart and composer-teacher Nadia Boulanger (1887–1979) to the formation of his famous ensembles, the Monteverdi Choir (1964), the English Baroque Soloists (1978), and the Orchestre Révolutionnaire et Romantique (1989), Gardiner brings a living presence not just to the music of Bach and Handel but to the Romantics and beyond. His recent book, *Music in the Castle of Heaven* (2013), marks the continuation of his research into and performances of the Bach Cantatas (Fig. 3).

This conversation took place during a two-day series of concerts of Handel's music in Kansas City's Folly Theater.

JOHN C. TIBBETTS: Last evening [23 February 1989, in Overland Park, Kansas] *we had the opportunity to hear you conduct the English Baroque Soloists and the Monteverdi Choir in Handel's* Israel in Egypt; *and today is a special day, isn't it?*
JOHN ELIOT GARDINER: Absolutely. Handel's birthday is today [i.e., 24 February]. Handel is the figure who has been most misinterpreted in the history of eighteenth-century Western music. He had the misfortune never to have been forgotten. He was always, always performed and always played and always sung from his death right up to today. Sounds strange to say that, but I believe it to be true, that very soon after his death—even at the end of his lifetime, when he was completely blind—there grew up a false mystique, and a false performing tradition around his music, which led to inflating it, using many, many more performers

Fig. 3 John Eliot Gardiner, with Handel in the background

than Handel ever had in his own orchestra and chorus to the point that in the nineteenth century in Britain and in North America and in Germany, too, performances of Handel were regularly done with literally hundreds, even thousands of performers on the stage.

Didn't Mozart play a part in that?
Yes, he did, incidentally. But that was to reinterpret Handel's music, which was then out of fashion in Mozart's day; so it's true the oratorios were done with larger

forces than Handel knew. But that was nothing compared to what went on in the nineteenth century. When we came to the Crystal Palace celebrations of 1850s [London], there were thousands of performers on the stage, more than there were in the auditorium! And people treated them as pop festivals, the "Woodstock" of the 1850s!

It seems that the great Romantic critics, like Berlioz and Schumann, talked a lot about Bach but not so much about Handel.
Well, you see, Handel was the Prodigal. He was the one who left home, who left Saxony, and who went off on his travels. He was very smart. He went to Italy, which was *the* place for music in the first third of the eighteenth century, and there he absorbed all that was up to date and the newest in fashion in European music. He met composers like [Arcangelo] Corelli [1653–1713] and composers associated with him in his circle, and he also encountered Italian architecture and painting, which made a tremendous impression on him. He was quite a collector, himself. Leaving his homeland, and especially pitching up in England, of all places, *das Land ohne Music* [the land without music] ...

Was England really called that?
Well, in the nineteenth century, yes, and in a sense, not totally without justification, because after the seventeenth century, which had been a great era of music in England, the eighteenth century was pretty arid. There was ballad opera,[4] there was chamber music, and some interesting opera going on, but in comparison with incredible events going on in Germany, France, and Italy, England was comparatively barren, and we owe it to foreigners, particularly Handel, to have revived and revitalized our culture.

But is it true that it took as late as the 1920s to hear the Handel operas again?
Yes, but you must remember that the whole idea of Handel opera in England was somewhat bizarre and very artificial in the sense that there was this German Saxon composer composing Italian opera seria for a London audience, half of whom probably didn't understand the words, although they would have understood the plot, assuming they looked up from their food and their drink and their cozy companions; but it was not until Handel began to write music for the British middle classes—and I'm thinking of the Biblical and dramatic oratorios—that he really made an impact on the British consciousness. And he was a great composer of ceremonial music, like the *Coronation Anthems* he wrote for George II and the *Funeral Anthem* he wrote for Queen Caroline. These things made him very dear to the English public, and they contributed to the kind of "fossilization" and monumentalizing of him after his death.

---

[4]An eighteenth-century English musical entertainment, with spoken dialogue in English. The most famous ballad opera remains *The Beggar's Opera* (1728), with music arranged mostly from popular songs of the day by John Christopher Pepusch (1667–1752).

I have for the last nine years been artistic director of the Göttingen Handel Festival, where I've sensed a kind of reticence among Germans toward Handel in comparison to the great Bach. Now this is changing in Germany. It seems that in the 1920s and 1930s in Germany they had to reinterpret Handel for themselves to make him acceptable again to their culture, and in the process they perpetrated the most appalling violence on his music. Can you imagine a piece like *Judas Maccabeus*—which of course celebrates the victories of the Jewish people [against the Romans], and also by association the British Protestants of the eighteenth century—being changed into a kind of document of early Naziism? Because that's how it was used. And the transition of all the castrato roles to the baritones and the changing of the tonalities and the orchestration made Handel's music completely unrecognizable.

Are you suggesting that early music revivals can do a disservice to a composer?
No, that's not what I'm saying. I wouldn't call that an "early music revival." I would call that an "early music *distortion*." What is currently accepted as an early music revival is a return to the sources, the historical sources, and the performing tradition of a given composer. And that is certainly what we try to do with the English Baroque Soloists and the Monteverdi Choir—to reconstruct, insofar as it is possible to re-create the kind of sounds that Handel and other composers of the Baroque actually heard and fostered. Of course, we're different from previous generations in that we hear music quite differently from the way our forefathers heard music and totally different from the way Handel and his generation heard music. Our ears have been enriched, if you like it, or polluted, if you don't like it, by all the music that's gone in between.

You have suggested that playing this music on modern instruments is asking the musicians to "miniaturize," which you will not do.
I feel it's misleading to ask the musician to play this old music on relatively modern instruments, which is to say instruments that may be old in derivation but modernized in the course of the nineteenth century to accommodate the larger halls. In a way you get a much more vibrant and exciting performance by going back to the instruments and the orchestrations of Handel's own day, where there's no question of minimalization or miniaturization. It's very intense and very full-blooded. And it's not kind of petite and dainty and effete and lacking in guts.

Were there conductors at all, and what kind of gestural technique might there have been?
There's a lot of conflicting evidence about it. There are descriptions of Bach leaping up from the keyboard, which I do not do (and I'm a lousy keyboard player!) and giving leads with his left hand, nodding at the same time, and using his feet and being imbued in general with the spirit of dance, which is how he transmitted to his performers the energy and the current he wanted in his music-making. We know Haydn stood to conduct certain of his works, but it was a collaboration also from the keyboard with the concertmaster of the orchestra, like [impresario Johann

Peter] Salomon [1745–1815] in London. Mozart would seize any instrument that came to hand and would leap up and conduct sometimes. But the notion of a conductor who was a non-performing leader is a late eighteenth/early nineteenth-century construct.

Did Mendelssohn help advance that idea?
Mendelssohn and Berlioz, above all. And [François] Habeneck, who is completely ignored today, was a German living in Paris who did the first thoroughly researched performances of the Beethoven symphonies. It had been more common before that to do them with very little rehearsal. Habeneck really subjected the Conservatoire Orchestra to lots and lots of rehearsals.

As for God smiting the Egyptians in Israel in Egypt: *how much of that is theatrical technique?*
It's not something I think about at all, or I'm aware of. I just want it to be effective and provoke the right kind of sounds that can be produced from a choir and an orchestra should conform to those for whom the music was written.

I guess I'm suggesting that music like this should be seen *as well as heard. Did Handel provide some theatrical stage directions, as it were?*
Well, he would, it seems likely, to have given theatrical representation to a lot of his oratorios. There was this ban, a veto, by the Church authorities in London on any theatrical representation of the Biblical Word. Now Handel was, first and foremost, a man of the theater, and having written so many operas, it was inconceivable, impossible, I would suspect, to have written musical theater without a sense of the stage scenery and the dramatic being in his imagination and present all the time, even if it's not actually on the stage. I'm very conscious all the time in works like *Hercules, Solomon, Jeptha, Israel in Egypt*, and *Acis in Galatea* (which was, of course, staged) that Handel was a master of theatrical craft.

Simon Preston: "Handel Was More a Man of the Theater Who Happened to Write Church Music"

John C. Tibbetts
10 March 1989 and 15 November 2002, both Kansas City, Missouri

Sir Simon Preston, CBE, is regarded as not only among the most distinguished organists of the twentieth century but also one of the leading figures in English church music. His astonishing organ discography amounts to well over 100 recordings, and his work with the choirs of Christ Church Oxford (1970–1981) and Westminster Abbey (where he served as Organist and Master of the Choristers from 1981–1987) set high standards of excellence that remain to the present day. In the words of Marc Rochester, Preston

Fig. 4 Simon Preston

"bestrides the globe as an Organ Colossus, wowing audiences with his inimitable charm, enthusiasm, and steely musical intensity" (Fig. 4).

    These conversations transpired during two of Preston's performances scheduled by Kansas City's Friends of Chamber Music.

JOHN C. TIBBETTS: You were appointed as Organist and Master of Choristers for Westminster Abbey in 1981. What kind of position is that, exactly?
SIMON PRESTON: That means I was in charge of all the music in Westminster Abbey. I trained the choir and took all the boys and men in rehearsals. It's a

professional choir, and it's a daily choir with at least one service every day. That was my first priority. This meant the whole day was taken up with rehearsals and performing, which calls for a lot of planning and administrative work. And I was in charge of the organ playing, as well. Although I had three very capable assistants to delegate some of the playing if I was conducting, I really felt I should do most of it, otherwise.

There must been times when you would enter the Abbey's organ loft and feel yourself surrounded by so many ghosts of the past ...
Yes, as a matter of fact, there is a board up in the organ loft that gives the dates and provenance of every organist who's been in Westminster Abbey; and it was daunting to look down this list and see Henry Purcell and Orlando Gibbons [1583–1625], for example. People like that, my predecessors. I felt I had to measure up to their standard! People seem to be endlessly fascinated by Westminster Abbey and Kings College Cambridge, you know, which I find extraordinary. Kings College is a musical place, whereas Westminster Abbey is a museum, really, and a national treasure house and location of the famous Poet's Corner and the place where all the Kings of England were crowned.

What's it been like since you left that post?
It feels wonderful! [laughs] I relish the musical freedom now. That was a bit of a problem at Westminster Abbey, unlike Christ Church, Oxford, where I enjoyed some freedom and which I regretted leaving. But I felt flattered to be asked to go to Westminster Abbey. It was a very busy place. And believe me, my time there had its moments. But it all wasn't Royal Weddings.

Wait a minute! Royal Weddings?
Didn't you know? Because the wedding of Prince Andrew and Fergie [Sara Ferguson] was in Westminster Abbey [in 1986], I was the organist, the director of the whole thing! It would have been very rude not to have been asked to be involved. And I must say, Prince Andrew and Fergie did it right!

There's something unique to your profession in that, unlike pianists who can take a keyboard with them, you have to travel to the organs of the world. They are there, waiting for you.
This means a *lot* of travelling, as a matter of fact. Nowadays, wherever I go I find wonderful organs, as you say, "waiting" for me. In America, or farther afield, like Australia and Japan, which are also burgeoning with wonderful instruments. I find people in Japan are increasingly fascinated by the organ, which I think has been rather alien to their nature.

What are some of the other organs and lofts that you especially enjoy?
I made some recordings not long ago in Lübeck in North Germany on a wonderful organ by a Danish builder in this beautiful church which had been devastated by British bombers during the War and had to be rebuilt. That gave me a certain perspective. On other occasions you can go to the Crystal Cathedral in California,

which gives you a different feeling. You're sitting at this extraordinary instrument, this immense instrument, nothing like it, which is so loud and wonderful. And there are these little cages of birds all around. These canaries all twittering away while you're playing Handel and Liszt and [Julius] Reubke [1834–1858].

What of your classic 1984 recording of the Handel Coronation Anthems *with the Choir of Westminster Abbey. It won a* Grand Prix du Disque *for Deutsche Grammophon.*
Don't forget our conductor, Trevor Pinnock, with the English Concert!

That was quite an occasion, wasn't it?
If you mean the Coronation Service for King George II and Queen Caroline [of England; 1653–1737], yes. It was at Westminster Abbey in 1727.

Okay, both occasions! By the way, should we refer to Handel as "George Frideric Händel" or "George Frederick Handel?"
I just call him "George Freddie!" We're quite close, you know.

What do you mean by that?
He's buried in Westminster Abbey, not far from the choir loft. He was just around the corner, the Poet's Corner, just south of the organ where I'm playing. I rather got to get to know Handel as a composer through the influence of Thurston Dart, who was the professor of music at Cambridge University when I was an undergraduate there. He was a great proponent, as it were, of Handel as one of the great genius composers of the world. And I remember that he once asked me who was my "desert island" composer. And I said, "Oh, I suppose it would be Bach"; and he said, "Well, not for me. It would be Handel, because he's a man for all seasons." I don't suppose his works have ever been out of concert repertory. In our own time we are seeing revivals of many of his stage and concert works. For me, whenever you're feeling down and low, Handel has really good cheer-you-up type music; and when you're over-ebullient and need bringing down to earth a little bit, Handel can do that as well.

And a man of many countries too.
Absolutely. He was much traveled, spoke several languages, although his English was apparently heavily accented.

Did he become an English citizen?
Yes, in 1727. He applied for what was called "naturalization." And he was officially dubbed "George Frideric Handel." But there's no question that he already regarded himself as a British subject. He lived almost exactly the same time as Bach, spanning the seventeenth and eighteenth centuries. But they couldn't be more different. Bach was basically a church composer and Handel was more a man of the theater who happened to write church music—but not so much in a

church setting. He could improvise wonderfully well to what was happening on the stage. I think that was his great gift. His music always sounded spontaneous.

At the time, I guess opera was essentially Italian *opera, yes?*
Well, it was, yes, and when that went out of fashion for a while, he changed to writing in English, although the change didn't happen straightaway. It seems he was rather reluctant at first. But when that failed, he invented this wonderful thing called oratorio, which was more of a concert performance than an opera, and usually on religious subjects, which allowed it to be done during the season of Lent, when theatrical pieces were not allowed. He was an opportunist. The Andrew Lloyd Webber of his day. If he saw a good thing he knew how to go for it! His most famous oratorio, *Messiah*, is just unparalleled, even today. Not all of them were on Biblical texts. There were dramatic secular pieces in English, like the pastoral ode *L'Allegro, il Penseroso ed il Moderato* ["The Cheerful, the Thoughtful, and the Moderate Man"].[5]

He seems to have been a rather rambunctious fellow, not necessarily subservient to the aristocracy. Is that correct?
I think that's probably right. I think he had a proper attitude to his own work as a composer and did not always have to be deferential to the high and mighty lords and ladies. Of course, it's true he was favored by King George I; and with the commission of the four *Coronation Anthems* for George II, he continued in that favor. But it seems that if anyone crossed him at all, he would give them a pretty sharp response.

What do we know about the genesis of Messiah? *By the way, it's not* "The" Messiah.
No, it's just *Messiah*, yes. We know he wrote it in 1742 in a terrific hurry. It was a late work. He seems to have gotten through it all under three weeks in August. An amazing achievement. It's quite long, and to perform the whole work takes the best part of three hours—an absolutely astonishing achievement. He did borrow a number of pieces from some of his previous works, to be sure, but you're not really aware of that at all. Handel was very good at recasting arias and choruses and things like that. And there's that marvelous libretto by Charles Jennens, chosen from the New Testament.

And that was something rather new at the time?
I suppose it was rather unusual, but brilliant. There was some controversy about singing from New Testament texts. After a successful performance in Ireland and a dismal performance in London, it soon went into the repertoire. He performed it a number of times before he died; and performances have been continuous ever since.

---

[5]Based on poetry by John Milton (1608–1674); a later poet, Charles Jennings, wrote lyrics for the *Moderato* portion of Handel's oratorio.

Do you believe those stories that say that Handel was divinely inspired—or at least thought he was?
Well, I wouldn't know, really. But there are those who insist on it. I think he was in a sense an opportunist. If somebody had asked him about that, he may have been sufficiently savvy to say, "Oh, yes, I had a divine inspiration straight down from heaven; and I just wrote as it came to me. I was just the vessel." And I think one has to take this with a bit of a pinch of salt. But there is no doubt that it was written in the white heat of some sort of inspiration, something that drove him intensely.

And it premiered in Dublin?
That's right, in the cathedral there in Dublin. They found one of the manuscripts years and years later, propping up the organ bench in the cathedral. Somebody had left it there.

You just said the premiere in London was unsuccessful; that it took a while to catch on.
Yes, that seems to have been true. It wasn't until the Foundling Hospital came into the picture that *Messiah* took off for English audiences. Quite a number of his pieces didn't have very good premieres.

How large were the ensembles for those first performances?
We know how large the forces were to begin with, because a set of orchestral parts was preserved in the Foundling Hospital. Handel was a benefactor for it. Those parts tell us how many string players there were, that there was a choir of twenty-seven singers, who the soloists were, and all that sort of thing. To begin with, the performance seems to have been a very small affair. But, you know, he was an opportunist, and if he had a chance to perform it with larger forces, he just changed it. If a soprano wasn't available or wasn't good enough, he made the change to a castrato, who could sing the part just as well.

And there was a woman named Susanna Cibber, for whom Handel wrote the alto solos in Messiah.
Yes, Mrs. Cibber, that's right. Something of a notorious character, an actress, you know, someone "with a past" who played with [David] Garrick. An actress singing sacred texts! Unthinkable! Her husband, Colley Cibber [1671–1757], was a play-wright and a friend of Handel's.

Do you have any preference yourself of the size of the forces in performing Messiah?
Do you know, it doesn't really worry me. If I'm going to do it with a small cham-ber choir, I enjoy that very much, because everything can be so neat and tidy and very, very crisp. The rhythms come dancing out, you know, and it's just thrilling. But at the same time, it would lack something of the sheer majesty of the piece. You have to remember that there are certain aspects of it, like the magnificent

"Halleluiah Chorus" and the "Amen Chorus," which might lose a little with a very small group. So in some ways I'm very happy with whatever forces I'm given. I think that's how Handel himself went on. He adapted it to suit available forces, which is why there are so many different alternatives to *Messiah*.

Now since you're an organist yourself, have you ever performed it on the organ while conducting?
No I haven't, no. No, no, I haven't. I suppose Handel might have. You know, he used to have an instrument which could serve as an organ and harpsichord at the same time.

Really?
Yes, it was all combined. It still exists. He could play and sort of wave his hand every now and then to start them off. But then he would go on playing continuo and nod at the strings and the singers. But those big, big performances with hundreds of performers came after his time. Then, a leader would have stood to conduct, but probably not yet with a baton. That came a lot later with musicians like Mendelssohn.

Come to think of it, have you ever had the privilege of performing on any of the instruments on which he actually played?
Any of the organs that I have played from Handel's time have been changed over the years. The first time I recorded the Handel organ concertos, I came across one of the organs that he knew quite well. Mainly, the organs that Handel would have played had been built by builders who built other organs which I have played. But I can't really claim that my fingers have actually caressed the same keys that the master did.

Now for Handel and film: I guess we don't immediately think of you as a movie star! What about that?
Well, Handel and the movies go hand in hand, you know. Come to think of it, there was an organ that I played in a movie about Handel that did belong to him. It was called *God Rot Tunbridge Wells*! [1985]. And it was directed by a British filmmaker named Tony Palmer. I had to dress up at one point and play an organ that Handel was reputed to have played. It was up at Chandos, where his patron, the Duke of Chandos lived. There's an organ there but it doesn't work at all, so I had to pretend that I was actually playing it, and then they later dubbed it with music.

Did you appear on camera?
Parts of me! In some scenes you see my hands and wrists only! Trevor Howard played the part of Handel. He was absolutely wonderful, because like Handel he was larger than life in every sense of the word. He was made to look like Handel. The rest of us were actually in modern dress. There's one scene where you see me in modern dress sitting next to Handel during a modern-day performance of *Messiah* by an amateur music club in Tunbridge Wells. Handel is listening to this awful performance, and he shouts, "God Rot Tunbridge Wells!" Supposedly something he really said.

A Clutch of Instruments

Introduction

Musical instruments can be found among the earliest surviving traces of human civilizations, mostly in various types of bone flutes. Additionally, images of instruments adorn caves, amulets, and pottery from millennia ago. As technology developed, so did musical instruments. String instrument manufacturing reached a Golden Age in Cremona, Italy, during the early seventeenth century. Makers such as Nicolò Amati (1596–1684) and Antonio Stradivari (1644–1737) provided exemplars of newly fashioned instruments designed for professional virtuosi.

During the Industrial Revolution of the nineteenth century, new technologies such as pistons and valves and developments in metallurgy allowed instrument makers to create and build improved versions of existing instruments. These were not only easier to play but also could better fill the larger acoustical spaces in which music was starting to be experienced. As instruments were being improved, composers were writing expressly for them and creating marvelous showpieces that allowed noted performers to exhibit the results of the new technologies.

In the interviews that follow, six noted instrumentalists—violinist Anne-Sophie Mutter, 'cellist Steven Isserlis, flutist Eugenia Zukerman, guitarist Christopher Parkening, horn player Barry Tuckwell, and concertmaster-ensemble director Iona Brown—offer insights into the histories, performance practices, and repertories of their respective instruments, including the modern symphony orchestra as a single performing entity rather than merely a collection of brass, percussion, string, and woodwind instruments. In addition to their other professional activities, each of these artists has championed new music (including film music) and enjoyed productive creative synergies with contemporary composers.

William Everett

© The Author(s) 2018
J. C. Tibbetts et al. (eds.), *Performing Music History*,
https://doi.org/10.1007/978-3-319-92471-7_4

Anne-Sophie Mutter: "The Greatest Compliment You Could Give Me Is to Have a Great Composer Write a Piece for Me"

John C. Tibbetts
31 March 2017; Kansas City, Missouri

Closely related to the viola and violoncello (or 'cello) as well as to the earlier rebec and vielle, the first modern violins were designed by members of the Amati family, Jakob Stainer, and Antonio Stradivari during the seventeenth and early eighteenth centuries. Slightly redesigned later, today's violins produce more sound than their ancestors, although mechanically amplified stroh violins also exist. The violin possesses an enormous repertory and has made its way into almost every kind of musical ensemble, including some jazz bands and Mannheim Steamroller, a quasi-rock group of the 1980s. During the 1970s avant-garde composer and performance artist Laurie Anderson manipulated an electrically amplified violin outfitted with a magnetic tape head in the bridge and played with a bow that uses recorded magnetic tape instead of horsehair (Fig. 1).

In August 1976, thirteen-year-old Anne-Sophie Mutter made her concert debut at the Lucerne Festival. Since then Mutter has established herself in the front rank of world-class violinists. Born in the German town of Rheinfelden, she skipped school and worked entirely with private teachers. In 1985 she was appointed professor of international violin studies and made an Honorary Fellow of the Royal Academy of Music. Her desire to promote the careers of young musicians led to the establishment of the Anne-Sophie Mutter Foundation. In 2009 Mutter became a Chevalier de la Legion d'honneur; in 2013 she became an Honorary Foreign Member of the American Academy of Arts and Letters.

This conversation took place before a concert by Mutter as part of the Harriman-Jewell Concert Series, Kansas City.

JOHN TIBBETTS: Your violin is always with you, yes? Tell me about this amazing instrument. It's never out of your reach, I guess.
ANNE-SOPHIE MUTTER: No, not often. At home it is out of my reach.

Is it a Strad?
It's a Stradivarius from 1710.

You have two?
I have two. The first one is 1703. That's the instrument I did for most of my recordings for [Herbert von] Karajan [1908–1989] in the 1980s. Then at the end of our collaboration—of course we didn't know that it would be the end, because he passed away—when I was in my beginning twenties, I felt the need for an

Fig. 1 Anne-Sophie Mutter

instrument with a larger dynamic range and even more layers of expressivity and a faster response; and that's the instrument from 1710, which I've been playing with since thirty years (Fig. 2).

Fig. 2   Anne-Sophie Mutter and Herbert von Karajan in the 1980s

You have spoken about your admiration for a number of great violinists of the past. Who were your heroes growing up?
Yes, I always begin with David Oistrakh. I did hear him only once. I was six years old and just starting to play the violin. He played the three Brahms sonatas. It was in Basel, and I was sitting in the balcony on the lap of my violin teacher. Back then there were no fire police rules, and I remember that students were sitting at his feet, on the floor. He was such a god. His sound was something I remember, even after the decades. And this is almost fifty years ago! It was a transcendental, life-changing experience. Later as a teenager I heard Nathan Milstein playing the Brahms Violin Concerto. He was around eighty and maybe there was a note or two "off," but his performance was unsurpassed in nobility.

What are the challenges in playing an instrument more than 300 years old?
Oh, these things can be very difficult to explain. The differences in sound you are going to achieve once you are really experimenting with the violin are huge. Consider just the left hand: how about different kinds of vibrato? Finger vibrato, hand vibrato, arm vibrato, even a *non vibrato*. Four kinds of vibrato. I'm not just

automatically vibrating, when some bad pianists put the foot down on the pedal, you know?[1] Every note has to go somewhere and it all comes from somewhere, so vibrato is an essential tool of the musical gesture of the sentence. I guess it's like with an athlete, who has to find the healthiest way to deal with his body. And this effortlessness, of course, also leads to longevity of performing, which we all want to achieve.

What about holding the bow?
That is what the right hand does. There is the Russian way to hold the bow, and a more French way. But the posture in general is what your body is able to naturally follow. You get the crooked back if you're not standing upright. I mean [Jascha] Heifetz had the pinnacle of great posture. I don't know if I could hold the violin up like that, erect. It's like in yoga: you try to just align your body and that's pretty much also in playing the violin. You align your body and you try to make the energy flow through the body as uninhibited as possible.

Do we know in the nineteenth century how some of the great violinists held themselves, how they held the violin? Do we know much about that, before we had photographs to document it?
Yes, there is a drawing of Regina Strinasacchi, who was a great composer in Mozart's day, and for whom Mozart also wrote a sonata [in 1784]. He comments very favorably in his letters to his father that she had this beautiful sound; and that because of the customs back then, which would not permit movement in a woman's upper body, she had to play with her arms totally folded to the body. So how you can do that is alien to me, but that was the custom for women back then. Strinasacchi was a big figure in Mozart's life. Not only was she a fabulous violinist but apparently also a composer.

I've heard you refer to your violin as a "she."
Right. In German it's *die Geige*. It's feminine. Or it's *she* or *he* or whatever! [laughs] This is a *transgender* violin! Very modern. I change the setup. I change the strings. I use softer ones. Strings that would put less pressure on the body. I changed the bridge. And the violin seriously sounds like it's hundred years younger! For me, the instrument becomes part of you and you are the transformer for a musical language from the 1800s.

Now, the violin itself is a Baroque instrument. But when you play, say, Vivaldi, on a modern instrument, are you playing it differently than if you were playing a Baroque violin?
Well, it's as if you would ask, "Would you play Shakespeare with men in women's clothes?" Well, we are not doing it! Today women are allowed on stage and we

---

[1]That is, overusing the "first" or "sustaining" pedal, on the right side of the modern piano's three pedals, which allows pianists to sustain sounds until they fade away.

can give to Shakespeare's plays all the depth of emotion by including both men and women. Something of the same thing with modern violins. However, I have often experimented with copies of Baroque bows in order to understand, particularly in the case of Bach, the original phrasing. Because in Bach's music, the original phrasing contributes so much to the musical gesture, although some of it is not physically doable—this is true for Beethoven as well—but it has to be thought as a *direction*. So even in the case of Beethoven, when there would be a slur over, let's say, four bars, which you physically could not do, you would understand that in the musical content it has to go there, even if you have to change the bow. What am I aiming at? Even if I don't play with a Baroque bow, I do know the character of these bows which have been extremely light in the frog [the heavy part of the bow], which permits you to play, let's say, eight notes together and one separate elegantly.

The Baroque bow was curved, right?
Yes, originally it was curved. The curved bow allows you to play all four strings together, but the real challenge is in the phrasing and in the gesture of the music. Occasionally in the Bach Partitas you have four notes you should hold together [i.e., play simultaneously on all four strings]. There are other elements for which you need to understand the swiftness of that bow in the seventeenth century, and you have to try to mimic that swiftness and lightness in all these dance movements.

Your Stradivarius was not designed and manufactured for music we hear now, was it?
The body of my Strad is original, the scroll is original, but everything in between isn't. The neck is much longer. The strings are obviously not gut strings. We tune higher. It's like great art. Look at Michelangelo [1475–1564]'s *David*; it's over five hundred years old. You stand in front of that sculpture, it's such perfection and mastery of the marble, that you wonder, how did he invent the tools to make it so that it "lives" today? I think that a great [old] violin, if properly cared for and carefully set up, can survive in our time. The aim as a string player is to very closely listen to how the instrument is developing over time; and I have noticed that over time that my instrument has started to sound more tired and gotten extremely sensitive to changes of temperature and humidity. So what do I do?

When did the violin-and-piano recital become an accepted practice?
Chamber music always was part of the life at the castles of the European autocrats. Think of Mozart's life and for example Beethoven's ten sonatas regularly performed by the composers together with their friends and patrons. But then came a time when you needed people to step out of the ordinary and become a prominent soloist, like Paganini or on the piano like Liszt. Great violinists were also contributing to the repertoire. I think of Pablo de Sarasate, for example, who brought great visibility to the violin soloist.

Many of today's composers are writing music for you.
Yes, let me point out Sofia Gubaidulina. She wrote a violin concerto for me, *In Tempus Praesens*, her second violin concerto, in 2007. Gubaidulina was born in the Soviet Union, and she was sometimes imprisoned in the sense that she was not allowed to travel abroad. She is a strong believer in individual power. Her modernism was opposed by the Soviet Union. In her concerto for me, she made my violin part the only violin in the score. The solo violin represents the Goddess of Wisdom—Sofia—and the orchestra is society trying to shut her down. She opposes society, and that is my role as a performer. There's a crucifixion in the middle of the piece, a struggle with God and a declamation of love. It's very, very touching to see how you can set that in music. But, you know, she once told me that she has musical visions, but she hasn't yet found the instrument to set them to.

Performing a new piece always brings new difficulties, I suppose.
Yes, but sometimes it is too much! [Krzysztof] Penderecki wrote for me his Second Violin Concerto, which he calls *Metamorphosen*. I first performed it in 1995. I met Penderecki in the early 1980s. His music is a physical and mental challenge, but I accept it with gratitude. I love the burial scene near the end of the concerto, when the soul is departing the dead body and going to heaven.

Do you work with these composers? Do they allow you in as part of the compositional process?
Nope. I do not want to interfere. I just want to be part of their initial process, but after that I'm basically out of the picture, unless they tell me they want some input. But to go to your first question: yes, there are difficulties in the writing [for the violin] that I might think are unplayable. *Seriously* unplayable! But I did play Penderecki's solo piece *La Folia*, which had some impossibilities, and his Sonata for Violin and Piano [1999].

Is this because Penderecki doesn't know the violin very well?
Oh no! He was a violinist. He admits he just loves to write things that are difficult as hell! And then he likes to hear from us violinists that [his music] *is* difficult as hell! So, he has achieved his goal! I admit it!

You play Brahms, and in years to come when we look back upon your career, will we say, "Here was a performer of Brahms," "Here was a musician who knew Brahms"? Would that be as good a compliment as you could get?
I don't know. I don't want compliments. The greatest compliment you could give me is to have a great composer write a piece for me. That's the greatest compliment I can receive because then my role as a muse has been fulfilled.

Steven Isserlis: "Rather a Lot of 'Cellos"

John C. Tibbetts
27 May 2008 and 29 November 2016, both in London, England

A close relative of the violin and viola, the violoncello—usually called the 'cello—was perfected in Italy during the sixteenth and seventeenth centuries; several of the great violin makers, including Amati and Stradivari, also made 'cellos. Originally considered a "bass violin," the 'cello is tuned in perfect fifths and has the basic violin shape. Italian musicians popularized the 'cello during the eighteenth century; Beethoven wrote sonatas for it, and Brahms wrote a Double Concerto for Violin and 'Cello (Fig. 3).

Dubbed "one of the top 'cellists in the world" by *Daily Telegraph* critic Elizabeth Grice, Sir Steven Isserlis, CBE, says he was "lucky" to have been brought up "in a house full of the sounds of music." In addition to performing around the world and commissioning composers to write for him, Isserlis

Fig. 3 Steven Isserlis

is passionate about telling musical stories through either film or by writing books for children, including *Why Beethoven Threw the Stew* (2001), and *Why Handel Waggled His Wig* (2006). In 2000 he was awarded the Schumann Prize in Zwickau, the city where the composer was born.

These conversations took place in Isserlis's London home. In addition to his performing career, he discusses his musical relationship with *avant-garde* composer György Kurtág.

Born in a small town in Rumania, *avant-garde* composer György Kurtág studied at the Liszt Ferenc Academy of Music in Budapest, where he earned a diploma in piano and chamber music in 1951 and a degree in composition four years later. After fleeing Hungary during the 1956 Revolution, Kurtág lived for several years in Paris, where he studied privately with Olivier Messiaen (1908–1992) and Darius Milhaud (1892–1974). After returning to Budapest in 1960, Kurtág worked for a while with the National Philharmonia; from 1968 until his retirement in 1993 he taught at the Liszt Academy, where he was appointed professor of piano and chamber music. In 1983 he was elected to UNESCO's International Roster of Composers. Kurtág's other awards include the Grand Cross of Merit of the Republic of Hungary, and the Golden Lion, presented to him during the 2009 Venice Biannale for lifetime achievement in music.

JOHN C. TIBBETTS: I see you've just been appointed a Commander of the Order of the British Empire [in 1998]. *Is it a medal, a certificate, a letter, prize money? How should I address you?*
STEVEN ISSERLIS: The CBE is just a medal. Nice to have, though! But, you know, the proper way to address me is, "Hey You!"

And there's the Schumann Prize in 2000.
Yes, I received that in Zwickau, Schumann's birthplace and the site of a very important museum and archive. It was given to me by the very dear friend, the former director, Gerd Nauhaus.

Why Robert Schumann? An abiding passion of yours.
Schumann is very much a part of my life. He is the ultimate Romantic artist. He invites us into his life. You don't think of any rules with him. Brahms will begin that way, and then pull away toward classicism. The more you read about [Schumann's] life, the more you know about the music; and the more you know the music, the more insights you get into his life. That's not always true. Think of Bach. But in the final analysis those aren't essentials to enjoy the music.

Take us back to when you first connected with Schumann.
I don't actually remember hearing Schumann for the first time. But when I was eleven or twelve, I remember picking up a volume of his letters. And I knew right away this was a wonderful man. It's very annoying how many of

his letters and such have yet to be translated into English. He's such a rounded, autobiographical composer, more than most composers. I remember my mother used to say her favorite music was Schumann's *Dichterliebe*, so I grew up with a feeling Schumann was a wonderful figure in music. I probably came on quite strongly about him when I organized a big eight-day Schumann festival in 1989, "Schumann and His Circle," at Wigmore Hall. We also had pieces by Schumann's friend, Ludwig Schuncke, and by Mendelssohn, Chopin, and Brahms. I'm very proud of that.

Which brings us to the Schumann Concerto for violoncello ...
I first performed that concerto when I was about eighteen. It was at Oberlin College, and I messed it up completely. I just didn't understand how to approach it. It wasn't until I heard [Pablo] Casals's recording of it that I was hooked. He made sense of it. I was forced to go back and reconsider it. It's such a personal piece. I want to do it as a kind of chamber piece. I can't think of a concerto that is more personal and intimate. The last movement is pretty classical, you know—first and second subject, development, recapitulation, that sort of [sonata-form] thing. I don't think he's experimenting particularly there. The first movement, however, is something else. There's such an inner struggle there.

How about some other issues at hand? Like hearing about your choice of instru-ments, your 'cellos, and their pedigrees? Why prefer one over the other? And what is it like traveling with a bulky instrument like the 'cello?
I have access to rather a lot of 'cellos. I play most of my concerts on the gor-geous "Marquis de Corberon" Stradivarius, kindly loaned to me by the Royal Academy of Music. It's a beautiful, aristocratic, poetic instrument, very close to my heart. But when I want to play "tougher" music, like the concertos of [Sergei] Prokofiev [1891–1953] and [Dmitri] Shostakovich [1906–1975], for instance, I usually play my own "Montagnana," which is strung up with steel strings. I would never put steel on the Strad. It's magnificent in its own, very different way. And then, I still occasionally play my former 'cello, a beautiful Guadagnini [made by Giovanni Battista Guadagnini (1711–1786)] with its own very special qualities. Finally, I own a fine modern 'cello by Robert Brewer Young, a copy of the "Marquis" Strad. I enjoy playing it a lot! It's named "The Lady Joanna," after my girlfriend!

These days do you find yourself performing either more or less on "period" and/ or "authentic" 'cellos?
Yes, I do play a lot with period instruments and orchestras. Recently, I've per-formed at the Beethovenhaus in Bonn, where I gave a recital with András Schiff playing fortepiano. I played on Beethoven's own 'cello! I loved it! Quite a gen-tle sound, but very beautiful—and quite easy to play. We performed three of the sonatas, one from each period. And I've just recorded on another, very unusual "period" instrument, the so-called "Trench 'cello." This was actually a "Holiday 'cello" built by W. H. Hills, and it ended up in the trenches in World War I. It

was originally played by its owner, a soldier named Harold Triggs, who much later sold it to my friend Charles Beare. This instrument has a fascinating history. It was made from an ammunition case and wood. I played it at a World War I Remembrance Service at Westminster Abbey. We got it going, and after awhile out came this rather wonderful plaintive, and poignant sound. I was so taken with it that I've included some items played on it on my 2017 album of 'cello music written during or just before the War.

How about travelling with these special instruments?
Of course, I've had endless experiences travelling with these 'cellos, some good, some bad. I remember once telling a hostess on a flight in the United States that my 'cello would only eat kosher food! She smiled politely—but then, ten minutes later, she came up and apologized abjectly for not having any on board!

I also understand that you are commissioning original works. From John Tavener [1944–2013], for example.
Yes, I asked John to write *Protecting the Veil*, a piece for me because I knew that he composed music in the Russian Orthodox style—I've always loved that music! I also thought it would go well on the 'cello. Of course, I had no idea when I asked him that it would be such a successful piece. I try to work with composers fairly regularly—it's one of the most interesting things a musician can do. I'm hoping that György Kurtág might write another short piece for me, soon. We'll see!

Regarding composers and commissions, let's talk about Kurtág. You've met him?
He's almost a sort of father-figure to me! I met him and his wife Márta more than twenty-five years ago, at IMS Prussia Cove in Cornwall. They visited there many times to teach. I remember one bleary morning in Cornwall, after having gone to bed far too late the night before, I staggered up to the main house in search of much-needed coffee: I encountered György outside one of the rooms. "Steven— you have to come and hear—Márta and some of the others are about to play through a Beethoven trio." I told him that I hadn't had my coffee yet! But he gave me a look that banished all thoughts of caffeine. "Beethoven first, then coffee!" he said firmly. It's a tribute to the beauty of the Beethoven that within a few bars I had forgotten all about the coffee (temporarily)!

You say he composed something for you …?
He composed a very special piece for me after the death of my wife, Pauline. And I have learned, performed, and recorded several of his 'cello pieces. I celebrated his ninetieth birthday last February [2016] by performing several of his works interspersed with the six Bach 'Cello Suites at London's Wigmore Hall.

How did you come to combine his music with the Bach?
Combining his music with Bach occurred to me when I realized that the dates on which I'd already agreed to play the Bach were all very close to Kurtág's birthday, on 19 February. I followed [Bach's] First 'Cello Suite with two pieces by Kurtág:

the *Hommage à John Cage* from 1987, and *Pilinszky János: Gérard de Nerval* from 1984.[2] Other pieces in the second half of the concert included his *Jelek 1* and *Jelek 2* from 1987. They are all from his *Signs, Games and Messages*.

For those of us unfamiliar with Kurtág's music, how would you describe it?
Signs, Games, Messages form the center of his output in recent years. The pieces are short—but they are not miniatures. Rather, Kurtág creates in every piece a separate self-contained world; each gesture is pared down to its inner core and is charged with maximum emotional commitment. There's a piece called *Shadows*, for example, that strays into the region of the barely audible. It calls for the heaviest possible mute, softening the 'cello playing of simple descending scales to an ethereal smolder. Another piece was written in the memory of the distinguished Hungarian musicologist György Kroó. It also calls for that same heavy mute. I wrote in my program notes that those slow descending scales seem to depict footsteps to—or within—another world. It seems as if the traveller's steps falter, as if he were finding his way in the darkness of night. It's almost impersonal; only the three "Gypsy" intervals—augmented seconds[3]—openly express a sense of loss. The rest is a luminous farewell, a last glimpse of one who has entered Shakespeare's "undiscovered country from whose bourn no traveler returns." Kurtág says these pieces should "never feel short," that you should not play a note "until you *have* to play it."

Working with him must be an unusual experience!
Yes! And I would never dare perform his music without studying it with him beforehand. As often as I can, I go to him for lessons on his music—sometimes even by telephone!—and these are amazing experiences. He is the most demanding of composers. It's exhilarating! I must have spent at least nine hours with him—or, rather, with him and Márta, since they are often both there—on just four short pieces. I can't imagine him without Márta. They are a unique couple, with the same intensity of outlook, and a matching passion for, and understanding of, his music. I saw them at a concert (which they said would be their last ever) in London a while ago. It was utterly magical: They sat facing away from the audience, playing on a muted upright piano, assisted with amplification by their son, György Kurtág, Jr. It was one of the most memorable concerts I have ever heard! They also interspersed Kurtág's music with Bach.

What is a session with him like?
His intensity is such that he cannot understand how anybody else's could possibly be less. He has an unshakeable vision of how each note must sound. He'll use a vast range of unexpected images to communicate that vision. He talks about

---

[2]Jânos Pilinsky was a twentieth-century Hungarian poet, Gérard de Nerval a nineteenth-century French poet and translator.

[3]Augmented seconds are identical in sound with minor thirds: thus C-D# = C-E flat.

the rhythmic properties, the dance properties, and sometimes requests the feel of a sicilienne, for instance, or of a wild folk-dance (he may ask you to "yodel"!). Underlying all his music is a strong sense of tonality, which gives the music such inevitability. I am so used to his unique voice. He will talk with a quiet desperation: "Er—er—how to tell you what I mean?" (He confesses that "stuttering is my natural language!") I have never encountered a musician for whom each note matters more. Every tone possesses for him a world of meaning, of narrative, of emotional depth. The satisfaction of coming close to pleasing him is indescribable. I come away from those sessions floating on air.

Eugenia Zukerman: "Good Music Is About Good Breathing, the Starting and Stopping, the Tension and Relaxation"

John C. Tibbetts
7 October 1986, Kansas City; and 12 October 2016, New York City

Before she embarked on her stellar career as a flutist and television broadcaster, Eugenia Rich Zukerman studied English at Barnard College. Zukerman's best-selling volumes include an anthology of essays, *In My Mother's Closet* (2003), and two novels, including *Taking the Heat* (1991). A student of Julius Baker at Juilliard, she won the Young Concert Artists Award for 1971 and made her formal New York debut to rave reviews; since then she has performed as a flutist around the world. From 1981–2005 Zukerman served as a special correspondent for *CBS News Sunday Morning* and interviewed on television more than 300 classical and popular artists as well as a few well-known actors (Fig. 4).

These conversations took place in conjunction with a Zukerman recital in Kansas City for the Harriman-Jewell Concert Series; and by telephone to Zukerman in her New York City home.

JOHN C. TIBBETTS: Practicing is a way of life, isn't it? And with the flute, you don't have to depend on driving cross- town to a piano. You can practice anywhere.
EUGENIA ZUKERMAN: I just flaunt my flute!

But I won't say "flautist", there's no such instrument as a "flaut." Right?
[Laughs]

You are in the vanguard, now, of a number of highly visible flute recitalists across the country. Galway, Rampal, Samuel Baron, Paula Robison—I mean, you're among a number of celebrity flute performers.
PANdemonium!

Fig. 4 Eugenia Zukerman

Right! It's becoming mythic! Is your career as a flute player occasionally fraught with pandemonium? You said last week you were not as organized as you would like to be.

Things are ever so chaotic when you're trying to do more than one thing, so I find sometimes that I have to shuffle and re-juggle things. But the one thing about being a performer, being a musician, in terms of being organized, is that there seems to be an inner biological rhythm, or clock, when you know that it's time to pre-pare something. And now, like most flute players, I play diverse kinds of things. There's a whole bunch of repertoire that I must keep learning. I never write down, say, okay, from October 17 to 19, I'd better practice this. And I don't know any

musicians who do. You just simply *know*—it seems to come into your consciousness early enough on, so you say, ooh, gee, it's January and I have to learn the
Mozart G major, I think I'll play that today. I think I'll see if I know it well enough.

*Surely one of the great virtues of flute literature is that a lot of the music that
you're going to perform will necessarily be lesser-known music, or music by
lesser-known composers. It gives us a chance to hear composers like [Friedrich]
Kuhlau [1786–1832], or [Jan Ladislav] Dussek [1760–1812].*
The repertory for flute is interesting. Some say it's limited. I'm not so convinced
about that. It's certainly smaller than piano or violin. But I think if we look at it
historically, we can understand what has happened in terms of composers who
have written for the flute. The flute had its golden age in the eighteenth century,
when Baroque composers used it as their favored melodic line. But as music
changed in the nineteenth century, and grew more heroic and larger, and the symphony became larger, and sounds became louder, the flute is an instrument became
relegated to "bird chirpings" in the background. We don't have any great Romantic
literature. We have no sonatas from Liszt or even Schubert. We have to constantly
pick away at the material to find more works that would work transcribed for flute.

*It seems that around the middle of the nineteenth century a lot of composers began
writing music that was easily transferable from one instrument to the other, that is
to say, for a flute or an oboe or a violin or a 'cello.*
Well, I think some of that was because of commissions. Publishers were saying,
well, could you make this for 'cello and for clarinet? And so there are many pieces
… However, in the twentieth century there has been a kind of renaissance of the
flute. In fact, it has become, in my opinion, the instrument of the hour. It's the
most popular instrument, I think, because, technically, things changed, and composers became aware of the potential of the instrument, and are using it in very
interesting ways.

Do you have a point at which you draw the line in transcriptions for flute?
Transcriptions can be wonderful, and they certainly make life interesting. But
there are certain things I wouldn't touch. I have certain performances that I can't
get out of my mind. For example, the [César] Franck [1822–1890] Violin Sonata
[1886] is played often on the flute. I would never do that. With other music that
I don't know that well, or that I don't have these monumental feelings about, I'm
happy to play on the flute.

*Are things happening with the flute like some of the things happening with the
piano: going inside and tinkering with the innards, or beating the instrument with
mallets? Are flute composers now trying to explore, the inner resources of your
instrument?*
Flutes are generally made of precious metals, so you're not going to bash a gold
flute around! You can't hit it too much or you'll bust the poor thing! What they
have tinkered with, and what we are experimenting with, is the natural resource

of the flute, and that is the *player*. The way you create the sound, the way you blow into the instrument, maybe singing and playing at the same time, blowing strangely into the instrument with almost shrieks and cries. Some performers are specializing in this sort of thing. One who comes to mind is the wonderful flutist Robert Dick. He commissions new works and he plays mainly contemporary music. He has almost redefined flute sound and flute technique.

Are composers like Steve Reich, John Adams, and Philip Glass writing for flute now?
Yes. In fact, Steve Reich was recently commissioned to do some pieces. The problem with commissioning is that it's extremely expensive, and you must have time to write for a grant to get someone to write you a piece, or you must have someone backing you. It's a complicated process. You can't simply say to a friend, "Hey, write me a piece," you know?

What do people want to know most about flute performance?
Mostly about how we hold our breath for so long. Which is interesting, because, of course, you're never holding it. You are taking a deep breath and you are letting it out. You have to find a way to save your air so that it lasts the longest possible time. Breath control is the unending struggle that a wind player has, and particularly flute, because you have no resistance. In other words, there's no reed in your mouth against which the air is resisting. So you are like a singer; you have to really dole it out.

And, like a singer, does it have to come from different parts of the torso, the stomach, the lungs?
The diaphragm plays as large a role, if not larger, than with a singer, and what you do is expand the lungs to their fullest capacity, and then you slowly squeeze the air out, using the diaphragm to push the air out. The control of that is the center of the art of playing the flute.

How much of that control is conscious and how much involuntary? Do you have to think how it's going to happen to help the body along?
By the time you've played for twenty years, there's a kind of a natural thing that takes over. But what is interesting about performing on the professional level and over a sustained period of time is how you deal with mood, emotion, and simply physical stress on stage. Because the first thing that goes when you're depressed or unhappy is your breath. I mean, you just feel—everything caves in, and it's just, you know, hard to take a breath. Good breathing is about feeling good, and that's not simply physical, it's also psychic, and so you have to find ways to feel good when you step out on that stage. Also, physically, if you have a cold, it's pretty tough to play the flute. It's possible, though.

Is there such a thing as a nasal intonation for the flute, as there is for singers?
I don't think so, so much. It's mainly a matter of the discomfort of the player. I've had to play with blocked ears, you know, with a really bad cold. That's the

worst thing. And you just don't know where you are on the instrument. And there are times you simply can't play. Prolonged phrasing is not natural; it's not part of human expression. We take breaths, we stop, we start, we begin again, we say something, we say it a little longer, but we generally have pauses in between. Another thing people say is, where do you get that sound, where does all that sound come from? Because, after all, it's just, you know, a pipe. And that's fascinating, to think of the physics of playing the flute, what it is that creates the sound.

And does the nature of the material that constitutes the flute itself affect the sound?
There is some controversy about that, although I think it's always more important for the player to just be comfortable. I played a silver flute for a very long time. And silver flutes have a silvery, bell-like, very direct, very piercing kind of a sound. Whereas, on a gold flute, you are able to create—or at least I, as a player, have the illusion of being able to create—a warmer, more golden, more mellow, more diffused sound. Whether this is true is disputable. It seems like the density of the metal has to come into play here, because gold is heavier than silver, and it is reflected in the sound that is created.

Are there flutes that come with pedigrees, as stringed instruments so often do? Does that make a difference, either the age of the instrument, or the maker?
Well, the maker for sure makes a difference. The flute became the instrument we know today in the 1840s when Theobald Boehm [1794–1881] revamped the mechanisms of the flute. Since then the flute hadn't really been tampered with until the last about fifteen years, when makers began to see that, if you move the tone holes just fractions of inches, you could get a different intonation. Since the tuning today is sharper, there has had to be this change in the mechanism. I play a flute made in Japan by the Sankyo Corporation that has something called "new scale", and that is slightly altered so that I feel that I can play better in tune. As to pedigrees with flutes, there are not too many. Unlike string instruments, the newer the flute, the better.

How about the so-called "authentic instrument revolution" that's maybe already old news by now? Has if affected flute players? Are there "original" flutes that people go back to?
People are playing Baroque flutes, which are the wooden flutes, five-keyed instruments; and there are many players who play them absolutely beautifully and brilliantly. I, myself, find it a limiting thing to do. I think that—and this might be iconoclastic—but I think composers would be delighted to have their compositions played as best as possible, and you play them best on modern instruments. Yes, it's an interesting phenomenon, this interest in funny instruments.

You said something a moment ago that I think is quite profound, the more I think about it. It's not a flute player holding his or her breath, it's exhaling it. That's where the music-making is.

It's also about giving. Music-making is about giving. It's an act of generosity, in a sense. I like to think it's not just letting the air out, but of giving something to your listeners. But now I get more nervous about performing than I used to. I'm not as sure of myself as when I was younger. I have to figure out strategies, you know? At my age, most flutists don't perform very much. You have to keep your facial muscles in shape. And I guess when I stop to think about it—which isn't very often!—I do see stopping my playing off in the distance.

Christopher Parkening: "My Life Is a Constant Process of 'Tuning Up'"

John C. Tibbetts
19 January 1989, Kansas City, Missouri; and 15 March 2017, Malibu, California

Although the modern guitar has many antecedents—the gittern, vihuela, and Baroque guitar among them—the fretted instrument we know today has six strings tuned E-A-D-G-B-E from lowest pitch to highest. (Guitars with four strings also continue to be played, although not as frequently.) Instruments resembling guitars appear in illustrations as much as 4000 years old, and some people believe the guitar's ancestor was the kithara of ancient Greece. The word "guitar," however, is derived from *qitara*, an Arabic word employed during the early Middle Ages in southern Spain. Classical guitars and steel-string or flattop guitars are similarly shaped, although flattops are larger and more heavily reinforced. Electric guitars, on the other hand, boast a variety of shapes and sizes; some of them are even equipped with pedal controls. Dismissed as an unimportant or merely "exotic" instrument by many Western composers throughout much of the eighteenth and nineteenth centuries, the classical guitar attracts much more attention today (Fig. 5).

Recognized as heir to the legacy of his mentor, Andrés Segovia, Christopher Parkening has been acknowledged by the *Washington Post* "as the leading guitar virtuoso of our day." Born in Los Angeles, Parkening performed around the world before retiring in 2013 from the concert stage. In addition to serving as Artistic Director of the Parkening International Guitar Competition (the world's most prestigious competition for the classical guitar), he holds the Christopher Parkening Chair in Classical Guitar at Pepperdine University in Malibu, California. His autobiography, *Grace Like a River*, was published in 2006.

These conversations transpired before Parkening's appearance with the Kansas City Symphony Orchestra, and via telephone with Parkening at his Malibu home.

Fig. 5 Christopher Parkening

JOHN C. TIBBETTS: As we speak, you are tuning your guitar. Take me through the process.
CHRISTOPHER PARKENING: Well, you temper-tune a guitar. I like to get a common A, whether the orchestra takes an A 440 or A 442 [that is, 440 or 442 vibrations per second], and then go from there and temper-tune the instrument. This is the correct way to tune a guitar, because there are so many variables with frets and strings. I like to tune to chords, a key that the piece might modulate to, for instance, and then tune the overall instrument that way. From my earliest recordings and performances I have used José Ramirez guitars exclusively. Their beautiful sound, appearance and musical expressiveness, I have found to be une-qualed by any other classical guitar.

Does it strike you that tuning an instrument can be compared to "tuning" our lives, too?
There certainly is a maturing process we go through, musically as well as spirit-ually. I started playing the guitar when I was eleven years old with the inspiration

of a cousin of mine, Jack Marshall. At that time Jack was staff guitarist at MGM Studios. When I asked him about studying the guitar, he suggested that I start with the classical style, because I could go from there into any style of playing with much more technique. I feel the classical guitar is a wonderful vehicle by which we can bring the beauty of classical music to the younger generation. It's the most popular instrument in the world. Young people might attend a classical guitar concert, just because they identify with the guitar itself.

What is it about this instrument that, up to a point, it is relatively accessible to players? Then—boom! Many beginners can't get beyond the chords.
True enough. Jack suggested I get the records of Andrés Segovia. Which I did. Then, I was fortunate enough in looking for a teacher that my family found the Romeros (considered "The Royal Family of the Guitar"), who had just come from Spain and were teaching privately. I first studied with Celedonio, and later, with Pepe. At fifteen, I was very fortunate to receive a scholarship to Segovia's first United States master class, held at the University of California, Berkeley. Without really knowing it, I was progressing toward a concert career. I had always been told by my father to work hard at whatever I do with maximum discipline, hard work, and study. I used to get up before school and practice; and then more practice after school. At the age of nineteen, I signed with Capitol Records for a series of six albums; and at twenty I signed with Columbia Artists Management in New York. That led to a tour of 72 concerts that first year and the start of a concert career that was very rewarding, musically and personally, as well as financially.

You mentioned the Romeros and Segovia. They are among several prominent guitarists you met during your studies, which also include composers Mario Castelnuovo-Tedesco [1895–1968] and Joaquín Rodrigo [1901–1999].
The first time I'd ever heard Segovia in concert, I was eleven years old. I went backstage and told him that I was interested in the classical guitar. I remember he patted me on the cheek. About three years later, I had the opportunity to perform the Concerto in D Major by Mario Castelnuovo-Tedesco with The Young Musicians Foundation Orchestra in Los Angeles. I really got to know him very well and was able to personally study that concerto, which was the first concerto ever written for guitar and orchestra in modern times. However, in 1963 Castelnuovo-Tedesco sent a tape of my performance of the First Concerto to Segovia, requesting a scholarship for me in his first United States master class. I then worked with Segovia for a month in that first class. I met Joaquín Rodrigo again in 1974; I had met him earlier when I had toured Spain but just very briefly. I was asked to go to Japan to perform fifteen concerts of both of his famous solo guitar concertos, the *Concierto de Aranjuez* and the *Fantasia para un Gentilhombre*.

Pepe Romero told me that the slow movement of the Concierto de Aranjuez *had something to do with the death of a child. Am I remembering that correctly?*

I have heard a similar story: that the end of the second movement is the child's soul going to heaven.

Now, about Maestro Segovia: do you recall your first meeting with him?
He was very overpowering to me. You suddenly realize that you're standing in front of—or playing for—the greatest guitarist that has ever lived. That is very intimidating! I was fifteen when I first studied with Segovia. He had selected nine performing students to perform in the class at Berkeley in the summer of 1964. And he would look through these very thick glasses at us and point his finger at you, and when he said your name, you had a mild heart attack! But he was also a very gracious man, a gentleman, in every sense of the word, and very, very witty. He loved to tell jokes and stories. In the classes he would demonstrate the pieces. But when he didn't like your playing, he had quite a hot temper. I remember when one guitarist played his own transcription of the Bach Chaconne for him. It was a very poor version, to say the least. Segovia allowed him to play it all the way through. (Segovia's own transcription is beautifully fingered, absolutely musical, in every sense of the word.) So, when this guitarist finished the performance, Segovia pointed to the door, and in Spanish he said, "Leave town!" That was his only comment about the performance. He could be very extreme in his anger! (Fig. 6).

Did you ever receive any of that anger?
I certainly did! As a matter of fact, on the same piece of music, my former teachers had re-fingered Segovia's version to make it simpler for the young guitarist.

Fig. 6 Christopher Parkening and Andrés Segovia

But it took all of the artistry and musicianship out of it. Now, I started playing that piece with Segovia listening, and I got about halfway through when, all of sudden, I heard the crash of his shoe hitting the stage floor. He went into an absolute tirade. He threw his hands up in the air. And he said, "Never in my life—How could I do such a thing?" His wife was trying to hold him back, and I was melting on stage. He said, "Why have you changed the fingering?" I told him that my teachers had changed it. And he said, "Who are your teachers?" And he mumbled something and said, "Change it back for tomorrow!" He was livid, absolutely livid. I remember literally having to go back and completely change the fingerings back to the original. He was soon appeased after that and two days later invited me to perform on the nationally televised segment of the class.

Would you flash forward to the last time you saw him?
The last time that I saw Segovia, I had toured Europe and came to Madrid in the fall of 1986. I called him. He invited me to his Madrid apartment. I went to see him there and spent about two and a half hours with him. It was a magical time. He got out several guitars to show me. I was so amazed that he would get out these absolutely beautiful instruments and ask me what I thought; and I said to myself, why does he even care what I think? There was memorabilia all over his apartment, and letters and pictures with kings and queens and presidents.... The last time I saw him, he was 93. He died the following year in June 1987. He was concertizing right up to the end.

Your career has been spectacular. And yet, you told me before we began this interview that early in your career you became burned out and dissatisfied. Would you care to explain?
I'd always loved music, but the big problem for me as a teenager was the many distractions in my life. I loved sports as a child, and I remember kids ringing the doorbell many times at my home to see if I could come out and play football or baseball. And I had to turn that down because of the necessity to practice. There was already somewhat of a struggle going on between my love for fishing, sports, the guitar, and of course, school. How to fit it all in? By the time I reached twenty, I was already thinking of retiring at an early age and maybe owning my own ranch and trout stream. I was playing so many concerts, about ninety a year at that time, and I became very tired of the concert life, the hotels, the airplanes, the loneliness. I had played the guitar partially as a goal to attain financial security at an early age. My father had retired at an early age, and I was kind of emulating his life. I was happiest on a trout stream. I had always had a great love for the out-of-doors and, in particular, fly-fishing for trout.

You can hardly carry your guitar while fishing for trout!
No, I couldn't, and I didn't. One day, at about the age of thirty, I called Capitol Records and Columbia Artist's Management and told them I was no longer going to make records or concertize. I found a beautiful ranch with a trout stream on it in the southwest part of the state of Montana so I moved up there. Apart from a small

amount of token teaching I did at Montana State University, I did not play the guitar at all for nearly four years.

Did you experience a healing process of some kind?
Well, I did at first. It was a great relief just to work on the ranch and then fly-fish to my heart's content. Not just on my own ranch but on other ranches and streams in the area. But after a while I didn't know what was happening. I was becoming unhappy with my life and I didn't really know why. About four years went by and I went down to Los Angeles to visit friends and family there. A neighbor leaned over a backyard fence and invited me to a Bible-teaching church. The pastor preached a sermon I'll never forget, based on a passage from Matthew in which Jesus said, "You will know a true Christian by their fruits or deeds. Not everyone who says, 'Lord, Lord,' will enter the kingdom of heaven. Many will say to me on that last day, 'Lord, Lord, haven't I done these things in your name?' And I will say unto them, 'Depart from me, I never knew you.'" Well, I had been raised in the "Christian" church, and I went to church occasionally, and my parents had me baptized at an early age. They told me that I was a Christian, so I had always believed that I was. Yet my life did not characterize anything that I know to be Christian. It was a real turning point in my life. I went home, really broken over the sins and selfishness in my life. I believed that Jesus Christ was the Son of God and that He had died for my sins, and the least I could do would be to use the ability or talent the Lord had given me for the purpose of glorifying Him. Bach has always been a great inspiration to me, not only musically but later when I found out what he wrote about music. He said, "The aim and final reason of all music is none else but the glory of God." And so I thought that would be the least that I could do: to go back on the road again to play with a different purpose. I thought that if Christ gave up everything for me that would be the least that I could do for Him.

What, precisely, was the inscription that Bach wrote on some of his manuscripts?
At the beginning of many manuscripts, he wrote the initials, "J. J." which meant in Latin, "Jesus help me." And at the end, he wrote, "S. D. G."—in Latin, *Solo Deo Gloria*, "for God alone the glory." That was a great testimony to his faith in Christ.

Would you say you were "tuning" your life, like you would the open strings of the guitar?
Yes, suddenly life had a new meaning for me and a new purpose. Jesus is both Savior and Lord, and I thought: whatever the Lord would have me do, I want to do. And I realized that there were only two things that I knew how to do; fly-fish for trout and play the guitar. The second seemed the better option. As a result, I actually ended up moving back to Los Angeles where I re-signed with Capitol. I made a record of transcriptions of sacred music for guitar, *Simple Gifts* [1982], and another of music for guitar and orchestra based on Bach's sacred cantatas, called *A Bach Celebration* [1985]. I also did an album with the soprano Kathleen Battle, *The Pleasure of Their Company* [1987].

That earned a Grammy nomination, I believe, for classical album of the year. But just as you always have to work to keep a guitar in tune, did you have to work to keep this new relationship with the Lord in tune as well?
Well, that's a very good question. For me, it is something that I work hard at, just as you have to practice an instrument in order to play it well, you have to discipline your life as a Christian. I have to spend time with the Bible each day to tune up my "strings," as you say. That is the bottom line. Having had many different religions sort of thrown at me at a young age, I came to the conclusion that the Bible was all that I needed. And to add to it or to take away from it, was wrong. I use the word of God to govern my life and it is a constant process of maturing and tuning up, so to speak.

Do you have an agent who arranges your performances, or do they just happen?
I do have a booking agent in New York. I have had the chance to be on a few television shows, which is a great opportunity for me to share the beauty of the guitar and classical music.

You've been on The Tonight Show, *haven't you? Do you feel that you stick out like a sore thumb against the usual rock singers and comedians?*
Yes, a little bit. I remember the particular show that I did when Liza Minnelli was also on. After I played, she told me that she absolutely loved the classical guitar, and she invited me to her subsequent performances in the Universal Amphitheatre, where she was performing.

Do any of these performers envy you because you don't need echo chambers, back-up singers, special reverbs, anything like that?
John, your question reminds me of something. The second time I appeared on the Grammy® Awards television show, a joke was played on me. I was onstage and all of a sudden some musicians with a heavy metal rock group wheeled in these gigantic amplifiers; and the guys came over and said, "Where do you want this plugged into your guitar?" And I said, "No, this is a classical guitar; there's no place to plug that in." They all burst into hysterical laughter.

Barry Tuckwell: "The Most Outstanding Characteristic of the Horn Is that It Is Capable of Producing a Beautiful Sound"

John C. Tibbetts
26 January 1992, Kansas City, Missouri

The horn appeared centuries ago in Europe, where it was known as the *cor de chasse* (hunting horn) or *Waldhorn* (forest horn) and, somewhat later, as the natural or "unvalved" horn. Modeled to some extent on the *shofar* or ram's

horn mentioned in the Old Testament, the modern instrument was rebuilt in 1818 by Heinrich Stölzel and Friedrich Blümel, who patented the first valved horn, with rotary valves; later, piston valves became standard. Hornists sometimes use their hands, inserted into their instruments' bells, to produce a variety of effects (i.e., "hand horns"), and crooks allow natural horns to play in different keys. It was the addition of valves that enabled performers to play in any key without changing instruments or crooks. Today the term "French horn" is antiquated even in English, and since 1971 the International Horn Society has preferred "horn" and "hornist" in professional circles (Fig. 7).

Barry Emmanuel Tuckwell is regarded as perhaps the preeminent French horn player or hornist of the later twentieth century. Born in Australia, Tuckwell studied piano, organ, and violin as a child in Sydney. He took up the horn at age thirteen; two years later he joined the Sydney Symphony, and in 1955 he was appointed principal horn of the London Symphony Orchestra. In 1968, however, he retired from orchestral work and devoted the rest of his career to solo appearances, orchestral conducting, chamber music, and master classes for advanced musicians. Tuckwell holds the Order of the British Empire, and in 1992 he was raised to the rank of Companion of the Order of Australia.

   This interview took place in conjunction with a concert appearance by Tuckwell at the Folly Theater, Kansas City.

JOHN C. TIBBETTS: I suppose general audiences probably have their own conceptions about horn playing and the so-called French horn specifically. What would you most like concert-going audiences to understand and even appreciate about your instrument?
BARRY TUCKWELL: That's difficult to answer because, on one hand, you get fed up with people saying, "Oh yes, the horn, that's the instrument that goes wrong!" You know, the horn is so *unreliable*. Because when it does go wrong, you want people to have some sympathy for you! [laughs] But I think more constructively, the thing that's perhaps the most outstanding characteristic of the horn is that it is capable of producing a beautiful sound, and it is a wonderful melody instrument that plays tunes very well.

That's a very nice way of putting it. How about our associations with the horn and the great forests? The Waldhorn, the sound of the hunt—that really does work, doesn't it?
Yes, except French hunting horn players didn't produce a wonderful, nostalgic, beautiful sound which you heard echoing around the woods. It was very loud, blasting with an excessive vibrato, with cracks in the note. The vibrato sound actually breaks. It can be quite frightening. [laughs] We must sound like Boy Scouts the way we play, because these fellows would really knock the hell out of these horns.

Fig. 7 Barry Tuckwell

What of the English and German traditions then?
I don't know what the German tradition is, because the people in Germany and Austria who play hunting horn music sound very polite about it. Otherwise, French players dress up in hunting garb and they go out to the hunts and they make records, and it's all documented in books as well as on recordings. In fact, I bought one of the first commercial recordings ever made—in 1890 or something—and one of them was a quartet of horns, which gives you a sense of how they used to play in the hunting fields.

But do there exist horns of that vintage, or horns without valves, that can be played today? Or are they reconstructed, as so many so-called "authentic" instruments are?
Yeah, I think you have to bear in mind that wind instruments wear out, so if you find an instrument from 1790 or 1832 or whatever, whether it's an oboe or horn, the likelihood is that, if it's in good working order, it hasn't been played *because* it was no good. If it doesn't work, it was probably a good instrument and was played and has worn out. Also, horns get dented often enough it ruins the sound. So people who play authentic music play on reproduction instruments. And horns are very easy to reconstruct. When I say it's easy, I mean it's not easy actually. It's easy in theory but always difficult in fact.

When did you first encounter the hand horn and is it an important part of your own performance?
I've never played in public with the *authentic* hand horn. I have one and I use it for practice purposes, because I believe you should understand what the player would have had in terms of phrasing and that way what the composer would have expected to hear. But I'm not too bothered about being authentic, because in fact the instrument I'm playing is an authentic instrument with valves on it. In many ways it's more problematic.

Does your horn have a pedigree like a Stradivarius violin? Are there certain kinds of horns the Cadillacs of the horn world?
Well, I play on a modern horn. Maybe it's, at the most, two years old. But it's a horn that I designed.

Give me the nomenclature, as it were.
It's made by the Frank Holton Company, which is a division of the G. Leblanc Corporation in Wisconsin. Model H-104, and it is called the Tuckwell Model. And over the years, I used to play a Holton, a Farkas Model. Philip Farkas is an eminent player and teacher.

Is your signature on this model as a famous baseball player's is on a bat?
[Whispering with mock secrecy] It's got my name on the mouth pipe, but it's very discreet. Very discreet. It's not like you're going to do a concert and you see STEINWAY written on the front of the piano. Nothing coarse. What we were trying to do was to try and reproduce the qualities of a particular instrument that is no longer made, called

a Kruspe, which is a German instrument from Erfurt in eastern Germany. These horns had a wonderful reputation. They were very popular in America. Beautiful, warm sound. And I think a lot of horn players who favor this particular type of instrument are looking for an instrument that plays in that way. Not every horn player likes this sort of horn. There are different people that want to produce a different sort of sound, or a horn with a certain characteristic that will help them. And we all have our weaknesses in our technique. You look for a horn that helps you where you know that you have a weakness. And if it's got a weakness where you're strong, you don't care so much because you know you can overcome that.

Must a horn be lived with, *and* seasoned, like a violin? *Or, can a horn be played satisfactorily right out of the shop?*
Some people will say so; I don't happen to think so. I tried a horn about a year and a half ago, and I didn't like it. I put it back in the case. And I left it in my home in Hagerstown, Maryland, and I came over for a week knowing that I didn't have any playing to do, but knowing that there was a horn there. So I thought, I'll practice using this horn that I don't like. I took it out of the case, but the valves wouldn't move, which happens if you don't play new horns. So I had to loosen [the horn], open it up, and it was not bad. And I've played it ever since. So virtually it's a brand-new horn.

Do you have a little tool kit with you on your travels?
Oh, yes. You have screwdrivers and things like that. You have the string on the back of the valves. It's curious in this modern space age that still most people prefer the lever to connect to the rotary valve with a piece of string. It works very well [laughs], but sometimes it breaks and you have to replace it.

How about an anecdote or two about when you were young, making a decision to play the horn. Is it the sort of decision that a young boy would be able to even make on his own, or was that a decision influenced by somebody?
I wasn't even aware of making a decision. When I was thirteen, I was lent a horn and given some lessons, and I just wanted to play it. I didn't think, "Ah, I will become a horn player." A couple of months went by, and I went and studied at the Sydney Conservatory with Alan Mann, a wonderful horn player. Eventually, somebody said, "Oh, go and play in the orchestra." *Play in the orchestra?* Fortunately, it was the *Seraglio* Overture by Mozart with horns pitched in C. I had to learn to transpose. If it had been a G or D horn, I wouldn't have known what to do, because I hadn't yet worked that out. Later I learned to transpose and that was it. I started getting gigs, jobs.

I hope you don't mind if I ask you, does it strike you as odd that making a living blowing into a piece of metal is ... strange?
Sometimes you think, "Why am I doing this?" "Because it hurts!" [laughs] True. Sometimes playing the horn is very painful. If you've got a sore lip or your lip's tired, yeah, it's not really very pleasant. It's unsanitary too [laughs].

We think of breath problems, but I've never heard the pain factor brought up. That's interesting.

Yes, and your cheeks begin to ache after a while if you get exhausted. That's why when brass players get tired, they start missing notes. There's no way you can control it, you know. If I had an announcement made that I have a sore lip—well, that's not allowed! You're not allowed to have that indulgence as a brass player. You have to go on and do it. If you don't get it right, they say you've gone off.

Do you keep a tube of gloss or balm or something?

Oh, I have stuff that I take around with me, yeah. Ointments and stuff, yes.

Who's the greatest horn player you ever heard in person?

I would say several, and of course that includes Dennis Brain; no question. I heard him when I first went to England, so I would have been nineteen. He was even better than the records. And I went 'round and said "hello" afterwards, and he was an extremely nice man. But the reason I said "including" is that there was another horn player who inspired me very greatly in Vienna: Gottfried von Freiburg. He was first horn with the Vienna Philharmonic and with the Opera. For me, he made the most glorious horn sound I have ever heard. What a sound! It's lived with me always.

Here's a tough question: Can you put into words what the "horn sound" is all about? When you strike a piano key or pluck a violin string, you produce a sound from the outside. *But the horn sound is coming from* within, *from your* insides.

Yes, to some extent the instrument makes the sound, but in the final analysis you get the sound *that you make.* I've experienced this with tests of different horns, blindfold tests just to see if people could recognize personal characteristics in a particular kind of horn. But what you end up with is that "Mr. A" always sounds like "Mr. A," no matter what horn he plays on. But there are certain instruments that will help you get what you want. Some violinists prefer a Guarnerius, some a Strad[ivarius] or some other make because it helps them get more of the sound *they* want. So, yes, the horn to some extent will help but it's *you*, it's the sounds *you want to make.* How you achieve that, I don't know, because I think it's a subconscious thing that you hear a sound and all the time you're experimenting with different tensions of the embouchure—the lips, tongue, and teeth—and the different placing of the hand in the bell, the different juxtaposition of air pressure with a particular note.

One thing you hear musicians talk about is making an instrument sing. *In your case it really does become a kind of* singing, *doesn't it?*

Yes. Well, obviously, you can't go on and on and on and on without a breath! That presents problems. Take the Schumann *Adagio and Allegro*, for example, a wonderful piece. It's a major piece for a horn with valves. It was one of the first important works written for that instrument. But it's terribly written for the instrument, in that it makes demands on your breath control. There is one passage in the "Adagio" section, where I think you have thirty-two measures without the possibility of a breath! Now, clearly you can't do that. You have to breathe!

Why did Schumann choose the valve horn?
It was there at the time! It came into the world before 1820, and Berlioz wrote for a valved horn. In the "March to the Scaffold" from the *Fantastic Symphony* he wants the hand effect, and he says, "From here to here, use the hand." Expressly saying, "Don't use the valves." So, to be authentic, you must use valve horns in the Berlioz *Fantastic Symphony*.

I think it was Berlioz who once directed the clarinet player to play with the clarinet in a sack. Have you ever had an odd direction like that one?
Well, when I was in the LSO [London Symphony Orchestra], we recorded for London Records the *Ring* of Wagner with Leopold Stokowski. Of course, that means all that horn work in "The Rhine Journey." At a certain spot, Stokowski instructed me toward the end to walk back into the hallway. He wanted the horn to come into prominence *acoustically*, otherwise it would get swallowed up by the orchestra. This is a practical thing, but kinda strange.

Composer Benjamin Britten [1913–1976] came along at an important time for you as a soloist.
My first meeting with him was in London during performances of [the opera] *The Turn of the Screw*. I was one of the horn players. After that I played for him in the orchestra at Aldeburgh and he said, "I wonder, would you like to take part in a series of recitals that the English Opera Group—as it was then called—are sponsoring at The Royal Court Theater in London for promising young musicians?" Of course I said, "Yes, thank you very much." And in fact that was my first London date. I think there were seven people in the audience!

When was that?
About 1956. A small audience, yes, but maybe the most distinguished audience you could have! There was Benjamin Britten, singer Peter Pears, and composer Imogen Holst [1907–1984]! There was also a critic from *The Daily Telegraph*.

Were you just beginning, not yet a seasoned player?
Well, I had been playing in the London Symphony for a couple of years and certainly I'd been a professional player, but I was still comparatively young. I suppose I was twenty-five years old, something like that. Later we recorded the *Serenade* [*for Tenor, Horn, and Strings*] and the *Third Canticle* ["Still Falls the Rain," for tenor, horn, and piano] and Britten conducted. We did lots of things with him. The *War Requiem* we recorded with him. It was a nice association.

Iona Brown: "I Direct from the Violin"

John C. Tibbetts
1 October 1987, Kansas City

By the seventeenth century, open or broken consorts often included flutes, lutes, string instruments of various kinds, and other instruments. Larger ensembles came into existence with the birth of opera; for his *L'Orfeo* (1607), Claudio Monteverdi called for cornettos (wooden trumpets), flutes, oboes, metal trumpets and trombones, violins and viols in various numbers, a harp, two harpsichords, and three small organs. The real ancestors of the modern orchestra, however, were the string ensembles of the seventeenth and eighteenth centuries, to which a few wind instruments were often added, and which included keyboard instruments for continuo support. Later eighteenth-century symphonic compositions were often published in sets of eight printed parts: one of the parts for two violins, another for two viols, and one part each for a single 'cello (or bassoon), a double bass, two oboes, and two horns. Haydn, Mozart, and Beethoven consolidated the basic modern orchestra: two flutes, oboes, clarinets, and bassoons, two or more horns, two modern trumpets and occasionally two or three trombones, two timpani, and larger numbers of violins, violas, 'cellos, and basses. A few composers, including Haydn and Beethoven, also called for cymbals, snare drum, and various noisemakers in their quasi-Turkish and military pieces. Berlioz, Wagner, Mahler, and their successors added more instruments. And, occasionally, noise makers to the mix: cannon fire for Tchaikovsky's *Overture 1812* (1872); a wind machine for *Don Quixote* (1897), a symphonic poem by Richard Strauss (1864–1949); and the sounds of airplane propellers and an air-raid siren for music George Antheil (1900–1959) composed for Fernand Léger's (1881–1955) otherwise silent animated film *Ballet Mécanique* (1924).

Early ensembles had no designated leaders, although seated first violinists—also known as concertmasters—often beat time for their colleagues. Later, composers stood to conduct their own works as well as those of others. Here Berlioz, Liszt, and Mendelssohn led the way, followed by Mahler. By the mid-twentieth century, symphony conductors had become stars in their own right; the most famous among them included Serge Koussevitsky (1874–1951), Arturo Toscanini (1867–1957), Leopold Stokowski (1882–1977), and Herbert von Karajan. Today, however, a few orchestras perform without conductors or are directed by members of their ensembles, usually violinists (Fig. 8).

Born in Salisbury, and into a family of English musicians, Iona Brown (1941–2004) worked for years under the aegis of Sir Neville Marriner (1924–2016), founder of the Academy of St. Martin in the Fields (ASMF), perhaps the most recorded classical ensemble in the world. After 1974 she served as the

Fig. 8 Iona Brown

Academy's director, and among her accomplishments was the soundtrack recording for Milos Forman's *Amadeus* (1985).

At the time of this interview, 1 October 1987, Brown was busily pursuing a complicated career with the ASMF, the Norwegian Chamber Orchestra (NCO) and the Los Angeles Chamber Orchestra (LACO). She gave her last performance with the ASMF in 1998.

JOHN C. TIBBETTS: Here we are, backstage at the Folly Theater, following a performance by the Academy of St. Martin in the Fields.
IONA BROWN: Yes, a wonderful evening here with Mozart [Symphony No. 29], Bach [Concerto for Oboe and Violin in D Minor], and Vivaldi [*The Four Seasons*]. I'm still a bit breathless!

We were just speaking about the thirtieth anniversary of the Academy. You almost cover that entire period. . . ?

Well, it's amazing, and quite frightening in a way. I joined the Academy in 1964, so I haven't quite been there from the beginning, which was in 1959; but the time has just flown past. I can't believe it, really. After sitting with Sir Neville [Marriner] for ten years, he offered me the Directorship in 1974. It came as a great shock. I was terrified. At first, I said no, I couldn't possibly do that, but I thought about it for about a year; and then I accepted.

Was that mere humility that made you say no?

I think it was actually a genuine fear, I mean—

Stark terror, in other words!

Stark terror, absolutely; because at that point in time the Academy already had an enormous name; the responsibility really was very daunting. He just said it's yours if you want it. I had spent my first ten years with the Academy sitting beside Sir Neville on the front deck. He directed from the violin in those early years, you see and he sort of handed it over to me, so I went from number two to number one, as it were. When I direct the Academy there's never a conductor; I'm the director, that's it. We play without a conductor. I wasn't prepared, you know. Neville wanted to develop his conducting career. He obviously saw some sort of leadership quality in me, I suppose, and had a lot of faith in me. I felt well, if he thinks I can do it, I must at least give it a try.

A good performer does not necessarily make a good conductor.

This is true, yes. And I had done nothing of this sort of thing before that time. Sitting in the hot seat is a totally different experience, of course. I direct from the violin, never with a baton. Not yet, anyway. When we started with the Academy, we were refugees from the whole conductor thing. So, it's a little bit ironic that Sir Neville has become a conductor! The Academy also has a small symphony orchestra, as well, which he conducts; but I continue to direct the chamber orchestra.

On the whole is the Academy the most recorded ensemble in the world?

I do think we know how to make records!I'm told we're up to around 400 recordings! [Note: the current count surpasses 500.] The problem is living up to those recordings when we play "live." This can be terrifying, sometimes, when people who have heard our recordings expect us in the flesh to live up to their expectations. I know there are collectors out there who boast they have all of our records. I think in a way we've almost done music and performance a disservice. I feel that the concert platform is a totally different world and one that I'm actually much more drawn to in fact, than in the recording studio. I've done a lot of recording but the live concert is what I really enjoy and feel that we're here for.

You say you're conducting from the bow, instead of from the keyboard?
I'm *directing* from the violin—that's right. Yes, I admit that sometimes the violin
bow sometimes turns into a baton. I wave it around quite a lot. Actually, I try to
keep my movements sort of undivulged, because I don't like to take away from the
music. I like to be fairly discreet but positive, you see; it's a thing of balance.

*It seems that you are one of the first women to take charge of a major orchestra.
Your discipline with ensembles is legendary. I suppose if you were a man, a critic
might describe you as "strong and charismatic", but—*
—but as a woman, "neurotic and difficult"? Yes, I admit, there have been some
occasions with various orchestras when I thought if I were a man, things might
go a little more easily working with players. Regardless, you have to be *looking* and *listening* to your ensemble all the time. There's a lot that goes on, which
sometimes the audience doesn't see. Sometimes they *do* see ... I did an interview
recently and somebody said I turn a certain "withering look" at the players—

–"withering look"?
—(laughs) and I thought, my goodness, I hope, because sometimes when you're
onstage, you know, you think you're in a private world. You forget the audience is
there; it can sort of turn into a party and you're unaware of what you do. And people pick it up, that "withering look"—I don't like it very much. So I think I'd like
to try and control it a bit better. Male or female, you have to have flexibility, discipline, iron-will; but you've got to be soft, sometimes, and sensitive. You mustn't
be thick-skinned. On the other hand, if you're not thick-skinned, you're going to
get wildly hurt if every word written in the newspaper isn't absolutely wonderful.
You've got to be able to take that.

Recently, I raided the Record Library at my radio station [KXTR FM Radio] *and
found that some of your recordings chart the progress of your own career—from
player to director to media celebrity. On the early albums your name is on the
back of the album, no picture. Then your name is on the front of the album, still no
picture. And now more recently with some of the Telemann recordings for Philips,
for example, here's your name and your picture on the front of the album.*
Well.

*It's a good barometer, isn't it? To be an "album-cover celebrity," if you'll forgive
that term, in the classical world. I guess that means somewhere there are pho-
tographers who meet with you for photo sessions now, correct?*
Yes. That's correct.

*Like this lovely pastel-colored cover on your Telemann Concerto album.
Somebody set that up? Somebody aimed the camera at you and said, do this and
do that?*
Yes, that's right. Actually, they came to my apartment. That's my apartment. With
the old-fashioned English chintz you see in the background! I think I always look

appalling in photographs, but they seemed to manage to some how to, I don't know, I can't comment on this.

It's just, is it one of the more unlikely aspects of being a classical musician? We think of this with pop stars, this sort of celebrity status.
Oh, I see what you mean. Well, I suppose publicity is terribly important and I suppose once I had employed a publicist only for three months. But I haven't really concentrated very hard on that side of things.

It looks to us like your career is in the ascendant—like the "Lark" in The Lark Ascending *by [Ralph] Vaughan Williams [1872–1958]. I believe your performance in that work as solo violinist under Marriner's leadership became one of your signature achievements.*
Thank you very much. I like to feel that I am not in a rut, that I'm developing, and that I'm hopefully contributing something to the musical world. That is absolutely vital to me. What is really fantastically exciting to me is that I can be anywhere—I can be in a tiny little town somewhere, or a large festival hall—and the most incredible moments are there.

What do we really know about this institution called "The Academy of St. Martin in the Fields"? Is it a real place? Some of us have an image of a rustic, small white building in the middle of a grassy field somewhere.
No, not exactly that. [laughs] Well, St. Martin-in-the-Fields is an eighteenth-century church in Trafalgar Square, the central heart of London. Of course, years ago, I suppose when it was built, it was literally in the fields. Now, it's amongst lots of other buildings; but it's still a beautiful church and has a lovely acoustic. We love playing there.

But I've also been hearing something about a new residence of some kind.
Yes, there is. That's in Wapping, in London by the river. We have a building, which was a pumping station in the late 1800s. It's a rather wonderful Victorian building and we hope to turn it into a recording studio and rehearsal hall. It will have a restaurant, a shop, a place that will be ours to work in and if possible give concerts in.

What kind of royal recognition of the orchestra has there been? Has there ever been an audience for the Queen?
Well, not yet. It's funny you mentioned that because I did actually go to a state banquet which was ? in honor of the King of Norway. So this was obviously to do with my activities in Norway. But funnily enough in two week times, I'm going to have lunch with the queen. Since you mention that. I'm very sorry that it's not the entire Academy but maybe one day we will actually play at Buckingham Palace. I would love to. It's a great thrill to go there, all the pageantry, it's tremendous, you know, I'm very excited about it.

You mentioned Norway. How many years now, have you been with the Norwegian Chamber Orchestra?
About seven years. Of course, they're much, much, much less experienced players than those with the Academy. I try not to compare the two because they are very, very different, Norwegians and English, you know, every group, and Americans, and the Symphony Orchestra in Birmingham. Every group of people is different. But the Norwegians have this amazing dedication. They're determined to really achieve something and that's so moving to me. I've got a responsibility to them and it's like, you know, they're almost like my children and I don't really want to say that but it does feel a bit like that because they need me and the Academy, it's a totally different thing. A lot of us have sort of grown up together.

Now, has the NCO itself encountered the withering look?
[Laughs] Yes, this was referred to at one of the NCO's concerts. But they know I love them dearly and there's total, mutual respect. I am a bit temperamental, I know, but they understand that my motives are always kind, and I always want the best for the music. I never get personal with people. I think they're all marvelous people. We get on fantastically well. But I have to insist that I will not lower my standards for anybody at all in this world. I just won't. I don't think one can face oneself if one does. And that does sometimes lead to not being the most popular person around but then I don't think that's the point, really. It's nice to be loved. But I was told by Sir Neville, when I took over the academy, he said, be prepared to be lonely and very disliked at times. And you do have to be prepared for that but I think that if your motives are right, you can face yourself, you know. If you can face yourself, you can certainly face anybody else. But you've got to be able to live with yourself and your decisions. They have to be based on the right reasons and then I think you're reasonably safe.

I know it must be impossible to go back over these years and select one or two times the road with your various ensembles, for a highlight or two...?
Do we have a week to talk about this? We're talking about more than twenty-five magnificent years playing in very possible venue. I remember outdoor concerts in the south of France, and playing underneath the Acropolis in Greece. And here in the Midwest, when the wind blows the music all over the place you have to use clothes pegs to fix the music sheets to the music stands.

And do you have experts in patching tires and tinkering with automobiles innards gone wrong?
Actually, we found we never have to deal with things like that. Travel-wise, I must say, we've been rather fortunate. There have been at times when we had to go by train rather than aeroplane and do a concert after an eleven-hour trip on a train. I do remember that happening in Spain, which was absolutely terrible. But on days like that, the concert tends to be even better. Because you've all had such a terrible day that it's a relief to get on the platform and play some music. You know, I remember once, we went to Bulgaria and eleven of us arrived with no suitcase.

The suitcases didn't arrive so we went onstage in our working, travelling clothes. I'm in my bare feet in my worst shoes, you know; but the concert was one of the best we've ever done. We had to because we looked so terrible! If you're a musician you want to communicate with those people out there who have taken the trouble to come out from their cozy homes, pay money and come and to listen to you. It's actually a very moving experience, even after all these years; and I've been playing concerts a long time.

I'd like to switch gears a moment if I may and find out more about Iona Brown at home. Where is home in the midst of all of this?
Well, that's a very good question. I do in fact have an apartment in London but my real love, I suppose, is my cottage, which is near where I was born in Salisbury, which is southeast, southern England.

So there is a little garden somewhere ...?
It's a beautiful, quite big garden. My garden is a great obsession. I wear lots of pairs of gloves and go out there alone and tend my garden. I really love it. I'm very old fashioned. I love antique furniture, I love old clothes. I love old plants that smell wonderful. New plants have bigger flowers but they don't have that wonderful fragrance. I'm a country person. I love going for walks alone in the countryside, and I need to be quiet and get away. Of course, I do see my family.

Do you wish on the whole there were more time for that or are you happy with the balance of things as they stand?
I have to admit, I miss my friends and they're very understanding and they know my life's totally impossible. But I would be impossible if I didn't have this artistic fulfillment. I'm very, very lucky to have that. But if I had one thing I could change, it would be that I just had a bit more time to just sit 'round the kitchen table with my friends and have dinner. Just be really a simple and quiet as possible because it's a very hectic life.

I'm going to close with something I'll never forget, and that's your performance this evening of the Vivaldi Four Seasons. *You and the players performed it in a way I've never seen before. But before I get to that, I have to wonder if we really know what Vivaldi's original scoring was for it?*
I'm not sure we know that definitively; I mean, you could of course play one instrument per part. You know, that's been done. It's the most extraordinarily versatile piece. I mean, obviously, one can do it with eight, six, four, four, two. I normally do it with six, four, two, two, one and I think that's a happy medium and it keeps it light but it's got some body.

Now, when you say six, four, two, two, one...
I mean, six first violins, four second violins—excuse me, four second violins, two violas, two 'cellos, one bass. I've in fact got three violas, three 'cellos, one bass because I like the middle and bass lines. I don't like an extremely light bass line.

*Do you think modern day audiences are more hungry for these original propor-
tions of sounds than they are for the more glitzed up, opulent sound that we've had
for so long?*
I think that, again, I think there's room for both. I think people love the intimate
qualities of a chamber orchestra and the fact that there's no conductor and everybody's looking at each other. It's sort of an enlarged string quartet sort of feeling
and people love this. It's very clear and sort of clean and very, very expressive. It's
a totally different experience.

But about tonight's performance of the Four Seasons.
Yes.

*There you were, tonight, on stage, all dressed in white, a tall, wand-like figure
interacting with the tight cluster of players seated in a semi-circle around you. You
moved from one to the other, almost as if you were a priestess with your acolytes,
anointing each player during each "season." I've never seen anything like that.
There was drama in* watching *it as well as listening.*
That's interesting you say that. I think sometimes in playing music with fellow
human beings you find yourself in a rarefied atmosphere. There's a lot of tension,
a lot is expected of you, and I love the feeling of the communication among musicians onstage. I think one becomes very close with the other players. It's sort of
indefinable, but I think it comes across to the audience.

*And your bowing arm would sort of soar off like a white flag, sometimes, and we
would follow it with our eyes.*
That's right. You can reveal lot with your body language, with your movements.
It's very, very important to be as free as you can without distracting the audience.
It's a question of giving everything you've got to the composer. A concert is here
today and gone tomorrow. It's a fleeting experience. But that is what makes it so
exciting.

Classical and Early Romantic Music

Introduction

Even while the contrapuntal complexities of the late Baroque were in full swing, alternative, melody-driven approaches to music that extolled lyricism and elegance were on the rise. The title of Jane Austen [1775–1817]'s novel *Sense and Sensibility* (1811) aptly captures the spirit of music written from roughly the mid-1700s through the first third of the 1800s, with logic and prudence joining both emotional longing and expressive restraint. These factors, when it came to music, resulted in a so-called classical style that stressed form and order, regularity, and predictability. Much of the music of the era reflected the principles of the Enlightenment, where reason and the pursuit of knowledge influenced the philosophical, literary, and political realms.

New relationships between music and text began to develop. Various types of opera flourished, including comic forms such as the Italian *opera buffa* ("comic opera"), the French *opéra comique* ("comic opera" that includes spoken dialogue) and the German *Singspiel* ("sing-play," also with spoken dialogue). *Lieder*, a typically German song tradition, has its roots during this period and reached a point of maturity with contributions to the genre by several important composers. Instrumental music also proliferated. In addition to multi-movement symphonies, string quartets, and piano sonatas intended for public performance, smaller works created for domestic settings appeared. Music making became a popular activity for the growing middle class, piano sales grew, and public concerts increased in number. In his interview, Malcolm Bilson explains that contemporary composers wrote for fortepianos, the precursor of our modern instrument, yet was significantly different from it.

Certain cities were becoming known for their impressive musical activities, most notably Vienna. Haydn, Mozart, Beethoven, and Schubert all spent significant parts of their careers in or near the city. Vienna was not the only musical

J. C. Tibbetts et al. (eds.), *Performing Music History*,
https://doi.org/10.1007/978-3-319-92471-7_5

center by any means. Paris, for example, gained fame for its lavish opera productions, musical instrument manufacturers that made vast improvements to existing instruments and created new ones, and towering musical figures, such as Hector Berlioz: an important figure discussed by John Nelson in his interview. Leipzig had its impressive Gewandhaus Orchestra, thanks to Mendelssohn's leadership, as well as a leading conservatory. Among his other accomplishments, as conductor Joshua Rifkin explains, Mendelssohn participated in the Bach revival that became central to nineteenth-century German musical culture. In Italy, cities such as Venice, Milan, Naples, and Rome championed opera, and composers such as Rossini, Vincenzo Bellini (1801–1835), and Gaetano Donizetti (1797–1848) developed a *bel canto* (beautiful singing) style characterized by virtuoso flourishes, elegant melodies, and transparent textures.

The late eighteenth and early nineteenth centuries also comprised an era in which composers were becoming known as especially significant creators in particular genres. In addition to the Italian opera composers mentioned above, Haydn earned a reputation as a master of the string quartet and the symphony (even called the "father" of both genres); Mozart of opera and piano concertos; Beethoven of symphonies, piano sonatas, and string quartets; Schubert of *Lieder* and piano sonatas; Frederic Chopin of the polonaises and mazurkas of his native Poland; and Robert Schumann of a widely ranging achievement many forms.

In the interviews that follow, Claude Frank and Richard Goode discuss Beethoven's sonatas and their own sonata performances; Paul Badura-Skoda and Brian Newbould concentrate on Schubert's works (some finished, some tantalizingly incomplete); and Elly Ameling and Thomas Hampson focus attention on Schumann's music; especially his *Lieder.*

William Everett and Michael Saffle

Claude Frank: "Good Music Is Always Better Than It Can Be Played!"

John C. Tibbetts
1984–1987, Lawrence, Kansas

Ludwig van Beethoven composed his first piano sonata, identified as Op. 2, no. 1, in F minor, in 1795. His composed his last, Op. 111 in C minor, in or around 1822. ("Op." stands for "opus" or work. Many composers' works are identified with opus numbers, usually arranged in the order of publication.) Together with his nine well-known symphonies and sixteen string quartets, Beethoven's thirty-two sonatas for solo piano have confirmed his reputation as perhaps *the* greatest Western composer. Not all of his sonatas resemble those of his contemporaries, although Beethoven studied with Haydn and borrowed certain gestures from Haydn's lively music. At the same time Beethoven's later sonatas achieved a sonic richness and variety, a mastery of

compositional techniques, and a seriousness of intention (offset, occasionally, by humorous gestures) that paved the way for many of his nineteenth-century followers, including Franz Liszt and Johannes Brahms (Fig. 1).
Claude Frank (born Claus Johannes Frank, 1925–2014) became an American citizen in 1944, before studying composition with Paul Dessau at Columbia University and conducting with Serge Koussevitsky at Tanglewood. Legendary pianist Artur Schnabel (1882–1951), however, served as Frank's

Fig. 1 Claude Frank

lifelong keyboard model and inspiration. (During the early 1930s, Schnabel became the first pianist to record all of Beethoven's piano sonatas. Frank followed suit in 1970.) After World War II ended, Frank taught at several institutions, including the Yale School of Music (1973–2006). His memoirs, co-authored with Hawley Roddick and titled *The Music That Saved My Life: From Hitler's Germany to the World's Concert Stages*, **remains unpublished at the time of this writing (2017). In 2008, along with nine another pianists, Frank took part in "The Olympic Centenary Piano Extravaganza of China."**

These conversations transpired over several years, during which Frank was Artist-in-Residence at the University of Kansas.

JOHN C. TIBBETTS: You're famous for your Beethoven performances. I'm curious to hear why you think that is …?
CLAUDE FRANK: The premise is wrong. Actually, without false modesty, what happens is that, in this country, you do more of something than of anything else, and you are apt to be stamped. And ever since I made my debut with the Beethoven Third [Piano Concerto, I've], played a lot of Beethoven, did all-Beethoven recitals, immediately one gets stamped as a Beethoven player. I don't mind that a bit, because I love it; but I wouldn't necessarily say I'm famous for it. I just do more Beethoven than anything else. Bach, Beethoven, Schubert, they are my gods. They do not err. By virtue of being gods, their music is impossible to play. I have to quote my teacher, Artur Schnabel, since it's a wonderful saying: "Good music is always better than it can be played." In other words, you can approach it, but you can't do full justice to it. Beethoven, for some reason or another, is more approachable, a little more human.

When did you begin playing the piano?
I started as a child in Nürnberg, Germany, my home town. The piano was in the living room, and my mother said I could sing and play recorder; and then at six she allowed me to play piano. From the time I took lessons, I took it very seriously. At age eleven, I played for Schnabel. He said to my mother, "Yes, this is serious; there's no reason why you shouldn't pursue this as a life."

Were you nervous before the great man?
No, not at all. Nervousness came in much later, in leaps and bounds! I practiced my stuff and I knew instinctively that Schnabel would recognize something that was there, whether I made mistakes or not. For better or for worse, I still feel that way. The perfect surface for me is not an end. I also feel if the perfect surface can be achieved without sacrificing something: that would be fine. Anyway, to get back to Schnabel for a moment, I wasn't worried about making a mistake. I probably did. I played a Schubert Impromptu for him, in A-Flat …

… to play Schubert for Schnabel!
I didn't know any better! I was eleven! I had heard that Schnabel played Beethoven. I didn't know that he also liked Schubert! [laughs] When it was over,

he said immediately, "Another piece," so I played a Beethoven Rondo, which I had heard on a recording by Schnabel, and I tried to play it exactly as he did. I remember that he talked a little about the importance of sight-reading, something about "getting inside the music," and things like that. Then he said to my mother. during a walk in the garden—this was all very old-fashioned and children weren't supposed to listen in on plans for their future—"Yes, there's no reason why he shouldn't make music his life, and I recommend that he'll be with me eventually, but he's still too young. For four or five years he should study with one of my most advanced pupils." He recommended one in Paris. And that's what we did! We were about to leave Germany anyway, for political reasons, [Adolf] Hitler [1889–1945] and all. Good time to leave anyway; and so, a year later we went to Paris and I studied with this French pupil of his, who died during the war. But Hitler saw to it that we left France before Schnabel had planned for us to leave. Three years later in America, in 1941, I knocked on Schnabel's door. I was barely fifteen, and I said, "Here I am." Schnabel heard me play and said, "Well, you're still a little young, but since you're here now, I'll take you." And so with him I studied, and with his son, Karl Ulrich, because Schnabel was often way on tour; and I went to his other lessons, too, of which Leon Fleisher was one. This went on for years and years, with interruptions—I was in the Army during World War II between 1944 and 1946. I went on to live in New York.

You began recording for RCA at some point?

Yes, I began with RCA in the mid-1960s with the Boston Chamber Players. Soon after that, RCA asked me to record all the Beethoven Sonatas. It took me two years to play them all. I completed them in 1969 in time for the "Beethoven Year" [i.e., 1970]. There wasn't much negotiating necessary with RCA, because they asked me and I said "Yes!" No questions asked.

Recording is important, but did you miss not having an audience?

Yes, I did. And I still do. There is a dimension missing in the recording process, yes. In public the audience is somewhat more *forgiving*. You do something, and there are three microphones ready to catch it all. Microphones are cruel. They are negative listeners; they are interested in what goes *wrong* than with what goes *right*. And audiences are the exact opposite. The audience *wants* to forgive.

Dare I ask if you have any favorites among the Sonatas?

If I say the Opus 31, No. 1, it's not because of its musical quality, no, but because of how important it was to me during the time after we left Germany during the War. I was just thirteen. We were in Madrid and I didn't have an overseas visa, without any legal right at all to be in Spain. [Francisco] Franco [1892–1975] was in power and Hitler was his ally. I could have been deported at any time. But then I was invited to the Brazilian Embassy to play for a diplomatic reception. I was pretty uncomfortable, but I decided to play the Opus 31. I knew only seven of the sonatas at that time, and the G-major was one of them.

I seem to recall that it's one of the longest of the sonatas.
Yes, that's so. But it was one that Schnabel had given me particular advice about. I remember him advising me how to play that long, long slow movement: "If you don't get bored with it, nobody else will!"And yes, somehow the guests stayed awake! Maybe it was me, just thirteen years old, or the music, or whatever. But when it was time to go, the Brazilian ambassador told me he was inviting me to Brazil. He was giving me and my parents visas.

Listening to your recordings recently, I was especially struck by the "Fantasy" sonata, with its almost free-form quality. In that work Beethoven really breaks down the barriers of sonata form, doesn't he?
Absolutely. This is where Beethoven came out of that "classical" shell.[1] He was probably the first one to do this kind of thing. You are thinking of the Opus 27, No. 1, the sister sonata of the famous "Moonlight" Sonata [Opus 27, No. 2]. Yes, for that time—I believe it was written around 1801—it was a tremendous thing, not to start with a fast movement and a slow movement ...

... and kind of a "whispering" introduction.
Again, it's so typical of Beethoven. When you break it down to the musical elements, there's no melody, to speak; there is no particular harmony to be interested in; no tonic, no tonic-first degree. Yet on the whole it emerges as an unbelievable spiritual experience.

And there are such vivid contrasts, episodes of dramatic contrasts.
And, of course, what he does in a German way, how he uses motifs, which recur during the whole piece.

And there's this gentle, rambling kind of mood, like in the "Pastoral" [Sonata, Op. 28], where the concluding pages, instead of being heaven-storming or broad, kind of just bubble along.
The last movement is just a pastoral meditation, as if Beethoven, only in his early thirties, already had the maturity of an older man.

But, for all that, you say he is always accessible.
The *Pathétique* [pathetic] Sonata [Op. 13], for example, is *approachable,* even with its unbelievable dramatic first movement, its solemn, religious second movement; his third movement mixes frivolity and deepest maturity.

In that third movement, do you think some pianists are tempted to treat it too frivolously?

---

[1]Sonata form involves a more or less fixed pattern of keys and melodic material that provides both variety and a return to earlier portions of relevant material near their conclusions. "Fantasy," on the other hand, is generally less prescribed.

Well, it's a problem that hasn't been solved. We don't really know whether Beethoven meant it gaily, in the old-fashioned sense, or tragically. And chances are he meant it as a mixture of the two. So I would agree with you that it shouldn't be too frivolous, yet, who knows? Maybe Beethoven played it that way himself, at one time or another. I'm sure he didn't always play it the same way.

Because the "Appassionata" and the "M" are so well known, do you think some pianists tend to play those too often, or should they explore the lesser-known sonatas as well?

Of the thirty-two sonatas, every one of them deserves to be well known, and one of the reasons some are well known is that they have names that, to a certain extent, were not given by Beethoven, but by a publisher. "Appassionata" was not Beethoven's term, but I don't think he would have disapproved of the name, because it fits the piece [Opus 57] very well. The "Moonlight" label was not by Beethoven but by a Swiss poet by the name of [Ludwig] Rellstab, who wrote the poems to which Schubert set a lot of *Lieder*; who was rowing on the lake once and was thinking of that particular sonata.

The later ones are not so easily tagged, so easily described. Those last three, for example—you're in another territory, aren't you?

You're in a totally different territory with Beethoven, who became metaphysical, highly philosophical and strangely enough—and this is where a lot of people disagree with me—very much "instrument" conscious. Now, people say in his last works Beethoven didn't write for the piano. I think it's wrong. I think it's totally wrong. I think the last sonatas, the Opus 109, Opus 110, Opus 111, are fantastic *for* the instrument. They reveal instrumental sounds which, until then, no other piano had done. Completely unique to that instrument. You think of Opus 111, there are certain places in that that couldn't be orchestrated.

They seem to permit a degree of communion between performer and instrument that we have not seen in music before.

Anywhere before and very rarely after. I will never forget how Schnabel played the Opus 111. No one has played those trills in the variations with the kind of magic, the subtlety, like he did. You would think time was standing still.

Richard Goode: "The Music Was Like a Thunderstorm, and the House Shook!"

John C. Tibbetts
11 September 1987, Kansas City, Missouri

A pupil of Claude Frank, pianist Richard W. Goode also studied with Rudolf Serkin at the Curtis Institute in Philadelphia; in 1966 he joined the faculty

Fig. 2 Richard Goode, with Beethoven in the background

of the Mannes School of Music, New York City. Together with clarinetist Richard Stoltzman, Goode won a 1983 Grammy for their recording of
Brahms's clarinet sonatas. Today Goode serves with Dame Mitsuko Uchida
as co-artistic director of the Marlboro Music School and Festival. In 1987 he
presented his first complete Beethoven sonata cycle in Kansas City and New
York; his recordings of the sonatas were originally released by the Book-of-
the-Month Record Club (Fig. 2).

This conversation took place on the stage of Kansas City's Folly Theater
during Goode's first series of performances of the complete Beethoven Piano
Sonatas.

*JOHN C. TIBBETTS: How would you describe your first "acquaintance" with the
music of Beethoven?*
RICHARD GOODE: I had a kind of, I guess you would say, atypical history
with Beethoven, because I remember as an adolescent loving the late music of
Beethoven. It is not only a summation of classical composition, but a gateway
into a different era. I immediately loved the late sonatas and started to learn them,
despite the advice you weren't supposed to learn them too early. My knowledge

of the early sonatas has come later. I was a kid growing up in Brooklyn when a young man came to the house and played the *Pathétique* on our upright piano. The impact of it was very strong. The music was like a thunderstorm, and the house shook. It embodied the assertiveness of the Beethoven personality. I began studying with a very fine teacher when I was a kid, Elvira Szigeti, a woman who was the aunt of Joseph Szigeti. She had graduated from the Budapest Conservatory and had a wonderful grounding in a fine musical tradition a great personal intensity. She introduced me to certain sonatas of Beethoven and a great deal of Bach and Bartók. I fell in love with pianos at that time. From then on, there was never a doubt that I wanted to be a musician. I then had a succession of excellent teachers, including Frank and Serkin at the Curtis Institute.

Can you recall when you first took to the stage with this music?
I remember playing the *Pathétique* when I was twelve at Mannes College.

And did the room shake?
[laughs] No, not as much as I would have liked!

When you finally encountered those earlier sonatas you found lots of unexpected things, even surprises?
That's always the case. There are certain relatively neglected sonatas, like the Opus 54, which stands midway between two of the most celebrated, the *Waldstein* and the *Appassionata*. This supposedly minor, two-movement work is played seldom; but it's a wonderful work of a different kind, of a kind of relaxed spontaneity, of the unexpected, even of the bizarre. This is when he takes an idea out as far as it can go in whatever directions it will go.

And Opus 27, No. 1, where there's nothing like rigid formula, the music changing and evolving all the time ...
That's a marvelous piece. There's a story about it. Shortly before I played it in New York, I went to my ear doctor, who had the distinction of studying with Emil von Sauer, the Liszt pupil, and for a short time had been a concert pianist and had given it up for medicine. (He had a Bösendorfer [piano] in his ante-room!) I mentioned the Opus 27 and he started singing it in a much faster tempo then I had been playing it. He said, "It seems to be based on a popular tune at time." And after hearing it, I decided I should play it from now on at that faster tempo! Anyway, compare this "evolving" quality you mentioned to somebody else, like Brahms, who I love very much, but whose works usually don't give you that sense of *anything can happen*. In that Opus 54, for example, you have an unusual first movement that is a curious double variation with a very courtly *menuetto*,[2] and then an explosion of almost brutal octaves and triplets, related, in a way, to some

---

[2]Or "minuet": a dance in triple meter that consists of two similar sections separated by a trio.

of Haydn's movements. Beethoven seems to be creating a "first movement" model as he's going along; and there was no limit to what he might try. That's one of the reasons why it's possible to play whole recitals of Beethoven sonatas because they all are so different.

That discursive, sweet ramble that opens the Opus 101. It just seems to drift, as if bar lines don't exist ...

That's one of the things that begins to happen in those late pieces, that all the voices become activated, a new polyphonic emphasis which makes for greater density and a richer melodic content. The middle pieces, like the *Waldstein* and the *Appassionata*, great as they are, subordinate their melodic content to the great architectural whole. In the late pieces, this profusion of exuberant melody becomes, in the opening of the Opus 101, a great dense, lyric web which defies you to take it to pieces. The movement begins in the middle of its statement and then goes on from there in its wonderful "in between" mood and doesn't achieve a tonic cadence until the end. Yes, its unpredictable.

Beethoven described himself as being in an "unbuttoned" mood. Is that appropriate here?

No! [laughs] There's nothing "unbuttoned" about this first movement, not if you think he meant by the word a kind of "wildness" of mood. I think of Karl-Ulrich Schnabel [1909–2001],[3] who reminded us that against Beethoven's music about 80% of it is *cheerful*. [laughs] And there are pieces that are gigantically cheerful and buoyant. There are minor-key endings for minor-key sonatas, but to think of a tragic mood that is sustained to the end, I think only of the *Appassionata*. And the "Funeral March" sonata [Opus 26] is generally rather light until the third movement, but after that comes the last movement, which pianist Claudio Arrau described as "the gentle awakening of nature." And there is a preponderance of lyric expression that is found everywhere in the 32 sonatas, like the last movement of Opus 79 and the first movement of Opus 109—which, by the way, is the only example I know of a "borrowing" of harmonic material between two separate sonatas. The number of sonatas in which the lyric impulse is paramount is striking.

Is it unfortunate that descriptive titles like "Funeral March" have been applied to some of the sonatas?

It's not generally known that Beethoven did contemplate poetic titles to his sonatas. He was dissuaded from that, except for the *Pathétique* and *Les Adieux* ["Farewell" Sonata, Op. 81a].

So many pianists have either recorded or performed—or both—the complete sonatas, that I wonder if that is intimidating to you as you take it up.

---

[3]Son of Artur Schnabel.

Tradition is a fine thing, until it becomes a burden. In my case, I try to be as independent of that as possible. I have in the past listened to a lot of performances of the sonatas, but I find as I have become more involved in my playing I hear "less" of other performances, if you know what I mean, and the less I want to hear; that I become specific about what I want to do for myself—to be more *unabashed* about it. The more I hear about tradition, the more I want to turn away to my own immediate experiences and to give back what I am hearing in them and play them as freshly as possible.

What is your strategy in your public performances of the sonatas? How do you arrange each program?
I want above all to ensure that each program has diversity; for example that each program would have a late sonata and an early sonata. Other than that, anything goes! Don't think, by the way, that an early sonata is necessarily a thing apart from the later ones. Beethoven did not take the "first" of any of his kinds of compositions lightly. He already had many of his works, some of them quite large, behind him when he wrote the very first of his piano sonatas, the one in F-minor—when he leaps into the arena. It's a very forceful and vehement expression that sets the precedent for the piano works to follow.

I was startled at that moment, when you—or Beethoven—virtually unleashed that storm. Suddenly, you saw in the young Beethoven a surprising premonition of things to come.
The music has been holding itself back until then. It's a stormy piece and that last movement is the most melodramatic of all the movements in the sonatas—quite a rabble-rousing declaration. And it's the young virtuoso showing what he can do, like the pure bravura he unleashes in that long cadenza of the First Concerto, which is full of an antic, almost slapstick humor.

When did you first perform all the sonatas in a series?
I haven't done it before! This is my first time! As I do them here, I also do them in New York. Not to say that I haven't performed most of the sonatas before, separately or on all-Beethoven programs; this cycle, here, is a first for me. I try to not lose the totality of each sonata in the face of performing all of them as a cycle.

So, as you begin this cycle, here and now, what's on your mind?
There are technical things. In the Opus 7 [Sonata], Beethoven writes in the score a *crescendo* [growing louder], even though the hands don't move. It's very necessary for a composer to indicate something like that. It's a good example of one of those "important impossibilities." A performer could convey that by body movement: You feel it within and the body would follow. We all know that once you strike the piano key, the sound begins to go away (our more modern pianos have a slower decay). Let's look for an example that illustrates that in a dramatic way: In Chopin's *Polonaise-Fantaisie* the brilliant coda dies down into a kind of soft "muttering" in the bass; and there are two quiet chords, the last of which is held by

the [sustaining] pedal; and then there is a *fortissimo* chord that ends the piece. The question is, *how is that be felt?* The *fortissimo* [very loud] chord is not the problem; it's what happens to the note after you strike it that determines how the whole piece is to be heard? The piano makes the *decrescendo* [growing softer] for you; and if you go along with the sound of the piano and simply take your hand off the keyboard quietly after the chord, you will hear, and the audience will hear, the piece ending by dying away—an elegiac dying away after that triumphant *clang!*

Things like that do come up in Beethoven. He is writing pieces that are not completely realized, but are realizable only by indirection. Like Schnabel says, the music is better than it can be played. I think Beethoven himself regarded the pianos he knew as inadequate for his desires. His piano and the music he wrote for it were not the same thing. Maybe the greatest praise is, the performance was "adequate"! This is not to say that while performing you have to be constantly evaluating and considering the music, it's not really a performance. You have to try to get rid of that part of your performing in order to be totally in the experience. At the same time, it's important to remember that the instrument and the sound and the audience are not the same as today.

How long will it take you to record them all?
I have already recorded thirteen of the sonatas, and there are the remaining nineteen this year. So, I am recording them simultaneously with the stage performances. George Spitzer of the Book-Of-The-Month Club Records asked me to record them. He liked my playing and wanted to start a series that was new and not a series of re-releases of previously recorded material. I am working in New York at the American Academy of Arts and Letters with Max Wilcox, who, I believe, also worked with Claude [Frank] on his cycle.

Like the Hammerklavier *Sonata. Seems like Beethoven is taking on the world with it!*
I think somewhere Beethoven wrote about it, "What I have now written bears no resemblance to what I have already written!" He was in his late forties then [1818], and it's his longest sonata, with technical difficulties far beyond the reach of amateur pianists. Not only does it challenge the performer, but it places demands on the keyboard itself, particularly those of Beethoven's day. It seems to demand our modern concert grand than a keyboard of his own time.

Can a pianist ever be fully prepared for something like the Hammerklavier, *or is it a bit of a crap shoot?*
It's interesting, because the dimensions of it are very unusual, having played it a number of times. You're not prepared for when the piece opens out after the second movement. The first movement is big, but not very long. Not I think longer than the first movements of some other sonatas. The second is very short. The third is the longest slow movement of anything he ever wrote for piano, a uniquely vast and spacious piece. And then the introduction and the fugue is something again huge. So the piece opens out from beginning to end; that's very unusual.

Have you ever played this on a piano close to Beethoven's own?
I've heard recently that Beethoven was fonder of the Streicher piano than the Broadwood. I think the music is more than his piano could ever take. It strains even the limits of our piano, in many ways. There are certain aspects of it that are specific to his piano, the soft pedal effect,[4] which is more drastic, and he uses it dramatically in the slow movement, and it's something he plays with. Otherwise, I'm not at all unhappy playing it on a modern piano.

Technically, is this just an overwhelming feat to bring off?
It's probably the most difficult of the sonatas, technically. For interesting reasons. In the later sonatas, there's more contrapuntal intricacy. I think even in the first movement there are two things involved that make it difficult. One is that it's very contrapuntally alive all the time. Things are going all over the place; there's many voices to take care of. That's one reason. The other is that it's more spread out over the regions of the keyboard than any other piece. It's seems immense not because of its length but because of the space. It just fills out the piano.

Musically speaking, in the bridge between the slow movement and the last movement, we find strange harmonic excursions Something very extravagant happens there.
Yeah. Well, in a way it's a written out improvisation in which he does what he's been doing all along, which is unifying it by descending thirds—in this case they are in the bass. It's in a way a transition in which he finds his way to the key, going through a series of thirds, of the Fugue. It's free music. And another way, it's also a very clear—just as Beethoven in the Ninth Symphony tries out the other movements to see if they give a possibility of going on; and then he finds the theme of the last movement—here he's doing the same thing, he's trying out possibilities of fugal writing, starting out with early, old music, medieval or Renaissance counterpoint (which he was very interested in); and tries it out three times, each time a little bit faster. The first one very quiet imitation; the third one is a Bachian fuguetta [a little fugue in the style of Bach]. Each time he breaks it off. And he resumes the improvisatory theme, and finally finds its way in a hair-raising explosion he finds his way to the proper place. The Introduction serves many purposes, one of which is to trace a little evolution of fugue, as if he's saying, "I'm going to write a fugue, but not something you've ever heard before." ... But it's all calculated, clearly calculated for the effect of that; but it's the end result of a long compositional process.

---

[4]The third pedal—also known as the *tre corde* [literally, three-strings] pedal, more often called the "soft" pedal, and on the left side of the modern piano's three pedals—can be used to create different sound effects on the modern piano, including "half-pedaled" or semi-muffled sounds. Its name comes from the fact that, when depressed, this pedal causes all the strings on the piano, including those notes with three strings, to shift to one; this allows pianists to play especially softly and create certain muted effects.

Beethoven doesn't seem too worried about the performer at this point. He's making very few concessions for ease of performance.
Yeah. I think he had a hard time with this sonata. He was fighting himself out of a period of compositional drought, the only one that ever afflicted him, for two years he hardly wrote anything. This sonata was an heroic thing for various reasons. That was probably reflected in the difficulty of playing. He did say it would give pianists something to play 50 years later. I find the contrapuntal side of Beethoven in the later pieces a great challenge, because the fugues have a lot of energy.

The Opus 111 is a two-movement work. And it ends with those amazing variations and the slow movement. Thomas Mann [1875–1955] in Dr. Faustus, *says, "This is the end of the piano sonata as we will ever know it."*
The end of anybody's? I'm glad Mann didn't advise composers to stop composing! I'm still thinking of the Mann quote! If Beethoven had stopped writing quartets with the *Grosse Fuge* we would think he had not wanted to write more quarters, but then we have the Opus 135 [Quartet]. There is something marvelous and unique about the Opus 111. The idea of the last movement, this set of variations, is among the strictest ever composed. Stricter than most in the sense that they're unified by tempo, like a Baroque set of variations. And more varied in mood than almost any variations could possibly be, except the Bach *Goldberg [Variations]*. There's an enormous variety of emotion and idea that Beethoven got into the variations. All unified by this tempo, the same tempo with diminishing rhythmic values. The piece is organized as a very slow theme and each succeeding variation doubles the note values. This is not so unusual, but to work with this elevated cantabile theme to an absolutely intoxicated rapture of the third variation, succeeded by its absolute opposite—this is the heart of that last movement. It's the way Beethoven goes from this fantastic kind of intoxicated dance of the third variation to a time-stopping variation, which is entirely the opposite.

You said it all when you said "time-stopping." Claude Frank said something like the same thing. I would think that would be a hazardous thing to bring off—time stands still, but the forward motion mustn't lapse.
The music goes on but you feel behind it this regularity and stillness behind all that. Unique. The use of the registers (high and low, extreme separations) … you have a combination of this shadowy darkness at the first part of each variation and the starlight of the second part, where everything is absolutely clear. And everything corresponds to the theme and moves to the dictates of the theme…. I don't think anybody wrote anything like that, before or since.

As we reach the end of our conversation—and the culmination of your recorded performances, what can we take away from the experience?
The combination of this tremendous charge one gets emotionally with these pieces with this extreme control of every moment in the music; that's something that never fails to amaze me. Everything somehow fits into this marvelous overall

shape in which everything seems to come out of necessity from what happened previously…. One thing arises out of the previous. That's something he was more preoccupied with than any composer since.

Malcolm Bilson: "Mozart Wrote, 'Vienna Is Piano Land!'"

John C. Tibbetts
Winter 1991, Kansas City, Missouri; September 16, Cornell University

Wolfgang Amadeus Mozart was the son of a talented composer and violinist living in Salzburg. Mozart achieved celebrity at an early age; later he moved to Vienna, where he composed hundreds of instrumental and vocal works. He died at an early age, possibly from poisoning, although there is no truth to the rumor that Antonio Salieri (1750–1825), a successful composer of Italian opera, murdered him.

Although other names have been applied to percussive keyboard instrument invented or modified during the seventeenth and eighteenth centuries, the fortepiano, as it is mostly known today, differs from modern concert pianos even as it inspired their designs. Softer and much more portable, fortepianos have leather-covered hammers used to strike thin, harpsichord-like wires or strings, and their frames are made entirely of wood rather than metal. All but forgotten during the nineteenth century; Bilson and several other artists, including Paul Badura-Skoda, have employed them with great success as part of the Early Music Revival (Fig. 3).

For more than forty years Malcolm Bilson has championed the fortepiano as performer and scholar. A graduate of Bard College with a D.M.A. degree from the University of Illinois, Bilson founded the Amadé Trio in 1974 and performed classic music with his colleagues on the fortepiano; later he was appointed Frederick J. Whiton Professor of Music at Cornell University. His many recordings include all of Mozart's Piano Concerto, together with John Eliot Gardiner and the English Baroque Soloists.

These conversations began in Kansas City in 1991, when Bilson performed a portion of his Mozart Piano Sonata Cycle at the Folly Theater; and they continued by email and telephone in 2016 while Bilson was teaching at Cornell University.

JOHN C. TIBBETTS: In his letters Mozart talks about a "pianoforte" and a "fortepiano." Are the terms interchangeable?
MALCOLM BILSON: Yes, they are interchangeable. You have a lot of different words. You had "Hammerflügel" and "Hammerklavier" and "fortepiano"—people tend to call these instruments "fortepianos" to distinguish them. But I don't think

On the occasion of the
Mozart Sonata Cycle
in the Folly Theater,
Winter 1991

Fig. 3 Malcolm Bilson, with Mozart in the background

that works very well. What are you going to call a piano Chopin played? This is a late eighteenth-century Viennese piano. That's what I call it.

And in Mozart's time, was the piano the preeminent solo instrument for him and his colleagues?
No question. Mozart writes to his father, "This is piano-land, Vienna." Around 1800 there were more than a hundred builders making these things. Every house had one. Certainly, it was the VCR of its day. [laughs] Everybody had one.
But he couldn't carry it with him ...?
Oh, yes, he took his own piano to the concerts, just as I do. It wasn't hard to move around.

That surprises me. I thought that, with coaches and carriages, a fortepiano would be pretty precarious baggage.

Why? If one was already in place, he played it. If he wanted one of his own, which is better—it's not such a big deal to bring his own. Like I brought mine, here. But when I go to California, I know I'll find nice pianos to play there; and I'm always glad to play them. On the other hand, if I lived in Santa Barbara and played in Los Angeles, I'd probably take my own. That's because I know every hammer and damper.

What did Mozart himself say about these instruments?

There are three detailed letters from him to his father in 1778, when he first encountered Stein's instruments. He goes on and on about how beautiful, how perfect they are. And indeed, there doesn't seem to be any way to *improve* on these instruments. In fact, they remained pretty much the same until, after 1800, when somebody made a *different* kind of piano. Most remarkable of all is the modern Steinway piano, which since 1870 has made no improvements. (Some will argue about this, but it would be good if we had a brand new 1870 Steinway to compare with one built today.) The fortepiano looked like a harpsichord and was called *piano* and *forte*, loud and soft. German and French harpsichords always had black naturals [i.e., keys] and white sharps. English and Italian had the white naturals and black sharps. After 1800 everybody goes to the standard modern way of having white naturals, probably due to the increased availability of ivory. Actually, this is very nice, having black naturals. If there's a stage with lights coming in from the side you don't see shadows, like on a modern piano. There's a knee lever that acts as a [soft] pedal and raises the dampers, and this particular piano has a hand-operated *celeste* stop, which introduces a cloth strip between the hammers and strings for a soft effect.

When should you use these effects?

When indeed! There's a whole question about the [sustaining] pedal. Mozart never wrote a pedal mark. Yet in his letters to his father, he talks about how wonderfully these knee-levers work in Stein's pianos. Basically, I think it's not like the [sustaining] pedal on the modern piano, which is often used as a general "sauce." I either don't use it at all, or use it a lot. For example, this famous passage from the second movement of Mozart's C Major Concerto [plays melody] shows I'm not changing the pedal at all. [plays] One probably wouldn't do this on a modern piano.

No way, I suppose, can we know if the sound emanating from this is in any way comparable to the sound emanating from a 1785 instrument? Is the sound of this anything like it would have been in 1785?

My fortepiano is a replica of a 1785 instrument. I can say that one of the things that is most disturbing to people who hear fortepianos for the first time, people who are used to the plush, homogenous sound of the modern instrument, is they're shocked by what seems the *thinness* of the sound. The fortepianist calls that "clarity," the *separation* of tones; the fact that you can hear clearly every note. In the 1790s instruments that Mozart, Haydn, and Beethoven played gave you every note clearly. In a way, it's harder to listen to that *because you have to pay attention more*. And people can be put off because there's so much more to follow.

Are there any materials in your replica that would not have been available then?
No. As a matter of fact, they seem to have had better materials in those days. But the builders are constantly getting better today. [plays] This instrument is out of tune, but it's cold. [plays] It'll get back in tune without me doing too much. They're all a little bit out. By the time it warms up it should be in pretty good tune.

But even during the process of performing, the instrument can go out of tune?
Well, you hit pianos pretty hard. You hit the strings hard. Spotlights give off heat. Wood expands with heat. Violins have to be tuned as well. Modern pianos are less sensitive than this one, because they're more massive; but the principle is the same. You have your pianos tuned as the season changes. Because the wood swells or dries out and the strings get shorter and longer.

So by necessity you have to have acute hearing?
No, you just have to know how to tune! When I was a kid there was a piano tuner who had no ear at all, but he knew how to tune! You listen to this and this should "beat" slowly and this should not "beat" at all, and this should "beat" slowly, etc.

Could you tell us what it would have been like at a Mozart concert? Would it have been successful?
There are several new books that I think show us that pretty much anything that you see in *Amadeus* is not only wrong, but probably completely wrong. Mozart seems to have been very successful and have earned quite a lot of money. It's fairly likely that his financial difficulties were due somewhat to his not knowing how much money was worth or how to run it. There are people who do not make very much money and have plenty and people who make a lot of money and have nothing. That's just a simple fact of life.

What does the term, "Early Music Revival," mean to you?
What is currently accepted as an early music revival is simply a return to the sources, a return to the historical sources and the performing tradition of a given composer. And that is certainly what we try to do with ensembles like the Monteverdi Choir and the English Baroque Soloists—to reconstruct, insofar as it is possible and attainable the kind of sounds that Handel and other composers of the Baroque actually heard and fostered. Of course, we're different from previous generations in that we hear music quite differently from the way our forefathers heard music and which is totally different from the way Handel and his generation heard music. Our ears have been enriched, if you like it, or polluted, if you don't like it, by all the music that's gone in between …

But what you do *hear is what you prefer to perform on so-called "authentic" instruments?*
I feel it's misleading to ask musicians to play this old music on relatively modern instruments—that is to say, on instruments that may have been modernized to accommodate larger halls. In a way you get a much more vibrant and exciting performance by going back to the instruments and the orchestrations of Handel and Mozart's own day. It's very intense and very full-blooded. And it's not kind of petite and dainty and lacking in guts ...

Speaking of authentic practices, do we know how Mozart conducted his orchestras?
Mozart would seize any instrument that came to hand and would leap up and conduct sometimes. But the notion of a conductor who was a non-performing leader is a late eighteenth-century, early nineteenth-century development.

Would someone like Mendelssohn have helped to advance that idea?
Well, Mendelssohn and Berlioz, above all. ... Now, I don't walk onto the platform wearing an eighteenth-century wig and frock coat when I conduct; and I don't take snuff. I'm a conductor in the modern age and conducting in the modern age and performing to contemporary musicians. No, I don't believe in the kind of hocus-pocus that goes along with that. But I do believe in the means of production, and the sounds that can be produced from a choir and an orchestra which conforms to those for whom the music was written.

You've had to become your own tuner and technician?
Yes, I had to learn to do everything myself! Whoever gets started in this learns that. I can tune a piano like this in twenty minutes; big nineteenth-century pianos take longer, of course.

You're working as we talk. Tell me when you first began playing replicas of fortepianos.
Back in 1969, a builder named Philip Belt brought me what he called a "Mozart piano." What Belt did in those days was quite remarkable. He left it with me for a week, and I practiced very hard on it. And what happened in that week was that I began to be not so much an elephant in a china shop but learned to adjust to the action. I began to appreciate it for its own sound. Much more than that, I began to see I was playing what was on the page.

[plays a few measures of Mozart] Take this Mozart sonata. Now, the expressive articulation slurs that Mozart puts there are very unequivocal. The first three notes have a slur, plus three dots; then another slur; then another. All of the sources in the eighteenth century say the bigger the break, the more expressive. It's very easy to sing, and you can do that on this piano. [plays] I didn't understand why at first, but the simple fact is that the modern piano, which is really an 1860–1870 piano, is designed to have the richest possible tone. Every piano that has three components to the sound—the *beginning* (attack), the *singing* part, and the *cutting off*. But what Steinway wanted was the best possible middle part of the tone, the *singing*, with a minimum of *attack* and *cutting off*. If what you want to do is play a long, uninflected line, the modern piano is superior, for the singing middle part of the tone carries so wonderfully. But the passage I was just playing from the Mozart sonata is full of small inflections that are almost impossible on the modern piano. So that's what got me going on these pianos.

Is an instrument like yours what Mozart himself would have owned?
It is based on Mozart's own pianos housed in the *Geburtshaus* [birth house] in Salzburg, and which is a very beautiful instrument.

What about volume? Do you have to be careful about the size of the hall?
The *size* of the hall is not as important as the acoustics. In Lincoln Center Tully Hall holds 1200 and Avery Fisher [Hall] holds 3000. But Avery Fisher is more resonant with a live acoustic. People tell me that at first the sound is a little soft, but they get used to it. I think it must be akin to somebody accustomed to orchestral concerts going to their first string quartet. That would seem "soft." But in many ways it's not so soft. If you took a Bartók string quartet, where you have the impression they're ripping the strings off the instruments, and heard it with a string orchestra, it would sound quite a bit louder but less savage, less gutsy.

Are there special problems in balancing the fortepiano sound with orchestral forces?
Have we got an hour!? [laughs] The standard way today is to play a Mozart concerto with an orchestra the size Mozart would have used, but with a modern piano, which is about ten times louder than [the piano] Mozart had. And what does that do for the balance? Mozart worked his balances out *so* carefully, to take an instrument like this one, with all its attributes (but which is not very loud), and make it *sound* loud and virtuosic. While the piano plays, the orchestra is fairly quiet; it is in the *tutti* that the band can play full out. Modern pianos turn on its head the whole effect of where the loud and soft places are. In addition, Mozart would not have sat out in front of the orchestra but rather sit inside the orchestra as part of it. That way you have all this back and forth, with moments for the solo instrument, others when the entire orchestra is playing full (when the piano plays the continuo or supporting part), and of course the chamber music aspect where the piano, the winds, and the strings all interact.

How far into the nineteenth century did this kind of piano enjoy general usage?
Well, the first half of Beethoven's piano sonatas should probably be played on a piano like this—probably the last instrument he was able to hear accurately. The modern piano does perhaps even more disservice to Beethoven than it does to Mozart. Let me go back to make a point: Basically, at that time there were two kinds of pianos, English pianos and Viennese pianos. The English pianos were really the antecedents of the modern pianos. They had much more of a middle

tone, a richer sound but with less clarity, less clear damping. And I think that when you talk about Chopin and Liszt, they played French pianos, Pleyels and Erards, which are the ancestors of Steinways; whereas Brahms played on Viennese pianos. You see in the music of Schubert and Brahms the same kind of articulation marks that you find in Mozart—also not observed by most modern pianists.

Joshua Rifkin: "One of the Great Agendas of the Romantic Era Was to Rediscover and Reclaim the Past"

John C. Tibbetts
21 October 1989, Lawrence, Kansas

Generally considered the greatest composer of the Baroque era and one of Protestant Christianity's foremost composers, Bach was "revived" during the early nineteenth century largely by the young Felix Mendelssohn, who arranged to have the *St. Matthew Passion* performed in Leipzig on 11 March 1829, almost exactly a century from the date of its first performance. Mendelssohn himself conducted. Because the event was a sellout, two more concerts had to be scheduled (Fig. 4).

Currently Professor of Music at Boston University, Joshua Rifkin is a conductor, keyboard artist, and scholar. He is perhaps best known for his assertion that Bach's choral works, especially the *St. Matthew Passion*, were performed by soloists, not large ensembles, with a single singer assigned to each part. Rifkin's 1981 recording of Bach's Mass in B minor won a Grammy for best choral performance, and his book *Bach's Choral Ideal* (2002) has won kudos from a number of musicologists. Rifkin is also known for his interest in ragtime and popular music; he has performed with Maria Muldauer, the Even Dozen Jug Band, and musical satirist Peter Schickele.

This conversation took place at the University of Kansas, where in 1989 Rifkin was a guest lecturer.

JOHN C. TIBBETTS: What were the circumstances surrounding this so-called "Bach Revival" by the Romantics?
JOSHUA RIFKIN: Really, since the early nineteenth century, the revival of Bach's music—not that it was unknown before, but the kind of revival that brought him to a much broader audience and made him much more integral to peoples' consciousness—was something that was fueled from the start by certain ideologies—a mix of political, national and religious ideologies that needed to create out of Bach a certain kind of figure that so well suited the needs of the time that, of course, this figure was received very enthusiastically. It has in a sense created a Bach, a wonderful Bach legend, a Bach myth that really has only glancing connection to the— if you'll forgive the term—historically grounded actuality in his life.

Fig. 4 Joshua Rifkin, between his heroes Scott Joplin and J. S. Bach

So, who was the historical Bach?
I find the "real" Bach a much more interesting figure. Always remembering, of course, there's no such thing as a "real Bach," because we're always recreating the past in our own image. And our real Bach is just as much a projection of our own needs as was the nineteenth century's Bach. That was, after all, to *them* the real Bach, you know.

Why did the Romantics try to reclaim him?
One of the great agendas of the Romantic era is in a sense to rediscover and reclaim the past. It's the first really history-conscious era that begun sort of in the century already before; but it's already a time when you're not only interested in what's current or what's from antiquity—but that there's a more recent past that's becoming very, very meaningful. It's when the classical music repertory begins to get set up and that's again very much part of that. They are discovering things that are no longer alive but that somehow are speaking to them and address their condition and they can claim as their own and shape into their own. And of course, when they discovered Bach, Bach was still enough in the recent past that they would not have a certain kind of historical distance, which meant that he was still in a way living repertory—repertory that was to be dealt with in the way you deal with living repertory. It's not that Bach's brutal or unethical, but he's very determined and he will cut through any obstacle to get there. He seems to be a man who is thoroughly at home with and basically accepts the tenets of his world. He's not a rebellious figure in those ways. He's very socially conservative; and he seems to feel the order of things is right. It is a role built on political absolutism and an absolute identity of church and state. Bach wasn't simply a church musician; he was actually a musician in the service of political entities, including churches. But since religious devotion was an integral part of state life, it becomes a great part of his duties. Which is not to say that he was not a religious man. He was, clearly. It all fits together in a way—it's part of the accepted order into which he fits. But into which he doesn't always fit the way he would like because of this really stubborn determination of his.

How do we distinguish between Bach's secular and religious works?
There is a distinction, but let's say they are points on a continuum rather than different things. The same music can serve in sacred and secular contexts and regularly did. And Bach could adapt secular works for sacred use very frequently. That was considered nothing wrong with this. And again, the lines are very finely drawn. An instance—one of the feats on the calendar on the St. Thomas Church in Leipzig was the Feast of the Celebration of the Inauguration of a new Town Council. And the Church stood under the directorship of the Town Council; so you see, it's a setup that in our post-Enlightenment world we can't really understand. It is so completely different than anything we know today. But there was simply no distinction. It was all considered part of a single, unified universe.

What was a public concert like in Bach's time?
We actually know very little about that. I think it's an area in which a lot of research remains to be done. But actually, it seems as if Bach himself were in on part of the ground floor. The activities he had with the Collegium Musicum of Leipzig, which he directed from 1729 for a number of years, seemed to have approximated—at least in several ways—modern concerts. They were not held in big halls. They didn't have concert halls, per se, then. But it does seem as if the audience bought tickets, came and listened to the music.

Here comes Felix Mendelssohn! Such a young man to take up the Bach cause!
Mendelssohn grew up in the context of early musical life, which was an absolute
hotbed of Bach enthusiasm. His teacher, a minor composer named Carl Friedrich
Zelter [1758–1832], was a great Bach fan and indeed owned a great many original manuscripts of Bach, and his Singakademie sometimes sang from Bach's
original materials. So, Mendelssohn came out of this background as a very young
man—you must remember he was twenty when he conducted the revival of the *St.
Matthew Passion*. He was fired with enthusiasm for the piece. Zelter was a little bit
skeptical about its chances of winning broader acceptance. But Mendelssohn and
his friends pushed this through. The performance, as you know, was a tremendous
success. Now, it had been well prepared by a press campaign.

And there were a number of points that Mendelssohn and his friends emphasized
about this music and about Bach that absolutely hit the temper of the time. I think
above all, it was the music's combined national-religious aspect. [Early nine-
teenth-century] Germany was a country that was fragmented and was beginning to
feel its fragmentation very keenly. And was very, very receptive to great German
figures. After all, in the arts Germany had always played second place to France
and Italy. So far. It was now beginning to assert its own identity. So, that there
would be a great German composer was terribly important. That German identity
was being sort of spear-headed in Prussia, which is where this all is taking place—
is yet another element. Moreover, there is a religious dimension here because
the striving for a unified Germany was very much bound up with the notion of
a unified people through the church—although Germany did have two religions.
The German unification was spearheaded though the Protestant territories. And so
there was a great expression of Lutheran faith, as they saw it, was yet another element that came into play here. Finally, of course, the dramatic style, the narrative,
the vocal style, the colors, the differences between choruses and arias—all of this
spoke very much to the Romantic sensibility. It was not simple keyboard music
or learned fugues; it was very dramatic, very vital, very operatic music. So all of
these elements come together.

There are revivals going on all the time, aren't there?
You can compare the revival of Bach, let's say, to the ongoing life of a Broadway
show. Take *Show Boat*,[5] which over the fifty odd years since its premiere has
stayed in repertory and has always changed, rearranged, re-orchestrated, shuffled
about, new cuts, modified to suit the present tastes, just as seventeenth and eighteenth-century French operas were. This is normal show-biz. Now, of course, we're
far enough away from the original *Show Boat* for John McGlinn to reconstruct the

---

[5]See the McGlinn interview in the present volume.

original and record it to great success, which also says something about the temper of *our* time. But with Bach, and his original rediscovery, nobody thought of this distance. It was just making it music that's part of your life. And that is how it happened and had it kept happening until more or less the present day.

Did Mendelssohn employ a "Romantic" orchestra or an original ensemble?
I don't think he thought of things in one way or another. He is using what he took to be appropriate for the music, which is in fact a Romantic orchestra. Because that is what they see as a proper orchestra.... Well, there was no one Romantic orchestra, any more than there is one Baroque orchestra. But Romantic orchestras are larger than your average ensemble of the eighteenth century. They have larger bodies of strings—I don't remember whether they doubled woodwinds or not in Mendelssohn's performance. Of course, the most dramatic difference to audiences today would be when Bach presented the *St. Matthew Passion*—and on this we have very solid evidence—he had basically eight singers for each choir. And Mendelssohn had a considerably larger number than that. I don't think anything near as large as the nineteenth century moved on—150, 200, 300. But he certainly had a very substantial group of singers and a group way larger than anything Bach could have imagined.

Was Mendelssohn's great friend, Robert Schumann, a part of this story?
I think Schumann felt a great affinity with Bach. He even wrote a number of fugues on the name "Bach", the B-A-C-H motive [i.e., B-flat /A /C /B natural]— that spells out Bach's name in [German] musical letters.[6] I think that all of this group, Mendelssohn, Schumann, all of that side of the Romantic musical movement felt a very strong affinity to Bach.

The other thing is, one has to remember that there was a central fascination with the Romantics for old things and antique things. They loved Gothic cathedrals. They loved ruins to the point of building their own ruins. And Bach fits very much in with this preoccupation as well.... The Romantics were perhaps the first—well, maybe not the first—but they certainly are a generation of artists who are really starting off with the perception of a "lost world." They have a very passionate involvement in the world in which they are living; but at the same time there is an intense fascination with the past, or with geographically distant places, and so forth. They want to live in two places—or many places—at once. And that is, I think, very much related to the Romantic sensibility.

---

[6]In German notation, "B" is B-flat and "H" is B natural.

Paul Badura-Skoda: "The Obligation of an Artist Is to Know that What He Plays Really Represents the Composer's Writing"

John C. Tibbetts
Summer 1987, College Park, Maryland

In addition to his hundreds of songs, Schubert wrote significantly for the piano, including twenty-one solo sonatas (according to the most common numbering system), various character pieces, and a substantial number of works for piano four-hands (Fig. 5).

Fig. 5 Paul Badura-Skoda

A student of Edwin Fleischer, Paul Badura-Skoda debuted in 1949 with conductors Wilhelm Furtwängler and Herbert von Karajan in Vienna. With his
wife, Eva Badura-Skoda, he has published *Schubert Studies: Problems of Style
and Chronology* (2008) as well as other books. He is the only pianist to have
recorded the complete piano sonatas of Mozart, Beethoven, and Schubert,
on both historic and modern instruments. Badura-Skoda is a *Chevalier de la
Légion d'honneur* (1993) and a *Commandeur des Arts et des Lettres* (1997).

   The following conversation transpired during the first William Kapell
International Piano Competition held at College Park, Maryland.

*JOHN C. TIBBETTS: You've won distinction as a pianist, as an editor of early
keyboard manuscripts, and as a historian and musicologist. Have these diverse
pursuits always been part of your ambitions?*
PAUL BADURA-SKODA: No, it hasn't been an ambition. It's just part of my personality, I suppose. It has something to do with my upbringing. I did not begin as
a concert pianist. And, although I've worked as hard as anybody, practicing the
piano for many hours, I have always used my spare time to look into the study of
musical texts and historical instruments.

*You were a pianist known to American audiences in the late 1940s, primarily
through your LP recordings.*
Yes, my recordings preceded me in many markets, not just America. And since I
was very young when I started in the early fifties to appear on the American mar-
ket, quite a few people are surprised to see that I'm only in my fifties [as of 1987]!
It's four decades since I started playing, so one can state that my career started
with my New York debut in 1953.

*On many of your early recordings for Westminster, you performed Schubert with
Jörg Demus. Historic recordings, I venture to suggest ...*
We shared honors in several music competitions. We were both young lads, teen-
agers, when we first met in the early 1950s—not in Vienna but in Geneva, and we
soon became very close friends.

*Do you remember how many recordings you did for Westminster, either by yourself
or with Mr. Demus?*
There must have been pretty close to a hundred, not just for Westminster but
for other labels, like Remington. I have a special fondness for the Schubert-
Westminster ones with Jörg for piano four-hands and for two pianos in the 1950s.
We both indeed share an affinity for Schubert, each in his own right as a solo pianist, and also, of course, playing Schubert's music together. One of the things we
regretted was that although we have been together for more than thirty years, we
have never were able to make a series of more modern recordings of Schubert's
four-hand piano works, just those early Westminster Records.

You've moved from performing Schubert to preparing an edition of his piano music, the sonatas especially.

My way of studying a work is to secure, first of all, the basic text as the composer wrote it or had it published. This is part of the obligation of an artist: to know that what he plays really represents the composer's writing, and not what certain editors, with good will or not-so-good will, have added a hundred years later. In the case of Schubert it was particularly interesting because at the time I recorded the complete Schubert sonatas, not one complete *modern* edition existed of certain works. Some of them I had to copy by hand, or make photocopies.

Were there editions that preceded yours?

We did have the excellent complete edition of Schubert's works published by Breitkopf & Härtel [of Leipzig]: one of the finest ever made; but it did contain quite a few errors. Of Schubert's twenty sonatas, only eleven or twelve appeared in the Henle edition. It was a fairly good one, but I'm still doing a lot of research, together with my wife.

It demonstrates that, although this music is over a century old, what we know about it is still ongoing. It's still very much a part of the present. Do you feel sometimes like a detective investigating a case?

Oh, indeed. I've gone through countless manuscripts, and interviewed my colleagues, as you interview me. I'll ask, "Why do you play this and that version?" My latest brainchild is working on Bach's ornamentations. My rather surprising conclusion [is] that the way the inverted mordent is played today is simply wrong. That means ninety percent of our performers are mistaken. This of course, again, entails a great deal of research, not only of historical material from old treatises and letters, and comparisons between the works, but going deeper into what is an ornament, how does it fit into the context? Can you really separate it from the music, and treat it as if it were an organism in itself?

Are any of Schubert's other keyboard works unknown, or at least not performed?—for example, missing sonatas, or fragments of sonatas, dances, that kind of thing?

No. I think somewhere the works might have been performed, but I believe I'm not mistaken in assuming that I gave the world's first performance of the Sonata in F-sharp minor, which was known as a fragment, and—actually, it was three fragments which I, by some research, and some combination, pieced together, finding out from extra-musical sources that they must have been written at the same time, that they belong together. One of the great discoveries was an unknown fantasy for piano written in Graz, which came to light some twelve years ago. But I don't expect an important and major work to come out of the dust. We know that half of one opera is missing forever, because the maid of Schubert's so-called friend [and minor composer Anselm] Hüttenbrenner [1794–1868] used it as heating material! So that opera, I mean the first acts, are lost unfortunately. It's like detective work. You find a piece of musical paper, and today, with the help of modern research, you can date it up to a few weeks with certain precision.

In looking back at your reconstructions of some of the sonatas, are you satisfied that you recaptured Schubert's intent and spirit?

I believe I did. Perhaps the test whether I did well was that I've played several of these movements to very good musicians, and to musicians who know Schubert's style, and not one of them could really tell where Schubert ends and where my reconstruction starts. It wasn't that difficult, because I was using throughout Schubert's own material, Schubert's own harmonies, and particularly, Schubert's own style of piano writing.

I'm curious about the resources, too, that you consulted. The Schubert houses, for example. In Vienna there must be several. What are they like? What kind of resources are available in these houses?

These houses are museums. They preserve portraits or objects, such as Schubert's eyeglasses or Schubert's last piano, busts, pictures of the landscape in Schubert's time, the certificate he received as a child, things like that. But for musical manuscripts, you would go to the Austrian National Library or to private libraries, which abound in Austria. And I did that. The most difficult part, actually, is when you try to find musical manuscripts which are in private possession. This is a real challenge. And here of course I have the advantage of being a traveling artist. When I know of a lady who has a valuable manuscript, I invite her to my concert, and I make personal contact, and in most cases I am successful in obtaining photocopies, or at least to have access to see the manuscript in question.

Will we ever really know what the piano sounded like in Beethoven's and Schubert's time? Has ageing and deterioration affected their sound today?

Unlike modern pianos, which age rather rapidly, old keyboard instruments, fortepianos and harpsichords, are like violins. They age very, very slowly. As we know, violins have been in their peak for over the last hundred years, and just now are very, very slowly losing a bit of their luster. Other violins which were made a little bit later are now coming into their prime. The construction of an early piano is somewhat similar. It's all wooden parts. The wires, the strings, are very, very thin and do not put too much tension on the frame, and although most of these instruments have been out of use for at least one hundred years, that means the strings didn't have the proper tension, and so you find them in very good condition. The actual proof of it is that reconstructions, replicas made today, come close to the sound quality and even to the volume of the old instruments, but never completely match them. This, I think, shows that some of the old instruments have been rather well-preserved.

How does the sound of the pianos used by Mozart, Schubert, and Beethoven differ from the sound of today's modern concert grands?

The question, of course, might be understood in two ways. The first reaction when you hear Beethoven on an original instrument is that it sounds a little strange. But you could also interpret your question another way, in the sense that an instrument which is a hundred fifty or two hundred years old, might have sounded differently, perhaps even better, when it was new. Even the best [fortepiano] replicas do not really produce a larger or better sound than the original instruments. I am the happy owner of a rather well-chosen, priceless collection of instruments, dating from harpsichords of Bach's time until, what I would say, Brahms or Debussy.

When did you begin to realize the superiority of these older instruments, either in the concert hall or in the recording studio?
I remember when the London Royal Association of Music invited me to compare playing Beethoven's *Appassionata* on a modern piano and an old 1803 Broadwood. I felt then that we would end up preferring the modern piano. I was wrong. The sound of the Broadwood was wonderful, a kind of delicate, silvery sound. The textures were clear, particularly in the lower register. The transparency was wonderful! And you know, I must admit there was a certain drama in the moment, wondering if the piano might break. Well, that suspense actually was part of the performance!

Is that why Liszt broke so many pianos? Was it a question of his own strength, or were the pianos too delicately constructed?
You could break such an instrument if you played music that's too heavy for it. Yet, they can take an enormous amount of beating if you remain within certain limits. It would never occur to me to break an instrument of that time playing a Chopin work, even a concerto. Beethoven did not really break instruments, but certainly he broke many strings. And that is perhaps the fascination. When you play on an old instrument, you could eventually break it. You come near a breaking point at least, which you would not possibly ever get on a modern piano. I can say that you have to have a very good technician standing by!

Are you talking about a Cristofori piano?
No, it was Anton Walter. [Bartolomeo] Cristofori [1655–1751] who was the inventor of the fortepiano nearly one century earlier. He invented single-handed the most perfect mechanism, an action which actually could only be equaled by the modern actions, but not surpassed, and his instruments reached great fame in the time of Bach and [Domenico] Scarlatti [1660–1725]. Today we assume that Scarlatti knew and played the instruments, that Scarlatti brought them to Portugal, and later to Spain, and that a number of his sonatas most likely were rather written for the piano than for the harpsichord. It's rather recent knowledge. With regard to Mozart, the piano had reached a perfect stage by then, a well-balanced instrument with a perfect sensitive action, enabling you to play practically everything. Its only disadvantage, of course, is that it didn't have the powerful tone of the modern grand, and was used in smaller hall or theatres, but still large enough to play with a chamber orchestra. I think I was one of the very first to make recordings on these historical keyboards.

When you perform, are you ever tempted to stop playing and tell us about your pianos and your researches? The performer-turned-educator! As a listener I would enjoy that very much.

Thank you. You encourage me. I did it in the beginning of my career, until I got a firm statement from my manager. He reprimanded me, "Our audiences do not want to be educated, they want to be entertained."

But better education contributes to one's entertainment, does it not?

I believe so. And recently I've done it again, particularly in France, strangely enough, and people just seem to love it. It not only [eases] the contact between audience and the artist, but also it establishes a familiarity. It shows how dear a work is to the artist, and what he sees in it. My introductions, of course, are rather personal. They are not dry historical introductions, but try to bring the composer, as a human being, nearer to the audiences. And I think it could be done more often. Of course, we have a wonderful precedent. I'm thinking of Leonard Bernstein's television broadcasts.[7]

If you could perform and talk about any composer, who would it be?

Well, Haydn is one of those great, great composers who is rather misunderstood up to our day. So I would immediately start with an all-Haydn program. The sonatas exceed in variety even the sonatas by Beethoven. What an incredible wealth of imagination, of invention, of beautiful piano sound we have! On the other hand, there are many composers in the Romantic era who have been half-forgotten. There has been a certain justice that, in many cases, a composer is neglected. I'm thinking of [Johann Nepomuk] Hummel [1778–1837]. Hummel was a contemporary of Beethoven and Schubert, who at that time enjoyed as much fame, more, actually, than Schubert and as much as Beethoven. And his fame dwindled away when Chopin came in, who was so much stronger. The same can be said about John Field [1782–1837]. Field's piano concertos are good stuff, and his nocturnes would be first rate if Chopin hadn't written better ones. But I think, still, discoveries are to be made.

Brian Newbould: "Have I Represented Schubert's Ideas Fairly?"

John C. Tibbetts
April 1985, Kansas City, Missouri; 10 April 2017, University of Hull, Great Britain

---

[7]Conductor-composer Leonard Bernstein (1918–1990) brought "classical" music to millions of Americans through his appearances on such TV series as *Omnibus* (1952–1961) and his own *Young People's Concerts* (1958–1972) series. Bernstein also wrote music for movies and Broadway shows, including *West Side Story* (1957 on stage, 1961 on film).

Schubert lived just thirty-one years, yet he completed almost 1000 composi-tions. He also left many incomplete sketches. Among Schubert's unfinished works are several sets of symphonic fragments in the form of keyboard drafts, orchestral sketches, or melodic and harmonic jottings. One incomplete work, the Eighth, or so-called Unfinished, Symphony in B minor, is often performed in its extant two-movement form. Yet another movement exists in keyboard form. Still other, recently completed symphonic movements and complete symphonies are available today on recordings (Fig. 6).

Fig. 6 Brian Newbould

Brian Newbould, Professor Emeritus of Music at the University of Hull, was educated at Gravesend Grammar School and earned a Bachelor of Music degree with top honors from the University of Bristol. Newbould's lifelong fascination with Schubert has established him in the forefront of Schubert scholarship. As a "musical detective," he has investigated the composer's unfinished symphonic sketches, revealing their completed symphonic potentials.

These conversations began during Newbould's visit to Kansas City in 1985; they concluded via email and letter while Newbould was at the University of Hull in 2017.

JOHN C. TIBBETTS: Perhaps we're more familiar with unfinished Schubert symphonies than we are with Brian Newbould! So, who is Brian Newbould?
BRIAN NEWBOULD: Well, he's just an ordinary chap who in his school days had a passionate interest in music and particularly what we would refer to as the Classical Period—Haydn, Mozart, Beethoven, Schubert. And I got to know an awful lot of his music because I loved it. And I suppose that before I left school at the age of eighteen, I knew all the Schubert symphonies—at least what we then thought of as the Schubert symphonies.

Had you already marked for yourself a career in music, or education, or composition, or all three?
Yes. I was going to do something in music, academic or compositional, rather more than performance, though I play instruments and conduct occasionally as well. Looking back on those days, I rather secretly wished that I had been born in about 1800 or 1810, because, in my view, the language of music was at its ripest. Healthcare and lifespan were another matter; but the opportunities for composition were absolutely marvelous at that time. The tonal system, the basic harmonic vocabulary associated with it, and the instrumental forms ideal for exploiting that were well-established, and the conditions for enriching the musical language and extending the emotional reach of music were more promising than ever—arguably before or since.

It's been suggested the Eighth [known as the "Unfinished"] Symphony was left unfinished because that was the period of Schubert's first serious illness, and that to complete the symphony later would have been to go back to a time that he wished to forget.
Well, it is the case that the illness became evident soon after the symphony was set aside. But there are also more general reasons for so many of Schubert's works being abandoned.

Was Schubert simply too impatient, were there too many ideas crowding upon him to complete any of them, or what?
Yes, he was probably impatient, but also easily sidetracked. I suspect he would get so far in a work and then go out for a drink and meet a friend who might say

"Franz, I've written this poem: will you set it?" We have to bear in mind that he was a "man-of-all-musical-media" (he began as many as eighteen stage works). His creative appetite (and some appetite it was!) covered symphonies, songs, string quartets, piano sonatas, keyboard dances, part-songs, violin sonatas, and more. Once he'd laid something aside for few days, an attractive new project may keep him away from the shelved one long enough to make a return to it that much more difficult.

Have you actually held in your hands and studied original Schubert manuscripts?
I've had that privilege. The first one I handled was the sketch of the Seventh Symphony and that's in London at the Royal College of Music. It's a beautiful document and the most extraordinary manuscript. It's complete, in the sense that all the paper Schubert needed to finish the symphony is there in this folio, and formatted for the purpose, as it were. It is written on orchestral paper with fourteen staves for all the instruments. And there can be little doubt that he composed it directly into the full score, which was his favorite way with symphonies.

Even the "Great" C major Ninth Symphony was composed in this way. But in the Seventh, the method let him down, in the sense that he didn't finish the piece. (In that sense, the "Great" was a creative triumph.) In fact, Schubert composed— simultaneously scoring—110 bars of the first movement in every detail. But from that point forwards he continued sketchily. For two-thirds of the four-movement symphony, only one instrumental line is given. Sometimes he added a snatch of bass, and at a few places up to seven of the fourteen staves are filled. The rest is empty full-size [i.e., landscape or oblong format] orchestral paper.

Perhaps Schubert already knew what should have been filled in?
At least, he knew that he could go back and realize the implications of what he had written so far, and thus complete the score. The advantage of this method is, of course, that the speed of writing only a single line gets close to keeping up with the pace of musical thought. With the Seventh, he obviously felt he didn't have time to write in all the other lines. It was holding him back and his thinking was moving faster so he went ahead and he completed not only the first movement but all four movements, more or less in that manner by writing the violin part or a leading woodwind instrument. It's clear to me that Schubert had the kind of aural grasp and aural memory attributed to Mozart.

We're talking about a remarkable mind. Perhaps the advent of computers has helped us understand what goes on in certain people's minds and how the human mind works.
You must be right in that. And while we are talking computers, you may be interested to know that because my life with Schubert has straddled the pre-computer age and the computer age itself, I completed my first effort—the Seventh Symphony—without the help of a computer, so I wrote every page by hand! This gave me some indication of how long our composer spent simply writing down

an orchestral score—probably 15–30 minutes for each page of full score, depending on the density of texture. Schubert was composing and scoring as one process, evidently.

What is the passion that drives you? This is no dry, methodological thing. There's a heart beating there too.
Absolutely. When I started work on that symphony, the Seventh, I said to myself, well, I'm just going to be carried along by the orchestral sweep of this sketch and pretend that I'm the composer. Yes, you have to take the part of composer and musicologist. My aim was to finish the very job he started. But at the same time I had to draw on everything known about Schubert and his style and his place in the linguistic development of music. The sketch was written in 1821, so the most obvious starting-point was the state of Schubert's style as the century's third decade began. All his resources of harmony and orchestration up to 1821 were relevant. But there were some less obvious considerations too. If the sketch seemed to look forward and anticipate the later symphonies, the [official] "Unfinished" or the "Great" C major, then I should try to underline that in my realization.

Does it make much difference to us if we know what it was happening to Schubert's health during the 1820s, his last decade?
Any aspect of a composer's life ought to be taken into account when we're trying to explain the mysteries of his creative processes and achievements. One of my interests is Schubert's why Schubert left certain works unfinished. If we can establish that there were medical reasons or medical reasons contributed towards this, I think that is important. It could be that when I said earlier on to you that Schubert was an easily distracted person, it could be in the later years that bouts of pain or discomforts of various sorts or thoughts of what lay ahead on him medically may well have helped to distract him…. Perhaps he was suffering from a syphilitic condition, but I'm not a medical expert.

All of this presupposes that a given symphony is incomplete in the first place, which itself presupposes the idea of a manuscript languishing someplace for decades, untouched, mislabeled and in some way unavailable. Where do we start with this? You said the Seventh Symphony was your first project, but there's another unfinished Schubert symphony. The "null opus," let's call it.
Yes, most of us that know that there are six youthful works, complete in every detail—and in my view composed directly into orchestral score, with astonishing confidence. But before Nos. One through Six we now have a sketch, well, in fact it's more than a sketch, it is several pages of actual score of a symphony we might as well call No. Zero. Only thirty bars have survived. He was fourteen when he wrote this. In his school orchestra, he played Beethoven's Second Symphony. We have it on the authority of people who knew him that he loved this work in particular, among the many played there. And in fact this Symphony No. 0 of Schubert's is very much modeled on Beethoven's Second.

How would you characterize this music? Is it important?
It's very accomplished in its use of the orchestra, within the parameters of orchestral usage of its day. I mean, he was only a fourteen-year-old lad and he jolly well
knew how to make a respectable orchestral sound, given a normal, small classical
orchestra, and oh yes, he had trombones in it.[8]

Really?
It's remarkable, because the First through Sixth Symphonies have no trombones.
They offer the smaller classical orchestra. And then it's in number seven that the
trombones come in and they stay then for Nos. Eight, the "Unfinished," and Nine,
the "Great." But in "Zero" he actually included trombones. No doubt he knew
about Beethoven's later symphonies, some of which introduced trombones. But he
didn't know how to notate them at first, and he got into awful difficulties with the
clef they use. As he was only now writing it down, he had to experiment with trial
and error to find the right notation.

*Which brings us to the Seventh. Or between the Sixth and the Seventh, we have
some fragments. Correct?*
We have some fragments. Now, shall I tell you about the history of the manuscript
because this is I think so important? There was a folio of sketches kept in the
Vienna State Library, kept there for years and years. This folio was looked at by
two famous musicologists about 1950 or the last 1940s: Otto Erich Deutsch, who
produced his catalogue of Schubert's works in 1951, and Maurice J. E. Brown, the
Englishman who wrote about Schubert fairly frequently. They looked at this folio
of piano sketches and on the first page of the manuscript saw the heading *Sinfonie*,
Schubert's signature, and the year 1818. Over on the next page the music stops
about a third of the way through, and then another movement is begun, and then
another and another. In all, Schubert tries to begin nine movements. And they're
all in D major or in close keys to D major. Close enough so that they could have
been the inner movements of a symphony or symphonies in D major. But I ought
to add that all nine sketches were different, on different themes. So he would actually have been ditching five lots of ideas, which is extraordinary. Schubert didn't
work like that. He got on with the job, he knew what his material was, and he
would compose it. However, all the evidence available to Brown and Deutsch
seemed to suggest that this is all it could be. It was all one folio; it must be a symphony in D, they thought. That was that.

It's interesting, by the way, that Beethoven's Second Symphony is in D, that
these sketches were in D, that Schubert's completed Symphony No.1 is in D,
Symphony No. 3 is in D, and the Tenth Symphony is in D. Schubert began thirteen

---

[8]The "classical" orchestra usually consisted of woodwinds (flutes, oboes, and bassoons) in pairs,
two or more horns, timpani, and strings, to which clarinets were added during Haydn's lifetime.
Trumpets and a few other instruments were sometimes added.

symphonies and in six of them he used D major. Was it all something he learned from Beethoven's Second what a good key it is for orchestral composition? I think probably it was.

Does key signature itself indicate a certain mood in Schubert or a certain kind of structure?

I have a theory of my own to explain this. It involves the French horn of Schubert's day, which was a natural instrument without valves and only certain notes could be played on it. Adjacent scale-notes were only available at the upper end of this range. One could raise that range of notes, or lower it, by fitting a 'crook' to the instrument. That would raise or lower the whole series of notes available according to the particular crook used. Now, if you're playing a symphony in D, you would fit a D crook to your horn, and that actually would bring the whole range of notes down into a much more useful range. So in effect, when Schubert or any composer of that time wrote for horns in D, they could make much more use of that instrument.

Okay, so: that brings us to the Seventh.

There was already an Eight and a Nine, so we actually have to squeeze in two fragmentary symphonies between them if we want to keep their chronology right. Anyway: for the Seventh we find four fragments, so he attempted all four movements. The first, second, and fourth movements remain fragments but the third movement, a scherzo, is sufficiently advanced in composition to be completed. So I have completed the scherzo and trio and it's quite a substantial movement, about seven minutes long, and the first two bars are the same as those beginning the Scherzo of the "Great" C major Symphony later on, so it's of special interest.

In other words, there is a point at which some of these movements are sufficiently sketched out so you feel encouraged to complete it as opposed to leaving it incomplete.

Yes. There has to be enough material if a fragment is to be completed.

Have critics of yours accused you of going too far in re-composing Schubert? Or hasn't that come up?

No, it hasn't come up but I think that maybe a lot of people who know intimately the "Unfinished" Symphony will probably feel there's not much point in finishing that work. But we'll come to that, no doubt.

Are we ready then for the Seventh? And why this particular symphony out of all of the others? Why has this gotten the most attention in terms of various versions?

My version is the most recent, and my reason for attempting the work is perhaps an unexpected one. In 1977, one year before the 150th anniversary of Schubert's death in 1978, I was employed by the University of Leeds, and the head of my department said to me, look we must celebrate Schubert next year with something exciting. You know that sketch of the Seventh Symphony? Would you have a look at it, and see if you can make anything of it, for performance by our students next year?

First reactions?
I was fascinated to see the sketch. I spent several weeks looking at it and scratch-
ing my head. Eventually I reached the point where, yes, I thought that I could
make the thing complete. It was a terribly bold decision, I know. And I suppose
some people would not understand my audacity, but there we are. I just had the
feeling that I could see what Schubert was getting at. And in any case, if our low-
key performance within the walls of the university was a flop, the whole venture
could be forgotten (or so I thought).

Why "or so I thought"?
Because I didn't learn until the last minute that representatives of the BBC had
been invited to the concert, in February 1978. And they liked the result enough
to program it twice that year, once with the BBC Symphony Orchestra at the
Cheltenham Festival.

How long did it take you to complete the Seventh Symphony?
Roughly the equivalent of six months full-time work.

And you first heard it performed in 1978. Did you conduct at that point?
No, I didn't. I was asked if I would like to conduct it. I said no. I felt that what
I badly needed to do was listen critically to the first performance and see if what
I thought I had done I had in fact done. I didn't even go to rehearsals, because the
inevitable inadequacies of student rehearsals would have left me with misleading
impressions of my own work.

*Now we come to the Eighth or official "Unfinished" Symphony. Probably the
single most famous composition of Schubert. Many people have felt that, after
that sublime second movement, nothing else is necessary. But you maintain that
Schubert did indeed intend on something else following it.*
Well, there's no doubt of that, because there's a complete piano sketch of the
scherzo. And not only that but he orchestrated some of it because a couple of
pages of the orchestral version have now been found. He may have orchestrated
more of it. It will be very interesting if more does come to light.

*That must be a question that haunts you. Will there be a discovery at some point in
the near future of pages orchestrated that you have since realized in existence and
how to compare them?*
Nobody would be more delighted than I would if that happened, because I would
so like to know what Schubert himself would have done.

*What are some of the reactions of people who have heard the Eighth Symphony
with a third movement? How do they feel about it?*
Much as I expected. The reason why I finished this symphony was not because
I've always had a burning ambition to complete the unfinished. After all, other
people have done it. And I don't think I would have done it at all had it not been

that conductor Neville Marriner and [representatives of] Philips, the firm issuing the complete recording of the symphonies, said to me: "Look, we're going to do all of your completions of the other symphonies; so wouldn't it make sense for you to complete the 'Unfinished' so that all the completions are by one hand?" I fell for that. Anyway, we have two complete movements of the "Unfinished," and it's even been suggested that Schubert himself regarded the work as finished in that form. That's absurd, of course, apart from the fact that he sketched a scherzo third movement, Schubert would not have ended a symphony (certainly not at this time of his life) in a key other than that in which it began. Of course, the fact that I had already worked with these other Schubert symphonies helped me to form an impression of how I should complete the scherzo of this symphony. Nevertheless, Schubert's "Unfinished" will continue to be known and performed as a two-movement torso. My effort is not an attempt to change that, but merely to give the non-reader of music a chance to hear where Schubert had thought of going after his ethereal slow movement.

Finally, what of the so-called Tenth Symphony?
The Tenth Symphony belongs to October and November 1828. During those last two months Schubert decided, oddly enough, that he needed counterpoint lessons, and went to a first lesson with one Simon Sechter on 4 November. Schubert died on 19 November, just two weeks later. The sketches for the slow movement of the symphony were begun on a page that already bore counterpoint exercises, probably written for Sechter. The last movement of the symphony is unprecedented in the variety and extent of contrapuntal devices it employs.

You say "oddly enough." Why?
Well, it seems rather strange that a composer with over 900 works behind him, many of them displaying contrapuntal mastery, would suddenly choose to have lessons in any aspect of his craft. In fact, it's less odd when we consider the stylistically progressive nature of that last symphony, progressive not just in its counterpoint. Schubert, I believe, simply wanted to extend his technical resources as a composer, in order to extend his expressive reach.

What condition was Schubert in during those months of October-November?
He was virtually on his deathbed. Schubert was clearly in a great hurry. You could say he almost knew what was coming, and he was determined that he was going to get this symphony down on paper. He ended his sketch of the first movement of this Tenth Symphony (as we now know it) by writing short modules of music, each about four measures long, and putting little continuation signs at the beginning and end of these, to show which ones connected with which others. My personal view is that that slow movement is most sublime and not only sublime but forward-looking. It looks back a little bit to the "Unfinished" but also to *Winterreise* [Winter Journey], that great and desolate song cycle, written the year before this last symphony. Yet there are also pre-echoes of Mahler, the Mahler of

the *Kindertotenlieder* [Songs of the Death of Chidlren]. It really is an astonishing piece of work.

You're suggesting that a man who may be on his deathbed nevertheless possesses a remarkably clear mind. Just what was Schubert composing on his deathbed? I've heard it was portions of the G major Quartet, the posthumous B-flat Piano Sonata, part of Winterreise—*and now the Tenth Symphony. Which one is it?*
The G-major Quartet was finished some time before, and the late piano sonatas in September of that last year, along with the String Quintet. It's likely that work on the Tenth Symphony was largely confined to October, and early November. All through his life, at least from the middle on, Schubert was moving about from one project to the other. Progress on an instrumental piece might be interrupted if a friend placed a potential song-text in front of him, or some occasional piece was needed. Recent research into Schubert's handwriting, the way it changed over the years, and the paper types that he used often help us say, with fair accuracy, in what month of what year a piece was written.

Now, the world at large didn't really know about the "Unfinished" Symphony until the 1860s. When did the world at large begin to become aware of a Tenth Symphony?
Only when some sketches hidden away in a library in Vienna were re-examined in 1978. Because I had experience in finishing Schubert, I bowed to encouragement from colleagues, sorted the many fragments into what I took to be their intended symphonic form, and began to convert the piano sketches into complete movements. And so the world heard Schubert's "Tenth" Symphony for the first time a century-and-a-half after his death.

Having come to the end of all of this now, can I ask you to sit back from it all and how do you feel personally? A great sense of fulfillment, of reward, for all of this? Are there things you would like to do all over again? Can you sum up where you stand in relationship to all of this scholarship?
I don't feel a total satisfaction. There are always those nagging questions. Have I represented Schubert's ideas fairly? Is it sometimes better to leave beautiful music unheard, as that is how the composer left it? But I feel a satisfaction in that my love of this music is deeper than ever. In a sense, to complete these fragmentary works I had to get to know the fragments themselves first, and get to know them so well and think around them so much that I developed a sort of proprietary relationship with them, as though I'd written them myself. I love some of the works that I have completed very dearly. And yes, I admit to enjoying the performances I hear. If others enjoy them, that's what really matters.[9]

---

[9]Thanks to the late Robert Kurth and his family who facilitated these conversations.

Elly Ameling: "There Is so Much You Can Sing by Schumann!"

John C. Tibbetts
October 1986, Kansas City, Missouri

Composer, critic, and founder of the *Neue Zeitschrift für Musik*—a "new music magazine" still in print—Robert Schumann planned a career as a concert pianist, then damaged his hand irreparably. Married to Clara Wieck (1819–1896), a pianist in her own right and one of the nineteenth century's

In memory of the
Schubert Abend,
15 october 1986,
with warmest regards.

Elly Ameling

Fig. 7 Elly Ameling

foremost women musicians, Schumann composed piano music, songs, symphonies, a celebrated piano concerto, and much else. Depressed and moody
throughout his adult life, he eventually fell into madness, attempted suicide in
1854, and spent the last two years of his life in an asylum (Fig. 7).

Dutch soprano Elisabeth "Elly" Sara Ameling completed her training with
Pierre Bernac in Paris. In 1956 she won first prize in the vocal competition
in s'Hertogenbosch, The Netherlands, but her career really took off after
she won at the 1958 Concours International de Musique' in Geneva. Since
then she has become a world-renowned concert and recital artist, with a few
excursions into opera, particularly Mozart. Among Ameling's honors are
three honorary degrees from colleges and universities in Canada and the
USA.

This conversation took place in Kansas City during Ms. Ameling's appearance at a master class sponsored by the Harriman-Jewell Concert Series.

*JOHN C. TIBBETTS: You embrace a wide range of vocal music, from Mozart
and Schubert to Schumann and [Richard] Strauss. Even the little-known Schubert
operas!*
ELLY AMELING: Oh, yes, the operas are pleasant music, quite touching, But
honestly, not in the same standard of emotional value and form as Schumann's
Lieder and his chamber music and orchestral works. It is his weakest part, I must
say, the melodies of Hugo Wolf [1860–1903] is more like a recitative. But with
Richard Strauss melody came back in a wonderful, opulent way.

The first time I heard you sing, you performed Schumann's Frauenliebe und
Leben.
I waited with that cycle. I waited very long before I ever dared sing it in public.
Jörg Demus always said to me: "But Elly, why don't we sing *Frauenliebe und
Leben* [Woman's Love and Life]? That is something for you!" And I said, "No,
Jörg, I think I don't dare yet. I don't feel ripe for it."

What did you mean?
Well, just maybe experience—life experience was holding me back. I had been such
a happy young person all the time. And here in the music is a woman who goes
through deep emotions of love and losing her husband in the course of the cycle.

Please talk about the last of the eight songs in that cycle. Everything points to it.
Yes, "Nun hast du mir den ersten Schmerz getan" [Now You Have Hurt Me for the
Last Time], about the death of her beloved. There's the famous postlude, where the
woman in the poem stands still and says she will turn back into herself, where she
believes she will recapture her lost happiness.

And you stand silent on stage for a long time while the piano concludes the cycle. What do you do during all that time?
When you stand there for several minutes, you should radiate, without singing, what the accompanist is playing: the return after much sorrow to this theme of happiness that began the cycle. You just express what the music says. That's the same thing when you have a pause in opera … and what do you express? You must express something! So I just *live* what I experience in the music and hopefully radiate that by whatever I do with my body—even standing still.

Let's talk about Schumann's Liederkreis *cycle, Op. 39? It is very special. Not at all like the* Frauenliebe *or* Dichterliebe.
You can absolutely not compare them. *Dichterliebe* [Poet's Love] has such a different subject: the ongoing love story of this man. The *Liederkreis* [Song Circle] is the love story of nature itself—nowhere else so much as in this cycle. The typical quality of these poems by [Joseph, Freiherr von] Eichendorff [1788–1857] is in the woods, and where the brooks are, and where the moon shines. It's the romantic spirit of nature, of love, of melancholy feeling. All of that together. And a great tenderness is in it. Something strong, but tenderness can also be strong. There can be great tenderness in a waterfall. And it's moving you to tears. It's the mark of the high German romantic poetry.

This raises the question whether it is best suited for a man or a woman.
There are women like my beloved Lotte Lehmann, who sang the *Dichterliebe*, which is really for a man; but it can be done. But there's so much else you can sing by Schumann. Why would a woman do the *Dichterliebe* at all? Everybody else sings it already! On the other hand, a man has yet to sing Schubert's "Gretchen am Spinnrade" [Gretchen at the Spinning Wheel]. Could you imagine a man singing that? In opera a woman can play "trouser roles," but a man can never dress like a woman, not in opera, not in song. I must say, I love to sing the *Liederkreis!* I believe it is a little better for a man. But only if you're quite aware of the social position of a man and a woman in those days. A woman, with a long skirt and high heels, wouldn't walk so freely in the woods as a man can. Women were just not so near to nature.

What are these twelve Liederkreis *songs about?*
Some are sad, about loss, like the first one, "In der Fremde" [Far from Home], when the singer walks in the woods and the red sky above is flashing with lightning. Others are like folk tales, like *Waldesgesprach*, which means "dialogue for the forest." The man in this song rides his horse into the woods and meets nobody but the Lorelei, yes? You know the story of the Lorelei? She is a siren who brings men to their death. The man looks into the water and sees her there, and he falls into her arms. She tells him at the end, "You will never get out of this wood again, because I have you and I will hold you, and keep you here!" Also "Im Walde" [In the Forest], when we hear hunting horns and see in the distance a marriage ceremony. And there is a picture of the moon in a starry sky, "Mondnacht" [Moonlight].

It's like a ray of moonlight, and the whole song is as still as a ray of moonshine. The same with "Auf einer Burg" [On a Castle]. It's almost a static picture—static, frozen, and dead. I think it is the hardest song for an audience to understand: this frozen song about the old knight of the castle, sitting in his stone chair above the valley. There's a German word, *Gipfelerlebnis*, which means being high up, here on top of a mountain looking across the valley. The knight was not *stoned* but became *stone* as he grew old! [laughs] I try to sing it without vibrato.

Are there any personal favorites?
I must say that "Wehmut" [Sadness] is maybe Schumann's most heartfelt song— "Ich kann wohl manchmal singen/Als ob ich froelich sei" [I can sing as if I were glad; but then tears flow]. Here again, *lachen und weinen*, laughter and tears, combined. What a beautiful melody there is to that song!

Thomas Hampson: "There Is a Great Mystery About Schumann's *Dichterliebe*"

John C. Tibbetts
11 September 1993, Omaha, Nebraska

On the operatic stage and the recital platform, Thomas Hampson has won praise as one of the world's great singers. A native of Indiana, Hampson studied at Fort Wayne College, then at the University of Southern California. In 1981, he was a winner in the Metropolitan Opera National Council Auditions national finals; best known as an operatic lyric baritone, he has sung in almost every major house in the world. In 1992 *Musical America* chose Hampson as "Singer of the Year": one of many important awards (Fig. 8).

This conversation took place on the occasion of a *Lieder* recital sponsored by the Omaha Concert Series, Omaha, Nebraska.

JOHN C. TIBBETTS: You have been working on your Dichterliebe *project for quite some time. What have been your primary concerns?*
THOMAS HAMPSON: Schumann's *Dichterliebe* belongs to that amazing burst of song-writing in the summer of 1840, before his marriage to Clara Wieck. We know the work and it is one of the most famous of all song cycles. Yet, there is a great mystery about it: In all of music there are few more vexing questions than why four songs from the original manuscript were omitted in the published first edition in 1844. He *never* spoke of it as a "sixteen-song cycle," even two years after its publication. He always talked about the "*twenty*-song cycle." The published version lacked four of those songs, and there were many changes in dynamic markings, tempo and phrase indications, the vocal *tessitura* at times was altered, the

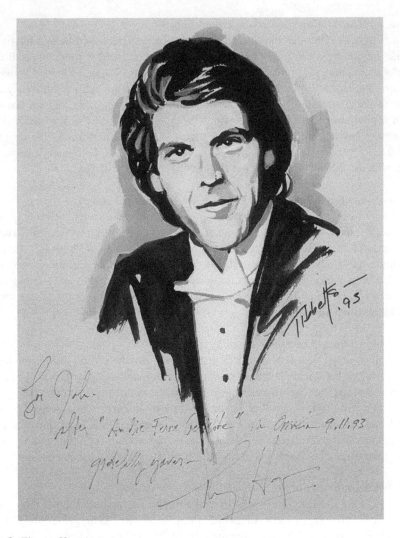

Fig. 8 Thomas Hampson

piano writing was full of jarring dissonances, and some of the postludes were longer.[10] The thematic material is more connected, song to song.

---

[10]*Tessitura* refers to the range of notes associated with sopranos, altos, and so on. Dissonance is often defined as the opposite of consonance: sour or jarring harmonies instead of sweet and soothing ones. A postlude concludes a piece of music or a series of pieces; Schumann added piano postludes to many of his *Lieder*.

How could he have overlooked such alterations?

Now, I'm not saying that the later, altered version was published behind his back. Quite the contrary. I'm not even saying what was published is illegitimate. But it marks a unique event in his *Lieder*. No evidence exists of what happened between the original manuscript with engraver's notes on it and the publication four years later of the first edition. The two versions differ so significantly that we are left with a plethora of ambiguous questions. Why the changes? I'm not saying I've found the answer or reasons for the changes, but I think performing the original manuscript version can be very enlightening with regard to Schumann's relationship with the fabled "irony" of poet Heinrich Heine [1797–1856].

Do we know if any of the songs were composed first *at the piano?*

We know from the sketches and from letters that only two songs were composed first at the piano, *for* the piano. Those are "Das ist ein Flöten und Geigen" [That's a flute and fiddle] and "Aus alten Märchen" [From old tales (or legends)]. I could not understand why some of the published songs had specific indications of tempo and dynamic markings throughout the song, yet others seemed to leave it up to the performer—sort of a "Do what you can with it!" In the manuscript, *all* the songs had interpretive markings.

Were they removed to preserve the unity of the cycle?

It's been assumed that Schumann did that himself. But there is no musical, autobiographical, or historical evidence anywhere that supports that conclusion. As far as I can determine, the exclusion of those four songs in no way improved the cyclic unity. His wife, Clara, said that the first edition of Robert's works were the final word, not the manuscripts. She was adamant about that. She even threatened to sue Johannes Brahms, her close friend, if he persisted studying Schumann's works from their original manuscripts rather than from their first published editions.

So what is your sense of the "proper" order of the songs?

Well, we have the first four songs from the published version. Then, I insert two of the removed songs, "Dein Angesicht" [Your face] and "Lehn deine Wang" [Let your cheek (touch mine)]—a passionate song of intense beauty—and right after that we go back to the published version with "Ich will meine Seele tauchen" [I would plunge my soul]; then later in the cycle, after "Am leuchtenden Sommermorgen" [On a radiant summer morning] comes the other two removed songs, "Es leuchtet meine Liebe" [My love shines], which is a fantastic song—so far ahead of its time it's frightening (you think you're listening to [Hugo] Wolf!—and then "Mein Wagen rollet langsam" [My coach rolls slowly]; and then you go to the end of the cycle.

Did you turn to any scholars for assistance or confirmation?

Yes, of course. We went right back to the first editions of any writings on the Schumann songs. We do know that Schumann was paid for *twenty* songs. Even when the cycle was at the publishers, he talked about twenty songs. As late as 1846, he *still* referred to his twenty-song cycle.

*We hear the usual charge that Schumann didn't carry through in his songs the bit-
ter irony of Heine's texts. What about that?*
There's a very important consideration here. When you restore the syncopations[11]
in the manuscript version of "Am leuchtenden Sommermorgen", for example, you
encounter a man who by that time in the cycle has broken his relationship with
nature and reality. He's living in a self-paradoxical world. Call it that for want of a
better term. What happens is that his conflicted notion of reality and nature, which
we know is disturbed, is conveyed in the syncopations. When he thinks the flowers
are talking to him—which is *his* perceived reality—that's when the rhythm stays
even.

Does Schumann's use of dissonance enhance these dislocations?
It bothers me a lot that Schumann's use of dissonance was so abrogated in the
first edition. For instance, when I first performed the original version of the first
song, "Im wunderschönen Monat Mai" [In the beautiful month of May], in Boston
and New York, the critics wrote, "Well what he [i.e., Hampson] did wasn't so
ingenious, he just doesn't perform the appoggiaturas in the first song." There's no
dissonance. But if you sing it the way Schumann actually wrote it, the vocal and
keyboard lines *diverge*, and what you have, all of a sudden, is a completely different thought process. The poet is speaking about when "love awoke at the same
time as the flowers, and I made it clear to my love"—he is already making it clear
that fate has denied him this love. Fate is the bad guy in this cycle, not the woman.
That is exactly what Heine was talking about: leaving the romantic world and ven-
turing into the modern world through his own poetry. I think Schumann understood that far better than we've given him credit for.

When did you first perform the "complete" cycle?
My first performances of the twenty-song cycle were in the fall of 1992, first in
Geneva and then in Vienna. It may or may not have been a public premiere. I also
performed it in Ann Arbor for Public Radio. I can't tell you who the accompanist
will be, but I can say at the moment he is a master of the repertoire.[12]

What is it that justifies all the time and effort you put into detective work?
You know, for me—not just with Schumann, but with composers in general and
works in general, those that keep grabbing me—are the composers and works that
ask questions but don't give answers. Mozart's *Don Giovanni*, for me, is a flawed
work, but the flaws make it universally accessible. I feel the same way about a
great deal of Schumann's music. You feel that he is a man struggling to articulate,

---

[11]Passages in which rhythmic emphasis occurs on unexpected notes and chords, producing a
bumpy sense of rhythm. Syncopation is especially important in ragtime; see the interviews with
Max Morath, and with William Bolcom and Joan Morris in the present volume.

[12]The accompanist was Wolfgang Sawallisch.

"Why?" Why life, why this context, why not another context; why not? Why the incongruities all around us?

It's not as if composers have access to the nuances of spoken language!
Yes, how to articulate those things in *music*, of all things? I think our responsibility as musicians—and I mean from both camps, the musicological side and the performing side—is to gather together, hand in hand, look at each composition, and figure out how to present it. Regardless of anything and everything else, it's our attempt to recreate the piece that transcends any knowledge of the piece. That's what interests me.

John Nelson: "Berlioz: I Want Berlioz!"

John W. Tibbetts
23 August 1991, New York City

Louis-Hector Berlioz struggled throughout his life to win acceptance for his work as an orchestral and operatic composer. Self-trained in childhood, Berlioz studied at the Paris Conservatoire. His *Symphonie fantastique*, performed for the first time in 1830 in an almost empty theater, remains perhaps his best-known work. A "programmatic" musician, he attached intriguing titles and even entire essays to some of his instrumental pieces; later he won international acclaim as a traveling orchestral conductor and wrote influential music criticism as well as a little fiction and a book about conducting. Berlioz's operas include *Béatrice et Bénédict*, *Benvenuto Cellini*, and *Les Troyens* [The Trojans]—the last based on portions of Virgil's *Aeneid*. In 1862, after years of struggle, Berlioz was made a Officer of the Legion of Honor (Fig. 9).

John Wilton Nelson was born in Costa Rica, where his parents worked as Protestant missionaries. Educated at Wheaton College and Juilliard, Nelson has championed the music of Berlioz throughout his career. In 1973 he conducted Berlioz's *The Trojans* for his debuts with both the New York City Opera and the Metropolitan Opera. From 1976–1987 he served as Music Director of the Indianapolis Symphony Orchestra, from 1985–1991 as Music Director of the Opera Theatre of Saint Louis, and from 1998–2008 as Music Director of the Ensemble Orchestral de Paris.

This conversation took place in Nelson's New York City apartment.

JOHN C. TIBBETTS: That headline above your desk: "Madman Attacks Maestro!" *What is that all about?*
JOHN NELSON: I was conducting *Scheherezade* [by Nikolai Rimsky-Korsakov (1844–1908)] in Central Park with the New York Philharmonic. It was on a hot summer night, before 250,000 spectators. It was an all-Russian program. And

Fig. 9 John Nelosn

after forty-two minutes of music, just as the concertmaster began playing his last solo after the shipwreck [movement]—this weirdo came from behind the basses, around the 'cellos, came toward me, no shirt on and Bermuda shorts, and pushed me aside as he went for the microphone. He grabbed the microphone and screamed into it, "Berlioz! I want Berlioz!" They wrestled him down. [pause] I feel like that sometimes!

You seem like the Scarlet Pimpernel[13]—*here, there, and everywhere!*
A concert schedule like I have is very typical of the conductor who must be on the road all the time. In five weeks I go to Lyon to do Berlioz's *Beatrice and Benedict*,[14] a new production at the biannual French Music Festival. Earlier, I did it in St. Louis, Indianapolis, and Paris. I'm a Berlioz freak. I tend to overlook—I even love—his defects. Because I know him. I really know him. I've read so much about him. I feel like he's a brother. I love the man, so I forgive him. And for every fault, I can cite five glorious things. I love Schumann too.

I can't imagine two more different characters than Berlioz and Schumann!
Yes, one is "inner," one is "outer." I grapple with that split between an earthy side and a more spiritual side—although I hate the word ["spiritual"]. I can enjoy the "Nocturne" in *Beatrice and Benedict*, on the one hand, and the exploding crucible in *Benvenuto Cellini*,[15] on the other. As critics, in Paris and in Germany, Berlioz and Schumann knew each other; and they even shared their readers. My goodness, both really knew how to *write!* Read Berlioz's *Memoirs*. Read the review that Schumann wrote on the *Symphonie Fantastique*—it's just marvelous. But Schumann was not the conductor that Berlioz was. Berlioz was not a pianist and not a violinist, so he made himself into a *professional* conductor. He even wrote a book about how to conduct!

Are we hearing enough of Berlioz, even now? I have yet in my life to hear a concert of his orchestral songs.
He will never be mainstream. It's impossible. He never was and he never will be. He wasn't in his lifetime. His music upset people then; it upsets people now. Time was when the main Berlioz conductors were British. But the French neglected him utterly; and they still do to an extent. It's still true that Berlioz is a little underplayed in Germany. You hear of his works being played in Vienna and German cities, but I think it's not a great success. Am I saying that all too often Germans find difficulty with non-German music?

Why the neglect?
For one thing, the music doesn't readily fall into categories. How do you program the orchestral songs? How do you program *Lélio* [sequel to the *Symphonie fantastique*]? And Berlioz had big ideas. *Big* ideas! He wrote a story about a fantasy city

---

[13]The protagonist in Hungarian-born British novelist Baroness Orczy's historical novel of the same name.

[14]Based on Shakespeare's comedy *Much Ado about Nothing*.

[15]Loosely based on the life and reminiscences of Cellini, a Renaissance sculptor.

he called "Euphonia": an ideal city where everybody was a musician and there were streets assigned to different musical professions. You had a whole street of sopranos and a street of piano tuners. Music critics were in another part of town. The opera house was always well supplied with singers and orchestras. Music was everything. But it's a fantasy, of course. And it was a fantasy that he expected his audiences to know their Shakespeare, their Virgil [(70 B.C.E.—19 C.E.], their Goethe, in order to really understand his music, or any advanced music of the nineteenth century.

Which works of Berlioz's, if any, still elude you, something that you have yet to perform?
Nothing yet. Because I haven't done everything yet! In time I'll do everything he wrote. My guess is that the most difficult things will be the incomplete things. And I always thought the *Grande Symphonie funèbreet triomphale* [Grand funeral and triumphal symphony, for wind instruments] is kinda crazy. But I've done it. I did it very successfully in Paris and plan to do it at the Aspen Festival [in Colorado]. You know, with all those kids who play clarinets! It has to be a band, a military band. A marching band, at that. We'll march through Aspen and end up at the festival tent. We might do it.

What do you do when the crucible explodes in Benvenuto Cellini *and all hell breaks loose?*
All the lights went out in my production in Lyon, including the stand lights in the pit! Pitch-black everywhere. That's supposed to happen at the end of the second act, not at the end of the opera!

Now, *The Trojans*—it's all possible in *The Trojans*. What he asks for can be ludicrous, like in the "Royal Hunt and Storm" and so forth, but it's all possible and makes great sense. And *Beatrice and Benedict* is a little jewel, which every opera company should be doing.

What about the "Royal Hunt and Storm" [In The Trojans]*? How do you handle the extravagant scenic effects?*
I've utilized every possible scenic possibility. At the Met they combined motion pictures and dance. Once I saw somebody do a marvelous version in Lyon where an actor playing Berlioz was in the midst of the whole thing. It was one of the stage directors who had a nose exactly like Berlioz's! So he himself got into the middle as somebody who was *dreaming* this fantasy of the hunt and storm. It was a delightful bit of stage surrealism.

You're in this for the long haul, I take it.
Berlioz will remain an important part of the repertoire, in general, at least as far as I'm concerned. For me, for the rest of my life, I'm committed to the man and the music. Before the end of my life I want to record everything.

The Romantic Piano

Introduction

With the possible exception of the guitar in contemporary popular music, the modern piano has proven itself the most popular Western musical instrument. Increasingly strengthened (with iron or steel frames replacing wooden ones), and increasingly refined in terms of percussive power and volume (hammers strike the strings in all pianos), glowing timbres, and social omnipresence (for decades almost every upper- and middle-class family in Europe and America owned one), the piano possesses a larger and even more variegated repertory than even the violin. Three pianists—two of them, the late Charles Rosen and Leslie Howard—have also contributed to musical scholarship. Garrick Ohlsson, the third, speaks about his own pianistic preferences without an interviewer's queries and prompts.

Michael Saffle

Charles Rosen: "During the Romantic Period, Piano Music was the Most Important Music Being Written"

John C. Tibbetts
21 January 1988, New York City

The piano became the nineteenth century's most popular and pervasive instrument, in part because more and more people could afford to purchase pianos and learn how to play them. During those same decades, the piano became associated especially with two areas of bourgeois life: the concert hall, where male pianists such as Liszt mostly ruled the roost; and the middle-class home, where "the girl and her piano" became established aspects of

© The Author(s) 2018
J. C. Tibbetts et al. (eds.), *Performing Music History*,
https://doi.org/10.1007/978-3-319-92471-7_6

Fig. 1 Charles Rosen, with Schumann in the background

gentility. During the early twentieth century and especially after World War I, piano purchases peaked, then fell off. Women as well as men had already become more frequently acknowledged as professional virtuosi, and in many homes the phonograph and even the player piano became increasingly commonplace.

A scholar as well as a pianist, Charles Rosen (1927–2012) began studies at Juilliard when he was only four; later he earned a Ph.D. at Princeton in French literature. Rosen won the National Book Award for *The Classical*

Style (1972); as a pianist he recorded works as different from one another as Bach's *Goldberg Variations* and—at the composer's invitation—Stravinsky's *Movements* for piano and orchestra. During the 1980–1981 academic year, Rosen held the Charles Eliot Norton Chair of Poetics at Harvard, and his Norton lectures served as the basis of *The Romantic Generation* (1995) (Fig. 1).

This conversation transpired in Rosen's New York apartment. He demonstrated his remarks at the keyboard.

JOHN C. TIBBETTS: Those years around 1810 seem to have been the cradle of musical Romanticism—
CHARLES ROSEN: —and 1803, if you want to include the birth of Hector Berlioz.

What's going on?
This was the period which all of these young people—Liszt, Schumann, Chopin, Mendelssohn, Wagner—were beginning to take off. There is this trust in spontaneity, in the primacy of the poetic impulse over the rational one, which is quite clear in German and French Romanticism. That generation tried to capture the originality of form and the exotic atmosphere of the literature and art and politics they had grown up with. That starts clear back in the middle of the eighteenth century with the *Sturm und Drang* and the young Goethe. Politically, of course, there had been the failure of the French Revolution. It was a tremendous disappointment, a great hope that everything would improve. But it turned out that things were not better but in some respects worse. A new conservatism crept in. In 1828 a big conservative reaction against the French Revolution was beginning to break down. Two years later you get the second French Revolution of 1830, which was in effect also international. Politically, it was a time where things were really starting to ferment again.

Was it accidental that the Shakespeare and Bach revivals were going on at this time?
There's this myth that the Romantics revived Shakespeare. Shakespeare had never been absent. But what happened with the Romantics was interesting. Before then, Shakespeare was criticized as a genius who was completely wild, who broke all the rules, a child of nature who simply wrote from the flood of his genius. In fact, that's basically what Shakespeare was considered during his lifetime by [Elizabethan playwright] Ben Jonson [c. 1572–1637]. When they told Ben Jonson that Shakespeare had never blotted a line, he said, I wish he'd blotted a thousand. But now [i.e., the early nineteenth century], Shakespeare began to be considered a role model. The founder of German Romanticism, Friedrich Schlegel [1772–1829], said that Shakespeare was the most "correct" poet that ever lived. Similarly, E. T. A. Hoffmann [1776–1822] wrote that Beethoven was not at all the wild, untamed genius that people think he is. He was actually the most sober and correct musician that ever lived. What Hoffmann was doing would have been understood

at the time, but might not be understood today: He was comparing Beethoven to Shakespeare and saying Beethoven is our Shakespeare in music.

What about Bach? The Romantics loved him, but was that more private than public?
We have the same kind of myth that Bach was "revived." He wasn't. There were generations of musicians who were influenced by Bach. Mozart discovers Bach and arranges the *Well-Tempered Clavier* for string quartet and for string trio. He even arranged one of the fugues from *Art of the Fugue*. Beethoven was brought up with the *Well-Tempered Clavier* and played a few of them from memory when he was thirteen years old. It got in the newspapers! [Carl] Czerny [1791–1857] published an edition of it. He taught it to Liszt. Chopin was raised on it. Schumann was raised on it. And we need to remember that the so-called "Bach Revival" was actually a revival of the *choral* works. The young Mendelssohn revived the *St. Matthew Passion* in a performance that was very heavily cut and abridged. From then on, Bach was regarded as the great composer of choral music.

Was the piano the best instrument for the Romantics' more personalized expression?
It was evolving, yes. During the 1830s, piano music was the most important music being written. It seems to me that one should play the music on the instruments that were inspired by the music. In other words, the imagination and vision of many composers exceed the instruments of their own time. So, you find in response to the new kind of music that was being written in the 1830s and 1840s further developments in the pianos of the 1850s and beyond. And there's no reason not to play Schumann and Chopin on the modern piano. It was due to the kind of music that Liszt was writing that Steinway invented the metal frame for the piano. I think it was Steinway who was the first to use steel for the frame. ... Basically, from the middle of the nineteenth century on, it's very close to the modern piano. The piano is sort of like a dinosaur right now. It's dying out. People don't buy concert pianos for the home. It's not big enough anymore ...

Let's talk about Schumann. When does his music first reach your ears and your fingers.
I've always liked to play Schumann. Even as a small child I used to play the *Album for the Young* with "The Happy Farmer" and "Knight Rupert" (who was like Santa Claus), and marvelous things like that. My teachers never gave me adaptations. It was important to play the real thing, the original. After the age of six, I don't think I played anything except really original pieces. There's an awful lot of easy work one can give children. I was taken to play for Leopold Godowsky when I was about eight. I was told he put me on his lap and said, "What do you want to be when you grow up?" And I said, "I want to be a pianist like Josef Hoffmann!" I'd never heard of Godowsky because he didn't play in public. He had a tremendous reputation for being the greatest pianist who only played in private. But Josef Hoffmann was the greatest pianist I'd ever heard.

Schumann was a great reader and literary figure. You must identify with that!
Thank you. Schumann certainly had his literary role models. Jean Paul Richter
[also known as "Jean Paul"; 1763–1825] was one, E. T. A. Hoffmann another.
Hoffmann was one of the greatest writers of the period. If you needed a Romantic
role model, he was about as good as they came. Hoffmann was also a fairly good
composer and a very great music critic. He knew a lot about music, obviously, and
was also the director of the Berlin opera.

Anyway, Hoffmann did become a terrific model for Schumann and Chopin and, a
little later, for Brahms. Schumann's *Kreisleriana*, for example, is derived directly
from Hoffmann. The title is Hoffmann's. It is one of Schumann's greatest compositions. And what it does contain is that wonderful contrast you get between
the extraordinarily wild Romanticism—like the life of the composer Johannes
Kreisler—and bitter satire. Chopin is different. Chopin, on the other hand, displays
little sense of humor, except in some of the early rondos.

You discovered a lot about Schumann's Fantasie, *Op. 17. What do we need to know
about that?*
There's a story behind how I came to perform the original text of the *Fantasie*,
originally entitled *Dichtungen*, or "Poems." The British [-Canadian music] historian Alan Walker discovered it in Budapest. It had been dedicated to Liszt and
the manuscript must have been given to him, which is how it came to be in the
Budapest Library. Walker learned that the last page is very different from the published last page. But in an article Walker published only sixteen out of the seventeen missing measures.

The original version ended with a return from the first movement of a melody
from Beethoven's *An die ferne Geliebte* [To the Distant Beloved] song cycle. But
with that return came an important change in the melody and harmony. When
Schumann came to publish it, however, he just crossed out the last page and sub-
stituted two measures of arpeggios. I think this original ending is quite beautiful.

*Schumann is not alone in cultivating this idea that he's making it up as he goes
along, is he?*
Yes, that last movement sounds like an improvisation. In a letter to Clara,
Schumann wrote, "I've been playing the melody from the last movement for
hours." And he probably just sat there playing that tune for hours on end, extending it with sequences. It's the sort of effect in Schumann, and sometimes in
Chopin, that you don't get in Haydn and Beethoven and Mozart....

The funny thing is that Schumann knew he revised badly. But he continued to
revise, he couldn't help himself. It's true of the poets: [William] Wordsworth
[1770–1850] revised badly—the original versions are much more spontaneous and
more interesting. I've always thought if you really want to see how this works is
with Chopin. [Novelist] George Sand [the pen name of Amantine Lucile Aurore
Dupin; 1804–1876] said that after Chopin composed something, he would start

revising it. He would work and work—he was never satisfied—and when he got finished he would publish the original version. That was [true] of *all* the composers of that particular period. I don't mean that Chopin was a greater composer than Schumann, but in a way he was a much more critical composer. Put it this way: There are very few failures in Chopin; there are a lot of failures in Schumann—pieces that don't come off. With maybe three or four exceptions, everything in Chopin comes off.

And Chopin did love Bach.
That extraordinary unity of sound Chopin gets is from his study of Bach's *Well–Tempered Clavier.* Chopin was the greater craftsman, probably the greatest master of counter-point since Mozart. The music is unbelievably, beautifully tailored—all the voices are wonderful. Take something like Chopin's *Préludes.* There are a lot of those preludes that don't make any sense unless you play the whole group. You really can't take them out of context. It's just such an extraordinary idea to write twenty-four preludes that make sense only if you just play them together. What you get is something that you call the "cycle," a set of pieces like the Schubert song cycles, *Die schöne Müllerin* [The Pretty Miller Maid] and the *Wintereisse,* where the songs are separate, but they only make sense if you play them as part of the cycle.

What music was Chopin hearing while he was growing up?
His education must have been rather strange. There's a lot of music that never got played in Warsaw. Basically, what he knew was Italian opera, especially Bellini, then the most popular form of music. Opera was completely international. Every place had Italian opera. And he knew the music of Bach, as I said, because that was how he learned to study the piano. When he went to Majorca with George Sand, the only piece of music he took was the *Well-Tempered Clavier.*

You say Chopin's music matures early; what about the later works?
Like a lot of people, Liszt was upset by the very last works of Chopin, which are unbelievably complex. The counterpoint becomes much more noticeable. The harmonies become extraordinarily modern. Liszt thought [Chopin's] mazurkas and the last *Ballade* and the *Polonaise-Fantaisie* were morbid. And Chopin was attacked by a lot of people because the music seemed sickly. Liszt said something very interesting: that the most morbid are the most interesting harmonically. It's only recently that people have become aware that far from being weak in the construction of large works, Chopin is in fact the only really great master of large forms in the 1830s and 1840s. He had much greater ease than Schumann and Liszt in writing a piece that was ten or eleven minutes long. Both Liszt and Schumann had trouble. They very rarely pulled off a long movement that was completely successful.

I know you love the mazurkas. I've always been struck that so many of the Romantic composers wrote dances, all kinds of dances—but not really to be danced to!
No, nobody's going to dance to the Chopin mazurkas! You really can't dance those in a salon.

Why do you say that?
Capturing the rhythm of a Chopin mazurka is, I must say, very interesting, at least to me. The last movement of the Second [Chopin Piano] Concerto has a mazurka in it. He's turning that into a great big virtuoso piece. What's interesting is that when Chopin played the concerto with Berlioz, Berlioz complained that Chopin was unable to play two measures in strict time! Everybody said about Chopin's mazurkas that most of them came out in 4/4 or 2/4 instead of 3/4. It's quite obvious that he used to elongate some of the beats more than others. He got very angry when you said that to him; and he would then laugh and say, well, that's the "national character"! The problem is, there is no such thing as a mazurka. There are about six different dances that were all called "mazurkas" at the time. Some of them have a long second beat, as in a waltz, and others a very long first beat. I remember going to play for Moritz Rosenthal when I was about ten, and he played the mazurkas. And there were some where he played the second beat so long it was twice as long as the first. I too play that way. In that particular rhythm. I don't do that ruthlessly all over the mazurkas; too systematic like that would be terrible. Chopin takes what was ordinarily a low form of salon entertainment and turns it into the greatest kind, the most profound kind of music you can write. That's very radical in Chopin. The only time Chopin writes a fugue is in a mazurka. But that's typical of Romanticism. The Romantics took forms and styles and things that were either despised or low or were considered not important and they made them as sublime and as important as anything else. I mean, the greatest example of early Romanticism are the *Songs of Innocence and Experience* by poet [William] Blake [1757–1827] What [Blake's] imitating are those moral forms that small children at the age of three and four were given. And he's turning out the most sublime poetry of his time in this form. They're certainly not for children any more.

Garrick Ohlsson: "Chopin and Schumann Present a very Interesting Comparison/Contrast Here!"

John C. Tibbetts
16 February 1989, Kansas City, MO

Born in Warsaw of middle-class parents and a child prodigy, educated in several local schools, Frédéric François [Fryderyk Franciszek] Chopin moved to Paris in 1830 and established himself as both teacher and composer. Chopin distinguished himself from other Romantic composers by writing almost

Fig. 2 Garrick Ohlsson

exclusively for solo piano. In 1835 he became a French citizen, although he loved his native land and employed Polish melodies in a number of works. A celebrated piano virtuoso who suffered from poor health—probably tuberculosis—throughout most of his life, Chopin performed publically in Paris on no more than thirty occasions.

The first American to win the prestigious International Frederick Chopin Competition in Warsaw, pianist Garrick Ohlsson embraces composers from Carl Maria von Weber (1786–1826) to Ferruccio Busoni (1866–1924). During the late 1980s Ohlsson recorded Chopin's complete solo piano works for

Arabesque Records. In 2008 he won a Grammy for Best Instrumental Soloist for his recording of Beethoven's Piano Sonatas (Fig. 2).

Our conversation was more a monologue than a dialogue; it is presented here without interruptions.

JOHN C. TIBBETTS: Who do you consider the early nineteenth century's greatest piano composers? And why?

GARRICK OHLSSON: Chopin and Schumann are the two greatest geniuses of the piano of their generation, with all due respect to Mendelssohn (who was more of a genius than many people think he was). In terms of sheer depth I think they both outclass Mendelssohn and Liszt at that time. But they didn't get along that well. Chopin's most Schumannesque piece is the F-major *Ballade*, which he dedicated to Schumann. It has that Florestan-Eusebius series of contrasts you might expect.[1] For such an elegant guy, Chopin's contrasts have no transitions at all; they are of such a brutality that they are almost unspeakable. But his music hangs together, nevertheless.

Chopin might have said, "Here, my dear Robert, this is you!" I do think that Schumann had a more generous temperament than Chopin. Schumann was more of a Californian, shall we say, in the sense of "Hey man, wow, isn't it cosmic!?" And that was his reaction when he heard Chopin. Chopin, being more the Old World arrogant snob and polished aristocrat, was perhaps a bit disdainful of this overly mammalian enthusiasm. You can see all sorts of reasons why the two men did not click. Chopin didn't think very much of Liszt, either, possibly for reasons of jealousy. And when Liszt began adding ornamentations to his Etudes, Chopin said, "Keep that pig out of my garden!".

We have a very interesting comparison/contrast here. Chopin has many things in common with Schumann. All the early Romantic composers did. They were all the children of [Karl Maria] von Weber. Because, although Weber was never as progressive harmonically as Beethoven or Schubert were in their last years—Schubert and Beethoven went way beyond anything Weber ever did and pointed directly to the end of the nineteenth century—but Weber invented the *sound* of the music of that generation around 1810–1813: Schumann, Chopin, Liszt, Mendelssohn and Berlioz. He almost invented these composers.

Chopin and Schumann could not have been possible before then. They have things in common that other famous pairs of composers have had in common. How many music lovers have said, "I can't tell the difference between Haydn and Mozart"? But the more you know about them, the more their differences become crystal clear. Now, Chopin was kind of an exotic in this middle European world. He was like a flower from Tahiti dropped into the Paris musical scene, with his wild,

---

[1]Schumann invented characters that expressed different aspects of his personality. "Florestan" represented his vigor, "Eusebius" his tendency to passivity.

Slavic temperament; but with aristocratic style and polish. He was the consummate technician and composer. And he had a sense of balance of texture and form that is really unparalleled. In small forms he a craftsman of a jeweler's precision.

My feeling about Chopin was that he was in touch with his deepest demons and could control them as you might control wild stallions. My feeling about Schumann was that his feelings got the best of him a lot of the time, compositionally and temperamentally. Schumann sometimes gets so carried away with himself that he loses me. I also think it has something to do with the sheer flow of his inspiration and emotional flow, that perhaps he didn't edit very carefully. I get the feeling with Chopin that he chewed on his ideas to the point where you don't recognize any mastication. It's all done for you. With Schumann, maybe he should have chewed a little bit more.

I am one of the pianists who has problems with Schumann. I don't know if the others pay him lip service or not. It's true that among musicians he's a deeply, deeply beloved figure. But at the same time, among chamber players, they do admit to problems. But generally, the heart is so warmed by the music, that most musicians feel, "Yes, it's problematic but deeply fulfilling." There's something about my temperament and Schumann's which don't mix. Which is my loss, I suppose. That doesn't mean that I'm problem-free with the music. I've played a great deal of Schumann, including the Piano Concerto and the solo works, including the *Abegg Variations* (one of my favorites), the *Davidsbündler*,[2] the *Carnaval*, the G-minor Sonata, the *Humoreske*, the *Symphonic Etudes* (which I've played only once). Just as like falling in love, but sometimes you might fall in love with somebody, and the more you get to know him or her, you realize you're not such a good match, after all. I personally have difficulties with motor rhythms. Thus, a lot of Baroque music is out the window for me. A lot of Schumann's music has tremendous Baroquish energy. It doesn't endear Schumann to me, but it does to a great many other people.

And when you come to the piano cycles, like the *Davidsbündler*, I confront a really personality thing. There is a lot of "in" stuff in Schumann—all the lettering and the names and the fact that the cycle goes toward the key of C in the middle and at the end—"C" means Clara—which is very beautiful and very touching. But sometimes I get impatient with "in" things and closed societies. Somehow I feel excluded. It makes me feel like I'm a voyeur peeking in on someone else's happy little thing. I don't mean to be nasty about this. I personally feel left out with all this "in" stuff, that I don't know the password to the secret door. Parts of the *Davidsbündler* are terribly beautiful, but I feel the whole of it starts to ramble—just as I am doing now! I just don't respond to this sort of thing. But maybe this is my own personal demon.

---

[2]Or "Band of David," Schumann's name for an imaginary band of musical revolutionaries.

Leslie Howard: "I Think We Have to Get Rid of the Liszt Stereotypes"

John C. Tibbetts
1989, Kansas City, MO; 1999 and 2007 in his London Home

Perhaps the most famous pianist who ever lived and one of the nine-teenth century's most celebrated composers, Franz Liszt was born in a village that then belonged to Hungary, spent most of his youth in Paris, later become known as a member of the New German School, and devoted much of his later life to teaching and religious composition. Liszt's name is almost

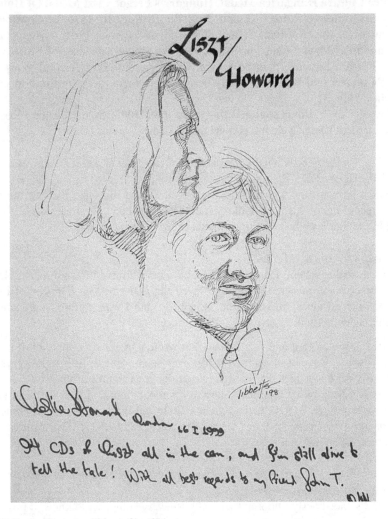

Fig. 3 Leslie Howard, with a profile of Liszt

invariably associated with "program music" and the "symphonic poem," neither of which he invented (although he popularized them through performances of his symphonic works). Liszt's elder daughter Blandine (1835–1862) married Emile Ollivier (1825–1913), who later became Prime Minister of France; Cosima (1837–1930), Liszt's younger daughter, married the pianist, composer, and conductor Hans von Bülow (1830–1894), then left him for Richard Wagner.

In 1986, the centenary of Liszt's death and the 175th anniversary of his birth, Leslie Howard began recording all of Liszt's solo-piano and piano-orchestral music: a feat unparalleled in recording history. Born in Melbourne, Howard has garnered many awards, including Membership in the Order of Australia, the Pro Cultura Hungarica Medal, Hungary's Ferenc Liszt Medal Of Honour, and—six times—France's Grand Prix du Disque. In 1876 he became an instructor at the Guildhall School of Music, and he also gives master classes at London's Royal College of Music and the Royal Academy of Music. The BBC *Music Magazine* praised Howard's "formidable intellectual grasp" of Liszt's music, and that "his vastly superior performances continue to carry the day" (Fig. 3).

These conversations spanned the years 1989–2007 when Howard recorded his Complete Liszt Cycle for Hyperion Records.

JOHN C. TIBBETTS: When did the music of Franz Liszt first reach your ears?
LESLIE HOWARD: Hearing Vladimir Horowitz's recording of the B-Minor Sonata. I have to say, with best respects to the great old man, that it's the only Liszt recording of his that I like. The piece grabbed me straightaway; and I couldn't imagine anybody writing a better piece of music than that.

How old were you at this time?
Oh, I was still at school. I suppose I must have been around fifteen. I mean, I knew some other piano pieces. Everybody played the *Liebesträume* [Dreams of Love] No. 3. I played the Sixth Hungarian Rhapsody, and I was starting to prepare the "Transcendental Etudes."

I started to look into it and found that Liszt wrote a tremendous amount of music, most of which was out of print (if it had ever been printed). Although everybody cautiously acknowledges that he was one of the great figures of the Romantic era, somehow a little bit of mud had clung to his reputation; and that had been sufficient for him never to have had so great a Collected Works edition as Brahms has had or like Wagner has had, or [Anton] Bruckner [1824–1896]. That struck me as something of an injustice.

Did your interest in Liszt also interest you in his life, his biography, the musicological aspects of the music itself?
I think it's enormously important with almost every composer to know, if possible, why a piece was written, or why a composer worked in the way he did—who he

knew, what were the influences in both directions. As far as I'm concerned, the more you find out, the better off you are, even if you can't actually pinpoint why it helps to know that Mozart played billiards. It's just part of knowing the sort of a bloke he was. You have to absorb everything you can to give as fair an account of a man's work as possible. That's why I've never understood piano players who don't go to the opera or don't listen to string quartets or don't accompany songs (let alone the ones who don't go to the theater or to art galleries).

Before we get to the music, what do we need to know about Liszt?
I think we have to get rid of some stereotypes. There's one time when, in a sort of tired, resigned mood, he said he was "half priest and half Zigeuner [i.e., Gypsy]." That was said to one of his students; but I don't think it was really meant to be taken seriously as his self-analysis! I think it's really rather appalling that Ernest Newman [1868–1959] seized upon it as the basis for a book which only can be described as unbridled character assassination! I think you have to throw out all of this rubbish about Liszt being only a flashy composer, simply because there was a certain amount of flashiness attributed to his performances when he was working as a concert pianist. Most people don't even stop to realize that this concert-playing period of Liszt's ran only from 1838 to 1847. But after that, he was as serious a musician as you would ever find. He was a serious musician before, of course. There's no doubt he was swayed by the business of playing, but he was also extremely tired of it well before he stopped. He heaved a great sigh of relief when he played his last recital in 1847.

Are the stories true of his platform antics, his breaking pianos and women throwing their gloves onto the stage?
I think all of that is true, but it would be wrong to assume that every time he played, that sort of thing happened. When he was touring Europe, he had to play on amazingly awful instruments. There are some splendid accounts of his tour in Britain in 1840, where half the pianos he played were those square pianos. If you can imagine what the "Norma" Fantasy must have sounded like on a square piano! I think it's a miracle that the thing wasn't completely destroyed. They just weren't designed for that kind of music.

People want to pin a "Mick Jagger" label onto him.
It's probably a fair commentary on his big concertizing period. He really was followed around by groupies wherever he went. In his case, the groupies were very frequently people with lots of spare time and lots of money. He had this ability to attract titled women wherever he went. But then, everybody was fascinated by him. He knew everybody.

Yet you say he gave up public recitals before he was forty years old.
I think he remains, like any human being, enormously complicated, but endlessly fascinating, because there was a lot of ego in what he was doing as a soloist. But he also spent a lot of time during that period—and certainly during the rest of his

life—trying more or less to recede into the background, even while he was try-ing to do new things musically. First, when he gave up playing in public, and he went to work in Weimar in the late 1840s, he bought back from his publishers all the plates of all of the music that had been printed of his original work—not of his transcriptions—so that he could rewrite these works and issue them in a form that showed what his brain was capable of doing. Then there was that dreadful manifesto[3] by Brahms and Joseph Joachim [1831–1907] suggesting that the "new music" coming out of Weimar by Liszt, Wagner, Berlioz, and [Peter] Cornelius [1824–1874] be stripped from the musical vocabulary. It was a critical cabal against him. Liszt actually asked his students not to play his music, and he asked his friends not to conduct it. "Don't perform my Mass in Paris, because it won't be successful." It's easy to knock him as a character because he lived his life under heavy public scrutiny. I'm sure there's many a composer in the nineteenth century who was extremely jealous of his popularity.

We can't go very far with Liszt before we realize how much time and energy he devoted to the music of others. I'm thinking now of his piano versions of songs, operas, and symphonies.
I think of Berlioz, who owed a great deal to Liszt and who ruefully remarked in his memoirs how wonderful it would be to play the piano like Liszt to get into places where he [Berlioz] couldn't go. And, of course, there's the famous story about the role Liszt played in getting the *Symphonie fantastique* before the public. The original score hadn't been published, and at the time Berlioz couldn't get it published. So Liszt made a piano transcription in 1834 with the sole purpose of bringing the piece to critical attention. It would be fourteen more years before the score was published. In the meantime, Liszt had circulated it in a form that was more accessible.

And, somehow, Schumann gets into the act and writes about it. Had he heard it in performance?
Not then. Schumann wrote a review of the [*Symphonie fantastique*] based on Liszt's transcription. There was no way he could have seen the original score, which Berlioz kept—as he did all of his music—in a suitcase, which he took with him wherever he went. But Liszt had indicated the instrumentation the best he could on two staves, and Schumann was able to get more than a rough idea of how the piece went. He wrote, I think, quite a perceptive and intelligent account of it.

Liszt started out transcribing with aims I suppose not much different from every-body else's—which was to say, that in the late 1820s, if you were a performer, you were expected to improvise on well-known themes from operas. You could write them down in order to make a little money. Liszt's first published venture in

---

[3]A derogatory document, probably in 1860 written by Brahms and eventually signed by some twenty musicians, that appeared in the Berlin music magazine *Echo* and was parodied in Schumann's *Neue Zeitschrift für Musik*.

this regard was based on a tune from a long-forgotten opera by [Daniel François Esprit] Auber [1782–1871], called *La Fiancée*. It's already more interesting than your average hack potpourri. It stretches piano technique. It already shows that Liszt at the age of nineteen was somebody to be reckoned with.

With all his paraphrases and transcriptions, Liszt temporarily became a traveling jukebox.

I suppose at one level he was, but every time he got hold of somebody's tune, he either had a duty to do something wonderful with it, or else write a whole new piece involving new decisions about structure and harmony and so on. The *Don Juan* fantasy, for example, is a pure piece of Liszt; somehow it manages to convey the drama in [Mozart's] opera [*Don Giovanni*] just by the way he combines the themes. You play a little fragment of "The Drinking Song" and the statue and his mysterious chromatic scales sort of creep into the middle of it so that you knew even before he sings the Don's "Drinking Song" that he's on a doomed road. It's really uncanny. I think his wisdom with other people's music was almost always spot on. There are very few of these transcriptions where you can say that he pulled a gaffe, because he didn't understand what the real spirit of the thing was.

Have any of these pieces ever tested your patience, if not your musicianship? Is he kind to the poor pianist? I mean, are these things playable*?*

A lot of people think that Liszt is basically unplayable altogether, but I think actually when you get close to it, you find that there are very, very few passages that resist a happy explanation technically, because he wrote so well. He never wrote anything that was sort of pigheadedly awkward. There's never anything in Liszt as awkward as the end of the Scherzo in Schubert's *Wanderer Fantasy*, for example. There *are* plenty of things in Liszt that look like they're hair-raisingly difficult—and make no mistake about it, you can't sight-read the transcription of the *Symphonie fantastique*!—but by and large, you can always stay within the bounds of possibility.

What part of Liszt's life and work do we find in your recordings that we didn't know about before?

I think you come away impressed with his devotion to the [Roman Catholic] Church. You have to take Liszt's Christianity absolutely as he tells it to you. Which is to say, when he was young, he was fanatically enthusiastic, and he had visions of being a priest-musician. And he used to go into fits of quasi-religious ecstasy when he was performing. That kind of religiosity, as it might be thought, never appealed to me particularly. But in Paris he went to the people he considered the most radical religious thinkers of the day and got to know them personally. Yet, even with his efforts to keep abreast of religious thinking, and to do everything else he was doing as a musician, it was only in his fifties that he took the formal [minor] orders of the priesthood and became Abbé Liszt. He became much more formal about his religion as he got older, but that was partly because he then got to know more clerics and, I think, suddenly enjoyed the traditions of the church better, and he liked the liturgy much better, too. Of course, he started writing motets when he was thirty, and he wrote his first mass when he was thirty-seven. Especially in the later years he wrote a lot more church music, and of course tried very hard to make a success of two completely different ways of writing oratorio, and by then you can see how very, very careful he is with the words. I always wonder how this relates to the perceived physical deterioration in his last years.

Were it not for you [and your Hyperion recordings], we would not know about the great majority of those pieces.
Hmmm. A lot of them. Liszt already realized that the church, in its wisdom, was a bit wary of his religious music, mostly without looking at it. Think of the number of *Ave Marias* [plural of "Hail Mary"] and *Pater nosters* [plural of "Our father"] and other such things that he published, that the church didn't quite take up. None of those motets ever achieved any kind of broader popularity, and they're only known to the people who've gone hunting for them. He did do piano versions of many of them. If we look at the collection called *Harmonies poétiques et religieuses*, or at least the set that he published, because that was in fact his third go at a volume of pieces under that title, the *Ave Maria* that's its second piece is quite a straightforward transcription of music for chorus and organ. You can't imagine why this wonderful work wouldn't be a satisfactory motet in a church and why it would never have achieved popularity.

Liszt's religious music is almost totally unknown, because people don't perform it. It's important that pianists should look at the transcriptions from *Christus* and from *St. Elizabeth*, because they're well worth playing. They're beautiful just to work at. And they come out sounding like quite a different composer, in many ways, from the chap who wrote the *Transcendental Etudes* some decades earlier. He reserves some of his most radical musical thoughts for some of his religious pieces. I mean, anyone who knows the *Via crucis* [Stations of the Cross] will know that he risked great opprobrium by trying to depict the sufferings of Jesus in such harmonically graphic terms. People thought he'd taken leave of his senses. His publisher rejected the work and sent it back. He knew he was right, and he made a version of it for solo piano, and a version of it for solo organ, and a version for piano duet, quietly confident that one day people would see the light and publish them. Which indeed they are doing as we speak. Actually, the *Via crucis* is the only one of Liszt's religious works that gets performed in Britain, along with the *Missa choralis*. There's a quality of thought in there which is quite astounding, and its musical form is different from anyone else's religious piece in all time as far as I can see.

Apparently, at least for you, Liszt is the best composer to live with year after year, decade after decade.
Well, he is, because he had the broadest mind, and he knew more music by other composers, I should think, than almost any composer ever. He was indefatigable in his interests outside his own work. The efforts to which he went to mount other

people's operas and to perform other people's orchestral music in Weimar, and to promote their piano music—not that he played it himself, but that he had his students play all sorts of musicians—shows a breadth of taste and knowledge which I don't think … it's certainly not equaled in the nineteenth century, or any century, for that matter.

For me, Liszt keeps being so interesting because you can never quite pin him down. He's always surprising you. Of all the great nineteenth century composers, he's the one who's been the most shamefully neglected, either in [terms of] serious musicology, serious performance, or publication. We don't bother to laugh about bad Beethoven or inferior Mozart or anything like that, and I think that it is high time that we stop worrying about Liszt's imperfections because there are too many things of real and genuine interest to get our teeth into.

From Romanticism Toward Modernism

Introduction

As the nineteenth century progressed, so did a growing infatuation with innovation. Philosophical discussions, national languages and literatures, new technologies, and the pure possibilities of sound were just some of the factors that shaped how composers, performers, and audiences thought about music.

In many circles concerts were viewed as religious experiences where spiritual truths were proffered by the musical geniuses that appeared on stage. Even the way concert halls were being designed—looking like Greek temples on the outside and churches on the inside—as well as how audiences were expected to behave—listening in devout silence—took on religious overtones. Russell Sherman deals in his interview with virtuosi such as Franz Liszt, who captivated audiences through the forces of their personalities and their music. Richard Wagner, Liszt's son-in-law, infused his music dramas with spiritual and philosophical resonances, and in later life Liszt turned to the church. Like Beethoven, Liszt, and several other nineteenth-century composers Wagner became a mythic figure, as noted filmmaker Tony Palmer tells us. To some extent, both Liszt and Wagner were musical "scientists," experimenting with new compositional methods and materials. Soon thereafter the phrase *avant-garde* (literally, "ahead of the troops") would be employed over and over again for Arnold Schoenberg, his followers, and other musical radicals of the twentieth century.

When it comes to issues of national identity, many nineteenth-century composers infused their music with idioms drawn either from actual folk songs or through convincing imitations of folk styles. A famous example of the latter is Bedřich Smetana [1824–1884]'s opera *Prodaná nevěsta* (*The Bartered Bride*, 1866), one of the most important Czech operas in the repertory. Although Smetana's opera includes genuine Czech folk music (in the furiant), early audiences thought the entire opera sounded "Czech" and decided that Smetana's style defined the

© The Author(s) 2018
J. C. Tibbetts et al. (eds.), *Performing Music History*,
https://doi.org/10.1007/978-3-319-92471-7_7

quintessential Czech sound. Qualifying any national—or regional—sound in music is an extremely complex and challenging affair, as both Leif Ove Andsnes and Rudolf Firkušńy explain in their respective discussions of Norwegian composer Edvard Grieg (1843–1907) and Moravian composer Leoš Janáček.

Musical nationalism rests near the idea of Modernism, whose practitioners felt that old, traditional models of expression and form—whether in literature, art, architecture, music, or any other creative manifestation—were irrelevant to an increasingly industrialized and urban society. Some composers, like many of the nationalists, turned to overt celebrations of the rural, the primitive, and the historical—in other words, the "pre-modern." In many ways Charles E. Ives (1874–1954), one of America's foremost art composers, was a nationalist; many of his orchestral compositions and songs draw upon patriotic and traditional melodies. Other composers championed abrupt breaks with the past and invented new modes of expression. Some, like Mahler and Béla Bartók, synthesized both national and aggressively experimental approaches to create highly distinctive musical languages that captivated such performers, as contralto Maureen Forrester and pianist György Sándor explain in their interviews. Although quite different from each other, Mahler and Bartók strove to create new worlds of sound that simultaneously looked backward *and* forward.

Other composers, including the "impressionist" Claude Debussy, focused on the qualities of sound itself, whether in terms of particular instruments or sonic textures that combined more complex timbres. Pianist Mark Markham deals with this subject in greater detail, but multi-dimensional envisioning of creative works, where boundaries broke down between music, theater, the visual arts, literature, and philosophy, was pioneered by Richard Wagner as well as later modernists.

William Everett and Michael Saffle

Russell Sherman: "Liszt Is a Thoroughly Modern Man … a Highly Speculative, Philosophical, and Religious Figure"

John C. Tibbetts
6 February 1991, Kansas City, Missouri

Russell Sherman (Fig. 1) **has been called "the thinking man's virtuoso pianist," celebrated both for his passionate devotion to teaching as Distinguished Artist-in-Residence at the New England Conservatory of Music, and for his devotion to the late works of Franz Liszt and other more contemporary composers. In 1996 Sherman published a collection of short essays entitled** *Piano Pieces*. **His most successful students include Marc-André Hamelin, Christopher O'Riley, and Tian Ying.**

During this interview, Sherman punctuated his remarks with demonstrations at the keyboard. He had been invited to give master classes at the University of Missouri-Kansas City.

Fig. 1 Russell Sherman, with an image of Liszt

JOHN C. TIBBETTS: You've said that Franz Liszt is one of the chief architects of modern music. What do you mean by that?
RUSSELL SHERMAN: It means something relevant and proven by the music and the evidence of Liszt's life. Here is a thoroughly *modern* man with many contradictions, one who was devoted to the frenzy of the masses and one who at the same time was a highly speculative, philosophical and religious figure who retreated to the abyss of his own privacy. And in his later music, especially, I feel something there that is pertinent, to the twentieth-century philosophy as found among the Existentialists: [Albert] Camus [1913–1960], [Jean-Paul] Sartre [1905–1980]. and [Martin] Heidegger [1889–1976].[1] There is that *nothingness* aspect, or simply that quality of life, which seems to behave in such irregular patterns, with so many variables clawing at each other in opposite directions. A kind of anarchy or chaos or nihilism is reached. I think the scientists are beginning to catch up with this now, that chaos itself has become a very dominant factor in the analysis of physical systems. An understanding that certain systems have in them these kinds of contradictory variables that cannot be sorted out as to make predictable patterns. But above all, what I feel in this late music of Liszt is the prophecy of that nothingness that happens after all of the illusions of progress and the march of history have been violated, have been betrayed, have been busted. Nothing is left but a sense of sheer astonishment and fright at the prospect that the human being turns in certain cycles, makes certain pretentions, ideals, utopias, and finds that they're always undermined and betrayed by elements in our own being, that we're all victims of some kind of universe that has in the philosophical sense no end, no beginning, no purpose.

It seems a realization that in its own way overtook all of the Romantics.
I think it is more pertinent in Liszt. You do make a good point. One can point out those qualities in [other] late Romantics, where the music drifts off into a kind of naïveté or innocence, a sort of prayer that our fundamental instincts might still retain some possibility of redemption. But Liszt seemed to me very uncompromising. He was a man with a bad conscience who, in facing the end of his life, thought: Well, maybe it's all been just a glorious cartoon, and now it's wasted, and I approach my death with no illusions. But I see it as something else. Really, what I feel is both the anticipation and consequences of a global war, and the way that the European culture, presumably divinely inspired, carried the seeds of its own destruction. In the end, tribalism and fury and misery and fear and anxiety—anxiety, above all—would be the dominant human characteristics. That fear, that anxiety, that emptiness seems to me an absolutely pertinent and absolutely brazen component of Liszt's music. It irritates many people and even many musicians. There are all kinds of serious musicians who find these late Liszt pieces just drivel, the outtakes of a distorted mind. I think that's very unfair.

---

[1]Liszt might have agreed with the depressive atmosphere associated with post-World War II existentialism in Europe, but he would have argued strongly against Sartre's adamant atheism.

How about audiences, how do they feel?
Audiences, audiences, audiences! You know, they're not homogenous and it really depends where one is. I think [we have] to realize that the portrait of "audience" as a fixed component with a certain degree of insight is just an illusion and depends upon the degree simply of cultivation within your audience.

I'm wondering too as we get into this late music if we also don't experience cul-minations of directions, harmonically speaking, that Liszt had embraced from the very beginning.
Infinitely so. Color and harmony and the dissolution of harmony and the dissolu-tion of tonality. The program that I played last night began and ended with Liszt. The *Jeux d'Eaux à la Villa d'Este* [Fountains of water at the Villa d'Este (outside Rome)] has in it all of the spells and all of the exquisite sonority and filigree of the Impressionist school and I've used it as a prelude to the Debussy's *Estampes* [Prints, as in etchings or lithographs]. But in these late pieces, tonality is severed, and what remains are these inconstant divisions of the octave into augmented chords and the whole-tone scale, where there is no tonic, no root tone.[2] [Instead], all the tones are freely swimming in some kind of solvent that just expands in a kind of entropy.

How do we hear this in the music?
I think the simplest way to demonstrate this is a late piece I've played many, many times, the *Nuages gris* [Grey clouds], which I think is a very pertinent example of these enigmatic processes of disillusion, nihilism, prophecy, and yet a grandeur at the mysterious powers of fate. [plays all of *Nuages gris*] Here you have the crisis, a piece that threatens at all times to become a domesticated G minor composition in its profoundly lyrical and prophetic quality. Yet, as soon as that elegiac tonality is heard, it is undermined by a sequence of augmented third chords and a trem-olo in the bass that rock the [key's] foundations and fall into a chasm and into an abyss. Again [Liszt] tries to propose a theme that has a certain symmetrical qual-ity, one that wants to become a nocturnal folk song or something like that. And as soon as it begins, this dark fluid of the draining abscess pulls it down, pulls it back, and [the music] dissolves into this kind of primordial ooze—before there were dinosaurs, and before dinosaurs there was algae, and before the algae there as just a bacterial soup, and before that there were certain chemicals. And it all ends in this vast and vastest of cycles from the beginning to the end. So, you see in that sense, one might say: "Well, what an extraordinary conceit and pretention! Here is somebody who is summarizing the history of the universe in one minute and forty-seven seconds or something like that!" But please, you know, one has to be a little fair. This is only a sketch, a vignette that portrays the virulent part of our natures and is a very active component in cycle of history.

---

[2]An example of an augmented chord or triad is [C – E - G-sharp]. A whole-tone scale beginning on C is spelled [C - D – E – F-sharp – G# – A-sharp /C].

At the same time, to aspire to this in the music is in itself a Romantic disposition, is it not? To find in tones some kind of source of all things ...

You're quite right, and yet we are a little bit misled in that attribution to the Romantics who presumably would absorb the lessons of painting, of philosophy, of poetry in their music, compared to the "pure" musicians like Bach, Haydn, Mozart [Anton von] Webern [1883–1945], and Schoenberg. But that's not really quite fair. It seems to me Mozart is also about a worldview and also about exquisite portraits of humans and animals and flowers in their various dances of love and desire. It is not so prescribed programmatically in Mozart as it might be in Liszt. But all music is about something else, and that something is life itself. The Romantics acknowledged that music, as one of the French poets said—[Paul] Valéry [1871–1945] or [Paul-Marie] Verlaine [1844–1896] or several others—is the condition to which all art aspires, and that in music we should hear always characterizations of not simply mood, not simply of emotion, not mere color. [Instead,] as Mendelssohn said, music is a far more specific way of rendering reality than words, which are full of ambiguities and always lead to mischief.

You mentioned the use of tremolo and augmented chords. What is a tremolo, exactly? The musicologist Hugh Macdonald told me the tremolo was at the very heart of Romanticism.

Think of the opening of the Ninth Symphony of Beethoven. This was the beginning of it. My teachers told me that the tremolo became a standard device in the late Romantics, like Liszt, Wagner, and Mahler. Unfortunately, we have today the simplistic notion that it was only a debased technique belonging to silent movie music. The point is, tremolos can be haunting, can be beautiful and can be beautifully etched and portrayed. For composers like [György] Ligeti [1923–2006], they move through the orchestral or string quartet fabric in the most haunting and magical way. They are the underground vibrations that bind together all the creatures of nature.

Liszt and the augmented chord seems a subject in itself, doesn't it?

Specifically, an augmented chord subdivides the octave by major thirds. [plays] As an equal subdivision [of an octave], each interval [possesses] the same tension as all the other intervals and therefore one can say there is no end and there is no beginning. There are three such chords—the augmented [triad], which splits the octave in thirds; the diminished fifth [interval]; and the devil's interval.[3] [plays] All those possibilities result in an equivalence that portrays beautifully that sense of boundlessness. And so for Liszt and for other composers, the augmented chord is the arch symbol of something that is eternally spinning and has neither inception nor conclusion ...

---

[3]Built on C, an augmented sixth is written C-A#. Built on C, the devil's interval—also known as the *diabolus in musica*—is written C-F#. Again, I'm not sure this note is necessary for the reasons stated earlier.

Liszt used the term "New Music." What do you think he meant by that??

I can only speak of that in a general way. Wagner resented the accusation that he stole his harmony from Liszt, even though it was quite true. In Liszt, and his confreres, you [encounter] the strain of composing in a way that contradicts the hierarchy of root tones and their consequences [i.e., associated harmonies], and the music begins to breakdown. There is a spirit of expiration, I think of democracy, in the sense that every note become liberated and is not simply fettered to a root tone. And this of course leads to atonality and the kinds of music that people are still not yet comfortable with, but which is beginning to infiltrate our consciousness. We listen now to Bartók and Stravinsky and even to Webern and Schoenberg in ways that were quite different twenty, thirty, forty years ago. Take a work like Liszt's B Minor Sonata, or his Second Piano Concerto, where one, two, three, or four motifs become the basis for the entire work. This is the signature of twentieth-century century music. A particularly redolent example of that is his late piece, the "Lugubrious Gondola" [i.e. *La lugubre gondola*], which has this quality of mystical retreat and darkness and prophecy. It is simply an essay in the languid entropic aspects of the augmented chord. [plays all of *La lugubre gondola*]. And the same chord, repeated a whole tone lower … one might mention the slimy grip of the augmented chord.

A premonition of Wagner's death, was it not?

Yes, yes, and finally, after those two statements, the tremolo,[4] which is an unyielding symbol of the shimmering evanescence of life, the "Gondola" comes to quite a thrilling climax. Even in a more conservative piece, like [one of] the *Petrarch Sonnet*[s], you find the tonic of the broken heart uprooted by an augmented chord. [plays one of Liszt's *Petrarch Sonnets*] This is the crisis chord, the symbol of an unrequited love. Of love unsatisfied and unconsummated.

And yet tonality haunts these pieces. Maybe it's a memory, maybe it's a hint, or even a premonition. But I think Leonard Bernstein said somewhere that we, as human beings, have a deep-seated need for a tonal center to give dramatic power to this kind of thing.

Yes, I know he said that, and in fact I can point to that firsthand. When I was an extremely young chap, perhaps nineteen or twenty, there was an informal competition to play with the New York Philharmonic. Bernstein was the conductor. I ended up playing the Brahms D-minor Concerto. I walked into his studio and the first thing we did was have a discussion about [the American composer] Roger Sessions [1896–1985]. I defended Sessions warmly, but Lenny was rather antagonistic. And again, it was this notion that somehow the absence of a strong tonal center was a sign that music was not coherent, rational, or civilized. However, I agree, in the sense that I remember the old phrase by [psychologist Jean] Piaget

---

[4]On the piano, a rapid alternation between any two notes or chords.

[1896–1980]: phylogeny recapitulates ontogeny. That somehow every one of us, individually, must recapitulate our ancestors and our roots. In that Jungian sense, we have to know not only our tonality, but also our dinosaurs, and our ooze, to have the fullest contact with our natures.[5] I don't think [tonality] was denied even by Schoenberg, even in the most idealistic sense of ridding us of this aristocratic and conservative, feudal specter of tonality. It was either desirable or possible and that it was simply used as one of the elements in constructing the psychological and artistic tableaux.

Tony Palmer: "Wagner's Work Grew Out of What He Perceived as Political Shambles in Germany"

John C. Tibbetts
February 2017, London

Wilhelm Richard Wagner is among the best-known, most beloved, and most despised figures in Western music history. Born in Leipzig, Wagner planned even in childhood to pursue a joint career in music and drama. His early operas brought him a certain measure of fame, but his participation in the Dresden Uprising of 1849 forced him to seek political asylum—first in Switzerland, then in Venice and Paris. In 1862 Wagner settled in Munich, where he became a favorite of Ludwig II, King of Bavaria; later he married Liszt's daughter Cosima. Before his death Wagner raised funds for a special theater, built in Bayreuth, where *Der Ring des Nibelungen*—four massive "music dramas" (rather than "mere operas," which were Italian) based loosely on medieval legends—received their first performances in 1876. In Nazi Germany Wagner won favor for his anti-Semitic writings; among musicians, however, he is best known for his use of *Leitmotive* ("leading" motifs, associated with individual characters, places, and objects) and for his invention of *Gesamtkunstwerke* or "total artworks" that combine music, poetry, and visual imagery.

A graduate of Cambridge University, Tony Palmer (Fig. 2) worked first with the BBC, then with Ken Russell and other major film figures—among them Frank Zappa (1940–1993; *200 Motels*, 1971) and a host of pop celebrities (*All You Need is Love*, 1976–1980). Later Palmer turned almost exclusively to classical music. Wagner has figured prominently in his film and television work; both *Wagner* (1983) and *Parsifal* (1997) conjoin music and biography with social and political commentary. Among his more than fifty awards are three Italia Prizes (television's most coveted award) as well as Gold Medals at

---

[5]Carl Gustav Jung (1875–1961) believed everyone is born with innate images or archetypes of such things as fatherhood, masculinity, femininity, and death.

the host (JT) with the most!
Tony many thanks

26-iv-03

Fig. 2 Tony Palmer

the New York Film and Television Festival. In 1989 Palmer became the first maker of arts films honored with a retrospective of his work at the National Film Theatre, London.

   The following interview took place in Palmer's London home.

JOHN C. TIBBETTS: You have devoted your career to making documentaries and theatrical biopics about many composers—[Giacomo] Puccini [1858–1924], Henry Purcell, Shostakovich, John Adams, and of course Wagner—as well as playwrights, musicians, and actors. Your research must be exhaustive!
TONY PALMER: Making biopics is not for the faint of heart! It's a dangerous business. First, you soon realize that more or less everyone knows or knew the

subject better than you. Next, you discover that the world is full of "experts" who are rapidly rewriting history to show themselves in the best possible light. Even more dangerous, assuming, of course, that it's the truth we are seeking, are those participants who seek to "interpret" the subject's life (and intentions) based on little evidence and less knowledge, except that they happen to be brother/sister/daughter/wife/confidante, etc., and thus (one would assume) possessed of invaluable insight.

I would think it's probably easier if your subject is still living ...
No, that's most treacherous of all. You risk trusting blindly the subject. He (or she) will twist and turn and cover his tracks and make your search as painful and perverse as he (or she) possibly can. I mean, how are we to believe what they are saying? But, you know, that allows for the kind of ambiguity between truth and fiction that I need.

What amazes me is that you entered the world of music documentaries and theatrical films with very little related cultural background.
It's true. As a boy, I had no formal musical training and very little experience with music, apart from listening to 78 rpm recordings and attending concerts. But that also meant I had no predispositions, good or bad, about music, pop or classical. I didn't have any formal training in making films, either, but I've been incredibly lucky. At the BBC as a trainee, I was fortunate to work with director Ken Russell and be involved in the world of BBC producers Humphrey Burton and Huw Wheldon. They were profoundly influential. I grew up at a time when you were encouraged to take risks.

Has anyone outside the BBC influenced your approach?
The best advice I've gotten was from Göran Wassberg, Ingmar Bergman's designer. Once Wasberg picked me up at the Stockholm Airport, and as he drove me in he asked me what I was doing that evening. He said he'd been invited to a dinner party and would I like to come? We arrived at this nondescript house. And there was Bergman, having a birthday party! I was completely tongue-tied! The conversation died down, because everyone was listening to Bergman as he explained: when you have an actor on stage, you must tell them where to come on, where to go off, and how to keep them from knocking over the furniture. That's the essence of it. Don't tell them any more. So, I listen to everybody and I try to figure out the truth of it all.

Please give us an overview of your work on operatic productions and opera films.
Operas have been an integral part of my career. There's really not a very great difference between directing a play, a film, or an opera. Whichever, there's a lot of "man management" involved. You have to assume that actors, like singers, are essentially like children. They need to be loved. They need a cuddle at the end of it. How could I have possibly told Placido Domingo what to do on stage, for example, in my *Parsifal*? I'm not going to tell him how to sing a line! Or Vanessa

Redgrave in my *Wagner*—I can't tell her how to say a line, but I can dress her up so that she can do her best. My job is to provide an atmosphere but not necessarily impose my ideas on them.

What especially of your biggest film project, Wagner*?*
Wagner was my first big theatrical film. I started from an admiration and fascination with the personality of the composer. For example, I was always gripped by the fact that a penniless, ruthless, anti-Semitic megalomaniac like Wagner could have "gotten away with it." He arrived in Zurich absolutely penniless, a political exile, found out who the richest man in Zurich was—one Otto Wesendonck—chatted him up, had dinner with him, and at the end of the evening not only had access to his bank account, but his wife and a cottage at the bottom of the garden. Come the premiere of *The Ring* years later, who came but Wesendonck? And they shook hands as friends! So I wondered, what was there about this man, unpleasant as he must have been, that was so charming and fun to be with? (I've often thought that in trying to find money for my films, I am a bit like Wagner visiting Wesendonck, although I do *not* make off with their wives—not all of them, anyway!)

What is it about Wagner's music that so attracts you?
Wagner comes the nearest any composer has ever come to capturing the sound of real speech in musical notes. Much of it is like sung dialogue. Rhythmically, it is endlessly subtle, bending and twisting according to the rhythm of the words. Harmonically, it is also constantly shifting, like the emotions it describes. Even today it sounds incredibly modern. My hunch is it will always sound modern.

But as a person... ?
You can know a lot from a very funny, but telling, anecdote about the man: Act I of *Parsifal* is a quasi-religious ceremony. I think it's actually a black [i.e., Satanic or parody] mass. At the world premiere in Bayreuth, at the end of that act, there was silence in the theater. Absolute silence. Wagner was horrified. And he was running around wondering what had happened. Unknown to Wagner, Cosima had told everybody this was such a great spiritual moment that it could only be greeted by silence. Applause would be vulgar. Wagner found this out and went about screaming, "How dare this horrible woman say that—I want applause. I love applause. Give me applause!" The idea of this horrid little man shouting that out at the top of his voice "I want applause" is hilarious. If you go to Bayreuth today, and people clap at the end of the first act of *Parsifal*, most go "Shhhh!" It is the case that we have become so entrenched in our view that classical music is somehow almost beyond criticism; that it expresses the soul in a way nothing else can; that only classical music is capable of subtlety and Art.

I see what you mean! But back to Wagner. *How did it all begin for you?*
We go back to John Culshaw's *Golden Ring*, a BBC production I worked on. Once I felt I had enough experience, I said to John, "I think I'm ready to do my own Wagner film." He took me to meet Wolfgang [Wagner] in Düsseldorf in 1977.

Here we were with this man, the composer's grandson, who had known his grandfather's only son, Siegfried, and who had actually known Cosima, his grandfather's widow. Cosima herself had personally known Ludwig [II] of Bavaria, Nietzsche, [Hans] von Bülow, and all the other incredible characters who had formed such an important part of Wagner's life![6] Amazing! Wolfgang told me that if his grandfather were alive today, he would want to work in Hollywood! He wished me good luck and offered to help. Eventually he became a true friend of the project, correcting various factual mistakes we made as we went along, giving us permission to film in his grandfather's theatre in Bayreuth, still the "temporary structure" his grandfather had built of wood in 1875 and still standing. He even allowed me to talk to his mother, the redoubtable Winifred, the friend of Hitler, who was no longer on speaking terms with *any* members of her family, including her younger son. She would not allow herself to be tape-recorded, nor could I take notes.

Did [Wolfgang Wagner] insist on script approval?
Once the script was finished—it took two years—we had to bring it back and show it to Wolfgang, not so he could veto anything, but so he could be appraised of the progress. He insisted that Charles Wood and I read the whole thing in front of him while his wife, Gudrun, translated the whole thing as we went. The script was 480 pages long! He didn't react at all, until we got to the scene when Ludwig's three ministers were discussing the *Ring*. When Gielgud said, in English, "And what's more, there's this *'Ring* thing'," Gudron translated it back into German as, *"Der Ring Ding."* Wolfgang thought that was the funniest thing he had ever heard. He went on and on, repeating it. For years, whenever I saw him, he kept repeating it. In any event, he approved of the whole project and granted us permission to use anything in Bayreuth we wanted.

Was Wagner *your most expensive film up to that time?*
We needed a substantial sum of money for *Wagner*. It cost around ten million dollars. That was in 1982, for the hundredth anniversary of the composer's death the following year. At the time we started the filming, I knew we didn't have enough to finish; so I just said, let's get on with it and worry as we go about more money. And the principals involved, including Richard Burton and Vanessa Redgrave, agreed to do it. Sir Georg Solti and Ivan Fischer conducted the music with the London Philharmonic and the Budapest and Vienna Symphony Orchestras. We filmed on locations where the composer lived and worked—Munich, Vienna, Siena, Budapest, Lucerne, Nuremberg, Bayreuth and Venice. The battle scenes we shot in Hungary. Most of the interiors were authentic. Many of the relics, too. We even had the ring that Ludwig gave Wagner. It took us twenty-six weeks to film and twenty-six weeks to edit (Fig. 3).

---

[6]Ludwig II (1854–1886) was King of Bavaria from 1864 until his death in 1886. Prior to German nationhood in 1871, Bavaria was an independent kingdom.

Fig. 3   Richard Burton and Tony Palmer on the set of *Wagner*

Do you see your Parsifal *as a kind of sequel to* Wagner?
I first did *Parsifal* on the stage for conductor Valery Gergiev in St. Petersburg. He had seen my *Wagner* and asked me to help restore Wagner, especially *Parsifal,* to the operatic repertory of the Mariinsky Theater. I had long thought I should do a "coda" to my *Wagner* film that would deal primarily with *Parsifal*. A lot of my ideas came from talking to Domingo. He narrates the film and, of course, appears in the operatic sections on stage. I wanted the myth of Parsifal to make sense to a Russian audience.

What do you mean by that?
Well, just as Wagner's work grew out of what he perceived as political shambles in Germany, so I wanted my film to speak to the chaos of contemporary Russian society. So we did it in terms of a Russian village that had awakened in the morning and then celebrated mass. The stage scenes you see in the film were extracted from my Mariinsky production. The Klingsor scenes were filmed in Italy, near Ravello, where Wagner had originally found his own inspiration.

You are quite concerned in the film with the whole subject of the Holy Grail.
The film includes a wonderful Biblical scholar named Karen Armstrong who tells us that the "Holy Grail" myth was invented in the thirteenth century; that it was a complete invention with no Biblical justification whatsoever. So, what does the symbol mean? She concludes that it is not a search for real truth at all, but a dangerous excuse that allows people to terrorize other people. We see examples of that in the interminable strife in Kosovo and the Middle East. Also, Wagner's great

biographer, Robert Gutman, whom we interviewed in the film, says that Wagner was after something very dangerous in his use of the Grail idea. Gutman points out that the story of Parsifal is about a small and diminishing band of knights whose leader, Amfortas, has been tainted by impure blood (he had sex with a non-Aryan). Thus, Parsifal's function is to come along and purify the blood. Gutman says he has no doubt that Wagner intended the ethnic cleansing of the pure German blood. And Hitler also believed that his mission was to purify the blood (Fig. 4).

Fig. 4 Marketing image for Tony Palmer's *Parsifal*

I can't help but note there are many erotic touches in your Parsifal.

Oh, you mean the underwater nudity! Well, that was only in the film! On stage, I do recall a great discussion we had about the behavior of the Flower Maidens. Six of them. They're seducing Parsifal, so I felt they had to be on the *move*, all the time; so there was that discussion. The Second Maiden, Anna Netrebko, agreed they could make it work. They were astonishing. They never stayed still for fifteen seconds. Once the scene got going in Act II, I told Domingo to just stand still while the Maidens were all over him!

On a more serious note, the political stance of your film is very clear at the end.

I took a lot of criticism for that. In the last scene you have Domingo facing the camera and saying that since the Second World War there have been eighty-five major wars, more refugees now than in the entire prior history of civilization, more people starving—facts we got from the United Nations. Then Domingo says that perhaps Wagner's anti-Semitism, unpleasant as that was, may have given us a clue in the text of the opera: that through redemption and suffering there is love. We filmed that in four different languages. I asked him if he realized that this is an overt political statement; was he sure he wanted to say this? But he insisted. It is, he told me, what *he* believed. And yet I was accused of putting these words in his mouth against his will. Rubbish! Unfortunately, the version first released on video was censored by the distributor, RM Associates. Domingo was furious. They should be ashamed of themselves. I vowed I would never work with them again.

Leif Ove Andsnes: "Grieg Was Restless, Wherever *He* Was!"

John C. Tibbetts

25 January 2005, Kansas City; and 12 June 2016, Bergen, Norway

Edvard Hagerup Grieg was introduced to the piano while still a child; later he studied at the Leipzig Conservatory. In 1861, Grieg made his debut as a concert pianist in Karlshamm, Sweden. He married his first cousin, a lyric soprano named Nina Hagerup, who pursued a successful musical career of her own. Both Liszt and Pytor Ilyich Tchaikovsky (1840–1893) praised Grieg's music, especially his celebrated Concerto in A minor for piano and orchestra. Grieg received honorary doctorates from Cambridge and Oxford, and in 1903 the Norwegian Government awarded him a pension: an unusual distinction at the time.

Born in 1970 in Karmoy, Norway, Leif Ove Andsnes (Fig. 5) **studied with Jiri Hlinka at the Bergen Conservatory and won his first major award, the Hindemith Prize, in 1987. Other prizes include the Norwegian Music Critics Prize in 1988, the Grieg Prize in 1990, the Deutsche Schallplattenkritik Award in 1991, the Dorothy B. Chandler Performing Arts Award in 1992, the coveted**

25. jan. 05

Talking about Grieg Best wishes,

Leif Ove Andsnes

Fig. 5 Leif Ove Andsnes, with Grieg in the background

***Choc du Monde de la Musique* magazine award (for his recording of the Brahms First Piano Concerto) in 1998, and the Norwegian Spellemannprisen in 2001.**

What follows is a conflation of two conversations—the first took place in Kansas City on the occasion of Andsnes's recital on the Harriman-Jewell Series; the second in Norway during the 2016 Bergen International Arts Festival.

JOHN C. TIBBETTS: Isn't Grieg your specialty?
LIEF ONE ANDSNES: The Grieg Concerto started it all for me here in Bergen. I was eighteen when I was asked to play it. It had such a *gravitas* that it was a

great honor for me. The Bergen Festival has a closing concert where that concerto is always performed. It always used to be the ending piece. In fact, I once heard a crazy concert where it followed a performance of the Mahler Ninth Symphony! Can you imagine? That's a very bad program. The funny thing was, I didn't really know the Concerto yet. Of course, I knew the opening chords, but I think that was very good, because I could feel every bar so freshly, so passionately. I didn't have any preconceptions of recordings in my head. Then, I made my American debut with the Cleveland Orchestra; and I played with the Berlin Philharmonic and everywhere with this piece. It's been a "door opener" for me, as it had been for Grieg himself. Sure, the music is sometimes simple in its childlike beauty, but it is never simplistic. It's never sentimental, never syrupy. I'll be playing and recording a lot of Grieg's music in the coming year. High on my list are the *Ballade* and the Sonata, two gigantic works that should be heard more often.

When I started out, I was careful to play not too many things. I wanted to master just those things that I was playing, particularly the Scandinavian composers. If Grieg's great friend, Rikard Nordraak had lived longer [he died at the age of twenty-four], he would have developed into an important composer, but at least he profoundly influenced Grieg in finding a specifically *Norwegian* expression in his music. And I played many of the smaller pieces by composer Agathe Backer-Grondahl [1847–1907] and others who are not well known outside Norway. After all, Norway is a young country. We only became independent in 1905, so I think it was important for our composers to find this nationalist expression in their music.

Apart from large-scale works such as the Concerto and the Third String Quartet, Grieg's best known works are perhaps the music from Peer Gynt *and a number of smaller solo piano pieces, including* Wedding Day at Troldhaugen *and* March of the Trolls. *They seem to pop up everywhere, in the soundtrack of Hollywood movies and cartoons, or in that notorious film bastardization of Grieg's life,* Song of Norway.

Yes! *Song of Norway*! Despite its awful reputation, it did bring a lot of music to millions of people. I think that's fine. The problem is that these "hits" have been used so often that it's hard to hear them anymore with a fresh ear. In our ignorance we think that his most popular piano piece, the *Wedding Day at Troldhaugen*, commemorates the silver anniversary of his marriage to Nina. But no, he had already composed this piece and called it "The Well-Wishers are Coming." People make a mistake when they hear in the middle section his thoughts about his wife. It's not true! He had someone else in mind when he composed it! But I always thought that the "Well-Wishers Are Coming" is the first and best way to describe the piece. It describes all of us who want to come to Troldhaugen and hear this music!

The piano pieces were very successful in Grieg's lifetime, you know. That's the reason he continued writing things like the *Lyric Pieces*. The first set is very much influenced by Mendelssohn's *Songs without Words*; but then it develops into a more Nordic language. Grieg has suffered from the sense that he's not seen as a "big" composer of big pieces. He had problems with the large forms. His fight with the material is part of the fascination. But he's not very advanced when it comes to counterpoint writing, as Brahms was. Nevertheless, his small pieces and his songs, for which he's not very well known (the reason for that is language, I think), the *Peasant Dances*, and the *Norwegian Folk Songs*, Opus 66 are amazing.

Grieg's sixty-six Lyric Pieces for piano span almost forty years of his life, from the first set, Op. 12, composed in 1866, to the Op. 71 set, composed in 1901 six years before his death. As you mentioned, they haven't always been admired. Debussy, for example, declared that they elicited "the bizarre and uncanny sensation of eating a pink bonbon stuffed with snow." And critic Eduard Hanslick dismissed Grieg himself as "a Mendelssohn sewed up in a sealskin."

You still hear that sort of thing. All I can say is, they are very forward looking, full of impressionistic atmospheres and chromatic adventures. Take something like *Bell-Ringing* from Book Five—it anticipates by almost twenty years Debussy's *La cathédrale engloutie* [The engulfed cathedral]. And in that last set of *Lyric Pieces*, Opus 71 you find harmonic language at its most advanced. But that was never Grieg's first priority. Some time late in his life, he said the most important thing in music is not originality, or novelty, but *truth in feeling*.

I understand you've played Grieg's own piano at his villa, Troldhaugen, where the composer lived from 1884 until his death in 1907.

I had gone to Troldhaugen before and played a few times and already knew the piano. Every time I had been there in earlier years I felt this piano is so right for this music. It's an 1892 Steinway, which had been presented to the composer by his wife, Nina, as a Silver Wedding gift. And it's been in the Grieg Museum at Troldhaugen ever since. He lived there for more than twenty years. Troldhaugen is just outside Bergen, on the west coast of Norway. It's about a twenty-minute drive from the center of the city. It's in a very beautiful surrounding, on top of a hill where you look out to the fjords and the islands. Outside the villa he had a little cottage where he composed, with just enough room for an upright piano and a desk. A very, very tiny place. And he would just sit there, looking out to the fjord. I'm sure it must have been very cold there at times, and probably the upright there was rather out of tune, too! He was such a small man. He used to sit on both volumes of the Beethoven sonatas to get high enough to reach the keyboard (Fig. 6)!

What other special qualities of Grieg's music continue to attract you?

Take something like *Homesickness*. [playing the piano] It's one of my favorites. Grieg is at his best in this, and in something else like the "Death of Ase" from *Peer Gynt*, where the harmonies makes you want to cry. Of course, there's an A-B-A form, which means the middle section is contrasting [or different music]. Here, it's *really* contrasting; and you can imagine Grieg thinking of home in this middle section, of a dance heard in the distance, from far away. I know of nothing quite like it in all of music.

Fig. 6 Grieg's Troldhaugen

[playing the piano] That's a Norwegian folk dance called a *halling*. The finale of the Piano Concerto, in particular, is dominated by the duple rhythms of the halling dance style. There's syncopation in the second bar, you see [playing], which makes it very folk-like. And there are plenty of examples of the halling everywhere in the *Lyric Pieces*. Grieg made piano transcriptions of famous peasant dances on the Hardanger fiddle, a folk instrument with four strings and four sympathetic strings under them. The beginning of "Morning" from *Peer Gynt* is derived from the open strings of the Hardanger fiddle. He used these intervals all the time, everywhere. When he was asked where his harmonies came from, he said he really couldn't separate the folk idioms from his own imagination.

[plays a passage from a piece called *Gone*] Toward the end of his life, Grieg became more and more chromatic. Even though he wasn't much influenced by Wagner, he did incorporate a lot of chromaticism. I've already mentioned similarities between some of Grieg's pieces and Debussy's.

What about the big pieces, the Ballade and the Sonata?
Well, the Sonata is early and is very much based on a sonata by the Danish composer Niels Gade [1817–1890], also in E minor. Gade was Grieg's teacher and gave him guidance. I love this piece. I think it's very beautiful, and I made a

recording of it in 1993 for the Grieg Anniversary. The Ballade is, of course, considered a major piece. Grieg said so himself. He wrote it after his mother died and it has this wonderfully beautiful, sad, melody. The title "Ballade" is misleading, by the way. It's actually variations on a little Norwegian folk song. You can feel he's struggling with the buildup. Grieg knew he was not a Beethoven or a Bach. He knew he couldn't build castles and palaces like them; but he wanted to build homes for people to feel comfortable in. That was his big gift. When he tried to write the bigger pieces, one feels this struggle.

Why, according to Grieg, are Norwegians never truly at home? I recall his famous remark that the Norwegian artist is a "strange bird," who one moment sings "Away! Away" and the next warbles "Home! Home!"
There is something right in that for many Norwegian artists. We are restless, wherever we are! Grieg was restless, wherever *he* was. He said no matter where he was his thoughts were always about Norway and Norwegians. But Grieg had a daughter that died, so he lost that kind of anchor. In those times Norway was far from other places he needed to go, so he tended to go on long tours for the whole winter. He longed to be back home, but when he came back he felt Bergen was much too provincial. We've made him such a symbol of Norwegian culture, but we still wonder *what that means*! Is he a nationalist; is he a cosmopolitan? Separate? At the same time? I wonder, why can't we have both?

Maureen Forrester: "Mahler Was a Man Who *Painted* Music"

John C. Tibbetts
1 January 1990, Kansas City, Missouri

A German-speaking Jew born in Bohemia, Gustav Mahler was celebrated during his lifetime more for his legendary conducting—for years he directed Vienna's Hofoper, arguably the most prestigious performance venue in Austria—than for his compositions. Shortly before he died Mahler completed his Ninth Symphony; he also served as conductor at the Metropolitan Opera in New York City. Louis Biancolli wrote that, "Mahler was the most uninhibited and subjective of composers. He conceals nothing from our ears—his nightmarish torments, his refuge in momentary illusions of joy, his shrill defiance of Providence." It was only after the removal in 1945 of the Nazi ban on his music, however, that his compositions were rediscovered and championed by his protegé, Bruno Walter, and a new generation of musicians and listeners, Leonard Bernstein and Maureen Forrester among them.

Born in Montréal, contralto Maureen Kathleen Stewart Forrester (1930–2010) left school at thirteen to help support her family. Celebrated for her

On the occasion of singing
Mahler's "Das Lied von du Erde"

1-1-90

Fig. 7 Maureen Forrester

performances of Mahler's vocal music, she also sang at the Metropolitan
Opera in New York City and helped revive Handel's *Giulio Cesare* and other
less familiar works; she also appeared in productions of Wagner's music dramas. A longtime champion of Canadian composers, she served for five years
on the Canadian Arts Council, was inducted into the Canadian Music Hall
of Fame, and was made an Officer of the National Order of Quebec. Her

autobiography *Out of Character*, **co-authored with Marci McDonald, appeared in 1986** (Fig. 7).

   This conversation took place during Ms. Forrester's visit to Kansas City to perform Mahler's *Das Lied von der Erde* with the Kansas City Symphony Orchestra.

JOHN C. TIBBETTS: You've said you've performed The Song of the Earth *[Mahler's* Das Lied von der Erde] *virtually everywhere and with everyone.*
MAUREEN FORRESTER: That's just about right, everywhere in Europe, in the whole of America at various festivals. I won't say it's a "bread-and-butter" piece, because it's a very long work and rather challenging for audiences; and the last song, by itself, is almost a half hour long.

Let's talk about that for a moment. Why don't we begin with that last song? What is an "Abschied" and what has it got to do with this piece?
It's a "Farewell," of somebody in touch with destiny. There's a rider somewhere off in the distance coming to take you somewhere else. The music says, *"ewig, ewig, ewig"*—"forever, forever, forever"—

And you sing it over, and over, and over...
It's very moving, that ending. It touches people so, because one is born and one dies, although you hope you'll live a long time! I think it is not Mahler turning to God, but to the earth itself. I think about that all the time. Here I am, going to be sixty in July, mind you, and I'm making my debut at La Scala in June [1990]. I think it's wonderful, playing an eighty-five-year old woman who dies in Tchaikovsky's *Queen of Spades*, which we do in Russian. If I can't be a heroine in an opera, at least I can get a "death scene."

Isn't it wonderful that you still have debuts to come!
I've sung on stage at La Scala, of course, many times with orchestra in concerts, but never [yet] in an opera.

People might wonder why we began this conversation with the closing music of Song of the Earth. *But don't you think it's important for us to know about that ending as we go into the piece? Because for Mahler it was a kind of penultimate "swan song."*
Yes, although that song doesn't really relate to the other songs.

Please take us through the sequences of the songs.
There are six individual songs, three for tenor and three for alto. The first one is a drinking song for tenor [*Das Trinklied vom Jammer der Erde*]. The second is my first song, a lonely song about autumn [*Einsame im Herbst*]—"Sun of love, will you never shine again?"—and it is very moody, very beautiful. The third one [*Von der Jugend*] is also for me, and it's about youth, it's light and charming, friends chattering around a little pool. The fourth and fifth are like folk songs. And the

last, as I said, is the famous "Farewell" and says that although Death is imminent, Spring is coming, "Forever and forever." It ends in C major. The two middle songs are both for tenor. They are very difficult and very high, and I'm certain [the late] John Gilmore is equipped to sing them, because I've sung the cycle with a lot of young people who *attempt* to do it, which is the best one can say. It really needs two tenors, a lyric tenor and a *Heldentenor* [heroic tenor], but John does it very well.

It might surprise some of us who think of Mahler as a very Central European composer to know that he's dealing in Das Lied *with Chinese texts.*
It's wrong to think those texts are translated from the Chinese. They're from a book by a guy who paraphrased versions of some [eighth-century] Chinese poems that had already been translated [by Hans Bethge]. Mahler saw in them a chance to *paint* music with many, many moods and many colors in his orchestration. While many others would just write a wonderful theme with a simple accompaniment, he makes of every instrument a solo voice. If you close your eyes, you can hear the themes pass from instrument to instrument, even the harp, the bassoon, the oboe, the flute; and every musician has to have a good night's sleep before he plays it! Everybody is very important to this piece. Technically, every mistake shows.

Your association with Mahler brings us to your work with Mahler's great friend and protégé, conductor Bruno Walter. How did you come to first meet him? Did you know from the beginning this was a career-making match?
You know, I started singing in church choirs in Montréal; music was just something I *did*. I never wanted to be a professional singer. I just sing to myself all the time, at home, on the street. People must stop in the street, and say, "There goes that crazy woman who talks to herself all the time!" But I am just humming next week's work! [laughs] But I like my work. And when I finish my career, I'll still sing; it's just a part of me. When I first auditioned for Bruno Walter, I didn't know anything of Mahler. But I had heard that Dr. Walter did, and my manager said, "Dr. Walter wants to hear you sing!" I just thought, oh, isn't that wonderful; it's just another audition. Everyone in Montréal was excited he was in town. I'll never forget meeting him. It was a Sunday evening in March. He asked me to prepare some Bach and Brahms.

You must have been terrified!
No, not at all. I thought of it as just another singing date. If it didn't go well, I still had to make a living somewhere else. So, I went down and met him. He was very kind. He wanted me to sing for him right away and so I sang the aria from Bach's *St. John Passion.* He told me later he made up his mind after just a few opening phrases. Then he asked me to sing something from Brahms's *Alto Rhapsody.* That had been a signature piece he did with Kathleen Ferrier. Immediately, Dr. Walter asked me, "Well, what are you doing next spring?" And I told him I was doing so-and-so, and I asked him, "Why?" And he said, "Because I want you to come

and sing for my last performance with the New York Philharmonic of Mahler's 'Resurrection' Symphony, and then later make a recording with me of Mahler's *Das Lied von der Erde*!" I said, "Oh! Gee, Dr. Walter, I'll see if I can change it! For you, I'll even drop dead!" That's how young I was. When word got out he wanted me to sing in the Mahler Second, every manager in New York wanted to take me on, because when Bruno Walter picked up a singer, it was like a stamp of approval.

It seems ironic that your contribution to the Resurrection Symphony *was quite brief, wasn't it?*
Yes, the *Urlicht* [primal or first light] is only about four minutes, but what a wonderful four minutes! I sang it—*"I am from God and will return to God"*—in 1957 with Dr. Walter and the New York Philharmonic at Carnegie Hall. We recorded it a few days later. When I first looked at my part, I wasn't very impressed. I wondered what all the fuss was about! It wasn't until I heard the full orchestra that I realized what depth it had. It's so moving, it really digs into you. I think I knew even then I would be singing Mahler for the rest of my life. That same year I first sang *Das Lied* with him. After that I started singing more Mahler, *The Songs of the Wayfarer* and the *Kindertotenlieder*. Dr. Walter wanted to record *Das Lied* with me, but my manager had just signed me to an RCA Victor contract and they wouldn't release me to sing with Dr. Walter, because he was with Columbia Records.

Talking with you here, now, I see a very happy and lively person ... not exactly somebody ideally suited to sing the mournful qualities in so much of Mahler.
I must tell you there is something in his pain and his nostalgia—and that sense of *melodrama*—that has always touched me. Maybe it's the reminder that not all of my own life has been a bed of roses. I don't dwell on it, but it's there. You know, you have to sit there on stage for such a long time through the first three movements before the solo in the fourth. The opening bars prepare me for memories that I otherwise keep stifled. They prepare me for what's to come.

Why do you think Mahler composed so much for the alto voice?
I knew he had had a terrible reputation with singers, as a tyrant, or something. But he gives a singer like me a chance to do things like those high *pianissimo* [very soft] phrases and many different rhythms. Mahler as a mostly sad composer, but there are a lot of "fun" things, like the *Des Knaben Wunderhorn* [The Boy's Magic Horn], which is wonderfully orchestrated and even silly at times. But yes, in his day, he was underrated and called "long-winded", but he did have a great sense of humor and sometimes must have had a twinkle in his eye.

Can you share an anecdote or two about insights Walter gave you about Mahler?
At the piano he mostly played and didn't talk very much, but I do remember there was a moment in the *Songs of a Wayfarer* that he said Mahler himself had explained to him. At the very beginning, there are bars of three, then four, alternating, changing tempo for quite awhile. That puzzled me. Dr. Walter explained

that Mahler had forgotten to indicate in the score that he wanted to convey that there were two parts in the scene: There was the wedding feast in a tavern, and there was the lovelorn wayfarer standing outside, watching his loved one marrying somebody else. Whenever I sing it now, I remember that, because that's what Bruno Walter said that Mahler intended. I also remember once him telling me to sing the music in a "masculine" way. That's the word he used, "masculine."

What is it about The Song of the Earth *in particular that has such special appeal for you?*
For one thing, I knew that Dr. Walter had been the first to perform it [in Munich in 1911]. Mahler had written it after his daughter's death. And he had just discovered his incurable illness. For me, it's also my favorite piece because, as a contralto, you're usually the "other woman" in an opera, some dying old hag, whatever. You never get to play the big roles. Mahler wrote a lot for either a low mezzo[-soprano] or contralto voice. And in *Song of the Earth*, in that last *Abschied,* you're standing on the stage and singing for a long time. It is quite a "sing," as I said. And the text really turns me on. It's full of regret and farewell and, at the same time, consolation. You have to be in good shape for it. It's very hard for youngsters to attack this work, because they don't have the staying power, to keep the voice fresh after the first ten minutes. Alas, I don't think Mahler ever heard it in public performance. He intended it to be his "Ninth" symphony, but not by that numbering. Maybe he was cheating fate by not officially numbering it as his "Ninth."

Besides Walter, you've worked with many other Mahler conductors.
Who have I *not* done Mahler with?! I've worked with many conductors, including Charles Munch. I recorded *Songs of a Wayfarer* with Dr. Munch. I remember that he didn't do a lot of Mahler, and when I arrived with the Boston Symphony to do *Songs of a Wayfarer* and *Kindertotenlieder*, he stood in front of the orchestra and said, "Madame, this is not really my music; I don't usually do Mahler; but you tell me what you want me to know and I'll do my best to work with you." That's a great man! Isn't that lovely? And I was a very young girl, about twenty-five or so, and for a man in his late sixties, maybe seventies, to admit that, I think that spoke very well for him.

Has that recording followed you over the years?
Yes, I was very young, very happy, very pregnant when I did *Songs of a Wayfarer* and the *Kindertotenlieder* with him; and the Boston orchestra has remained one of my very favorite orchestras. But now, I've lived a lot, I've had happiness, I've had sorrow, like everyone—life is a learning process—and I probably sing those songs quite differently now. I made that recording back in the mid-1950s, and I have to confess I haven't listened to it in a long time. [laughs] It's sometimes thought of as a man's story: about a young man who's had an unhappy love affair, so he wanders on and achieves a sense of resignation: "Well, no matter what you had in life, tomorrow is another day." But *Kindertotenlieder* is something else, because it talks about the death of children. But always, as in Mahler, it starts out with a

certain melancholy and sadness, but at the end you have, "I will be with them forever; those eyes up in the sky will be there, always. I know they're in their beloved
mother's arms."

Are Mahler's song cycles an extension of the traditional German Lieder *cycle?*
Oh, yes, *Wayfarer* is kind of a *Schöne Müllerin,* you could say, and maybe the
Kindertotenlieder, too. But *Song of the Earth*, as I said, he really wrote as a symphony, a vocal symphony with movements. They are not much related to each
other, like a *Lieder* cycle, where you have a continuing story. For me, most of it is
written in the right range for a contralto.

*And I would think a different kind of voice is needed for the more intimate Lieder
cycles.*
Oh, yes. All singers have their own way of explaining how they do what they do.
For me, singing is like weight-lifting. People ask, how can you make that "big"
sound? You use a different set of muscles if you pick up a tennis ball as opposed
to lifting a bowling ball. It's all in the diaphragm and the breath technique that
supports the sound. It's like picking up something heavy and placing it on a shelf,
which is to say, projecting the sound out to an audience. You can't sing *Lieder*
with the same muscles, so to speak, as for the heavy dark voice of a big Mahler
work. By contrast, when I do those brief songs, *Lieder*, every one is a test of shifting moods and intensities. I think of my head and shoulders and chest as a ball of
helium when I'm singing one of those songs, and that there's a little thread in the
middle, which I just *pull through*. But there's air all around.

Does the Lieder *recital play an important part in your career?*
I think the practice of the *Lieder* recital is dying out. This is a very sad thing.
Everybody wants to go for the big, brassy orchestra things. And always the same,
familiar things in the repertoire. I don't think enough young singers sing *new*
music. And too many want to go right into operas. They think they can do Lieder
when they're old. Let me tell you, doing a whole *Lieder* evening is much harder
than singing a whole opera! You're changing character, weight of the voice, every
five minutes. In an opera, you're one character with one main theme going through
the whole opera.

You're known as a champion of new composers.
Being a Canadian, I was for five years chairman of the Canadian Arts Council, and
I know the plight of the artist. I always program a Canadian work, especially when
I leave my country, and that's how I try to further the work of my contemporaries.
When I give a master class at a school, I'll ask the publishing company to send
copies of the Canadian works, and I'll put them at the back of the room and tell
the teachers to put down their names and have the publishers send copies to them.
Too many performers will not allow someone else to perform something written
for them—not until they're dead! That's silly.

Finally, do you feel limited, sometimes, in the choice of roles available to you?
I do a fair amount of opera. Of course, I do all these dying old ladies. I have to make you laugh, or I die! Never the bride! A Canadian, Paul Warrack, wrote this for me during a show, and I must say, it describes my whole life:

> You never let me play the bride,
> Although I've got a lot of passion;
> On stage it's always been denied
> A low voice is not in fashion.

And so on.

This should be printed and placed in every green room[7] and rehearsal hall!
It's my encore piece! It's a great piece: Never take yourself so seriously. Know what you can do and what you can't do.

Mark Markham: "The Music of the French Impressionists Is All About Sound!"

John C. Tibbetts
15 June 2017, Florence, Italy

The term "impressionism," borrowed from the visual arts for some of the music composed in France during the late nineteenth and early twentieth centuries, has been contested. Yet it's stuck for a long time and has generally been associated with musical "suggestions" of clouds, flowers, and pretty girls, as well as poetic compositional titles, harmonic ambiguity achieved through extensive use of unusual scales, augmented triads, half-diminished chords, parallel chord progressions, and ninth, eleventh, and even thirteenth major chords; (e.g., a C Major triad [C – E – G]—topped with a B, a D, or even an F). The most celebrated Impressionist composers are Achille-Claude Debussy and Joseph Maurice Ravel (1875–1937). Others include Henri Duparc (1848–1933), Grieg (although a Scandinavian composer), and Ernest Chausson (1855–1899). Some of Chopin's and especially Liszt's piano pieces have also been called "Impressionistic."

A native of Florida, and a graduate of the Peabody Conservatory in Baltimore (where he has also taught), pianist and voice coach Mark Markham (Fig. 8) **possesses an international reputation as a collaborator and a jazz as well as classical keyboard soloist. In 1987 Markham was appointed pianist of the Contemporary Music Forum in Washington, DC. For more than**

---

[7]A "green room" serves as a waiting room for musicians before and after a performance as well as during concerts when they're not called upon to perform.

twenty years he has been Jessye Norman's collaborator of choice, and he has worked with the Britten-Pears School and the Norfolk Chamber Festival of Yale University. Critics have described Markham's playing as "brilliant," "exquisitely sensitive," and "in full service to the music."

Fig. 8 Mark Markham

The conversation that follows took place during Markham's Summer 2017 tour of Tuscany, Italy.

JOHN C. TIBBETTS: This thing called "French Impressionism," what is it, exactly—a mood, a style, a perception? Something unique to French culture in the years between the nineteenth and twentieth centuries?
MARK MARKHAM: Yes, yes, and yes!

Painting and music seem to blur together! Seems hard to separate them.
Right. And don't forget about poetry. We want to lump them all together. We love our labels! They simplify things. But that label gets us into trouble. We think we know that Ravel and Debussy are *the* "Impressionist" composers. Maybe. I'm no historian, but the better I know them, and the more I consider other French composers of their generation, easy definitions fall apart. I do know that Ravel and Debussy both hated the term, and conservative composers like [Camille] Saint-Saëns [1835–1921] hated *them*. Ravel's teacher, Gabriel Fauré [1845–1894], is more a classicist than an Impressionist. And one of Ravel's favorite painters was not an Impressionist but the eighteenth-century classicist [Jacques Louis] David [1748–1825]. What about stodgy old César Franck and brash young Emanuel Chabrier [1841–1894]? Chausson and Georges Bizet [1838–1875] died prematurely, before the end of the nineteenth century. [Érik] Satie [1866–1925]—well, who was *he*, really? He cared little about conventions and went his own way. These composers roughly all occupy the same time frame, and of course they were all French. To say everything they wrote can be described as "Impressionistic"?— of course not. You couldn't even say that of Debussy, who is most closely associated with the term Impressionism. Early Debussy is not much like late Debussy, which goes from a sensuous sound to a more austere [style of] expression. And Ravel's life and music are very different from Debussy's, in many ways.

Their Paris was a different place before the Franco-Prussian War and after World War I.
Right. Politics, culture—a volatile mix! The influence of late German Romanticism is in question. Wagner—you love him, you hate him. But you can't entirely get away from him. "Realism" is not just a copy of life, but a matter of the senses. Debussy is a "realist," at least in the sense that, like the painters [Pierre-Auguste] Renoir [1841–1919] and [Claude] Monet [1840–1926]. he is fascinated by atmosphere, light, and color in nature. Music is not a collection of rules but a search for the sheer *sensuousness* of sound.

It must have been an unusual time, where painters and composers were influencing each other.
That's difficult to know, precisely. Maybe it's more for the historian and the academic to know, than for the artist. But something called "impressionism" was in the air as a short-hand term for what's happening. And we shouldn't forget a new interest in Spanish and Russian music. That was going on, too.

Let's back up for a moment. What were your own first experiences with French music?
My first French piano piece was the *Prélude* to Debussy's *Suite Bergamasque* [1903]. I was twelve. I grew up in the Deep South, in the town of Pensacola, Florida. There was a great musical community there. I won't describe that piece as exactly a "Eureka" moment, but I sensed this strange combination of a "classical" sound with a kind of *fantaisie*, too. I knew even then that I have found "shoes" I can walk in. *So, let's walk!*

And I guess you kept "walking," as you say, in your later studies?
[laughs] I owe so much to Ann Schein at Peabody. She studied with Artur Rubinstein, who had so many connections with the French musical tradition. She's a wonderful pianist.

Did she, or anybody else, connect you with French music?
Well, we all knew about [pianist] Marguerite Long, whose devotion to Ravel is legendary. She knew him and toured with him. She premiered his *Le Tombeau de Couperin* [1917] and his G Major Piano Concerto [1932].

Did Long also know Debussy?
Yes, she studied with him in the years just before his death; but she said on several occasions she didn't really understand his music. She didn't make many recordings, which is a shame. But we know she had a wonderful sound and has become an example for us, particularly with Ravel.

Meanwhile, as a pianist, you've not only performed things like the Ravel Concerto, but also acquired a reputation as an authority on piano accompanying ...
... or *collaborating*, more exactly. My dissertation was on the piano writing of the songs of Francis Poulenc [1899–1963]. I looked at all the different ways that he exploited the piano throughout his career. That's just a part of my interest in the evolution of piano writing for the *mélodie*, which we can trace back to Berlioz, who hated the piano, and later to Fauré, Duparc, Ravel, and Debussy, who *loved* the piano and transformed it into an essential *partner* of the poetic text. And on to Olivier Messiaen. I've always had a strong interest in Messiaen. He stands in a direct line from Ravel and Debussy, yet crafted his own distinctive sound. I've performed almost all his vocal music.

Can we talk specifically about the relationship specifically between Ravel and Debussy? Where do we start?
They were so different, in so many ways. Debussy is the more important composer, I feel, because he points the way to Modernism. He leaves behind the French sensibility, which is a kind of *herd* instinct. It is very rare that someone actually breaks out of that, like Debussy did. Debussy's music has more warmth, is more visceral, than Ravel's, which is incredibly refined in all ways. Debussy was a burly guy and a hedonist. Ravel was slight in build and intensely private,

something of a loner. He was a very shy person and he kept everything inside of him. I think this comes out in his music. You always sense in Ravel a *concealment*, an underlying sadness. And there's more of a *control* factor than in Debussy. Even in his ballet *Daphnis et Chloé* [1912], or in *La Valse* [1919], Ravel is very much in control. He once said, "I am Basque and feel things violently"; but then he was quick to add, "but I hide it."

Did they know each other?
Of course, and they respected each other, but I believe there was some sort of falling out later over a dispute with their mutual friend, Erik Satie.

Can we identify a few things their music has in common?
Okay, let's talk about a kind of *stasis* in their work. No wonder they rejected Wagner, whose music is all about tension and release. Their music is all about *sound*. We think of Debussy, always moving back and forth around dissonant seventh and ninth chords, moving four [beats] against three, blurring tonalities. That leaves things floating in the air. And it can leave the pianist sometimes afloat, too! All those double sharps and double flats. It's exhausting! But the results! Think of those most important works from those amazing years, 1895–1905, the opera *Pelléas et Mélisande*, the *Prelude to the Afternoon of a Faun,* and *La Mer* [The Sea]. Everything changed after Debussy's *Pelléas*! There was no looking back!

In my opinion, Ravel's music from this time belongs in that same company.
Oh, yes. I've performed his *Sheherazade* song cycle [1903] with Jessye Norman many times. And there's the *Rapsodie espagnole* [1907], where the sensuousness of the *sound* is intoxicating. Perhaps, though, we find the really essential Ravel in those little piano pieces he wrote at this time, the *Miroirs* [1904]. They're beautifully crafted, tightly controlled miniatures, mostly descriptive of nature.

This must be the first time anybody wrote music about moths!
You mean the *Noctuelles*, sure. You hear the flutterings of moths as they flicker in and out of the light; and the strange *oiseaux triste* or "sad birds," which has an entirely different kind of pulse. I mean, what are "sad birds"? Another piece, *Une bateau sur l'océan* [A boat on the ocean] has more water in it, so to speak, which is all about the [soft] pedal, which muffles all the edges. But again, even here, everything is all very *private,* somehow. Even in the larger G Major Piano Concerto you find this really private Ravel in the second movement. There's an almost Mozartean clarity that conceals its heart. It's terrifying to play. It's *too there*.

You mentioned the use of the piano's [sustaining] pedal. It's very important to both men, yes?
That's tricky. You can start with the fact that Ravel will use very little [sustaining] pedal in his *Sonatine* [1905], allowing every note to achieve crystal clarity. Debussy, though, in pieces like the *Bruyère* [Community; from the *Préludes*, Book

Two, 1913], asks to have the [sustaining] pedal [pushed] all the way down. But even saying that is too simplistic. This pedal [shouldn't] always go all the way down. There are so many gradations. Your foot has to move according to your *ear*. You might push it down three-quarters, and let up only a bit; or all the way. And there's the middle pedal. I'm using it a lot. It's a big question, did Debussy and Ravel know about the middle pedal and did they use it? It did exist at the time; we're sure of that. You can do many things with it. In things like Ravel's *Alborado del gracioso* [from the *Miroirs*], there are a lot of places with a held chord and pizzicatos. Without the middle pedal, there is no way to do it. You can hold a chord with the middle pedal and you have a little pizzicato in the left hand.

We hear a lot about both composers using pentatonic and whole-tone scales.
That's where the influence of Russian music comes in. In the whole-tone scale there's a whole step between each note. You don't have these leading tones anymore. There's always a full step between them. The pentatonic scale[8] creates a sense of *float*, which is not what you find in Germanic music, but in Asian music, which is very *freeing*, harmonically. Liszt at the end of his life was already going into these things. His late piece *Nuages gris* is a great example. This is maybe helps explain where the word "impressionism" comes from, something that is more *suggested* than declared.

Were Debussy and Ravel both superior pianists?
I've always loved what Debussy said when he was asked about how to play his music: "Play so that you forget that the piano has hammers!" In the beginning he and Ravel were exceptional pianists; but in his later years, Ravel was ill and didn't play so well.

Have you traveled much to the places where these composers lived and worked?
If you want to understand and perform these composers [s music], you [need to] go where they lived and *feel* the world they lived in. I lived in France twelve years. You know, the light in France is not the same light as in Germany. The weather is not the same as in Italy. Money is never discussed; that is only an American thing. And how they control their *language*, what is *in* and what is not. They're always meeting and talking about the French language. That's a level of control that is mind-boggling. They're very serious about it. A great example is how they regard the French *mélodie*. In contrast to the German *Lieder*, which are transposed all the time to suit the singer's specific vocal range, French songs are written in a *particular key* and for *only* that key. And they are very gender-specific. You don't replace male with female, or female with male. You don't transpose down a fifth. No, what you have is what the composer wanted. That way everybody in every vocal range is not taking the same bloody song and putting it in any key they want. That's great!

---

[8]Or "five-note" scale. On C the five notes are C, D, E, G, and A.

Let's conclude with some observations about how Debussy and Ravel lived. Have you seen their homes?

I have not yet tried to find Debussy's home in the Bois de Boulogne neighborhood of Paris, where he lived with Emma Bardac in the years before his death. His domestic arrangements, unlike Ravel's, were scandalous and pretty messy, you know. But I understand he lived rather fashionably at the time and kept a well-ordered studio. I have seen the two accessible Ravel houses. The house where he was born, in Ciboure in Basque country, has nothing much to see. But the house at Montfort l'Amaury, where he spent time near the end of his life, has been left the way it was. To walk into the house, to see the rooms, to see the piano, to see how things are placed—.

I understand that Ravel's favorite toys and glass objects are still there, in his house.

Yes, you can see all of that. He loved miniature things, mechanical toys. They remind you of his empathy with the world of children, of those tiny musical worlds we hear, for example, in the *Mother Goose Suite* [1908]. (You know, as lovely as is his orchestral version, I still prefer the piano original). And there were hundreds of tiny glass things, Spanish and Japanese things. It's very moving to see them. He didn't have many friends, you know; I don't even think there was ever a lover or mistress. But here, they seem to "tell" us so much about him. You find all the artificialness and the intensity that mark so much of his music.

Rudolf Firkušňy: "My Duty as a Musician Is to Do the Best I Can for My Country by Playing Czech Music"

John C. Tibbetts
3 November 1985, New York City

Bohemian, Moravian, and Silesian composers and performers have made tremendous contributions to Central European music. Long before there was a "Czechoslovakia" (a post-World War I nation, put together from parts of the defeated Austro-Hungarian Empire) or a "Czech Republic" (a nation that separated itself from what is now Slovakia after the Soviet Union collapsed at the beginning of the 1990s), Czech and Moravian culture gave the world the Bohemian polka, the cimbalom, teachers, and composers such as Czerny, and the music of Heinrich Biber (1644–1704), Antonin Dvořák (1841–1904), Bedřich Smetana, Jan Stamic (1717–1757),[9] and a host of other creative geniuses.

---

[9]In previous generations, Czech and Slovak proper names were often "Germanized": thus "Jan Stamic" became "Johann Stamitz." Today Czech and Slovak names are more often spelled in their original forms.

Fig. 9   Rudolf Firkušńy

When **Rudolf Firkušńy** (Fig. 9) **returned to Prague in 1990, after a self-im-
posed forty-four year exile in protest of Communist oppression, he was
greeted as a returning hero, a patriot and a poet-statesman. Firkušńy held
the Czech Republic's highest civilian honor, the Order of Tomas G. Masaryk.
Born in Napajedla, a Moravian village, Firkušńy studied with Alfred Cortot,
composer Leoš Janáček, and Artur Schnabel. In 1939 Firkušńy fled to Paris to**

escape the Nazis; later he became an American citizen. After receiving an honorary doctorate from Charles University in Prague. He observed that, although he was "just a piano player," he joined philosophers and artists in the "eternal search at every step for the meaning of things."

This conversation took place in Firkušńy's apartment in New York City; his wife Tatiana was also present.

JOHN TIBBETTS: It seems the neighbors [in your building] complain about the "noise" of your piano playing.
RUDOLF FIRKUŠŃY: I didn't have this problem for a long time, but now new neighbors live under me and they don't like the sound of my practicing. We'll have to do some readjustment to deaden the sound. Of course, now I can't play nights, and I can't start mornings before 9:00 and not too much on weekends. But I was relatively lucky until this last time when I had trouble with the neighbors.

Please talk about your upbringing in Brno and the man who greatly influenced your life, Leoš Janáček.
I was only five when I first met Janáček. That was in 1917. Janáček lived in Brno. Looking back, I realize how much has changed since then. I still remember kerosene lamps in the houses in the village. And draught horses delivered beer barrels. I remember one day my mother took me to a parade, and the sounds the marching bands really thrilled me. I felt my whole body moving to the music. There was a woman standing next to us who told my mother that I seemed very taken with the music. Why couldn't I be given some music lessons? I started playing the piano. I just liked to play, and I was very desperate because I wanted to be better. I wanted a teacher, but because I was very young, nobody wanted to take me. They said, "Wait until he goes to school and then we will see." Then, finally, I met a musician who was not a piano teacher but a flute player in the Brno orchestra. He told my mother that he would give me some lessons. Nobody in my family knew anything about music—my father had died—so he took me and we started my first piano lessons: how to put the hand on the piano and how to read the music.

How would you describe yourself as the boy that was?
I was a bit spoiled! I had a good memory; and I always played at home what I heard. This was during the War. I remember telling my mother that I didn't have to take lessons anymore, since I now knew how to play the piano! But a man came and said, "This child seems to be talented. It would be a good idea to see an authority about his true talent." The greatest musical authority in Brno was Janáček. My mother thought if it could be arranged, why not? But she was warned that he might be very unpleasant and difficult. He didn't have the best reputation as a patient man—he had quite a bit of temper.

What do you remember of that meeting?
He gave me a real audition, like he would give any normal student. He said I had absolute pitch, and he examined my hands very carefully, so there was no trouble

about that. Then he asked me some general questions, and then I played for him a tune from one of his operas. He decided I am talented and he told my mother, "Look, this child has a great talent for music. If you trust me, I am willing to take him under my guidance and guide his musical development." That is how it started.

He played the last movement from [Beethoven's] *Moonlight* sonata. He was a very good pianist, by the way. He didn't play very much, except for himself; but when he did he had a very nice touch, very soft, gentle. The only thing to know is that Janáček was quite fond of *rubato*.[10] He liked freedom. He found a teacher for piano for me, because he decided the teacher I had before was no good. And I took lessons with him in theory and harmony and you name it. Then of course he became friendlier, because he was extremely fond of me.

Were you a precocious student?
No, I was not a child prodigy. Janáček was known to dislike child prodigies. I had just been playing for pleasure the way other children played with their toys. He was extremely nice and full of attention for a small child, which was rather surprising. I loved him, even though as a child I didn't realize how great and famous he was. I almost thought of him as a kind of father. He took a great interest in everything about me—and not only in musical terms, but in my financial situation and in doing things for me.

Was he a strict teacher?
I think he was a man of great curiosity. He wanted to see the development of a child, you know; perhaps for him I was an interesting experiment in a way. I was his "project." I was practically nursed with his music from the very beginning. His teaching was very unorthodox and individual. He wrote an interesting book about harmony, you know, which is quite extraordinary, because it is very close to Schoenberg, although Janáček didn't know of Schoenberg at the time. This harmonic method was not accepted at the Brno Conservatory because they thought it was much too advanced.

When did you get to know his music? Did he share that with you?
Yes, we played his music together; and when he had a new score coming he asked me to play four hands with him. I remember studying his scores with him, like his First String Quartet. He was inconsistent about how he wanted his music played. One day he would tell me one thing, another day something else. He was also interested in the music of his contemporaries—[Vítězslav] Novák [1870–1949], [Josef] Suk [1874–1935], Karel Jirák [1891–1972], and the Slovaks [Alexander] Moyzes [1906–1984] and [Eugen] Suchoň [1908–1993]—although he always

---

[10]With rhythmic freedom. *Rubato* is often employed in Romantic piano music, less often in Classical and modern music.

loved most of all the music of Dvořák. Automatically, of course, I knew I would play his music all my life: one, because I love his music; and two, because I owed it to him. I had the advantage in my youth of hearing Janáček's music in the narrow circle of his students before it was known more widely. For a long time it was not especially recognized internationally. Even in Czechoslovakia I was one of the first that started to play his music all the time. Now he's an established figure on the international scene; everybody's playing it. The only trouble is that he didn't write very much for piano.

How long did you continue your study with him?
At one point, he decided I should go to the Conservatory, so I ceased to visit him as a student. I continued to visit him just to play his works. I saw him for the last time in June 1928. He died in August 1928. At that time I was studying harmony, counterpoint at the Conservatory. My professor in Prague was Vilém Kurz, who was a student of Jakub Virgilius Holfeld. He had been in turn a pupil of Josef Proksch; and one of Proksch's students was the young Smetana. Through Kurz I learned the Dvořák tradition. Kurz had had direct contact with Dvořák and knew his concepts of the pieces. And from Suk, my composition teacher (and Dvořák's son-in-law), I learned more about Dvořák interpretation.

You were in a position to learn and perform directly from Janáček some of his greatest works. I think we share a particular love for the cycles On an Overgrown Path [1901–1912] …
Indeed we do! I must tell you, when I was young and started my career, I was a Czech pianist living in Czechoslovakia, and I felt a strong obligation to do something for the music of my country. Unfortunately, though, most of the piano music of the great Czech composers has not been popular. The "Overgrown Path" is full of intimate pieces. They are small pieces, actually written originally for [the small organ called a] harmonium, not for piano. The harmonium by this time was a more popular instrument. The schools in the small villages didn't have a piano, but they had a harmonium. Sometimes even in the church. You know, he lost his daughter Olga when she was about twenty-one years old. Some of these pieces were written as recollections of the days they spent together and of those days after she died. So they are very intimate, extremely personal. Also, the titles somehow are very poetic, I think: *Our Evenings, A Blown-Away Leaf, The Barn Owl Has Not Flown Away.* There is a folk tale associated with *The Barn Owl Has Not Flown Away.* In Czech folk stories an owl appears near the house when somebody is going to die. And that's the reason the last piece has an owl that doesn't fly away. Janáček told me to play it rapidly, to "try to chase away the owl!" He also told me to play the arpeggios at the end very loud—again, as if to drive away the owl. In another piano piece, *In the Mist* [1912], he comes back to that theme of the owl. You know, the word 'mist' is not a mist in the real sense of the word, it's the more psychic, interior mist. Janáček was having a difficult time in his life, with much illness, but was starting somehow to see the light at the end of the tunnel. But still, this music is not quiet, you know? It is full of struggle. The work had such a big meaning for Janáček. I played it for him and he gave me ideas about it.

The Piano Sonata [1905] *has a peculiar title ...*
Yes, *From the Street: 1 October, 1905.* This sonata is one of the first important
pieces Janáček wrote for piano. The city where he lived at the time, Brno, was pre-
dominantly German. Czechs were a minority. Janáček was a very great patriot and
a passionate Czech. He resented the Germans; so much so he wouldn't take the
streetcars because the stops were [printed] in German. He helped the resistance to
preserve Czech culture. Well, the Austrian government sent an army of soldiers to
the rally, and they killed one man, a simple working man. Janáček was impressed
by the idea that a simple man gave his life for the idea of higher teaching. He
was inspired to write this piece in the man's memory. Sometimes his music looks
like it might be a little bit rough, even brutal in a way. But he never liked it like
that. He preferred that everything be lyrical. Originally it was in three movements
called *Street Scene*; but he destroyed the third movement.

*You said that Janáček loved Dvořák. I know you have recorded a lot of Dvořák's
piano music. What are your favorites?*
Although Dvořák wrote quite a great deal of music for piano—I play quite often
the *Theme and Variations* [1876] and sometimes the *"American" Suite* for piano
[1894]—to tell the truth, the other pieces, charming and lovely as they are, are all
small pieces. The *Poetic Pieces* [1889] are nice, but they're quite difficult to make
an interesting selection from them. The Piano Concerto [1876] is another matter.

We weren't hearing the Concerto until you began playing it after World War II.
Actually, I had been engaged earlier by Sir Thomas Beecham to play it in London
in 1939, but when the Germans invaded Czechoslovakia, I was unable to meet
the engagement. But I had the orchestral and piano parts and I brought them to
America a year later. I played it with Beecham at the Ravinia Festival. It was this
performance that not only helped launch my career in this country but also, at long
last, spurred interest in Dvořák's neglected opus.

It's always been a personal thing for me. I was practically the only person who
played it at the time. It is not a concerto in the way of a virtuoso concerto; it is a
symphony, and the orchestra is very important and it is beautifully orchestrated.
It is a very, very difficult work—what you call non-pianistic. But my teacher,
Mr. Kurz, decided he would "improve" it with more flashy writing. And he did a
good job, changing little of it, really. I played it in the beginning in this version,
because that was how I had learned it from him. I didn't get the original version
until much later. By then I decided that the only way to play it was the Dvořák
way. I played it when I returned to Prague after the War for the 1946 Festival, with
Rafael Kubelik conducting.

And we can't leave out Smetana! Talk about difficulty! Those Czech Dances ...
Wow!
[laughs] I loved Smetana very much. He was our national composer. In a way, he
was even more than a composer. He was a kind of national prophet, a symbol of

the new Czechoslovakia. Smetana was a wonderful pianist and wrote beautiful, virtuoso works for the piano. Yes, the *Czech Dances* make great demands upon the technique. But again, Smetana didn't write a sonata, a really major work. He wrote dances, polkas, short pieces. Always the problem is where to put them on a program? I tried putting all the dances on a program once, but I found it was not such a good idea. It was too much of a good thing. Like trying to play all the mazurkas of Chopin at one time. And I always am very unhappy that Smetana didn't write a Piano Concerto. Because he wrote a beautiful piano part in his G-minor Trio.

By the late 1930s you were traveling a lot, weren't you?
Yes, this was one summer shortly after Hitler took over Germany. At Lake Como I met George Szell and his great friend, Artur Schnabel. Maestro Szell wanted me to perform with him; but I reminded him he had never heard me play. He said that Schnabel had told him about me and that was good enough for him! From that moment, we clicked, and we grew extremely fond of each other, playing together in Scotland, America, everywhere. Since I was already shaped by the time we worked together, we worked as equals. We never disagreed, actually; even when there was a matter to discuss, we did so in a very civilized way.

When did you first come to America? Did you play Czech music there?
That was in 1938 for my first American tour. I felt it more necessary to perform music from American and South and Central America. I gave premieres of American works by Howard Hanson [1896–1981], Samuel Barber [1910–1981], and Gian-Carlo Menotti [1911–2007].

You spent time with Bohuslav Martinů during those American years, didn't you? Were you playing his music at that time?
Yes, but I already knew him from Prague at the Conservatory, and we were together in Paris in the early 1930s. And our friendship deepened during our stay in the United States during World War II. I premiered many of his piano works, either in private or in concert. The greatest gift he ever gave me was his *Fantaisie et Toccata*, which he had written a little earlier, in Aix-en-Provence, while we were waiting to leave Occupied France for the United States. It was an anxious time for us. We had arrived in New York practically empty-handed.... Martinů was one of my closest friends, and he lived next door when I was living in Prague. We were together every day, practically, and everything he wrote for piano I played.

How did your music sustain you during all those years away from Czechoslovakia?
For me as a musician, this was the only means of expressing disagreement with the situation in my country, of protesting the totalitarian subjugation of my homeland, and—to paraphrase [statesman] Vaclav Havel [1936–2011]—the only way to avoid playing according to the rules of a game I detested.

What must you have felt, coming back to Prague! What did you play?
There was never any question that I would play Martinů's Second Piano Concerto!
Martinů was a very dear friend of mine, and he was writing this concerto for me. I
had performed it for the first time in Prague. And Martinů hoped to go back to his
native country. Unfortunately, he wasn't able to; because when he was supposed
to come in 1946 he had a very bad accident that made him miserable for a long
time. And then of course the Communist administration began. Finally, he died.
I'm proud to tell you that after a performance of his music, President Václav Havel
led the crowd in a standing ovation.

Did you meet friends who still remembered you?
It was a great emotional event. Coming back after forty-four years of absence is
not easy. I realized fully that I would not find anyone from my generation, or very
few; so I really was going to a "new land." For many years, you see, I was taboo—
they weren't allowed to hear about me or my activities. But my reception was
absolutely overwhelming, the greatest welcome I ever had. And from the young
people, which made me doubly happy. When I went to Prague for the rehearsal
to the Hall with the Czech Philharmonic, which had all new people, you know—
no more old timers—it seemed that nothing had changed: I played my 'A' so the
orchestra could tune, and we started. It was like coming home.

Did you see yourself as a political figure?
I was never a statesman. I was never interested in internal politics. I was a musician. I served the music. I decided that being a musician, my duty is to do the best
I can for my country by playing Czech music. That is all I did. Nothing more. I
hope that I achieved some kind of result that the Czech music became more popular and better known than it was before.

It's such a pleasure to see you here. In your home element!
I'm happy to say that, because of this centenary of Dvořák's American visit—and
thanks to Dr. Botstein [president of Bard College], who had the idea to put Dvořák
at the center of this Festival—the time has come. It's been long overdue. I am so
happy that I could participate. Not only as a tribute to Dvořák, but to the others
who followed him. The programming was absolutely first rate, including Czech
composers like [Zdeněk] Fibich [1850–1900] and Novák—who no one had ever
heard of—and who may eventually become more in demand. All of the composers represented here—Novák, Martinů, Janáček, Suk—I knew them all! So many
memories ...

Yet so much yet to come!
[flashing an impish grin] No time to sit down and look back on my achievement.
Because I am a musician and because I love music, I always know there is a long
way to go.

György Sándor: "Bartók Was a Colossal Musician; I Owe Him a Great Deal"

John C. Tibbetts
November 1988, New York City; and 18 August 1995, Bard College

Born in Nagyszentmiklós, then part of the Kingdom of Hungary (and since 1920 known as Sannicolau Mare, now part of Rumania), Béla Viktor János Bartók learned how to play the piano at a surprisingly early age. Later he studied at the Liszt Academy of Music in Budapest with István Thomán, himself a pupil of Liszt. Bartók was a superb pianist, the composer of six of the most important twentieth-century string quartets and of much of its best keyboard music. In Budapest Bartók met Zoltán Kodály (1882–1967), a lifelong friend; in 1909, working with Kodály, Bartók became one of the founders of modern ethnomusicology. Despising the Nazis (he stopped concertizing in Germany after Hitler came to power), he fled Hungary and in 1940 settled in New York City. Among Bartók's last works were an important ethnomusicological study, *Serbo-Croatian Folk Songs*, and four masterpieces, including the *Concerto for Orchestra* and the Third Piano Concerto.

Born in Budapest, pianist György Sándor (1912–2005; Fig. 10) studied with Bartókand Kodály, then became an American citizen in 1940, ten years after making his concert debut. During World War II, Sándor served in the U.S. Signal Corps. He taught at Southern Methodist University, then from 1961– 1981 at the University of Michigan, and after 1982 at Juilliard. Sándor's recordings of Bartók's complete piano works for Vox won him a *Grand Prix du Disque* in 1965. In 1996 New York University gave him an honorary doctorate.

   What follows is a conflation of several conversations that began in 1988, in Sándor's New York City apartment, and concluded during the 1995 "Bela Bartok Festival" held at Bard College.

JOHN C. TIBBETTS: You studied with Bartók at the Franz Liszt Academy of Music in Budapest. How did that come to pass?
GYÖRGY SÁNDOR: I was eighteen when I gave my first public concert in Budapest and was supposed to be taught by the Academy's director, [Ernst von] Dohnányi [1877–1960]. But Dohnányi was unavailable at the time, so I turned instead to Bartók. He agreed to accept me as a pupil, but because his own schedule was full, he offered to see me on a private basis. I think he welcomed me because I was already studying composition with his great friend Kodály. So, I visited him on a weekly basis in his apartment in the Kavics ucca in Buda.[11]

---

[11]Budapest became a single city in 1873, when Buda was joined by Buda and Óbuda (both on one side of the Danube) and Pest (on the other side).

Fig. 10 György Sándor, with Bartók in the background

Who were some of the other students in those years?
There was the conductor, Georg Solti. He was a terrific pianist, a student of Zoltán
Székely and Dohnányi. I must say, I'm really the only student of Bartók's who's
internationally active in concerts. I was one of his last students.

What do you remember about Bartók's manner, his style of teaching, etc.?
Let me put it this way: I would say that most of what I know about music, not
necessarily just piano playing, I have thank Bartók. At first I hardly dared to speak,
and he was also silent for much of the time. It was mostly with music that we
communicated. At first, I would play something for him by Mozart or Brahms, or
Liszt—or some of his own, more accessible pieces—and without any comment,

except, "Good, good, Mr. Sándor," Then he would sit down and play me his own interpretation. Anything he touched, he performed in his own personal way. He was very spontaneous and very imaginative. I learned a great deal. He was one of the greatest pianists of his day, a phenomenal pianist.

You said you played his simpler pieces at first. When did you take on the harder work?
It was only in my third year that I learned things like his Piano Sonata [1926]. In those days, few of us understood Bartók's music. The Piano Sonata I didn't understand at all. But after months and months with him, I began to understand and feel what he meant in his music. I have included much of what I know in my book, *On Piano Playing* [1981].

What do you say to those who said Bartók was a rather cold and humorless person, and that his music was harsh, even brutal?
Bartók was an extremely civilized, intelligent, and honest human being. He had a wonderful sense of humor. He spoke more than a dozen languages and knew their dialects. He loved most of all those things that were natural, that were close to the soil. Like folksongs, like animals and insects (which he collected), like gardening, sunbathing. Despite ill health, he loved exercise and mountain climbing. It is true that Bartók had little patience with those things not connected with his work, and at times he could seem distant and serious. But to those of us who studied with him, we knew full well the more humorous side of him. Unfortunately, you don't see that in most of the photographs, where he hardly looks human. But I can tell you, when he smiled, his face lit up completely. I even have a picture of him smiling! In those days some Parisians held a very aggressive, condemning opinion of Bartók and his friend, Kodály, because their music was so different from the prevailing German and post-Germanic music. They called Bartók and Kodály the "Young Hungarian Barbarians." So, as a joke, Bartók took a piece he originally called *Allegro in F-sharp Major* and changed the title to *Allegro Barbaro*. Not because it's "barbaric"—it's just an ordinary, common march. He did it only to mock these critics.

We always hear that his music is percussive and mechanical—"motoric." I think it's unfortunate that so many of his works are performed this way. Bartók never played that way with me! He had a virile, dancelike energy, not the sadistic and destructive piano bashing you hear so often today. I heard him play many times, and he always varied everything tremendously. He produced the most aggressive, yet the most subtle sounds; the most imaginative, colorful, half-pedaled and fully-pedaled sounds. He was a very free, improvising type of artist. His playing was full of *rubato*. Listen to any of his recordings. In the two *Rumanian Dances* in C minor he starts in a certain tempo and finishes in a very different tempo. He used irregular rhythmic units, which under no circumstances should be played evenly. Bartók wrote music for every mood. It's like prose, which avoids the strophic beat; or speech, which should never be monotonous. And that's how his music must be played." Recently the Hungarians brought out a collection of recordings. Unfortunately, very few of them are very good. They were made 60–80 years ago, when recording technology was very unsatisfactory. But he has some good recordings for Columbia he made in this country—like the *Mikrokosmos* [1926–1939], his Sonata No. 2 [1926] and a few others.

It seems to me we never hear in concerts some of his little pieces, like the Mikrokosmos.

Actually, I did give two programs in New York some years ago where I played the entire set, all six volumes in two programs. Each of the more than 150 pieces is a masterpiece. Some are teaching pieces, some are homages, some are derived from folk sources, etc. But for a public concert, I don't think it's a very good idea. It's too much.

You haven't always been labeled as a "Bartók" pianist, have you?

No, not at all. When I arrived here [i.e., in America], I was then known as a "Liszt pianist," because I came from Hungary. But I am no specialist in Liszt, and I would argue that I'm not the last word in Bartók, either, or in Prokofiev. I play everything equally badly, or well, I hope. I just love good repertory.

Certainly, Bartók's music has its own distinctive "sound," does it not?

May I answer this in a roundabout way? I think the first earmark of a great composer is that he's universal. He's capable of making people respond to any kind of human emotion. Now we're used to hearing that Beethoven is a robust, heavy composer; and that Bartók is percussive. But I think they both wrote for any mood and any sound. No, I don't think there's any particular "Bartók sound." It's varied so tremendously. He produced the most aggressive, most subtle sounds; the most imaginative, colorful, half-pedaled and fully-pedaled sounds. He was frail, yes; but he was a powerful, spontaneous, accurate interpreter.

The word "modernist" comes to mind. Do you classify him as a "modernist" composer?

You must understand that Bartók's music, like Debussy's, actually goes back to Palestrina. Various "aberrations" have been explored during the last hundred years—and I include the so-called polytonal, atonal, dodecaphonic compositional styles, which are rather sterile music.[12] Bartók's line was tonal writing. But tonal writing his way sounded different than Mozart's. Bartók never wrote atonal

---

[12]Often employed erroneously as synonyms for each other, "atonal" music is simply music without a discernible key. "Polytonal" music employs two or more keys at the same time. "Dodecaphonic" or twelve-tone music, on the other hand, was a strict system of atonal composition more or less invented by Schoenberg and practiced by Webern and Alban Berg (1885–1935). It was considered the most characteristic kind of "modern" art music until the 1960s and 1970s introduced minimalism, paper music, and other postmodern musical styles.

or bitonal music, in spite of what his critics have said. Every piece he wrote has a tonal center. Even the two Violin Sonatas, the First Piano Concerto, and the Second String Quartet. He knew the dodecaphonic and rejected it. There's a very good explanation why it's invalid. Compositions based on it don't make any sense. Furthermore, if you don't have a tonal center to which you can refer—no tension, when you go away from the tonic, or release, when you return. When you have an arbitrary set of notes not tied to a tonal center, there's no tension.

Do you think there's almost a philosophical aspect to all this? That deep inside we need a "truth," an answer?
It all comes from physiological phenomena, from the vibration of air, and from nature. Dissonance creates tension, not only in the air but in the human ear too. A conflict of harmonics, and nobody can deny this conflict exists. Bartók knew this from his studies of nature. He realized that the origins of music lie in the sounds of nature. Listen to the fourth movement of the *Out of Doors* suite, to all those little noises of the night, those little stylized twitters and flutings of frogs and insects. At night everything is obscured. So, the sounds are hazy, notes blurred together, to evoke that sensation. And Bartók knew music itself is based on vibrations in air.[13] The pentatonic scale exists in nature: it is the one scale where vibration is least interfered with. Folklore, whether Hungarian or Romanian or Chinese or Indian, is based on the pentatonic scale. From that came the modes, the diatonic, the chromatic, his own scales. And the pentatonic scale is the one where the air vibration is the least interfered with. He wasn't unique; at the turn of the [last] century people were going back to origins.

But our ears think there's a lot of dissonance going on!
What creates that impression is that Bartók often synchronizes the functions of, say, the tonic and subdominant, at the same time; or he gives equal meaning to certain notes and those notes closest to them, which I call "derived notes." Let me go back to the piano. [plays] Now what Bartók does most of the time is feature the grace note *together* with the main note. That's a very strong dissonance, but we know the D-sharp leads to the E. That's not two tonalities, that's one tonality either upper or lower. As for "derived notes": if you have a C that's part of the melody, that C is the source of several other notes, the C-sharp, the C-flat.

You're saying the "C-majorness" remains supreme.
The "C-ness," as you put it, is neither major nor minor. Most of Bartók's compositions stand on one basic note and use practically all the twelve notes that are around the diatonic scale. He can use any of those notes. He simultaneously uses neighboring, or derived notes. We as musicians should know which are the

---

[13]Every vibrating body within an atmosphere produces overtones, notes above the primary note. The first few overtones outline a tonic chord.

ornamental notes and which are the main notes. The inner structure is there, but it's covered up by neighboring notes or derived notes.

But it's a challenge to ears accustomed to a more consonant sound.
Let's not forget that there was a Liszt before Bartók, and a [Max] Reger [1873–1916], and a Ravel!

But was Bartók aware that some people found his music offensive?
Oh yes. Attacks? Nothing but. He had a few close friends around him who respected and admired him. The rest were shocked. And I don't blame them, because whenever I hear something really new or different, I don't know what to do with it. Let's face the fact: Music does not appeal to reason. It is purely emotional and physiological. When you hear a major chord, it is not by accident that it sounds uncomplicated. That's simply because the harmonics are undisturbed. If you add any notes that do not figure in the "harmonic ladder" of the bottom note, then you have either a depressing or stimulating result. It's in our hearing apparatus; it is innate.

Toward the end of his life did his music become more accessible?
Not necessarily, when you consider the Viola Sonata and the Solo Violin Sonata; but I must say the Third Piano Concerto is, how we say, more "audience friendly." At least, it was more easily accepted than either the First or Second Concertos.

Let's talk about that. The Third Concerto occupies a special place in your life, doesn't it? You premiered it with Eugene Ormandy and the Philadelphia Orchestra.
Maybe our "ears" have gotten more used to it. Now, when Bartók died in 1945 in New York, his music was already starting to spread. His Third Piano Concerto was one of his more mature works but perhaps more economical than in the First and Second Concertos. Somebody once said to me that Bartók must have lowered its standards to make money. That's pure nonsense. All great composers learn how to economize and distill their music. Prokofiev's Ninth Piano Sonata is much simpler than the early ones. The Third Concerto's form is just as wonderful and perfect as the Second. But Bartók used fewer notes. It's an error to think it a weak or decadent composition, just because Bartók was sick and dying. It is one of the very robust works. When we presented it with Ormandy in 1946, [composer and critic] Virgil Thomson [1896–1989] wrote that here is a new work by Bartók that is very pleasing and very well done—and that now we have something that will last a season or two. People could not really evaluate his work—even in those days.

Was it understood during its composition that you would premiere it?
Not at all. I was with Bartók in his last days. He knew the end was near when, a few days before his death, emaciated and too weak to work, he scrawled the word *Vege*—"The End"—on the last page of the Concerto. He had never put those words at the end of a composition before. He was in a hurry to finish it, to leave it

as a legacy for his wife, who was also a pianist. He was very anxious to send the *Concerto for Orchestra* to Boosey and Hawkes to have it published. The deadline was September 30, 1945; and he died only a few days earlier. About a week before that, he gave me the score to correct the second proofs and mail them to Boosey and Hawkes, which I did. All that time he never said one word to me about the Third Piano Concerto. Then, in 1945, December, I had a phone call from Tibor Serly [1901–1978], who orchestrated the last seventeen measures of the *Concerto for Orchestra*. Serly told me then about the Third Concerto and asked me if I wanted to play it, since Ditta[14] was quite sick and unable to play much at the time. So, of course, I agreed.

Speaking of premieres, you've hinted that you're soon going to premiere another Bartók work. What was that all about?
What I showed you were some photostats of Bartók's handwriting of the piano version of his *Concerto for Orchestra*, which he composed in the fall of 1943. Shortly after the first performance with the Boston Symphony Orchestra under Koussevitsky, there was talk of performing the *Concerto* as a ballet for the Ballet Theater of New York. Bartók was asked to work out a piano reduction for rehearsal purposes. He prepared a compressed, two-hand piano version in just ten days, but it was never performed. The Concerto is one of the most colorful of orchestra pieces, and it must have been tough to do.

Is this piano version technically challenging for the pianist?
Even [Beethoven's] *Für Elise* is difficult! Of course, it's not an easy piece at all. Many passages were indicated with additional staves, making it virtually unplayable for ten fingers! When I mentioned this to Peter Bartók, the composer's son, he told me to do whatever was necessary to present those voices clearly. No orchestral score is easy to play on the piano.

Playing this transcription, after all these years, must have inspired renewed contact with Bartók.
I enjoyed every moment! It's about thirty-seven minutes long, and thus not an easy thing to put on a recital program. The five movements are rather detached and independent; any of those can be played alone. I will play both the complete version and separate movements, depending on the circumstances.

Is this the only example of Bartók's piano reduction of his orchestral works?
Not at all. He also adapted the *Dance Suite for Orchestra* [1923] for piano. And of his *Petite Suite*, selections from his Violin Duos.

---

[14]Ditta Pásztorsy-Bartók (1903–1982), Hungarian pianist and Bartók's second wife.

It's ironic, I guess, that Bartók's music enjoyed an upswing in performance and acceptance immediately after his death.

The real Bartók "cult" only arose after his death. But this is obvious: Any great composer who starts his own idiom has to wait until the public assimilates and enjoys his work. And so you see that within the next four years there were premieres of works, and performance cycles of his string quartets and stage works, like *Bluebeard's Castle* and *The Miraculous Mandarin* (Fig. 11).

Epilogue

In November 1988, I listened with Sándor to a tape of Bartók speaking in Hungarian. The voice was a pleasantly soft, baritone sound, yet strong and assured. I asked Sándor to identify the words in question.

Fig. 11 György Sándor and Béla Bartók, New York City, 1943

SÁNDOR: [Bartók]'s reading the text from his *Cantata Profana*. He always felt very close to that work.

Why is that?
He once said that it contained his own philosophical credo. He composed it in 1930, and it is based on an old Rumanian folk ballad, *The Hunting Boys Turned into Stags*.

With a title like that, you'd better explain!
[laughs] It's about nine sons who have been trained by their father to be excellent hunters. When they enter the forest to hunt a "magic deer," they are transformed into stags. The father follows them and confronts the stags. He doesn't recognize his sons, of course, and he aims his rifle. Suddenly, the tallest stag says, "We're your sons! Don't fire your rifle, or we'll chase you and crush you on the mountain rocks." The stag explains they can't return with him because their antlers won't fit into the door; that their furry coats won't permit them to wear clothing; and only clear lake water can quench their thirst.

And from this you take what meaning?
I think Bartók saw it as about his last years in America. He had left Hungary and he knew there would be no return. He was in a New World, a new way of life, and since he couldn't return, he kept moving forward with his music. It was all he could do.

What about those last days? When did you last see him? How well do you remember it?
Very well. He passed away on 26 September 1945. I happened to be in his apartment when they took him to the hospital. That was just a week before he died. He looked very emaciated and was terribly weak. And then I went to the hospital, not every day but every second day, at least. The last time I saw him was about three days before he died. As I told you, he asked me to correct the second proofs of the *Concerto for Orchestra*, which were supposed to be sent to Boosey and Hawkes by September 30. He asked very politely if I would; of course. I took it home for about three days. He died on the 26th. When I went back to visit him the day before he died, I wasn't allowed in. He'd gotten a blood transfusion; and the next day he was gone.

The Art of the Accompanist

Introduction

The art of "accompanying" another musician scarcely existed as a performance category before the eighteenth century; the *Oxford English Dictionary* gives 1768 as the first appearance of the word "accompanist" in our language, Nevertheless, instrumentalists of many kinds—percussionists, keyboard musicians, guitarists, lutenists, and so on—have supported singers and even other instrumentalists for centuries. Writing for *The Guardian* as recently as 2012, Tom Service expressed pity for "the poor accompanist" (by which he means the collaborative pianist) "condemned to sit in the shadow of the great voices and the even greater egos of today's singers." This is not quite true. More than a few accompanists, almost all of them pianists, have made names for themselves on the concert platform and through recordings of various kinds.

Today, pianist-accompanists regularly collaborate with other musicians—sometimes with several at a time—in performances of *Lieder* and other songs; sonatas for solo instruments and piano—violin, clarinet, and so on; and chamber works such as piano trios (piano, violin, and 'cello), piano quartets (piano and three other instruments), and piano quintets (piano and string quartet). In both rehearsals and concerts pianists often work with choruses and play for dance rehearsals and recitals. Advertisements for "collaborative accompanists"—today the approved term—appear in many places, and the contemporary solo-vocal and chamber-music worlds could not survive without them.

Samuel Sanders and Martin Katz concentrate in their interviews on their own experiences as keyboard collaborators, while Graham Johnson concentrates on his keyboard experiences with British composer Benjamin Britten (1913–1976) and members of Britten's musical circle.

Michael Saffle

© The Author(s) 2018
J. C. Tibbetts et al. (eds.), *Performing Music History*,
https://doi.org/10.1007/978-3-319-92471-7_8

Samuel Sanders: "I'm Always Telling Students, 'Don't Slouch Like That; The Song Is Not Over yet!'"

John C. Tibbetts
13 May 1987, New York City

Samuel Sanders (1937–1999) studied at Hunter College and Juilliard; he later taught at Juilliard. During his career Sanders worked with a host of singers and instrumentalists, including soprano Jessye Norman. For thirty years he collaborated with violinist Itzhak Perlman; together they made twelve recordings and earned two GRAMMYs. Sanders founded the Cape and Islands Chamber Music Festival on Cape Cod. He received honorary doctorates from several universities as well as an honorary award at the 1966 Tchaikovsky International Competition in Moscow, and he performed at the White House for five different presidents (Fig. 1).

The following interview took place in New York City following a concert appearance with Sanders and Itzhak Perlman. He demonstrates his remarks at the keyboard.

JOHN C. TIBBETTS: How often are you referred to as an "accompany-ist" rather than an "accompanist"? You must get that a lot!
SAMUEL SANDERS: Yeah. I got it yesterday, actually! There's no such word!

And "accompanist" is a term you don't shy away from. You seem to be in the vanguard of those people who actually studied accompanying in an academic setting.
Yes. I did. I studied at Juilliard, and my accompanying teacher there was a very great accompanist, as well as a voice teacher, which is unique. Sergius Kagen, who's very prominent to this day—though he died in 1964—did many editions for different composers, like Debussy, Brahms, Purcell, and so forth. He was a very learned, musician, and a terrific pianist. But he was also a voice teacher, and one of his students was Jan DeGaetani.

Is this a new academic discipline?
Yes, yes. It is certainly thriving. USC [University of Southern California] pioneered the degree in accompanying. When I was on the faculty at Juilliard, they did not have such a degree. Now they do. I admit I take a little bit of credit for starting that masters program there. Though I still teach at Juilliard, I do most of my teaching out at Peabody; and they have a degree in chamber arts, rather than calling it "accompanying." Now there are a number of other schools in the country that have degrees. Illinois, for example, with John Westmund, who's quite fabulous; and Martin Katz at the University of Michigan. I know that there are other schools—the Manhattan School of Music—and I believe Akron University has a degree, along with maybe eight or nine others.

Fig. 1 Samuel Sanders

For me the name "Gerald Moore" stands foremost as one of the deans of this whole profession. "The unashamed accompanist" was his term.

I would say he's my idol, quite unashamedly, one of my dearest colleagues. Unfortunately, he just died two months ago [i.e., on 13 March 1987] at the age of eighty-seven, and … well, he was to accompanying what Pablo Casals was to the 'cello and Segovia to the guitar. He really legitimized the profession and made people aware of the essential aspect of what the person who's playing the piano is all about.

You've been quoted as saying that, when it comes to being a virtuoso pianist, the heck with it. You have no truck with showing off in competitions.

I have mixed feelings about competitions in general, anyway. I did partake in competitions when I was a solo pianist. I did okay. I played with the Young People's Concerts with the New York Philharmonic when I was sixteen, when I was playing solo music. The reason I really got into piano playing was simply because my mother told me to play the piano! With my heart condition, she didn't think I could do much else. She didn't say it in those words, exactly, but I really was a problem; and there wasn't much that I could do. I don't feel any competition, frankly, with any of my colleagues who specialize in this field. I think, if anything, we have to help each other, because accompanying is a slightly misunderstood field. I love music. I wouldn't say that I love the piano as a solo instrument. The reason that I chose chamber music and accompanying was because I happen to like the sound of the piano in conjunction with other instruments. Had I been born healthy, I probably would've chosen the bassoon! That happens to be my favorite. Don't ask me why. I just like the sound of it better.

I love the analogy you once used of the soloist as baseball pitcher and the accompanist as catcher! Are you "calling signals," in effect, to your singer, too?

You know, the more experienced a pitcher is, the less a catcher has to take care of him, baby-sit him, in a sense, through the game. When I'm working with a young performer, I'm almost extra-cautious. When I'm working with a more experienced person, I know that if something happens, that person will be able to handle himself.

Forgive me for saying it, but like a ballplayer, you have to sit on the bench!

[laughs] Uh… sit on… Oh, right. Right. That's true!

Now, this art song business is really a curious beast, isn't it? And the song cycle. I guess in the nineteenth century you really wouldn't have heard a complete song cycle often in concert.

I think Schubert is really credited with creating the so-called *Lied* in its pure form, in a sense that the piano and the voice are inextricably combined. And in Schumann, you hear the opening of something like the *Dichterliebe*, which is … [starts playing] This is all piano. And then all of the sudden the singer comes in. [stops playing] See, and it's linked together. I mean, the piano part and the voice part are part of a large fabric.

And you're saying that before then—

Yeah, before then there were exceptions, Mozart and Beethoven and so forth— but I think before that, the piano didn't really play the role that it played with Schubert and Brahms and Wolf and so forth. It was more of an accompanying feature than an inextricable part. Mozart wrote some beautiful songs that are very much part and parcel of the song. But still, the piano is more in the nature of an accessory, beautifully written [for], yes, but not really with a major role. When you talk about a Schubert song or a Wolf song or a Brahms song, the piano is one of the *charac-ters* in that song. Let's put it this way: your leg and your arm and your neck are part of your body. You couldn't conceive of your body without those parts, could you? But perhaps with composers before that, you might think of them separately, like the shoe that you put on your foot. You see what I mean?

As in Schubert's Wohin?
Yeah, you have this piano pattern, here, which is the stream. [plays] And the singer is saying, "Whither?" [i.e., *wohin*]. The poet is addressing the stream. And that happens all the time, where a line might be started, for example, in the piano, and finished in the voice, or vice versa. There's a wonderful book by [Dietrich] Fischer-Dieskau with a lot of translations of German songs; and in his preface he writes this better than I can say. I never realized what a scholar Fischer-Dieskau was!

There have been those who suggest, too, that when you find these piano patterns in a composer's music, you can find similar patterns occurring in his or her solo piano music, and find that they are very consistent in how and when they employ these patterns, correlated to emotions and things.
Exactly. Mr. Kagen, my teacher, always said you can't play the opening of the Schumann Piano Concerto really properly [plays briefly] until you know some of the Schumann songs and chamber pieces that are very similar in certain gestures.

What goes through the minds of the singers you've worked with? What do they do on stage during the long epilogue you've mentioned?
If they're thoughtful musicians, they realize that the piece is not over until the last note has been played. They will be in the world of that song, of that poem, until the last note has been struck. I'm always telling my students "Don't slouch like that, the song is not over yet." In a sense, you're an actor or an actress. When you see a great actor or actress on stage, sometimes their whole body language, or body position, without ever saying a word, is saying so much. This is either before they've spoken or after they've completely done their speaking part. You see what I mean? There's a wonderful piece that I've played frequently called the *Voice of the Whale* by [*avant-gardist*] George Crumb for piano, 'cello, and flute. And the players are wearing masks so that, in a sense, they're dehumanized. The music has to match geological eras, really, more than anything else, Paleozoic and Mesozoic and so forth. And the last instruction that Crumb, one of our best com-posers, gives, is: after all the notes are struck, the pianist should mime seven or eight notes. In other words, time is endless. It's a kind of infinity. I think, to me, that's what he's saying.

On the other hand, there are times when your part has to be heard, the keys have to be struck ferociously, as in Schubert's Erlkönig.
I never really look forward to that one! The "Erlking" is just a killer for any pia-nist. It's hellishly difficult to play unless you have machine-gun wrists, because

of these repeated octaves that never let up. Balance is a problem, a major problem. And, in fact, when you're dealing with a piece like the [Sergei] Rachmaninoff
[1873–1943] 'Cello Sonata, you could blast the 'cellist right off the stage if you
wanted to. There's constant adjustments being made in terms of balance, always. It
depends on the size of the hall, on the weather, on the quality of the instrument, on
the player, you name it. All kinds of things.

Finally, you share with Itzhak Perlman an interest in benefits for the disabled.
Perlman's big cause is building facilities that assist the handicapped, because of
his own handicap, brought about by polio. I don't know why we were brought
together, by fate, or something, but I think it's fitting in a way. I was born with a
very serious heart defect. The trouble is, you can't see a heart defect as readily as
you can somebody who has crutches, but it's been a huge handicap for me, for my
entire life, and it's included three surgical procedures—three heart operations, that
is. And a lot of the problems that I have to face, and people with handicaps, are the
same problems that I have to face, so what he's accomplishing for so many people,
he's also accomplishing for me. So I have my own personal debt of gratitude to
him.

Graham Johnson: "The Whole World of Song Proliferated Outwards from Britten"

John C. Tibbetts
10 January 1999, London

**Born in Southern Rhodesia, Graham Johnson, OBE, studied at London's
Royal Academy of Music. Johnson's work with famed collaborative pianist
Gerald Moore as well as with composer Benjamin Britten and singer Peter
Pears was crucial in his development as an artist and scholar. Today Johnson
holds a Senior Professorship in Accompaniment in the Guildhall School
of Music and Drama; he also continues to record. In 2002 he was created a
Chevalier in the *Ordre des Arts et des Lettres* by the French government. In all
Johnson has won four Grammys as "solo vocal awards": in 1989 (with Dame
Janet Baker), 1996 (with Ian Bostridge), 1997 (with Christine Schäfer), and
2001 (with Magdalena Kožená) (Fig. 2).**
  This conversation transpired in Johnson's London home.

*JOHN C. TIBBETTS: You grew up in Zimbabwe, where I assume your exposure to
classical music was rather limited.*
GRAHAM JOHNSON: Yes, apart from the parlor piano and radio, there wasn't
much to go on. I remember as a little boy being enchanted by a tune from a radio
program called *Let's Be Serious*, which spoke to me in an incredible way. I found
out later it was Gerald Moore's famous solo piano transcription of Schubert's *An*

Fig. 2 Graham Johnson and image of Schubert

die Musik [To music], a recording Moore made in the 1940s. The die was cast. What also fascinated me, very early on, was language. At school I was fortunate to learn French grammar. I remember longing to learn and understand German, even at the age of ten or eleven. And poetry always fascinated me. So, the *Lied*, the song form, was waiting to happen to me. Then I discovered that piano playing could be allied with the glamour of languages and the power of poetry.

I started off playing solo piano. When I came to England I discovered I loved chamber music. I formed a duo with a 'cellist and investigated all the repertoire of Beethoven. Beethoven became my god. The piano trios, the violin and 'cello sonatas, particularly. And the Brahms sonatas, Debussy, Britten. At eighteen or nineteen I became terribly absorbed in the music of Benjamin Britten. Above all, the vocal music of Britten appealed to me: *Peter Grimes, War Requiem*, the song cycle, *Les Illuminations*. I wrote to Britten and got an immediate reply, which I've always kept. And I got to know both Britten and Peter Pears. I got a scholarship to study here at the Royal Academy of Music. That led to Britten's festivals at Aldeburgh, and to meeting for the first time the composer of these great operas. And on a mind-blowing occasion in 1971, I actually heard him perform *Winterreise* at Aldeburgh. That was a turning point. I had originally wanted to be a composer. But when I heard him playing the piano in the Schubert, and it was a revelation. Everything seemed to come like a blinding flash—this is what I must do; this I understand; this I could do…. Soon afterward I plunged into Hugo Wolf, and I'd always been attracted to French music.

The sudden awareness of what lay out there coincided with being asked to play with Peter Pears for a master class. After this I met Flora Nielsen, Felicity Lott's teacher. Then Pierre Bernac, who was connected with [Francis] Poulenc. The whole world of song proliferated outwards from Britten. And as a young man I met Eric Sams, the great expert on Wolf and Schumann. All these people came into my life at the same time. It became obvious to me that my mental attitude, my interests in programming were awakened—the idea that songs *meant* something, that they were from a background, from a period, from a past, and that each song had in it a double life—the life of the composer, the life of the poet, the double reason for existing. They had two conflicting and sometimes complementary biographical reasons for existing. Because the poem had to be written at a certain time, just as the song did. And how they describe something more specifically and more completely—perhaps more *intimately*—than absolute music, which is not trammeled by these specificities. On the other hand, they have an historical immediacy, a sociological immediacy that's actually lacking in other music and which exists in the song form.

During recording sessions you create a "virtual space" as opposed to real space?
That's right. You put your finger on it. You create a balancing in recording that is a "virtual reality," or space, a different reality than the reality itself.

And, for your recordings, you write your own program notes. The term is inadequate. These are not merely "notes," but scholarly annotations.
Writing gives me the type of fulfillment that I lack when I realized I would not be a composer.

Who are the writers who have had a formative influence on you?
Among the musical writers who have influenced me is Eric Sams, who has continued to be a godfather to my writing and whom I first met him when I was twenty-one at a party. Ever since then, he's been my mentor. He uses language in the most unbelievably pellucid and witty way. He's a person who in a sense is my own Cambridge or Oxford tutor. Because I went straight from school into performing, I'm a total autodidact. Other writers I've admired include Saul Bellow [1915–2005], W. H. Auden [(1907–1973), and] Willa Cather [1873–1947]. I was very moved as a young man by [novelist] Mary Renault [1905–1983], whose specialty was writing about the ancient Greeks. Her books were formative influences

on me. She and I engaged in a correspondence, you know, that lasted many years. Another author who makes me shake with admiration for his generosity of spirit is [poet] Walt Whitman [1819–1892].

Martin Katz: "Watch with Your Ears!"

John C. Tibbetts
September 1988 and March 2017, Kansas City, Missouri

Martin Katz has worked with more of today's stellar singers and instrumentalists than perhaps any accompanist in history. During 1966–1969, and as a member of the U.S. Army, Katz served as piano soloist and accompanist with the Army Chorus. Since 1984 he has served as Earl V. Moore Collegiate Professor of Music at University of Michigan, where he chairs a program in Collaborative Piano. Voted *Musical America*'s 1998 "Accompanist of the Year," Katz wrote *The Complete Collaborator: The Pianist as Partner*, was published in 2009 by Oxford University Press (Fig. 3).

JOHN C. TIBBETTS: In the annals of great musical teams we've had wonderful examples: Brooks Smith with Jascha Heifetz, and Jörg Demus with Dietrich Fischer-Dieskau. How did you come to work with world-class performers like these?
MARTIN KATZ: I studied accompanying as a major in college. Very few schools offer this, especially at the undergraduate level. But the University of Southern California does have a major devoted specifically to accompanying. I'm proud to be the head of the accompanying major at the University of Michigan. It exists only on the graduate level. USC may be the only one that has it also on the undergraduate level. When I got a piano scholarship to USC, I was all set to register for piano but noticed that they had accompanying. I had played for the choir and played songs at Rotary Club luncheons and things like that, and I thought, I think I'm pretty good at that; I'm going to check that box instead of the piano box. And low and behold, the teacher I was lucky enough to get was Gwendolyn Koldofsky. She was my mentor for four years and some incredible opportunities came about in a professional way during my four years there. I'm not going to be falsely immodest, but that is really what I'm good at, as opposed to playing a Rachmaninoff concerto.

Nevertheless, the bottom line is, *you have to be able to play the piano*! Long ago, accompanying ceased to be a dumping ground for people who loved to play but really couldn't play. That's not acceptable anymore. That may have something to do with universities beginning to teach accompanying seriously. I hope the audience will never know whose idea some aspect of the performance is; it comes across as a communal idea. If bothers your ego, then you're not cut out to be an accompanist.

Fig. 3 Martin Katz

With whom have you had the longest association?
Probably with [mezzo-sopranos] Marilyn Horne and Frederica von Stade than with anybody else that I play for. Marilyn and I will have been together nineteen years this coming February [1988]; with Frederica, maybe twelve. They're both in addition to other fabulous colleagues, dear friends. I know their families; they know my family. I've cried with them and laughed with them over things that have nothing to do with our work; but that can be part of the union with them on stage.

How did you come to work with Renata Tebaldi?
When I was a high school student at sixteen, somebody gave me a record for my birthday of her original performance in Puccini's opera *La Bohème*. As a piano student, I didn't know anything about Puccini's operas, because there's no piano music written in that style. So, I heard her voice and this music, and the experience was one of the cornerstones of my going into accompanying profession. When I began to play for her in the early 1970s, she was near the end of her career, but it was very exciting to me. I wanted to tell her so much that this was like playing for my godmother, in a way, something that had turned my life around. But I felt sheepish about it, and I never did tell her that. Maybe she'll listen to this interview!

What kind of give and take do you have with a singing partner—Kiri Te Kanawa, for example?
She may convey a programmatic or emotional expression, rather than an actual musical expression. She doesn't usually say, "Oh, lift your right foot here" or "Be sure you change the pedal there," or something like that. She may say instead, "I need more silence there." Sometimes if she's doing something for the first time so, how I'm playing it becomes part of how she will think about the piece. You see, it depends very much on whether somebody comes to you having already performed something before. I'll use Mr. Hakan Hakegard as an example. We collaborated on Schubert's *Winterreise* a couple of times. He's done the *Winterreise* since he was seventeen years old, maybe forty, fifty times. And this was my third crack at the whole thing. He didn't need me to tell him how the *Winterreise* goes! I was the one who really needed his experience to help me out. You know, Americans don't get that many chances to do long song cycles like that, because our audiences are not so crazy about them over here as they are in Salzburg.[1]

I guess you have to develop a facility for sounding out the performer that you're with. What kind of mood are they in? When can you talk things out and when do you have to be quiet?
Oh you're absolutely right. That's very perceptive of you. There are certain days when no performer wants to hear anything in the way of a correction or criticism or a suggestion. Other days they're just wide open for it, so you have to be a little bit of an amateur psychologist to know the difference.

You worked with other seasoned artists while you were quite young. How did you handle the discrepancy in age and experience?
Two stories come to my mind. Once with Tebaldi, we were scheduled to perform two concerts at La Scala in Milan. Tebaldi's from Milan and had not sung in Milan for thirteen years. That rivalry with Maria Callas. I had just learned Italian, and

---

[1]Here the annual Salzburg Music Festival, founded in 1920. See below.

here I was, going to Milan with a legend like that! The pressure of that night, and the love, was more intense than I've ever felt on the stage. I also remember very well the first time I ever played in Salzburg. I was just a little American kid at this Mount Olympus of European Festivals. This was with Marilyn Horne. She'd been singing opera in Salzburg that summer. We were to do a recital in the middle of her opera run. Well, the response to her opera performance had been mixed, and I know that she felt a certain pressure to really show her worth in the recital. For me, it was my first time at the Festival, and I was all nerves. Backstage we were *both* nervous. Just basket cases you know? But when we got on stage, something happened. It was magical, we were together on everything, no matter how complicated the music was. That's something I'll treasure all my life so.

What distinctions do you make between art-song performance and opera performance?
I think that's terribly important for today's young singers to learn. I try to tell them that there's no longer this hard and fast distinction between "I do concert singing" and "I do opera singing" and "I do oratorio singing." Today's singers are more versatile than any in history. They have to be. That's the way the economics go these days and just the way the world is. I don't understand that just because someone has specialized in art songs, she isn't necessarily not as good at other kinds of performance. If you know what the words are and what your technique allows you to do, why can't you perform in an opera as well as you sing songs?
We've not yet talked about how you work with page turners.

I have a real easy answer: I never, ever use a page turner, under any circumstances. Well, there is one exception: if I'm performing outside, say, in the Hollywood Bowl, I might have a page turner, because when the wind comes up, there's no way the music is going to stay on the rack. Otherwise, I can't bear to have one. The soloist and I are working like Trojans to create a mood, and nothing can disrupt that like a page turner jumping up at an inopportune time.

When we attend a performance by a singer and an accompanist, what should we watch for that we haven't been noticing?
That's a wonderful question. You "watch" with your ears! You listen for the organic combination between the accompaniment and the singer much as you would in a Wagner opera between the orchestra and the voice. It's really that sort of hand-in-glove partnership. You appreciate it when it exists and you're impatient with it if it doesn't. The piano may come before the first note of the singer and after the last word. Sometimes the pianist is saying even more through his notes than the voice says with the poem.

Musical Multiplicities in the Twentieth and Twenty-First Centuries

Introduction

Since we are still close in time to the music of the past 125 years or so, it is difficult if not impossible for us to see the "big picture" of what has happened recently and is still happening in Western music. Even though Baroque music, for instance, has many sub-styles, we have a general sense of what "Baroque" means. For much of the music of the twentieth and twenty-first centuries, however, we can only look at individual trees or groves, not the entire forest.

As music grew more complex harmonically and structurally—one thinks of Mahler's enormous symphonies and Wagner's music dramas, which require entire evenings for complete performances—it also grew less complex. For example, in the USA during the 1880s and 1890s, some composers strove to create music with immediate popular appeal. As Max Morath demonstrates, and as composer-performer duo William Bolcom and Joan Morris explain, ragtime piano pieces and songs were two important popular forms; so were vaudeville songs; so were songs drawn from various musical stages. With its distinctive syncopations (in which melodic notes and chords don't line up rhythmically with accompaniment notes and chords), ragtime quickly became both famous and infamous—the latter attitude prevalent among conservative concert-goers. The blues, based largely on certain chord progressions, grew increasingly familiar.

Both ragtime and blues overlapped to some extent with early jazz. Perhaps the most original American art form, jazz began sometime in the late nineteenth century, probably in Louisiana; the first famous jazz musicians came from New Orleans. A difficult genre to describe, early jazz combined elements of African American, African Caribbean, and Western European music. Almost all early "jazzers" were African Americans; their performances depended largely upon improvisation, and most of them performed exclusively in ensembles, including the "big bands" of the 1920s, 1930s, and early 1940s. Early jazz was more or less

© The Author(s) 2018
J. C. Tibbetts et al. (eds.), *Performing Music History*,
https://doi.org/10.1007/978-3-319-92471-7_9

"popular" in sound and reception, but after the 1930s jazz became a kind of "art" music that featured ever more complex harmonies and paid less attention to familiar pop-song melodies.

During the early 1920s, jazz was taken up by popular white composers and performers, George Gershwin (1898–1937) and cornetist-composer Bix Beiderbecke (1903–1931) among them. Especially in the form of "big band" dance music or "swing," jazz rose to national prominence until the bands began to break up during the 1950s (Ragtime also served briefly as dance music.). During the 1930s and early 1940s, however, jazz was transformed by a small number of black artists into bebop: virtuoso and harmonically sophisticated music at once cerebral and passionate. Pianist and bandleader Jay McShann discusses the birth of bebop and "Kansas City" jazz, while the late pianist and composer George Shearing explains the classical as well as popular song and "cool" jazz influences in his own work.

Other musicians chose a very different direction, eschewing even suggestions of the "popular." Some of them became true iconoclasts, attacking conventional notions of what Romantic and Modernist music could be. Arnold Schoenberg and his disciples practiced highly systematic dodecaphony, or twelve-tone compositional procedures. Other, quite different innovators were George Antheil, John Cage, and Harry Partch (1901–1974), all of whom experimented with new sounds and musical "circumstances" (or performance venues). Still others, including George Crumb, continue to experiment today. As Cage himself relates, audiences often became perplexed when they encountered his radically unfamiliar musical utterances. Nevertheless, Cage has become almost a household name, at least among modern-music fans.

Twentieth- and twenty-first century composers have often combined stylistic elements to create their own, distinctive compositional voices. Carlisle Floyd's *Susannah* references the folklore of the Southern States. In *Cold Mountain*, Jennifer Higdon conflates symphonic sounds with echoes of Appalachian music. Chinese-American artists Chen Yi and Zhou Long explain in their joint interview how they combine Chinese musical traditions with Western genres and instruments. Nor is this all: today, musical genres continue to proliferate. So-called rock music has given birth, in one way or another, to such varied styles as glam rock, alternative rock, and metal music. Today hip hop, yet another product of African American artists, continues to influence genres beyond itself.

William Everett and Michael Saffle

Max Morath: "Livin' the Ragtime Life!"

John C. Tibbetts
5 June 1993, Lawrence, Kansas

Initially improvised by piano-players, ragtime was a syncopated form of the military march. Between c. 1896 and c. 1920, thousands of rags were

composed mostly by African American artists, including Scott Joplin (1867/1868–1917) and James Scott (1885–1938); other important composers included Joseph Lamb (1887–1960), who was of Irish descent. Keyboard gestures employed in ragtime were adapted to a variety of dances, including cakewalks and even a few foxtrots; ragtime rhythms also figured in stride piano-playing, the novelty piano numbers of the 1920s, and compositions by Debussy, Stravinsky, and other so-called art composers. Revived for the first time during the 1940s, ragtime underwent a second and longer-lasting revival during the 1970s, when Joplin's opera *Treemonisha* (1910) was performed for the first time in 1973. Joplin's music was featured in *The Sting* (1974), a major Hollywood motion picture, and E. L. Doctorow's 1975 novel *Ragtime* enjoyed considerable popularity and became the basis for a highly successful Broadway musical in 1996.

Performer, scholar, and entrepreneur, Max Morath has been acknowledged as a leading authority on the American Ragtime Era. A native of Colorado Springs, Morath (Fig. 1) has tirelessly worked as a pianist, radio announcer, actor, author, composer, and producer for National Public Radio and PBS Television. Since 2006, his thirteen-episode series for WFMT radio, *Ragtime to the Max*, has been heard worldwide on WFMT affiliates and on XM Satellite Radio. According to scholar Edward A. Berlin, "Max Morath … strikes a fine balance between entertainment values and historical veracity, a quality he pursues assiduously."

JOHN C. TIBBETTS: What follows is an account of my witnessing Max's performance of his one-man show, "Livin' the Ragtime Life", in Liberty Hall, Lawrence, Kansas. Permission for publishing this account courtesy of Max Morath.
It's show time. On stage, flanking the grand piano, its raised lid draped with a tasseled coverlet, is the Edison cylinder machine at stage left and a chair and table and hat rack at stage right. An offstage voice is heard: "The right time is ragtime, sung by Max Morath, Edison Records." Strains of music, the words scratchy and tinny, emerge from the gramophone:

> All night long, constant syncopations;
> Crazy songs, raggy conversations.
> Put your arms around me to the 'Grizzly Bear';
> Cuddle up a little closer, honey, I don't care.
> Here's your chance, light fantastic trippers;
> Dance that dance, in patent leather slippers.
> What's this world coming to, the Turkey Trot and Hitchy-Koo …

Lights full up. Max briskly strides onstage in a natty grey suit with a red bowtie and matching pocket kerchief. Without missing a beat, he takes up the song in his clear, declamatory voice:

Fig. 1 Max Morath

Everybody's rarin' to rag.
I'm gonna stay up late, I'm gonna syncopate;
Everybody's doin' it and I can't wait—

After tossing off a few more lyrics, he moves to the hat rack, doffs his straw hat, and launches into a few brief remarks about our tendency to dismiss Edison's "miracle" of recorded sound as something by and for "old fogies." No," he declares, "those are young people you're listening to. Kids. Popular music has always belonged to the kids. Ragtime was America's first popular music ...*rag time*. Two words in those days."

Moving to the piano, he belts out his signature tune, "Living the Ragtime Life," composed in 1900 by Gene Jefferson and Bob Roberts:

Got more trouble than I can stand;
Ever since ragtime struck the land.
I never saw the like in all my days
Everybody's got the ragtime craze ...

After a deft transition to Joplin's "Maple Leaf Rag," he returns to Jefferson and Roberts (Fig. 2):

Ragtime's everywhere.
Ragtime's rife.
And I'm certainly living the ragtime life!

Applause. Up from the keyboard, Max takes a bow. "Think about it," he says, "it's been almost a century since Gene and Bobby left their Indiana home to follow a ragtime dream. And here I am, living the ragtime life, still. Has it changed? Show business stays the same—late hours, hotel rooms, booze, tawdry women..." A pause. "I love it! ... [applause] It's our music that labels our history ... more than our wars; more than our politicians!"

For the next ninety minutes Max commands the stage, moving from keyboard to easy chair and back, delivering an easy flow of music, patter, historical detail, and amusing anecdotes. His timing is razor-sharp, every detail carefully honed and polished. He delivers a brief chronology of American social history, from the Chicago World's Fair to World War I—"hardly the Good Old Days!" He performs a series of musical demonstrations devoted to different entertainers and their styles—including performances of Eubie Blake's *The Charleston Rag*, a medley of Prohibition songs (does anybody remember Ernest R. Ball's *Saloon*?), a tribute to the influential music publishers John Stark of St. Louis and to composer James Scott of Kansas City. Then, Scott Joplin. After playing Joplin's *Easy Winners*, Max quips: "Joplin published his *Easy Winners* in 1901, the same year the American Federation of Musicians, our union, passed a unanimous resolution condemning

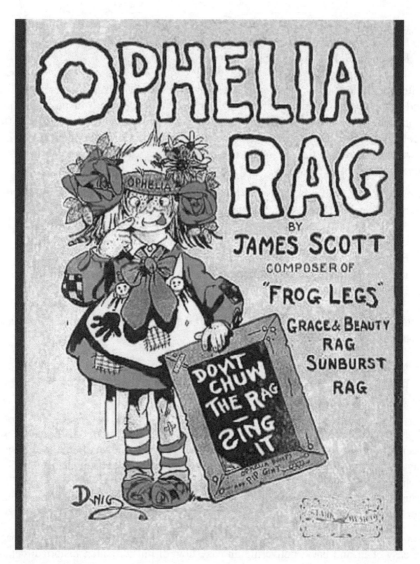

Fig. 2 Sheet music cover for James Scott's *Ophelia Rag*

ragtime and urging members not to play it!" Pause. "If you think that's weird, the following year the teamsters came out against *trucks*!"

The place of turn-of-the-last-century women in one of Morath's recurring themes. A famed entertainer named May Irwin scandalized the nation at the turn of century with rowdy syncopated songs like *The Money Song* ("If you don't have any money / Don't you bother coming 'round"), and she appeared in a sixteen-second Edison film called *The Kiss* that elicited outrage from the pulpits. Many white women, moreover, introduced ragtime sheet music into the parlors of middle-class

America. One of them, eighteen-year old composer Adaline Shepherd [1883–1950] wrote the *Pickles and Peppers* rag, which became the campaign song of William Jennings Bryan's 1908 Presidential bid. Bryan lost.

Max continually rejects the nostalgic haze that has accrued around ragtime. He admits, however, that, "if I could go back in a time machine, I'd visit Big Tom Turpin's Rose Bud Café in St. Louis. Maybe Scott Joplin would be there, or James Scott from Kansas City, or Eubie Blake. Tough competitors. Maybe on *this* time machine [gesturing at the piano], we can hear Joplin himself at the Rose Bud, playing this …" [followed by a rather melancholy performance of Joplin's *Solace*].

Finally Max produces with a flourish an antique piano roll. He inserts it into the piano, settles himself back on the bench and engages in a musical "dual": first the roll, then his fingers. Past and present, recorded and "live," back and forth, separate and together. They "talk" to each other, as it were, finishing each other's musical sentences.

Applause. And more applause. Max bows and exits the stage—but not before bestowing an affectionate gesture to the Edison gramophone.

William Bolcom & Joan Morris: Ragtime Song—"It's What Our Lives Have Become!"

John C. Tibbetts
5 June 1993, Sedalia, Missouri, and 4 October 2016, Ann Arbor, Michigan

In addition to innumerable piano pieces, ragtime composers wrote songs—many of them ethnically or racially "inflected." The most common of these were the so-called coon songs, and coon shouters like May Irwin became famous as a white woman who mimicked black performance styles and gestures on stage. Not all racist songs made fun of African Americans, however, and not all "coon songs" featured ugly lyrics and grotesque colored sheet music covers. A number of black composers—among them James Weldon Johnson (1871–1938), co-founder of the National Association for the Advancement of Colored People, or NAACP, and his brother J. Rosamund Johnson (1873–1954)—published, separately or together with Bob Cole (1868–1911), less offensive popular numbers, including "Tell Me, Dusky Maiden" (1901) and "My Castle on the Nile" (1901). Almost forgotten today, smaller numbers of Chinese- and Japanese-themed, German-themed, Irish-themed, and Jewish-themed ragtime songs can be found in a number of public libraries and archives (Fig. 3).

In 1988 William Elden Bolcom won the Pulitzer Prize in Music for *12 New Etudes for Piano*. The composer of many other works—including three operas, nine symphonies, twelve string quartets, and several concerted works

Fig. 3 William Bolcom

for strings and piano—Bolcom was named Ross Lee Finney Distinguished University Professor of Composition in 1994 at the University of Michigan; in 2006, he was awarded the National Medal of Arts. Nevertheless, Bolcom is perhaps best known for his collaboration with wife and musical partner,

**mezzo-soprano Joan Morris, and for their joint recordings of ragtime, vaude-
ville, and popular songs by brothers George and Ira (1896–1983) Gershwin;
by Richard Rodgers (1902–1979) of musical theater fame; and by "crossover"
artist Mike Stoller, who—together with Jerry Leiber (1933–2011)—helped
shape 1950s rock 'n' roll.**

**Born in Portland, Oregon, Joan Morris taught a cabaret class at the
University of Michigan from 1981–2009. She joined other musicians in a 2004
performance of her husband's *Songs of Innocence and Experience*; in 2006
the Naxos recording of that performance earned four Grammys for her and
her husband, including Best Classical Album of the Year.**

**These conversations began at the Scott Joplin Ragtime Festival in Sedalia,
Missouri in 1993, and concluded in the home of Bolcom and Morris in Ann
Arbor, Michigan.**

*JOHN C. TIBBETTS: Bill, you may be the most prominent composer these days to
have written ragtime.*
WILLIAM BOLCOM: In the 1960s a lot of us were starting to chafe at the
"International Fellowship Style"[1] as we used to call it: the [compositional methods of the] post-Webern period, which is the way you should write—you haven't
heard that before?—or the guys wouldn't give you a hearing. Still true, by the way.
To a great extent if you wanted to get a Guggenheim [Fellowship], you'd better
go with the flow or forget it. Unless, of course, if you happen to be somebody
known as a maverick, and then they have to give it to you, but only grudgingly. I
got tired of hearing it! I suddenly found myself getting involved with Scott Joplin,
and it felt so liberating to write tunes in A-flat Major with four flats and harmonies
you could understand. That could also have been nostalgia, and I suppose it was
considered—and still is—considered by the establishment as copping out. But it's
because we didn't follow that party line.

What was it about Joplin that attracted you?
The reason, I guess, that Joplin was such a good transition toward a more open
attitude toward musical style was because he was so good. The details were so
good; they bear scrutiny. Like Chopin mazurkas, rags are a body of music that
people think they can do themselves. I delighted in them because I could sit down
and write in two-four, in key signatures, and have [tonic] cadences at the end! The
voice leading, the way they're *made,* is so good. And so there was a whole spate
for about ten years when a bunch of us were writing a lot of rags. Bill Albright
[1944–1998] and I started exchanging our little pieces in the mail. Like sending
postcards. It felt so good after being a card-carrying Modernist all those years!

---

[1]More precisely, the dodecaphonic, or twelve-tone, compositional method [I cut the end of this
note, since it's in the introduction to the section just a few pages earlier].

I love the titles of your rags: "Incinerator Rag," "The Tabby Cat Walk,"
"Serpent's Kiss"—
—Eubie Blake loved that one![2] He always asked me to play it!

Then there was your "Poltergeist Rag." Do you remember what John [Graziano]
said about it?
Remind me!

He said something like, "Bill must have written it when they had a sale in acciden-
tals at K-Mart one day!"
[laughs]: Be afraid, be very afraid! You know, I still get rags sent to me by young
guys who want to write a rag. Maybe they're a good way to get a person started to
be careful about writing. It's a good exercise; maybe I should get people to write
rags as beginning exercises for a student.

JOAN MORRIS: My piano teacher in Ann Arbor said that when young kids of
eleven or twelve—she has students of all ages—when they're beginning to lose
interest, and when the practicing is getting to them, she'll give them a rag; and
they get all excited because the rhythm really turns them on. They're working on
something that's difficult harmonically, but it's all in the service of this rhythm.

It's hard to realize now that there was a time when Joplin's rags weren't well
known at all!
BOLCOM: Yeah, in 1967 few people even knew who Scott Joplin was. Many
of the jazz folks dismissed him as "academic." To them he seemed stiff, somebody you didn't fool around with. I mean, the notes were *there*. I knew *The*
Maple Leaf Rag, but that was about all. My friend, Norman Lloyd, then head
of the music division for the Rockefeller Foundation, mentioned a Joplin "ragtime" opera called *Treemonisha*. I was intrigued. No one, not even at the Library
at Lincoln Center, had it. But Rudi Blesh, my colleague at Queens, told me he
had the piano-vocal score and that it was absolutely charming. T.J. Anderson,
an African-American composer, and I worked out a performing version with a
theater orchestra of sixteen pieces as a kind of "home-made" opera. Then I went
to Vera [Brodsky] Lawrence, who was working on a big [American composer
Louis Moreau] Gottschalk [1829–1869] project, and played her some Joplin rags.
She decided that collecting Joplin's rags and staging his *Treemonisha* would be
her next project. Meanwhile, I had already gotten hold of some of Joplin's rags
from Max Morath. I talked with Josh[ua] Rifkin about them and he recorded three
albums for Nonesuch in 1970. Between that, the movie *The Sting*, and the heroic
work of our good friend, Max Morath—well, the rest is history.

---

[2]James Hubert ("Eubie") Blake (1997–1983), musician and composer, was one of many African
American ragtime stars.

How exciting it must have been to see Treemonisha *in a full-scale stage spectacular!*
[pauses and looks to Morris for confirmation]: Lawrence acquired the royalties from the Joplin estate, which accrued to her own benefit. She wanted the opera "big." But then, somehow, the charm gets lost. It needs to be done *small*.

Some time during all this, the two of you begin performing ragtime and vaudeville songs together.
MORRIS: Bill and I met in 1972, and we gave our very first concert in New York on 5 January 1973. So when we came to Sedalia, Missouri—Joplin's home town—in 1974, that was really one of the first occasions that we performed together.

BOLCOM: I think that might have been your maiden voyage doing *Pineapple Rag.*

MORRIS: It sure was. I can remember the utter terror I felt when I was standing back stage and going over the words, like a mantra. There really is no time to breathe in that song. Now I don't have as much fear about it, because I've done it so many times. Someone said, "My god, that's really a weird song!" And is, too! It was a weird one to start with!

> Come honey love, my money love, slide me;
> Come syncopate, don't hesitate, glide me,
> Say, you're a daisy, I'm going crazy,
> Oh, that Pine Apple Rag!

But it was good, because it prepared me later for all those Cole Porter [1891–1964] "list" songs, where you don't have to time to think.[3]

Who wrote the lyrics for Pineapple Rag*?*
It seems to have been a fellow named Joe Snyder. The music came out in 1909 and the lyrics a year later. Not many people are singing these things any more. Joplin wrote lyrics, too. He wrote the words to one of his earliest songs, *The Ragtime Dance*. You have words like—[half sings and recites]

> I attended a ball last Thursday night …
> It certainly was a sight to see.
> So many colored folks there without a razor fight
> T'was a great surprise to me!

---

[3]"Patter" or "list" songs, featuring rapid-fire lyrics and music, are mostly associated with opera and musical theatre.

Oh my! Razors! I hardly need remind you that, in an age of cultural diversity, lyr-
ics in songs like seem shocking. Is that a problem for both of you? How do you
deal with that?

BOLCOM: That's the trouble with many ragtime songs. And that's the thing people are very tough about, words like "razors," "coons" [i.e., African Americans],
"niggers." My feeling is that either you don't perform these songs at all, or you
perform them when everybody understands the [cultural] context. I don't know,
my feeling—and I think Joan agrees with me—is that we'd rather not do the song.
About ten years ago we used to do one of the old Babe Conners numbers that May
Irwin performed quite often, called "The Bully Song." Which is full of just exactly
that kind of thing.

Is that the same May Irwin who appeared in an early Thomas Edison short called
May Irwin's Kiss?

MORRIS: I believe so. Irwin was very popular around the turn of the century. But
what's been forgotten is that she introduced the syncopated song in a Broadway
musical. She also introduced probably the most famous song of the century, "After
the Ball" [by Charles K. Harris (1867–1930)]; she had her own stage company;
and she sometimes sang what was called "Negro dialect." Here she was, a white
woman, popularizing "coon" songs as early as 1895.

BOLCOM: Which is where we get her "Bully Song."

MORRIS: Right. We performed things like that at the Yale Cabaret and all the
black students came up to us afterward and said, "Oh, thank you! We've always
wanted to know what they [coon songs] were like." The only real problem you'd
have today would be from a certain kind of white liberal who gets upset about
political correctness. It isn't the people *involved* that seem to object. To me we're
talking about a form of political bigotry.

Eubie [Blake] used to talk about being called an "Uncle Tom" for doing this kind
of material. They've really got a nerve, if you ask me, getting upset [even though
they have nothing to do with] the people that actually suffered through it at the
time. I don't think you can have a healthy attitude about these things unless you
can see what was there. Now, I think you should at least have the courtesy to say,
"This is the way it was; this is not the way we are now. But look at it, don't be
afraid of it." Let's get rid of the shame; let's look at it for what it was. Let's not
have this false Mrs. Grundy attitude: "Oh, we can't touch that." If you sweep it
under the carpet, you're just going to be dealing with fear and anger because you
haven't faced up to it.

When people object, do you make any apologies for performing these songs?
BOLCOM: You're bound to have some people object. I would imagine if you did
it, even here [in Sedalia], you'd have to preface it by saying, "Listen, this is the
way it is, we're going to do it unexpurgated. Stop wincing and get used to the fact
that this is the way your grandfathers used to do it."

Does it break your heart, though? Because there must be some songs you'd love to perform, but somehow feel reluctant to.

MORRIS: Yeah, you bet. The one Bill mentioned, the "Bully Song," it's a great character song. About this big black guy who who's not scared of anybody since he's stronger than anybody and carries that dangerous razor. And then his enemy [half sings, recites]—

> When I walk that levee 'round, 'round, 'round,
> I'm lookin' for that bully, and he must be found!
> —you get such a charge out of being somebody else! But you can't do it now, you know.

BOLCOM: It's very frustrating. If you were going to perform it here, you'd have to do it in quotes. I do feel that the time has come for people to put aside their fears and realize that's what people were like [before World War I, when these songs were being published]. But they won't; and they're just trying to justify their squeamishness. Music, any music, has no real race or ownership. No one "owns" ragtime. Once it's out, it's in the world and then it's for everybody.

Epilogue
The following transpired in the Bolcom-Morris home in Ann Arbor, Michigan.

MORRIS: Retirement—if that is what it is—is still busy for both of us. Bill's 1992 opera *McTeague* was just revived in February at Landestheater Linz. A program of Bill's *Cabaret Songs*, co-written with Arnold Weinstein, was performed in April at Manhattan's Café Sabarsky. Two months later Bill's Trombone Concerto was given its world premiere by the New York Philharmonic, led by Alan Gilbert, with soloist Joseph Alessi.

BOLCOM: Yes, and some other new works are on the way. I just finished a new piano rag for Joan. It's called *Contentment*. Nothing showy; more like a Joplin rag.

TIBBETTS: I understand you're working on a new opera, Bill.

BOLCOM: It's based on *Dinner at Eight*. Mark [Campbell] is working on the libretto. It's not based on the classic MGM film, with Marie Dressler, Wallace Beery, and John Barrymore. I had to sign a paper saying we would not use certain things from the film. I went back to the Edna Ferber/George S. Kaufman play, which was produced a year earlier [Opened on Broadway at the Music Box Theatre on 22 October 1932]. Unlike the movie, it's a serio-tragedy, more edgy, a little darker. I plan to open it on March 11 next year [2017] at Ordway Hall in St. Paul.

MORRIS: And I'm working on a new book, *An Actress Who Sings*. In a way, I've been working on it for forty years. It's been difficult to find time for it while we're on the road; but now that we're slowing down and thinking of retiring, I'm going to finish it. I'll mix in my research into performing instructions and notes with anecdotes about our career and the many people we have met and worked with along the way.

BOLCOM: By the way, Joan and I are planning to perform *The Pineapple Rag* again at Ann Arbor at the Kerrytown Hall and then later in New York City at the Metropolitan Room. Reading through our interview with you a few years ago, John, is prompting us to take on the song again. It's part of our agenda these days to not perform so often, but only selectively.

Jay McShann: "I Crashed the Notes!"

John C. Tibbetts
2 January 1987, Kansas City, Missouri

During the 1930s and 1940s, the so-called Kansas City jazz style emerged, combining upbeat blues with a flexible, increasingly harmonically complex improvisatory style. Its legacy was soon felt in the bebop movement led by Charlie "Bird" Parker (1920–1955). A thriving, wide-open town under the benign dictatorship of "Boss" Tom Pendergast (1872–1945), pre-World War II Kansas City was a crossroads for the Union Pacific and Atchison, Topeka & Santa Fe railroads, and a temporary home for the "territory" bands that restlessly crisscrossed the Midwest. Many of the city's night clubs, dance halls, brothels, and vaudeville houses passed into legend, including the Reno Club, the Paseo Ballroom, the Cherry Blossom, and the Hi Hat, but several remain in the 18th and Vine Historic District, including the Gem Theater and the Blue Room.

Born in Muskogee, Oklahoma, James Columbus ("Jay") McShann learned from and worked initially with jazz pianist Earl ("Fatha") Hines (1903–1983). In 1936, McShann to Kansas City, Missouri, where the Jay McShann Orchestra included such legendary performers as saxophonists Ben Webster (1909–1973) and Charlie Parker; in 1940 Parker made his first recording with McShann. The band broke up in 1944, when McShann was drafted into the army, and in later life he mostly performed as a pianist and singer with collaborators that violinist Claude Williams (1908–2004). In 1988 McShann was inducted into the Blues Hall of Fame. He made his last recording, *Hootie Blues*, in February 2001 (Fig. 4).

The conversation that follows took place in 1987 in McShann's Kansas City home. I am indebted to the late Dick Wright, jazz historian at the University of Kansas, for arranging the meeting. McShann had just received news that the National Endowment of the Arts (NEA) was planning a cere-mony to designate him as an American Jazz Master and award him a stipend of $20,000.

Fig. 4 Jay McShann

JOHN C. TIBBETTS: Jay, how long have you been playing?
JAY MCSHANN: Well, I've made the three-score, or whatever.

What were your impressions of Kansas City when you first arrived in 1936?
When I came to Kansas City, the town was wide open, jumpin', no curfew, and joints stayin' open twenty-four hours [a day]. You'd see the porter come in about 6:30 or 7 in the mornin', and we'd just move over to one side while he cleaned up; and when he finished, we'd move back over where we was [and keep playing]. You'd see guys on the street during the spook breakfasts, waitin' to catch the streetcar, with their dinner buckets, you know, and they'd hear that blowin' and they'd come in and order a drink. By noon, they'd never gotten to work, still sittin' and still tastin'.[4] Meanwhile, we'd be playin', Maybe just start with two or three players but finally end up with ten or twelve in a real jam session. The piano players got worked real hard. Maybe you'd have lots of horns waitin' to play, but there'd be just one piano player, goin' all the time! That killed piano players, drummers and bass men!

When was this?
When I came to Kansas City, this was already goin' on. Any time you have a town that's wide open you gonna find all the chicks there, you gonna find all the pimps there, you gonna find the gamblers, the musicians coming from north, east, south and west. It makes for good times. And everything just *moves*. You could go from club to club, the Lone Star, the Sunset, the Subway, the Reno Club where [William James ("Count")] Basie [1904–1984] was.

When you arrived in Kansas City, how aware were you of the so-called "Kansas City" style?
Here's what you were hearing; you got these cats comin' from all over. And every time a new cat would come in, we'd ask, "Who's this new cat in town? Bring him down to the session. We'd find out what the cats from the West Coast was doin'. So when he sits in and blows, we all had our eyes on him. And when he hears the other cats here in town, he'd say, "This is some different stuff." Then, when cats from the Midwest would go east, they'd take their own thing there. Bands were passin' through, comin' and goin' all the time. I wasn't real conscious of that; I was just tryin' to play. I'll say this, when I got to Kansas City, I hadn't heard anything like it. Joe Turner [1907–1990] and Pete Johnson [1904–1967], doin' what they were doin'. Pete would play for about twenty minutes with the rhythm section, and Joe would sing for about twenty minutes. Then another ten minutes from each—and that was the first set! And that just excited me, and I would just

---

[4]"Spook breakfasts," popular events in mid-1930s Kansas City establishments like the Reno Club, featured jam sessions and "cutting" contests for jazz musicians who drifted in and out of such clubs from the early morning hours of Sunday into the next day. Spook breakfasts were recreated in Robert Altman's 1996 film *Kansas City*.

stand there with my eyes bugged out. I didn't realize that Joe was just rollin' those words right off his head. I hated to go to bed for fear I was gonna miss somethin'. I was just glad to be there and sit and just listen. We all listened to each other.

Your band had that great rhythm section, with Gus Johnson on drums and Gene Ramey on bass.
Oh, we played lots of other places, too. I understand both of them are in New York now [1987]. We got together a few years ago and had sort of a reunion, you know?

Tell me about Charlie Parker.
We were both so young, not even out of our teens! Parker was the kind of person you *remember*! [laughs] He was a lively person. He loved to live. And he wanted to get everything he could get out of life. He was burnin' all the time, like me. But he had me beat! I first heard him in a club with a sound I had never heard before. He was already blowing it hard. He sat in with me and blew with Harlan Leonard's band, too. But I think he always felt more comfortable with me. My first recordings were all with Parker [1940]. We hit it big in New York at the Savoy [Ballroom]. But all that was over when the Army drafted me and Parker moved on.

What about that nickname "Bird"?
We were drivin' to a job in Nebraska when our car struck a chicken. Charlie yelled, "Back up! You hit a yardbird!" He got out and carried it on to Lincoln, where he cooked it and ate it all!

That's the story?
That's the story.

You talk about the boogie-woogie style. How would you describe it?
You take Pete Johnson. He did a lot of boogie-woogie; he was one of the greatest." [plays and riffs with the right hand over a rock-solid left hand] There's different ways you could play that left hand to get a different feel, fast or medium slow, like the old days with [boogie-woogie stylist] Mama Yancey [1896–1986].

I notice you have no hesitation in playing two notes together.
That's right. That's another thing I liked about Pete; he could just crash those notes.

Crash the notes?
Yeah, you can get those notes close together and crash them. Like you're trying to slide in and out of the notes [demonstrates with his right hand].

More than a few musicologists go nuts trying to break down those dissonances!
You just play your cards, number the notes, all the way from 1 [i.e., the tonic] to the dominant seventh. *Downbeat* magazine one time broke down Ben Webster's chords and sent them him to check for accuracy. Ben took one look and said, "I

can't play that!" But he *had* played it! Your two hands are like an orchestra, and when you're doin' a single, you can play with your right hand like the brass and the left like the percussion.

How did Moten Swing *become a Kansas City trademark tune?*
That's been around a long time. It was a tune that Bennie Moten [1894–1935] wrote and Basie played. The idea for it was what we always did, where we'd take one number off another number and them combine them. They took *Moten Swing* off *You're Drivin' Me Crazy*. [plays *Moten Swing* and gradually merges it with the pop standard] We'd start with one and move on into the other.

When did you start doing your own vocals?
I wasn't doin' any vocals at all for a long time. During the time I had my band, I always liked good singers, like Walter Brown [1917–1956] and Al Hibbler [1915–2001]. I found Walter in a little club in Kansas City. He was a great blues singer and Al was a great ballad singer. So I had all I needed! But on a lot of my jobs, some of the guys in the band would say, "Go ahead and sing!" So I did, more and more, on into the 1950s. I realized I could do some jiving on my own with the vocals. Just enough to get by. I believe Nat [King] Cole started singin' like that. I guess my singin' is no different than my playin'.

Why do they call you "Hootie"?
Oh, I hadn't been in Kansas City very long when I knew the bartenders were always trying out new drinks on the musicians. Somebody asked the bartender to fix me a new drink he'd been talking about. So he fixed me a 3-2 [i.e., 3.2% alcohol] beer and put alcohol in that beer,[5] and it got really cold, with all that foam runnin' down the outside. He passed it over to me, and it tasted so good I really hated to turn it down. The guys knew that was gonna happen. So finally they said, "Are you ready to sit in and play?" I'd say, "Yeah," but when I got ready to get up, I couldn't get up! So they started calling me the cat that got "hooted."

Let's talk about the NEA stipend you just received.
Right now, all I've heard is that there'll be a presentation of some kind this year. I'm glad they looked out for me. Past folks that have been honored I believe are [composers] Dizzy [i.e., John Birks] Gillespie [1917–1993], Roy Eldridge [1889–1960], Jo Jones [1911–1985], and Thelonious Monk [1917–1982]. The two with me this year are Cleo Brown [c. 1907–1995] and Melba Liston [1929–1999]. I was with Cleo a couple of years ago in Denver at a party. She was at one of these retirement homes. She's into these church things, now, and she played piano for some gospel. But then, before we left, she broke down and did some

---

[5]Probably a "boilermaker": a glass of beer with a shot of whiskey or vodka.

boogie-woogie for us [laughs]; and she's still got that left hand workin' beautiful. Melba's a fine trombonist who was around Kansas City a lot. She was with Diz for awhile.

Melba's an educator, a teacher, right?
I believe so. That's right. As for the money, I'll believe it when I see it! That's always the best buy. And then I'll start making plans. Maybe I'll just take it easy. The last ten or twelve years I've been all over the world with my music.

Will you write a book?
Well, I've been workin' on some stuff. There's a guy [at the] University of Minnesota wrote me a couple of days ago, wantin' to know what I'm gonna do; so we'll see what happens.

So I guess you'll be looking back at pictures and letters and things you've kept?
Oh, no! I'm the worst in the world! [laughs] But I'm workin' on getting some things together.

And your music will just keep on keepin' on, won't it?
No other way to go.

George Shearing: "'Classical,' 'Jazz'—Don't These Musics Call upon One Another as Parts of a Larger Idea?"

John C. Tibbetts
10 October 1987, Kansas City, Missouri

"I consider him one of the greatest musical minds I've ever been around," said Dave Brubeck (1920–2012) of blind jazz and fusion artist George Shearing. Born in England, Shearing was blind from birth and received little formal education; nevertheless, by 1937 he had begun broadcasting on BBC radio. In 1947 Shearing emigrated to the USA, where he became a citizen in 1956, and where he spent most of the rest of his professional life. In addition to numerous recordings and concert tours, he won fame for his "cool" jazz arrangements and for his use of "locked-hands" melodic improvisation (also known as "Shearing's voicing") that added harmonic richness to his music-making. A fan of classical music as well as jazz, he appeared occasionally throughout the 1950s and 1960s with symphonic orchestras and chamber ensembles. In addition to a number of awards, including two Grammys and several honorary degrees, Shearing was knighted by Queen Elizabeth II in 2007 (Fig. 5).

This conversation transpired on the Folly Theater stage in Kansas City prior to his evening concert.

Fig. 5 George Shearing

JOHN C. TIBBETTS: You find much in common between classical music and jazz.
GEORGE SHEARING: Yes, indeed. Because, you know, music is music is music. And then there's rock and roll! No, no, I'm sorry. But you know, everything, whether its jazz or classical music must have architecture, it must have *direction*. I think if Johann Sebastian Bach were alive today, he'd be a marvelous jazz musician.

What happened to "freezing" music on the page?
Something had to be done to preserve a text.[6] Think of all the various and sundry additions and alternatives that were going around. So musical rules became stricter. "Thou shalt nots" came into being. No more consecutive fifths![7] [laughs] You finally get to the point where the poor student coming out of school is totally inhibited and is afraid to put his hands on the keyboard unless he's got something [printed] up in front of him. I know, my wife is a musician, but I can't get her beyond the first four bars of "Autumn in New York!" Only the jazz musician feels free [today] to improvise and swing the music.

Which, in a way, is what you are doing when you bring classical elements and quotations into popular songs. I remember how delighted I was to hear you quoting Frederick Delius [1862–1934] in Berkeley Square.

---

[6]Prior to the invention of the phonograph and other recording machines, most music simply disappeared. Hand-copied, printed, or "frozen" music, on the other hand, survived.

[7]"Parallel fifths" (for example, [C - G] moving immediately to [D – A] in the same vocal line or lines) were avoided by many composers from the fifteenth through the nineteenth centuries because they were thought to interfere with proper voice leading.

Ah, right. *[On Hearing the] First Cuckoo in Spring*. Well, Delius is really one of my very favorite composers, along with other English composers at that time, like [Australian composer and ethnographer] Percy Grainger [1882–1961].

Well, Delius and Grainger would have approved, wouldn't they?
I think so. I think so. In fact, when my wife was working one day with the New York Philharmonic doing the Bach B-minor Mass, some of the players during the intermission asked me to do something on my own. So I played the *Kerry Dances*.

Why in the world did you do that?
Well, I played the *Kerry Dances* and used it with as a fugue subject from the opening of Bach's Kyrie. So it became, you see, the *Kyrie Dances*! You have in the left hand the Kyrie [hums] and in the right the tune from *Kerry Dances*. [sings]

A knowledgeable audience must have had a ball with that!
Yeah. It was fun. I do that all the time in the clubs when I know there's a classical table there. I'll do it, and they're the only ones who laugh and the rest of the room is, shhh! You know, shush!

Any more examples of this sort of thing?
Sure, the so-called American Songbook is ripe for that.[8] I've always gotten a kick of out of weaving counterpoint around "Easy to Love." And I've always loved the second movement from Rachmaninoff's Second [Piano Concerto], which goes nicely with *Tenderly*. I'll work in Debussy and Ravel whenever I can. And Poulenc: There's a lovely *Perpetual Movement* [No. 3] that I use in "On the Street Where You Live." Do you know "It Never Entered My Mind," a great Rodgers and [Lorenz] Hart [1895–1943] standard? Well, a little Satie [the first *Gymnopedie*] goes with it beautifully! There's "Taking a Chance on Love," which has always had for me the stately tread of a Bach Chorale Prelude. And *How Insensitive* by [Brazilian composer] Antonio Carlos Jobim [1927–1994] seems to evoke one of the Chopin preludes—the No. 4, I think.

You don't see this sort of thing as a stunt?
Not at all! Yes, I have fun with it, but really, don't these musics sort of "call upon" one another? Parts of a larger idea?

Just a year ago [1986], you partnered with Barry Tuckwell, possibly the finest horn player in the world.
I met Barry at a concert in London. I was playing Mozart in the first half and he was playing in the second half. I admired him very much. And just as I went to meet him, there was a knock on my door, and there was Barry! We got to

---

[8]More often called the "Great American Songbook" and also known as "American Standards": an imaginary collection of popular songs mostly composed during the 1920s–1950s.

talking away about various things, and he said, "Look, when it comes to giving me an encore, why don't we play that number that you made with Richard Russell Bennett [1936–2012], based on music by Jerome Kern [1885–1945]?" We worked it out. And then afterwards, we both said, "Why don't we make a record?" That's how it happened. *George Shearing & Barry Tuckwell Play George Shearing.* Says it all! We had a string quartet join us on some of those tracks.

Please talk about your classical training.
I wouldn't exactly call it that. I was born in Battersea, a London suburb, and at first just memorized tunes I heard on the radio and picked them out on the piano. After some lessons from a local teacher, I studied with a blind teacher at the Linden Lodge School. That was between the ages of twelve and sixteen.

Was that difficult, or awkward?
It wasn't until I was twenty-one that I really forced myself to learn Braille music.[9] There are no staves and no clefs. We have the same six dots in Braille for letters, music, and everything else. You have only a bunch of combinations of six or fewer dots. It's not music notation, per se.

When did you realize that you did not have to be confined to the printed page, braille or otherwise? I mean, you must have a natural ear. Or can you develop an ear?
You can develop your ear to a point, but I don't know whether you can develop it to the point where somebody plays a ten-note chord and you can play it right after them. And I could do that. Somebody hits a chord, bang, bang, and you know, all ten notes. I think it's kind of a gift. And my music teacher, in case I didn't realize it, said to my parents when I was sixteen, "Further study of classical music with this young man would be a waste of time. It's obvious that he's going to become a jazz pianist." But I've kept on doing both. I learned a lot in the clubs listening to Teddy Wilson [1912–1986] and [composer and pianist] Fats Waller [1904–1943]. Sometimes I was allowed to play along with some of the visiting American musicians, like [composer and saxophonist] Coleman Hawkins [1904–1969]. And later after coming to America, there were times with many of the major symphony orchestras throughout the country here. Mozart and Bach concerti and stuff like that.

Are you ever tempted, perhaps playing a Mozart concerto, to add your own cadenzas right on the spot?
I resist the temptation—sometimes! I remember once I had a thirty-bar memory lapse. And I turned my left ear to the orchestra and improvised in the Mozart style around the chords that I heard the orchestra playing. Until my memory came back. It was the most nerve-wracking experience I've ever had in my life.

---

[9]Braille is a form of "tangible writing," consisting of raised impressions (dots) that can be read with the fingertips.

But, with all apologies to Mozart, I bet it was the highlight of the evening.
I tried to pay as much homage and respect to Mozart as I can. I've done it a number of times. Nowadays I don't practice much, unless I have a concert like that coming up. I don't learn from braille anymore. I learn from listening to tapes. I do not suggest to the parents of blind children, though, that they have another [pianist-song writer] Ray Charles [1930–2004] or George Shearing on their hands. "Oh boy," they say, "he put his hands on the piano twice today!" But, you know, maybe the kid has a tin ear. Blindness has nothing to do with musical gifts. The only benefit I can see is that if you are forced to gather information that's less available to you than it would be to a sighted person, you will cherish it more, memorize it longer, and pick it up as soon as you can.

My father, who was a jazz musician back in Kansas City's great jazz days, cherishes the small jazz combo that you formed, beginning in the 1950s.
The Quintet? That started in 1949. It was almost an accident, really. I had been working in the clubs on 52nd Street in Manhattan, when at the last minute I had to form a new group for a recording date. My clarinetist [Buddy DeFranco] was unavailable, and I added Chuck Wayne on guitar and Margie Hyams on vibraharp to our bass player John Levy and drummer Denzil Best. Yes, it was something fresh and mellow to what we then called "bop." Two of my own hit songs came from those early days: "September in the Rain" and "Lullaby of Birdland."

What is "Birdland" really about? And just what was—or is—Birdland?
Birdland was a club owned by Morris Levy. It was named after your own Kansas City great, Charlie "Bird" Parker. Levy wanted a theme song for his nightly radio broadcast from the club. [The melody] came to me quickly. I tell everybody the whole thing took only ten minutes to work it out. It became a bebop standard, you know.

And you sing it, sometimes!
Let's just say that [composer as well as singer] Mel [Tormé; 1925–1999] has allowed it, on occasion!

Will the Shearing Quintet sound ever come back?
No, it won't come back. When I broke it up in 1978, I said it would only return if Standard Oil or Sinatra wants it! Standard Oil never did come through, though Frank Sinatra did; so we played for two weeks in Carnegie Hall with Frank. And we played for a week in Boston with Frank and we've done some benefit [concerts] together.

In fact, one of those benefits I believe was for a cancer foundation.
That's right. For the Sloan-Kettering Fund we raised two million dollars in one night. Luciano Pavarotti and Frank and I.

In addition to making wonderful music, what kind of an extra kick do you get, knowing that you've contributed to a cause like that?
Not only did I realize that I was giving my services to a very wonderful cause, but I was presented with the most wonderful citation. [It came] in a beautiful leather box, and a beautiful leather book bound in the box, and it was given by the Rockefellers. Frank came out and said, "I've been blind a number of times in my life [!], so I'll read it for you." It was in print as well as Braille!

You mentioned Mel Tormé a minute ago. What of your work with him? If there is a pop-song equivalent today to the art song, your work with Mel would have to be it. When did that start?
Thanks are really due to George Wein, the JVC Jazz Festival impresario. It used to be called "Newport Jazz," and then "Cool Jazz," then JVC. I think George paired us together first in 1976 at Carnegie Hall. We first met when I was playing at a club in San Francisco. I remember hanging out with Mel until three and four in the morning, talking about mutual interests in classical composers like Delius and Debussy. I've always felt that Mel is the greatest all-around talent in the business. I can't imagine a more compatible musical partner. It is like a musical marriage, and we literally breathe together during our performances. Our workload together has increased immeasurably as the years have passed. And, it's a joy, 'cause that man, if I changed one chord tonight, he would change a note to go with that chord. This is how these "Berkeley Square" and "It Might as Well Be Spring" things come about. They're never the same two nights running.

In other words, your ear is as much attuned to him as to your instrument. So, when do you rehearse with him?
Maybe the day before a gig.

You're kidding?
No.

That's it?
That's it. I call us two bodies with one musical mind.

Magnificent. What about an album from George Shearing in which you pair up with Mel Tormé for a number of Christmas Carols, like you did for a PBS television special?
Yes. Yes, I've wanted to do it for the longest time. I hope I can sell Carl Jefferson of Concord on the idea one day. How about swinging *Away in a Manger* to Brahms's "Lullaby"?

Carlisle Floyd: "My Own Approach Is to Create a Completely True, Credible, Dramatic Life on the Stage"

John C. Tibbetts
September 1991, Kansas City, Missouri

Opera houses first appeared in North America during the eighteenth century, and ever since, American composers have created operas to fill their stages. It is often a very rocky road, and the performance of an American opera is still a noteworthy occurrence. Notable opera companies have contributed significantly to the art form in America. Founded in 1854, Manhattan's Academy of Music offered both grand opera and (later) vaudeville to the city's cognoscenti; the Academy closed its doors in 1926, decades after New York's Metropolitan Opera was established in 1883. The "Met," perhaps the most prestigious American opera company, moved to Lincoln Center in 1966; today its performances reach millions via digital broadcasts to movie theaters all over the world (Fig. 6).

Fig. 6 Carlisle Floyd

A graduate of Converse College and Syracuse University, Carlisle Floyd joined the piano faculty at Florida State University where he later received a Distinguished Professor award; his other prizes include a Guggenheim Fellowship, induction into the American Academy of Arts and Letters, and the National Medal of Arts, presented to him by President George W. Bush. Critic Joshua Kosman praised Floyd as "one of the living masters of contemporary American opera"—this on behalf of Floyd's most famous opera *Susannah* (1955), today second only to *Porgy and Bess* in popularity and number of performances. Floyd's other operas include *Of Mice and Men* (1970) and *Cold Sassy Tree* (2000).

This conversation transpired in 1991 as Floyd was assisting in the preparation of *Susannah* for the Lyric Opera of Kansas City.

JOHN TIBBETTS: How did Susannah *come to pass? Sounds Biblical, doesn't it?*
CARLISLE FLOYD: [laughs] Appropriately enough! Well, it actually came to pass, as you say, in 1955 at Florida State University, where it had its first performance. Actually, its first *professional* premiere was one year later in New York. Although, in a sense, the one at Florida State University in Tallahassee was professional in that the two leads were imported, Phyllis Curtin in the title role and Mack Harrell as the Reverend Olin Blitch. Curtin then went on to do it at the New York City Opera.

How soon did you know that Susannah *would achieve its currency and popularity?*
I don't think I really had any idea. I remember my mother saying to me, "Son, did you expect so much to come so quickly from it?"
And you said to her ... ?
I said, "No," although I have to admit it was being considered by the then-existing NBC Opera Company, which was the first television opera company, the brainchild of Samuel Chotzinoff for production before the [New York] City Opera did it. Their concern was that because of its regional flavor it would really have a currency only in about three southern states, which of course has not quite turned out to be the case since. I think by now it's probably been performed in most of the fifty states.

I think you estimate 650 performances ... and counting?
Well, that's not an estimate, that's an actual count!

And as a World's Fair opera, in Brussels in 1958?
It was selected after it had had its New York premiere and was in the repertoire of the New York City Opera for four years running. A production was mounted expressly with the idea of taking it to the Brussels Fair. And it's one of those things that went through all of the bureaucratic channels before the State Department sent it over as its official American entry in the field of opera.

Before we discuss the plot, please say something about Susannah*'s American theme and setting.*
The story's hardly restricted to one or two Southern states. Many people in unlikely places tell me it evokes memories of their childhoods. It goes into a very strong fundamentalist strain, a religious fervor, throughout our country—whether Missouri Lutherans, the Mormons, or the Seventh Day Adventists. I must emphasize, though, that this story is a more general take on a kind of puritanical fundamentalism that crosses the country really.

What about the plot of Susannah*?*
It's set against the background of a revival meeting, an evangelical meeting, in the mountains of Tennessee.[10] It opens with a square dance and we see that the church wives are jealous of Susannah's beauty. A newcomer to the community, the Reverand Blitch. asks her to dance. The next morning Susannah, who is a very spirited, strong-willed young mountain girl, is discovered very discreetly and privately taking her bath in the nude in on a creek near her own house. Four elders are looking for a baptismal creek because of the new evangelist's revival meeting. Because of their inability to control their feelings after discovering her, they brand her as lecherous, as evil. She's told she must make a public confession concerning allegations that she has seduced one of the members of the congregation. There's a deadlock between this very, very strong-spirited mountain girl who refuses to acknowledge any guilt, and the concerted efforts of the community to extort a public confession from her. Olin Blitch offers to pray for her soul, but he succumbs to the weakness of his flesh and seduces her. She later says, simply, she is "too tired for it to make any difference." Susannah's brother Sam murders Blitch and the community tries to drive Susannah out of the valley. She defies them with a shotgun. They retreat.

It's certainly a far cry from typical grand opera's exotic settings and characters.
Well, "grand opera" is a term that I get a little impatient with, because there are only a few real grand operas. *Turandot,* maybe, and the second act of *Aïda.* What people overlook with *Aïda* is that the other three acts are quite intimate. Certainly, people think of opera as being exotic, something far away, not really dealing with flesh and blood human beings.

Please describe the musical profile of Susannah. *Are there arias and hummable tunes?*
Well, actually, there are plenty of those! "Ain't It a Pretty Night?" is a long psychological working through of a young girl who wants to find out what life is like beyond the mountains; at the same time she's concerned that if she leaves, she won't be able to get back to the things she loves about her home. And there's

---

[10]To some extent the plot of Floyd's opera parallels the story of Susanna (or Shoshana) and the Elders in the Old Testament Book of *Daniel*, chapter 13.

Susannah's second act aria, "The Trees on the Mountain," which is far darker and more elegiac, but which has proven to be very popular. And from there into my use of very recognizable folk tunes. Folk elements appear all the way through the piece, including the hymns in the revival meeting, although they're all original, both words and music. I use them to suggest immediately the flavor of a place and also what's going on.

Of course, your own Southern upbringing suggests that you were steeped in this kind of music and mood.
Well, yes, my father was a minister in the Methodist church. Of course, the kind of evangelical meeting I'm dealing with in *Susannah* is on a much more primitive level than anything he was ever involved with.

Did you get caught up in that fervor sometimes?
Not caught up, exactly; I mean, my reaction to revival meetings as a child was what I think most people's is, and that was really one of abject terror. It seemed the whole thrust of the sermon in a revival meeting was to simply frighten people into something they think must be "salvation." I didn't intend my revival meeting in *Susannah* to be a parody in any way. It's not a caricature; it's a very solemn and, I hope, a terrifying scene.

I'm thinking of the rich atmosphere of your opera. Has anybody ever staged it in Tennessee in an outdoor theater, maybe on a summer night?
Nobody. I did stage it myself about three years ago, in Knoxville, for the Knoxville Opera. Of course there are references to Knoxville in the text, when Susannah sings about the world outside of the mountains.

Which of your other operas are available on recordings today?
None at this point! Recordings of complete operas are like hen's teeth in this country, because of the enormous expense involved through [musicians'] unions. I experienced this with my opera, *Willy Stark* [*All the King's Men*], which was done ten years ago [i.e., in 1981] on PBS's *Great Performances*. I knew we'd have to pay very high union costs to the orchestra. But what really stunned me was the expense of the copyists who prepared the orchestral parts, something the average audience member isn't even aware of, but which is very expensive. The copyists had to be paid *twice*—this time for the *television* production as opposed to the *stage* production, although they only worked once. Bottom line: the best time to record an opera is *when it's in production*, so then you save rehearsal costs for the orchestra and the singers. There have been moves to record *Susannah*, and there's a very serious one right now. [The opera has since been recorded.]

So: how can you make a living as an opera composer? Is it possible?
Probably my operas have been performed a great deal more often than those of any other American opera composer. But it's a very uncertain income: one year it can be very large and the next year it can fall off. I started out, of course, in a

university and went into the professional music world, which is backwards from the way most people do it. I have been in both worlds ever since.

That's really important today, combining the academic with the professional.
We have to look at academic support as a modern-day version of the old patronage of nobility. Opera never paid for itself except in the late seventeenth century, when it was popular entertainment. But the point is, it's an expensive art form; and in the past we had the nobility or the wealthy families to underwrite expenses. Now, that kind of refuge for composers and artists is in universities, where it is possible to earn a livelihood while practicing their art professionally.

John Cage: "I Noticed Rather Quickly that People Were Having Difficulty with My Work!"

John C. Tibbetts
12 April 1988, Kansas City, Missouri

Among the many movements in twentieth-century music are several highly experimental styles, including minimalism, aleatoric or "chance" music (in which performers choose what to play and when to play it), "ambient" music (in which surrounding sounds, often drawn from nature, are incorporated into compositions), computer-generated "art music," and performance art (in which place and audience largely govern what happens). Of these movements, minimalism occupies a somewhat ill-defined place. Often associated with Philip Glass and Terry Riley, minimalist and "chance" composers often insist that "less is more," that music can and even should be constructed of a very few subtly changing harmonic or melodic patterns.

A predecessor of mid-twentieth-century minimalism, Erik Satie wrote one short piano piece he specified should be performed 840 times. Laurie Anderson, a composer-performer and experimenter with electronic media, briefly became famous in pop-rock circles for *O Superman*, a 1981 piece of "performance art" consisting of a single repeated note, two chords, electronically modified vocals, and a concluding passage featuring ambient sounds (Fig. 7).

Composer John Milton Cage, Jr. studied with Schoenberg and Henry Cowell (1897–1965); he also worked closely with choreographer Merce Cunningham (1919–2009), with whom he lived for much of his life. A proponent of aleatoric music, Cage pioneered experiments with ambient sounds in musical or quasi-musical contexts. His most famous work, *4′33″* (generally called "Four Minutes and Thirty-three Seconds") consists both of a pianist playing nothing and of the sounds made by audience members during the piece's duration. Cage was also important in the fields of electroacoustic music and the use of prepared pianos and toy pianos in concert compositions. Cage's *Europeras*,

Fig. 7 John Cage

a "light- and soundscape" opera in five parts (sometimes identified as "five operas"), exemplifies the composer's fascination with indeterminacy.

The following conversation took place in Vanderslice Hall on the campus of the Kansas City Art Institute.

JOHN C. TIBBETTS: Let's talk about your life in the arts. I understand that two of the great influences on your work are Satie and Arnold Schoenberg.
JOHN CAGE: Well, I've had many, many guides. They were two of them.

Do they represent two opposite positions in your approaches to music?
They're two different centers. I don't think they're opposites, because each one was so unique. I never met Satie but was in my teens when I first heard his music.

What was it about this gentleman—
—that made me like him?

Indeed.
Well, if you love someone or something, are you able to say what it was that attracted you? I don't think so. Just anything about that person pleases you, and that's my case with Satie. You know, he wrote all kinds of music, even at the age of forty, he went back to school to study counterpoint. And his music has a great deal of variety. And even at the end he was writing, well, *Mercure* and *Relache*; and those ballets introduced the use of popular tunes, and this was found shocking by many of the young composers who had taken him as master. They called him the *maitre d'Arcueil*.[11] But he was able to change music much more profoundly than others did. Most people find one way to do things and stick with it, but he didn't do that. That may be why I like him so much, because I've done that myself. Not all of my pieces have no sounds in them.

You did study with Schoenberg, though. Was that when he taught in Los Angeles?
He was first at home in Hollywood, and then he gave lectures at USC [University of Southern California]; later he was at home in Brentwood and he taught at UCLA [University of California, Los Angeles]. The reason I mentioned his homes is that he taught at home, too. And I went to all of his classes, whether they were at home or in the schools. When I first went to him asking him to teach me, I told him I couldn't give him any money. He said, "Will you devote your life to music?" and I promised that I would. I remember one day at USC he was saying, in front of a large class, "My purpose in teaching you is to make it impossible for you to write music." I literally worshiped the man. When he said that he wanted to make composing impossible, I determined to do it even more than I had determined before.

---

[11]Arcueil is a suburb of Paris. The phrase is both respectful and satiric: the "master of a village" rather than of Paris or any other important city.

Which of your works had he encountered before he died?
None, as far as I know. I think he heard about my work, because he was asked by
the conductor Hermann Scherchen whether he had any interesting American students. And he said, no, there weren't any; but then he smiled, and mentioned my
name. He said, "Of course he's not a composer, but he's an inventor."

What kind of reception did you have with your concerts?
When I gave concerts during the 1940s, and even a bit into the 1950s, I had to persuade people to come to them! [laughs] And I did all the—I designed the programs
and the announcements and everything. So. I took advantage of everything I could
to somehow get an audience. I used to be able to get a hundred people to come and
listen.

I understand you have recently composed an opera.
The first performance was in Frankfurt, in Germany a few months ago. I think it
was the third of December. It was supposed to be in November, about the fifteenth,
but the opera house burned. It burned, and I don't think anyone really knows how
it actually happened. The story that was publicized, printed in the newspaper, was
that someone had come from East Berlin, and being hungry and poor, climbed into
the opera house to find some food; and finding no food decided to build a fire at
the very point where a smoke alarm would not work. It's clearly an unbelievable
story.

*That seems indicative of the great number of conflagrations that have sprung up in
your wake over the years!*
Well, it was dramatic!

What's the name of your opera?
Europeras: One and Two, which are the words "Europe" and "opera" put together.
People say it's really the same work in two parts, but that's not true because it has
different singers. It's two different pieces. And the time lengths are different. The
first one is slow and the action is less concentrated than in the second one. It's an
extension of the way I worked for years with Merce Cunningham, where we bring
about a separation of the music in the dance, so that each one exists on its own,
and together they make an interpenetration in time. And here that's extended to all
the other aspects of theater, including the lighting.

Has it been performed in the United States?
It will be in July, they say. In Purchase. It's outside of New York. It's part of what's
called Summer Fair, or the Pepsi Cola Festival. We're heaving several festivals in
New York now, in the summers, all over the city of New York, and not just indoors,
but outdoors, too.

Did it ever upset you when your listeners, or maybe some of them, reacted nega-tively to your works?
No, I thought that was very encouraging. Because I knew that if they all liked it, that I was probably doing the wrong thing. I didn't have a very high regard for— what shall I say?—I like people, but I notice that they don't like experiences that they haven't had before. So many of them have trouble with new experiences. So, if they don't have trouble then it can't be very new, don't you think?

But hostile critics: was it difficult for you to withstand their barbs, their negative energies?
Well, I got used to it rather quickly. You see, my first concerts were given at the Cornish School in Seattle. I had given a few private concerts at home, so to speak, in Santa Monica, but the first public ones, where tickets were sold and all, were in Seattle. And I noticed rather quickly that people were having difficulty with the work; and that that was a way of knowing whether or not I was going in a new direction. Each audience became a kind of thermometer of whether I was doing my proper work, which was, I thought—because of my father perhaps—to find something new. I didn't really think of myself, and Schoenberg didn't either, as someone who had something to say in the way of expressing himself. I've never been interested in self-expression. I've been interested in invention and discovery. And now that I'm older, I'm afraid I have to confess that I keep on discovering the same thing all the time. I don't really discover anything that I didn't already dis-cover. It's very strange.

[Speaking of an installation in Cage's honor at the University of Kansas]: Never did the term "found object" more literally apply than to arrowheads and fossils!
Mmm. I have a garden in New York, and I think that this has been noised about that I'm a kind of magnet for stones.

We're in a garden, all right—a garden of sights and sounds, right here! There's a typewriter chattering away, there's some explosion sounds, phones ringing in the distance, a wall plastered with words and random numbers, etc.
As you come into the entrance, you hear the sounds and patterns of light. It's very lively. You don't see or hear things very clearly. There's a kind of smokiness, or absence of sharp edges everywhere, so you feel that you are dreaming rather than being wide awake. The letters and words are not an alphabet but a fantasy. It's poetic. It puts you in a kind of—well, it made tears come to my eyes.

It seems ironic that we have to come here to appreciate the sounds that are really all around us in everyday life.
I think more and more people are hearing the environmental sounds and enjoy-ing them. You know, one of the first ones to make publicly clear that that was a pleasure was Henry David Thoreau. I recall a remark by [Canadian pianist] Glenn Gould to the effect that the act of listening to the sounds, such as the sounds that are coming in the window now, is in fact a *musical* pleasure. It's been that way for

me all along. People ask me what music I prefer, and I tell them, no music at all. Just what happens to be audible wherever I am.

So that expression "hunter of sounds" that's been applied to you may not be quite correct. Because you don't have to hunt *for sounds; they're already all around us.* No, but you have to pay attention.

Audiences for your 4′33″, for example, may have been startled to realize that the sounds they were listening to came not from the piano up on a platform, but from themselves.
I understand there are people in Woodstock, where that piece was first played by David Tudor [1926–1996], who are *still* angry. I'm told that by the widow of Henry Cowell, who lives there. She lives in a suburb of Woodstock.

And those are probably the same people who were angry at Cowell's Banshee*!*
[laughs] I think so. But, along with the people who are angry, there are many people who, you know, enjoy what has happened to music. I think music has become more— more *open*, particularly to noises; and there are many listeners, now, who are more in the same way.

The idea that you could be called a member of an avant garde *strikes me as odd, because there's a very common-sensical aspect to your approach to life and art.*
"Common-sensical." I like that!

Is that a word? I'm not sure.
I like it. It's so close to "nonsensical!" I think *nonsense* is much more—well, it's more engaging than, you know, than *sense*. They teach it in the universities in Japan, did you know that?

Nonsense?
Yes. A Professor of Nonsense went all the way from Tokyo to Toronto as a guest to give some lectures on "Nonsense" there. [Pauses and goes over to the window, looks out, ears cocked to the sounds below – the tinkling sounds of a passing ice cream truck can be faintly heard].

What are you—
—I'm listening to the ice cream truck! [returns to his chair] I once wrote some music like that … for a toy piano. You know, the ones we play as children? Back to this whole notion of common sense. My father was an inventor. He liked the idea of common sense. And he objected to things like the square root of minus one. I grew up around machines, but I was always frightened of electricity. I was afraid I would get a shock. I must have gotten one right off the bat, so that I didn't want to have any more!

How long ago was that?
While I was a child and still living at home, in Los Angeles. We had a beautiful big bungalow, which I remember as being big, and surrounded by roses, arbors of roses. Recently I was taken to visit that house and I found that it's now in a kind of slum area, and it also looks much smaller. As people get older they become less tall, and apparently the houses we used to live in also shrink. It's just amazing.

Maybe that's more a fault of our perspective than the world, huh?
Well, it's something. It's very surprising. We have actually no clue—of course, we were smaller then, so things looked larger.

Now, at the age of seventy, what's your perspective on things?
I'm going on seventy-six now. My birthday was on 5 September [1988].

How does the world look to you now, bigger, smaller?
It looks more and more interesting. I'm always astonished at the things that I didn't take time to be interested in when I was younger. And if by circumstances I get an experience of the things of which I had no experience, I see that there's that much more; and the implication is that there are countless things to be interested in.

I love that kind of child-like sensibility—that before we learn languages and musical systems, words, colors, sounds are vivid and alive all on their own. Have you ever heard the marvelous quote by Chesterton when he came to New York in 1922, stood in Times Square amid all the flashing lights of the city, and said, "What a garden of wonders this would be for someone who did not know how to read"?
How true that is! A matter of perception. That reminds me of a painter in Virginia, where I was last week, who invited me there, who makes paintings from high points in Manhattan. He treats what he sees as though he were not in a city at all, but in a mountain range or in some natural spot. It's a strange idea.

Jennifer Higdon: "Yes, I'm a Hunter of Sounds!"

John C. Tibbetts and William Everett
15 March 2017, Kansas City, Missouri

Pulitzer Prize-winning composer Jennifer Higdon holds a Ph.D. in Composition from the University of Pennsylvania. Higdon's *Cold Mountain*, an opera co-commissioned by the Santa Fe, Philadelphia, and Minnesota opera companies, was premiered in August 2015. Her *Blue Cathedral* is one of the most performed contemporary American orchestral compositions. Among Hidgon's honors are two awards from the American Academy of Arts and Letters, and the Delaware Symphony's A.I. DuPont Award. Currently

Fig. 8 Jennifer Higdon

she holds the Milton L. Rock Chair in Composition Studies in Philadelphia's Curtis Institute of Music (Fig. 8).
What follows here is taken from observations presented by Ms. Higdon before various groups of students at the University of Missouri-Kansas City Conservatory of Music and Dance, where she was a Barr Institute Laureate.

JOHN C. TIBBETTS and WILLIAM EVERETT: Let's regard this moment as a snapshot in time. What's up with you at this very moment?
JENNIFER HIGDON: My Viola Concerto is now finished and there's a CD just out on Naxos. And there's an Oboe Concerto and a tone poem I call *All Things Majestic*. I wrote it for the Grand Teton Festival in honor of our National Parks.

Any works in progress?
I'm finishing a Tuba Concerto right now for the Pittsburgh Symphony, Royal Scottish Orchestra and Curtis; and I'm about to start a little brass concerto for three trombones and tuba. After that's a chamber opera for Opera Philadelphia.

What of Blue Cathedral? *Did you have a plan at the outset, how to structure the opera?*
I wasn't sure how it was going to unfold because I don't use established forms. I write instinctively. I think about what sounds sound interesting, what sounds cool, and how can you build that into something that's interesting for the performers and the audience. But, yes, I had to have some sort of logic for the order of the solos. I thought, "Well, I'm the older sibling, so I'm going to bring the flute solo in first and then my brother's clarinet solo, since he is a year and a half younger than me." And then I have the violin join in. In the slower middle section there are a whole lot of solos for individual players, and this is where I think of all the kids at Curtis, where I teach.

How about the selection of the color "blue" for the title?
My brother's middle name is Blue. He had been given the name by my dad, he said; in case he ever wants to be an artist, he could go by "Blue." So, I was thinking about Andy's middle name. And I was thinking about blue sky and the image of a cathedral.

Why a cathedral?
In a way, the cathedral is a touchstone in our lives, you know, for baptisms, weddings, funerals, sometimes fellowshipping, gatherings with people that you know, or maybe you don't know. Also, my brother had been living in Baltimore at the time on Cathedral Street. As for the music, I didn't want the pieces to sound too "square," you know? Normally, music is in 3/4, 2/4, 4/4, maybe 6/8, but I made the crazy decision to put it in 5/4, which is unusual. If you're used to 4/4, you don't think about that extra beat. Pop music is [almost] always in 4/4. You know where the strong beat is going to be, but having the 5/4 there gave the music a floating quality. None of the players are sleeping through the piece, I can tell you,

because they must count! Andy was a visual artist, and so I imagined floating in from the church at the back entrance all the way up toward the front.

Your music seems to build and build, until—
—actually, until all the instruments and the rhythms start aligning, and there's a brass fanfare, and it just *explodes*, all sixteenth notes, the equivalent of flying up toward the roof; and then the roof opening and flying into the sky. So, you see, I also realized that this piece was not about dying but about *living*. My brother Andy would have preferred that I look at life that way. So I knew there was going to be some sort of climactic point, and that brass fanfare would be like an opening of the roof. I remember thinking, "The horns sound so cool when they're up high, so at the loudest point I want to make this moment the top of a horn line." To write that I had to back up and write the measures leading up to that. Horn players need the line to ascend. It's cruel and unusual punishment to make them just suddenly pop out like that. The four horns have that kind of a confident liftoff moment. But where do you go from there? It just felt like the right thing for that piece was to bring the sound back down from that climax, to take it back to those opening textures.

Would you describe how you got those effects, almost of "celestial" music?
You're flying up in the stars, but what would that sound like musically? I remember the moment: I'm staring out the window of my place in Philadelphia and someone had given me a little box of Chinese bells. I wondered, "Can I put that sound into the piece?" I wanted a kind of ethereal sound, and so, these bells come in very quietly, emerge out of the instrumental texture just a little bit, and they go right up until the end. And there are a bunch of little percussion instruments playing clock-like patterns at the end.

And there's this weird effect of a piano playing just a little out of tune.
The way I got this sound was to put a small screw between two of the different pitches [i.e., strings], to give the piano a slightly out-of-tune sound, so it sounds like a clock you're hearing in the distance.[12] Because my brother was thirty-three when he passed away, I [also] put thirty-three gongs in there, like a little Morse code, as if to say, "Here, Andy, here's your piece."

What was the public premiere like?
For the performance at Curtis, they engaged Robert Spano, who'd been my conducting teacher at Bowling Green. He told me that he loved the piece and wanted to record it, so the next year I went down to Atlanta and we recorded the work. When that commercial CD was sent out to radio stations, news about the piece spread. It took three years between the first performance and the next series of

---

[12]The result is known as a "prepared piano."

performances beyond Atlanta. But before long, orchestras started calling and asking about that piece. We've now had, I think, about 800 performances of the work.

I can't help but wonder if what you heard in concert at all was like what you had been hearing in your head?
I think at the time that I wrote *Blue Cathedral* I probably was 60% accurate in anticipating how the music would actually sound. So now I'm much more practiced in being able to figure out what I'm going to hear. Even though I've worked with orchestras a lot, combining the sounds, trying to figure out how these things collect together, I still have to project in my head what is it going to be like in a hall? And the momentum, the tempo, varies a lot with how many instruments you are using. A small ensemble's thinner sound changes everything. It's a bit of a guessing game, especially in the early stages when you're writing. You're always trying to figure out, "Will this work, and what does it sound like?" And the piece also changes depending on when you're working with professionals or if it's a junior high band!

Hearing the sounds you produce in Blue Cathedral *reminds us that the orchestra of today is a very different animal from orchestras of 150 years ago. Is there a "contemporary" orchestra, as opposed to the "classical" orchestra of the past?*
Well, the "Great Beast," as I call any orchestra, has changed a bit over the centuries, particularly in the improvement of some instruments and the addition of new ones, like saxophones. The percussion sections today are huge. The string instruments have gotten a little bit better. String players can afford better bows and that makes a big difference in the sound. The flutes have also improved. We now have multiple-size tubas, and that makes a big difference in the repertory, whether you've got the low end or the high end of the tuba. I shiver when I think about what Beethoven must have heard, because the playing was not good and the instruments were not as good. I believe that players today have gotten so much better.

Yesterday, you told a student that you were a "hunter of sound."
Yes, I'm a hunter of sounds. I'm always *listening* for new sounds. I mean, literally. If someone drops something, my brain automatically thinks, "Was that metal, was it wood? How far did it fall? What is the thing it hit?" I mean, we had an incident amongst the composers who were going into a restaurant and someone dropped their keys accidentally down a grate, and people were like, "Oh, no, the car keys!" I said, "It sounded like they dropped ten feet!" And everyone stopped and they're like, "How can you tell?" In my music I'm always layering sounds, and finding ways to boost the sound. For instance, there may be a trumpet solo that needs a little reinforcing without the listener realizing what's happening. I'll have the flute play maybe an octave down, or in unison. People can't hear the flute, but it thickens the sound a little bit. Like a chef looking for the right spice.

You've said that you worry your young students suffer from what you call a "Masterpiece Complex."

Too many students worry that they can't write a "masterpiece." They start to write a string quartet and they cry, "Oh, there are [already] these incredible string quartets. Look at these string quartets Beethoven wrote!" So they get paralyzed, they can't write because they're worried that what they're writing doesn't sound good enough. It's a creative paralysis. My way of dealing with that is just to keep writing as fast as I can [laughs] and spend so much time writing that it's like not letting something catch me! I have a healthy respect for the Classical canon, because I realize how much work goes into writing music. It's torture in some ways. I'm sure for Mozart it was a lot easier, but musicologists have discovered that the romantic idea of Mozart directly putting everything on the page is mistaken. They've looked at the layers of ink, and they've realized he actually went back and made changes and filled things in.

And today: has there been a breakdown in traditional formulas, like sonata-allegro form, or genres?

Yeah, it's easier for composers when you're working in traditional forms than when you're trying to build something from scratch with no predetermined form. It's like architecture; there are certain kinds of A-frame houses all over the world because that's an easy, pre-determined way of doing things. But when you're trying to make something original that doesn't have a typical shape or form, it's actually a lot more challenging. You're making it up as you go; but the thing still has to work.

Can you take us back to your own student days? Were you a go-getter, a shy-retiring type, what?

Well I grew up in a family of freelancing artists, so I knew I couldn't be a shy, retiring person in getting commissions! I knew that you had to kind of be on top of everything all the time.

The first time you filled out an employment form or went through Customs at the airport, how did you list your occupation?

Classical composer.

Classical?

Yes, and the conversation always goes: "What does that mean?" I say, "I write music." They go, "You write music?!? Would I know any of your music?" I go, "I don't know. Do you listen to classical music?" They say, "Well, I listen to some; are you any good?" I'm like, "Well, I don't know. I'm not sure how to answer that."

You yourself are careful to say that between classical and rock there should not be any boundaries.

Yeah, that's right. There doesn't have to be boundaries. Other people put the boundaries there. They're not there in my head. It's just that mostly classical groups that commission me.

But when you do something like a bluegrass concerto ... ?
—which is a "Classical-bluegrass-hybrid" at the request of the orchestra. That's how it's been described to me. It's not bluegrass like [songwriter] Bill Monroe [1911–1996] wrote. I think the guys doing bluegrass are doing it so well, why would I? I may pull in other elements of other musics, but the people who are asking me to write are very specific about it being classical.

Now we come to your first opera, Cold Mountain. *You must have poured all your experience into it.*
Yes, indeed!

You've talked about your own personal contacts with the story. Please explain.
In a way, the story is very familiar to me, although I didn't realize that until after I had already started the opera project. I was reading the novel through for the fourth time, and I looked carefully at the map in the front, and I suddenly realized that the farm I lived on in East Tennessee was right over the [Great] Smoky Mountains; on the other side was Cold Mountain. So the reason this novel felt familiar to me was because I knew these people, I knew the landscape, I knew their spoken language. But it's fairly terrifying, because when opera companies mount a brand new production, it usually costs them between one and three million dollars. I'm inexperienced with putting big things on stage that tell a story, and I knew that somebody was spending a lot of money on this and I'd be responsible! It always comes down to the composer. It doesn't matter whether the set's great or not, or the scene's good or not, they always listen to the music, the composer. But having a familiar story was a big thing for me. Now the story has a lot of characters in it, so my librettist Jean Scheer and I culled it down to an outline. My rule going into this was it had to be two and a half hours or less. It could easily have been the *Ring* cycle over several nights! We tried to pick out characters we thought would be interesting to interact with Inman, the main character.

Were you familiar with the music by Gabriel Yared for Anthony Minghella's movie version [2003]?
No, but I do love film music.

Are there film composers you like?
Yes! John Williams. He's one of the few people who get a "star-struck" moment from me! I just got a letter from him, you know. He was with the Philly Orchestra last spring, late in the spring, and I missed him. I asked the orchestra if they would give him a letter. I just wanted to thank him for *Star Wars*, which was probably the first real "classical music" I got to know. I wrote him and said, "I think you're the most amazing artist-citizen. Your behavior in the world, in general, has taught me how to be a good citizen to go out into the world. And I'm very conscientious about orchestration because of the way you handled those soundtracks. I must have played them forever, over and over and over again." I added, "I know that through all the things I've done, and even the awards I've won, there's a little bit

of you in it." And he wrote back a week later. I'm like, "Oh, my gosh, it's John Williams!" I was afraid to open the thing.

You're a fan!
He was so sweet. He said, "Thank you. Your letter actually meant so much to me." I know he gets accolades from everyone. If you think about it, his music is probably heard by more citizens in the world than a lot of the stuff we term as classical music.

What of the author of Cold Mountain, *Charles Frazier? Had you read his book?*
Oh, yes. He was unfamiliar with opera, in general. He loved music, but something more like mountain and rock music. Opera was a very foreign entity to him. I told him, "Mr. Frazier, I love this novel and I promise I will take care of your characters"; but all the time I'm thinking, "He knows Inman, he knows Ada, and he knows Ruby." And I've got to do a good job with this, making the ten years he worked on that novel come together in two and a half hours.

I understand that Frazier's based his book on real-life events.
I found out that the Confederate soldier, W. P. Inman, was a real person, one of Frazier's relatives, who actually went AWOL[13] during the war. Apparently, a lot of people were going AWOL, but the Confederate army would take you back if you'd sign up and take a new oath. The story is set in the fourth year of the Civil War. Inman is in a hospital in Richmond. He decides he's going to go AWOL and walk back to Cold Mountain. He wants to rejoin this young lady he met just before the beginning of the war, Ada Monroe. Although they didn't get to know each other very well, they quickly fell in love. On the way back, while avoiding the Home Guard, Inman encounters a lot of characters, half of whom are trying to kill him. Another character is Ruby, who comes to help Ada make a living on Black Cove Farm. Ada doesn't know how to do anything. She's been raised to speak French, play the piano, paint, write poetry, look at the stars. She doesn't know how to cook. I mean, she's completely clueless and starving. Ruby, on the other hand, is a young mountain girl who's learned to survive. Ruby makes a deal with Ada: she'll teach her how to farm the land, fix up the barn, make things work, and they'll grow crops. Later, Ruby's father returns from the war.

And that's just the bare bones of the story! How did you come to terms with such a massive project?
When I began designing the opera, I used a huge sketch pad with drawings of each scene which indicated how intense I thought the music would be; and it helped me keep track of all the characters as they went on and off stage. This was so

---

[13]"Absent Without Official Leave."

important, because you have to chart how to get them on and off stage, when they have their costume changes, that sort of thing.

A writer gives his characters individual traits and ways of speaking. How do you pull that off in music?
There are a lot of characters and I had to figure out a way to make them have their own distinct sound. What makes Ada sound like Ada, Inman sound like Inman, Ruby sound like Ruby, Stobrod [Ruby's estranged father] sound like Stobrod? Everyone has a different rhythm of speaking, a different speed of speaking, different diction, etc. For the bad guy, Teague, the leader of the Home Guard, I have "snake-like" sounds, something nasty and kind of pinched. So I like to use a lot of stopped horns, because that's a pinched sound. Ruby is always nervous, so her music moves at a fast clip, because she's making lists. I don't think the audience even realizes this, but the beauty of it is you've got these contrasting personalities in the music. Inman described himself as empty, hollow inside, so I took out the middle thirds of his chords, leaving only the interval of a fifth, so you can't tell if it's major or minor.

Most writers say their characters sometimes "speak" to them. Does that happen to the composer, too?
Good question. By the time I was into the second act, I knew the characters so well they started *telling me* what their music was supposed to be. After I started composing in January 2012, these characters never left me. They were in my sleep, every day and every night. Seven days a week I was composing about seven to eight hours a day. And I'd get done at the end of the day; I'd be completely exhausted. I worked on Inman's death scene for an entire week. I had a physical reaction when I finally had to kill him off at the end, like in the novel. It was horrible! I had spent two years keeping this guy alive, and now it was over for him. So, I began fantasizing: "Maybe he sneaked off through the night, maybe he got out, maybe he went to find Ada." But no, he had to die. At one point I had to go into the hospital to have my throat checked, because I'd been singing through all the characters. So I asked Frazier, I said, "My god, you've been working on this for ten years. Did these people ever leave you alone?" He said, "No, they stay there." So I have to be careful for the next opera!

A trial by fire, eh?
Two and a half hours is a lot of music! I mapped out on another chart about how many people were singing in each scene, and I talked with the librettist about designing it so we made sure that there was a chorus at the beginning and end of the first act and another two thirds of the way through the second. The volume of sound was critical; we had to know when there were lots of people singing versus maybe a duet and an aria.

You seem to be working with a lot of Appalachian or bluegrass sounds. Are we correct in that?

I wanted a supposedly "authentic" mountain sound, so there are instrumented sections that coincide with the open strings on the violin. And at points where I want a harmonica sound, all three percussionists are blowing the exact same pitches into their pitch pipes. It's an A, a D, a G, an E. It sounds just like a harmonica coming out of the pit. I remember when I was growing up, I used to go to Old Timers Day in the Smoky Mountains, and they always depended on open strings to make pedal tones,[14] which is very typical of folk music. And they would play by ear; I'm not sure any of them actually read music. It was pretty wild to watch them, too, because instead of using a string bass, they would use a broom handle attached to a washtub with a string.[15] It's all handed down, over the generations. These are the weird practical things I had to think about while composing.

What about the violence in a story like this? And lots of gunplay. Can you simulate gunshots with musical instruments, as Aaron Copland [1900–1990] does in Appalachian Spring?

Oh, we used real guns with blanks in them! We calculated the exact number of gunshots we needed. And there was blood, too! We even had one entire meeting about blood, how much blood we'd need, and how much is too much because they put blood packs in the costumes for when people are getting shot. They wanted it to look realistic. So I think we started out with two gallons of blood.

Take us to Santa Fe, where Cold Mountain *was premiered. Paint us a scene. Were you there?*

It was the most exhausting thing I've ever gone through! The tech rehearsals ran from midnight 'til the wee hours of the morning. There are union rules for who can come into sing what and who has to do the gun training. I'm rewriting things for singers because we're at a high altitude, you know, trying to figure out what needs to be adjusted in the orchestra, because we were recording it. Believe me, in the fight scenes people would come out gasping for breath because of the thinner air. I'm also learning of the dangers of somebody maybe falling off the set!

Were you on a perpetual search for copyists?

I remember, when I was coming out of grad school, we weren't using computer programs, so I was trained as a copyist. I did the ink copying, so I know exactly what that's like and how hard it is on your hands, your back and your eyes. I'm like eternally grateful for computers because I can make quick adjustments in my scores. I remember once removing twenty-eight measures in one of the acts of *Cold Mountain*, and the computer did the recalculation. It was a scary set.

---

[14]A single sustained note, usually a low note, against which the rest of the music is played. Bagpipes combine pedal tones with melodic lines.

[15]Known as a "washtub bass."

What do you mean, a "scary set?"
A scary set has a lot of odd angles painted black, and it goes up two stories, and you're trying to align with the conductor literally like thirty feet below. And the lights aren't quite set right so the light's in your eyes. And you're in an outdoor venue, and here comes a thunderstorm out of the distance!

Was Cold Mountain *recorded for compact disc?*
They're recording it now [2017] for a commercial CD, so you don't want to mess up. You don't want to drop the singer off the side of the stage, and you can't trip, because you might fall and break something. And you're trying to see the conductor and hear what's going on with the orchestra. The wind's blowing a certain way and the temperature changes from night to night, so the sound projects differently. On warmer nights, the sound was more "lethargic," I guess you could say, and it wasn't projecting out as far. The thickness of the air affected that. It would take probably a decade to explain all the problems. I got basically no sleep for two months!

Chen Yi and Zhou Long: "We Strive to Combine the Culture and Inspiration of East and West"

William Everett and John Tibbetts
Kansas City, 25 August 2017

Modern classical music isn't the exclusive property of Western nations. As long ago as the seventeenth century, missionary Matteo Ricci (1552–1610) introduced European keyboard instruments to the then-Emperor of China. During the New Culture Movement of the 1910s and 1920s, Chinese musicians turned more enthusiastically toward the West. Shortly after World War I, jazz reached Shanghai, and as recently as 2012 that city's Peace Hotel Orchestra included a few of its early twentieth-century jazz-band members. Today, increasing numbers of Chinese "classical" composers have achieved international fame, including Bright Sheng and Tan Dun, while Zhou Long won an Academy Award for his score to the film *Crouching Tiger, Hidden Dragon* (2000) (Fig. 9).

A prolific composer who blends Chinese and Western sounds, thereby transcending cultural and musical boundaries, Chen Yi—the Lorena Search Cravens/Millsap/Missouri Distinguished Professor of Composition at the University of Missouri, Kansas City—was inducted in 2005 into the American Academy of Arts and Letters. Born in China, Chen Yi earned degrees from the Central Conservatory in Beijing and Columbia University. Her composition teachers have included Wu Zu-Qiang, Chou Wen-Chung, Mario

Fig. 9 Zhou Long and Chen Yi

Davidovsky, and Alexander Goehr. She has received numerous prestigious awards, including a Guggenheim Fellowship and the Charles Ives Living Composer Award. Her works are regularly commissioned and performed by leading ensembles worldwide.

Born into an artistic family in China, Zhou Long began piano lessons at an early age. During the Cultural Revolution Zhou Long, like his wife, Chen Yi, was sent to a rural state farm. He resumed his musical training in 1973, and in 1977 he enrolled in Beijing's Central Conservatory of Music; he also attended Columbia University, where he studied with Chou Wen-Chung, Mario Davidovsky, and George Edwards. In 2011 Zhou Long won the Pulitzer Prize in Music for his opera *Madame White Snake*; in 1999 he received ASCAP's Adventurous Programming Award and in 2011 that organization's Concert Music Award. His music is heard regularly in concert halls around the world.

WILLIAM EVERETT: How would you describe your music?
CHEN YI: My music might be a kind of a combination, with the culture and inspiration from both East and West, and including Western instruments and also Chinese instruments. I also write for chorus, but basically orchestral and chamber works.

JOHN TIBBETTS: And the texts for the choral works?
The texts are mostly sung in Chinese, but many works are sung in English. Because in some universities, when they commission the pieces, they want to learn them quickly, like in a semester. So they may not want to have them sung in a foreign language. But many commissions have come for works to be sung in Chinese, if they want to learn the language. In choral music, like in other vocal works, the language is closely related to the pitches.

WILLIAM EVERETT: Since Chinese is a tonal language?
Right, and so they wanted them to be sung in Chinese. So it's according to the needs. Sometimes I make the decision. And when the commissions come in and they ask me to write "whatever you want"—and even the text, they don't limit to any idea or anything—I would choose the poems on my own. The poems are mostly taken from ancient Chinese literature, the old poems.

Why do you choose old poems?
First of all, they are very inspiring. In ancient China you considered the Renaissance men who would be the intellectuals, who wrote the poems, and who would also write choreography. Their poems would go with singing and might go with dancing. They talk about their landscape and eventually about the meaning behind the scenes. So I took those inspirations. And also it's easier to deal with copyright because if you take somebody else's words, you have to go back and forth to get permission. Sometimes I write words for my own pieces. And also I could translate all the poems into English to be sung.

Have you written for groups other than choirs, orchestras, and chamber groups?
Yes. The band culture is very popular in the United States, so I have written a lot for band.

Zhou Long, how about the same question—how would you describe your music?
ZHOU LONG: Very similar because we have similar backgrounds. Some critics describe my music as "angular impressionism." I think that means maybe oil painting with watercolor. My music is also highly influenced by the Tang [Dynasty] culture. This was a flourishing period in history—poetry, painting, and descriptions of music, for no music survives—from roughly 600 to 900. My orchestral work is inspired from the Tang poetry, and some of my choral works and some for voice use Tang poems in Chinese or in English translation. I've only done one opera; most of my pieces are for orchestra.

Can you please talk about your opera?
The opera is called *Madame White Snake*. We started the project in 2006. The librettist [Cerise Lim Jacobs] is an attorney, not a professional writer. She studied comparative literature and later decided to study law at Harvard. She's an immigrant from Singapore, Singaporean American now. She was a prosecutor in public service for years and then started her own law firm in the New England area and was in practice for thirty-five years. She and her [now] late husband were both crazy about opera, and he purchased an apartment right at Lincoln Center so they could go to the Met. The first thing she wanted to do after retiring was to give her husband a gift for his birthday and came up with *Madame White Snake*.

Her plan, her dream, was just an aria, not an opera. She tried to find a composer and asked a friend in Boston. I received an e-mail saying this woman was trying to find a composer to write *Madame White Snake*, an opera. Everybody knows the story; it's very popular in China and East Asia. In Hong Kong they made a movie of it, and in China they have a television series. It has also been adapted in many different [Chinese] provinces for their own local opera with different dialogue and styles. This is the first English Western-style opera [based] on the story.

JOHN TIBBETTS: Is the story well known in the West?
Not really. But the theme is [like] a Western story: a demon becomes a female human being in love with a gentleman. Now came the reality of how to get it performed. We contacted Opera Boston. Gil Rose, the conductor, was music director. He knew my music but we didn't know each other personally. The librettist interviewed a dozen composers, Chinese and American, and Opera Boston said, "You have to pick this one."

CHEN YI: I thought that we should go to New York to meet them. And they listened to all his CDs. His mom was a vocal teacher, a professor at the Beijing Central Conservatory, and he grew up listening to opera. They decided to invite him to write.

ZHOU LONG: The person contacted me first. And I said that maybe we two could work together. But Chen Yi was too busy, and I said I would compose the opera. In 2006 we started to develop the script into four acts. I suggested turning the story into a prologue, four acts, and an epilogue. So six parts for a 106-minute piece. For the style, we wanted a Peking Opera actor, but decided not to because the libretto is in English.

WILLIAM EVERETT: So were you involved with choosing the cast?
Yes. Not only choosing the cast but also fund raising. At first when we talked I told them I don't want to be involved in fundraising, casting, and interviews. And

they decided that "you must." I don't have that much time. I attended two major fundraising events. So we raised some money. Like a half million, almost. The whole production [cost] 1.2 million [dollars].

How did you cast the title role?
Most of the professional singers, even if they have new opera experience, when they look at the score they can't do it. It's too hard. But in the end we found Ying Huang from Shanghai.

CHEN YI: Her manager brought her to the audition and pushed the librettist and said that she would be a perfect fit. And she herself also was passionate and said, "I know Chinese style." And although others might be more famous, they might be too tall or their voices not flexible enough.

ZHOU LONG: She had very good experience and made a movie with a French company (i.e., Frédéric Mitterrand's 1995 film adaptation of *Madama Butterfly*).

CHEN YI: And also she is a Metropolitan Opera singer. She's singing main roles.

ZHOU LONG: But she never attended graduate school. She graduated from the Shanghai Conservatory with her undergrad and then began her professional career.

CHEN YI: She made her name in Europe singing. Several people have played this role, and she is thirty-one. She learned the score first. It definitely is hardest for the first person. Others could listen to her recording.

Have there been other productions?
ZHOU LONG: Yes, it had its second production in Boston in 2016.

CHEN YI: The second production was brand new, completely new staging, new sets.

ZHOU LONG: We didn't ask Huang Ying, because she was in Shanghai. We auditioned four singers; they all dropped. In the end there's only five weeks left. A young singer [Susannah Biller], in her thirties, had already worked with San Francisco Opera and Houston Opera. She's very smart. In five weeks she memorized the role.

CHEN YI: More presenters came up for the second production. They loved the stage setting. The Hong Kong Arts Festival will do it in two years. The first production was also done in the Beijing International Music Festival the same year as the premiere because it was a co-commission. When the director of the Beijing Festival met us, he asked Zhou Long, "What are you doing?" Zhou Long said, "I'm writing a new opera for Opera Boston." And he asked, "What's the title?" And then he said, "In that case it's not good. It's a scary story for a Western audience." But he said he was interested in co-commissioning the piece, so that's why he supported the production in Beijing and the Festival paid for the whole production.

The director of the Beijing International Music Festival, Yu Long, is also the music director of the China Philharmonic, the Shanghai Symphony, and the Guangzhou Symphony. And so after this opera we have had some other collaborations with him. He commissioned us to write a large-scale symphony for the Guangzhou Symphony Orchestra, which won the China National Competition First Prize.

Was that something you worked on together?
Yes. *Symphony: Humen 1839*. It was on the Naxos CD that was the second Grammy nomination for the New Zealand Symphony. That was his commission. He has done our works with the Shanghai Symphony and other orchestras.

On Stage and Screen

Introduction

Crafting music for dramatic purposes, whether on stage or on screen, requires a highly specialized skill set. In some cases music must dominate and carry the weight of the storytelling; in others it must assume a more subservient role. When characters sing, as in opera, their music should, and often does, tell us a great deal about their personalities and motivations, going beyond what words alone can accomplish.

In the early twentieth century, before the invention of synchronized sound for motion pictures, every movie theater of any importance employed instrumentalists that would perform as each film was screened. Sometimes scores would be sent with films; more often a music director would choose appropriate music for each filmic scene. This art of creating original music for silent movies has found new life in the latter part of the twentieth century. Philip Glass, for example, has created operas in which singers stand in front of screens on which silent films are projected; he has also scored many films, both silent and sound. In his interview, composer Carl Davis discusses scoring dozens of silent films, notably the epic five-hour *Napoléon* (1927). Davis has also composed music for many new television programs and films, including the second iteration of BBC's celebrated series *Upstairs, Downstairs* (2010–2012).

Glass is still associated with *avant-garde* musical experimentation, although his score for *The Truman Show* (1999) won fame with Hollywood film fans as well as a Golden Globe award. In the realm of popular musical theater, however, other composers employ pastiche techniques to evoke the music of earlier epochs. Among artists who epitomize this approach are Jerome Kern and John Kander. In *Show Boat* (1927), Kern used music to evoke various time periods in a multi-generational storyline. In his own musicals, Broadway composer John Kander provides vivid aural backdrops for nineteenth-century minstrelsy in *The Scottsboro*

© The Author(s) 2018
J. C. Tibbetts et al. (eds.), *Performing Music History*,
https://doi.org/10.1007/978-3-319-92471-7_10

Boys (2010), the "Roaring 1920s" in *Chicago* (1975), and 1930s Berlin in *Cabaret* (1966), to list a few examples. Singer, dancer and choreographer Tommy Tune has worked both with older shows and helped get new Broadway musicals off the ground. His interview mentions his work with filmmaker Ken Russell (*The Boy Friend*) and the stage show *The Will Rogers Follies*.

All this leads to complex questions of authenticity. Kander's pastiches are so well crafted that they can easily be mistaken for older music; "Tomorrow Belongs to Me" from *Cabaret* (1966 on stage, 1972 on film) has sometimes been accepted as an actual Nazi song. Closely related to original "antique" stage and screen music composition is the restoration of classic musicals. Conductor and scholar John McGlinn has been deeply concerned with this possibility and has recreated historic shows, including *Show Boat* (1927), in as authentic a manner as possible. The issues McGlinn raises in his interview concern not only the Broadway canon, but any established work in need of restoration.

William Everett

Philip Glass: "I'm Starting to Write Works That Will Be More Dramatic Theatrically"

John C. Tibbetts
Lawrence, KS, 24 October 1985, Lawrence, Kansas; 1995, Kansas City, Missouri; and 12 June 2016, Bergen, Norway.

During the 1960s an emerging New York school of minimalist composers made familiar harmonies and easy-to-follow repeated statements acceptably *avant-garde***. Steve Reich, for instance, employed tape loops to create "phasing patterns": musical motifs and harmonies offset in time to create slowly shifting wholes. Terry Riley's** *In C* **(1964), which combines aleatoric freedom with phasing patterns, quickly became a hallmark work of minimalist music. Although he later dismissed the term "minimalism" (preferring "theater music") for his own work, Philip Glass was profoundly influenced by Reich, and he quickly eschewed academic dissonance in favor of a radically "consonant vocabulary." The 1950s and 1960s witnessed similar revolutions in the visual arts, with Andy Warhol (1928–1987), Roy Lichtenstein (1923–1997), and other painters rejecting abstract expressionism in favor of what came to be known as representational "pop art." Within a few years "rock" also became more experimental, with albums such as Pink Floyd's** *Dark Side of the Moon* **(1973) outfitted with tape loops and comparatively complex harmonies.**

As a "crossover" artist, Philip Morris Glass (Fig. 1) **has successfully bridged the classical and popular worlds of late twentieth—and early twenty-first-century music. A student of Vincent Persichetti (1915–1987) at Juilliard and**

Fig. 1 Philip Glass

Darius Milhaud in Colorado, Glass worked for a time as a public school-teacher before spending years in Paris and India. Often identified as a "minimalist," he is best known for compositions he describes as "music with repetitive structures." He is also a keyboardist. Among his most popular works are his film scores, including those he wrote for Godfrey Reggio's trilogy, *Koyaanisqatsi* (1981), *Powaqqatsi* (1988), and *Nagoygatsi* (2002); for Stephen Daltrey's *The Hours* (2002); and for Peter Weir's *The Truman Show* (1999). For the last score he won that year's Golden Globe and was nominated for an Oscar. Glass's recent opera *The Perfect American* (2011) concerns the life of Walt Disney (1901–1966), although his most famous opera remains *Einstein on the Beach* (1976).

In the conversations recorded below, Glass discusses his scoring of silent and sound films, including the celebrated *Koyanisqaatsi Trilogy*. He concludes with brief remarks on his new opera, *The Perfect American*.

JOHN C. TIBBETTS: To begin with, do you object to calling your music "minimalist"?

PHILIP GLASS: A fellow composer, Tom Johnson, wrote for *The Village Voice*, and he came up with the idea. He considered himself a minimalist composer. He just retired from journalism and is now a full-time composer again. One of the last things he wrote for the *Voice* was a retraction about that term, "minimalism." He said he was sorry he started the whole thing. Thanks, Tom! Anyway, he was famous for an opera called *The Four-Note Opera* [1972]. Now, I've never gotten down to four notes, even in my most reductive period! The idea came at a time when my generation of composers was reacting, maybe even over-reacting to the experimental and twelve-tone music of the mid-1960s. This generation was looking for a music that was based on rhythmic structures, that had a very regular beat to it, that was very tonal. The credo of minimalism was "less is more," that was what we used to say in those days. But the thing about theater work, as you probably know, is that really *more* is more. It's really the opposite. You know, in theater you work with designers, with dancers, with directors, with lighting people, with writers sometimes. But minimalism, yes, is a way of developing music through gradual changes, through very slow changes over a long period of time.

Let's talk about your work on the films of Godfrey Reggio.

When you get to know Godfrey, it's very clear he has tremendous concentration and determination. He made *Koyaanisqatsi* against all odds. It was a non-commercial movie, he did it outside of the industry; he raised the money himself; and he has a tremendous belief in his goals. He is a very centered kind of person, and you can see that this guy could easily have spent fourteen years being a Jesuit.

How did you come to the project in the first place?

He called me up. I don't really look for film work; it's not my favorite kind of work really. The trouble with film is that once you've done it, you can never reinterpret it. There's something so final about it that I find it very off-putting in a way. I don't like the medium for that reason, though I work very well in it. I mean, I know how to work with image and time, because I've worked in the theater and I know how to work in film. Godfrey's film wasn't done when I began to work with him. I was looking at unassembled footage. The last two and a half years of the film, I was with him about once a month. I flew from New York to L.A. and spent long weekends with him looking at new footage and talking about the structure. It was a real collaboration. I wrote a score to fit the script; that's the way I would write an opera, to fit a libretto. Then Godfrey cut the film and the music together, and I had to rewrite the music to fit the new cut. In other words, I had to write the score twice. If I were an industry film composer, I never would have done it.

For better or for worse, your name will be forever linked to that film. On the whole, is that a good thing for you?
I don't mind. At first, I objected. But not now. We recently did a live presentation of it in New York at Avery Fisher Hall. I got an orchestra of about twenty-four together and Michael Riesman conducted. He did a storyboard in the score and he followed the score and the pictures. He rehearsed with a video and the score before we even rehearsed with the musicians. I would say that Michael knows that film rather well now! [laughs].

So he actually has drawings in front of him?
Michael has drawn pictures into his score that tell him what he should be seeing on the screen at every moment. Now, I don't know how well you know this film, but Michael was never more than a handful of frames out of synch. That means much less than a second. I'd say he was never more than half a second away from perfect synch, or rather, when I say perfect synch, I mean the synch we are accustomed to seeing the film in. In fact, the synch that it was cut to. At this point, we are in the middle of a twenty-five city tour.

You've taken Koyaanisqatsi *on the road, with live accompaniment. You told me a couple of years ago that you regretted linking the score with a film, as if setting the music in cement. But I guess with a "live" performance, it's different?*
Right. We've on a twenty-five city tour with these "live" presentations. As I said, Michael learned to coordinate the music with the image—a technical problem that had to be solved. We also solved the problem of adapting symphonic music for a traveling ensemble of around twelve or fourteen people. Then we had to book the tour. Now the music is very alive and responsive to the film. Last night at the performance, I noticed that Michael was creating dynamic shadings that weren't in the original score. He was responding the way any good musician will respond to a piece of music. You give musicians a piano piece, and after they play it for ten or fifteen times, they begin to personalize it. That's what you want from a sensitive interpreter. The conductor has to be the interpreter. He has a very precise sense of time, which I don't have so much. My sense of metronomic time is not at all accurate. But Michael is extremely accurate and he was the right person to do that.

It's nice to think too that the music acquires a life of its own in that way.
Well, it acquires, let's say, a living relationship to something else. I think even the most ardent film buff will agree that the problem with film is that it's *frozen* in place, in a way. It can't be changed. I suppose you can go back and change it, but it's very difficult to do. Sometimes you can't even find the original prints. There's a story that as an old man, the great French painter [Camille] Pissarro [1830–1903], would be found in the museums in Paris touching up his pictures,

Museum attendants must have loved that!
The guards would throw him out! But he was doing what any artist wants to do, you know, we are all trying to keep the piece alive; and that's very hard to do with

film. When we look at a film like *Citizen Kane* [1941], what invariably happens is that we are forced to include an element of nostalgia in what we're looking at, since what's old can't become new again. Films become history quicker than any other art. They're set and finished and I can't do much about them. By contrast, we just did a revival of my music for *Satyagrahaii* [1980] in Chicago and it's being done differently now than it was eight years ago, even though they are following the score exactly. People ask, how can that be? But that's the way an actor will read Shakespeare differently when he's fifty than he reads it when he's twenty-five.

You say you're preparing a second film with Reggio?
Powaqqatsi is all finished, by the way [1985] and in the lab being color-corrected. I'm going to see the final print I guess in about a week. It was filmed in South America and parts of Africa and India. *Powaqqatsi* means "transformation," from a Hopi [American Indian] word; the transformation of the southern hemisphere by the northern hemisphere. But it becomes more complicated than that. In fact, it turned out to be a lot about the resiliency and the independence and authenticity of a southern hemisphere culture. I was along for the shoot. I think Godfrey had some idea that the southern hemisphere had been more the recipient of culture rather than the originator of it and what we discovered, in fact, was a very strong and very lively cultural life. In *Powaqqatsi* we actually reached the point where I wrote music for scenes before they were shot. I played them for the cameraman before he shot the film.

So, you knew the nature of the scene that was going to be shot?
Yes. For I already had found documentary footage that existed of the mines in northern Brazil, so I studied it. We went down there with the music, we filmed it, and we played it for the people who were in the film, for the miners.

This reminds me of Arnold Schoenberg in Hollywood, who thought the purpose of the film composer was to write the music before the filmmakers came up with the images.
We actually have come fairly close to that in some cases. I think you would be impressed with how precise Godfrey's visual plan is. When he first went on location, he actually planned the shots and knew where he would put his tripod. When he went back with two crews, he had precise ideas of how many days he would have to be in Lima, what parts of the city to go to, what he wanted to get on film.

It must have been different working with other Hollywood directors, like Paul Schrader.
I scored *Mishima* for Schrader. Motion pictures can be a very autocratic experience for some directors. I was on set watching Schrader making *Mishima*, and he was all over the place. Now, his cinematographer is the great John Bailey, but Schrader was looking through the lens, telling him how to do the lights. He was

everywhere. Besides that, he wrote the damned thing with his brother! I don't see a lot of directors stepping aside and inviting people to help them direct their films.

How did you come to the idea of writing original scores for the films of Jean Cocteau [1889–1963]?
Cocteau was an artist, he was a painter, he was a designer, he was a writer, he was a man who approached film as an art form. He really thought of it as an art form.

Those were the days!
You know, movies are not really part of the art world anymore. When a film like *Jurassic Park* [1993] comes out, the big news is how much money it made on the first weekend, not the qualities of the movie itself. Now, Cocteau and Milhaud were among a group of artists who in the twenties were making music theater experiments. Georges Auric [1899–1983] was another one. He went on to score three very important Cocteau films. The first is *La Belle et le Bête* [1946], the second *Orphée* [1949], and the third is a film called *Les Enfants terrible*, which I'm currently working on. I had already studied in France in 1954; and again in 1962, when I spent three years studying with Nadia Boulanger. We sometimes say about American composers that we either take the German route or the French route. Well, I very definitely took the French route.[1] You could see French films like the Cocteaus in the 1950s—very soon after they were made. I saw them when they were new, in other words. I've lived long enough to see them become classic films. So when I began thinking about the film medium, the films of Cocteau appealed to me.

So anyway I began, I picked three of Cocteau's films. *Orphée* sets the myth of Orpheus in modern France in about 1950. The second, *La Belle*, we'll see tomorrow night. The third was a film called *Les Enfants terrible*, which is the one I'm currently working on. I have to tell you that when I began to score my own music to an opera version of *Orphée*, I really didn't know how to go about it. My favorite way of working is to create a situation in which I don't know what I'm doing, and then I have to figure it out. I usually find other people to work with me, and we try to solve the problems together. Cocteau's scenario is just all the dialogue, just like a play. I did a very simple thing: I turned the scenario into a libretto and I made an opera based on that. We then staged it in Boston and New York. Another production was done in Germany.

At the time I guess it was unusual to write an opera based on a movie.
That was already quite unusual. When I look at the movie, *Orphée*, I understand that the director really determines what I look at—close-ups, things in the distance, all these things are determined by the director. When we set it on the stage it wasn't like that. You see the whole stage. The dramatic development happens quite differently. Something can be happening over here and something can be

---

[1]Other composers who took the same "route" were Copland and Stravinsky.

happening over there. You can develop a kind of a dramatic counterpoint where things happen simultaneously. The movie took ninety minutes; the opera took about one hundred and ten minutes. We tend to sing more slowly than we speak. Still, every word that is sung comes from the movie.

In the case of La Belle *you're writing your own score for a movie that already has a score!*
This was a much more radical approach. I took the film itself and put a time code on it. It's a little digital clock, and I spent about three weeks writing down the exact time of every word in the movie. [laughs] You have to be a little obsessed to do this kind of thing. I took the movie and divided it into nineteen scenes. There are actually about twenty or so scenes. I don't mean shots, I mean actual scenes. But I put some of them together because I wanted to have longer passages of music. Then I wrote the music for each scene without putting the words in. Using a metronome and a calculator, I figured out where in the score each word would appear. Right? It's not that hard to figure out, it's just arithmetic. Then I set the words rhythmically in the score and wrote the melodies for the words. I have to tell you, no one really knew what I was doing. We recorded the whole score exactly in the tempo and then synched the film with it. Suddenly the film was an opera! Instead of talking, people were singing. But there was a problem. Films run at a different speed in Europe. I think they use thirty frames per second, and we use twenty-four. I went back and readjusted the music, which meant I had to rewrite the vocal parts. Then we projected the film and hired singers; and then Michael Riesman watched the film and began to learn the score. Michael has an amazingly accurate sense of time. He has perfect pitch, but he also has perfect tempo, which is something I didn't realize that you could have—but he has it. What I was really doing was writing an opera with a film as a backdrop.

And now it's "live" on stage too?
When you see our "live" presentation of *La Belle* it'll be more an *opera* than a *movie*. We spent weeks putting it together scene by scene, but couldn't really see what was happening yet. We opened it in Italy, where we did a series of concerts; then went to Spain. We did it about ten or twelve times, and the piece started to come together. There will be platforms in front of the screen for the singers. During the show they will move to different platforms, different placements. In front of them is my ensemble of three synthesizers, three keyboards, and three woodwind players. I'm on one of the synthesizers. Michael Riesman is the only one who is actually watching the film; the rest of us are watching *him*. I want to emphasize the *operatic* nature of this exercise and not the film part, so I have had to work on the relationship of the live singer to the person up there on the screen. It's not like an oratory where people sit up and sing, and then they sit down again. We create physical relationships with the screen images and with the audience. We've done about sixty performances so far, with thirty more to go. The relationship of the film to the live performance is very tight now. We're actually interpreting the film.

That's a lot different than synchronizing live performance with film, isn't it?
I always had the idea that somehow they would *interact*. But the film is so beautiful it could overpower the music. In fact, the live performers have no trouble standing up to the film. Live performance is so attractive as a modality. That's why we still go to the theater. That's why movies haven't really replaced theater. So that what's been interesting, to see the power that a live performer has and that it can actually hold the space in front of the movie.

Watching you and your musicians during "live" performances of motion pictures, I could actually see all of you below the screen. It looked like you were a kind of human scaffolding, holding up the screen on your shoulders.
That's interesting. Well, we do wear black coveralls since we don't want to distract too much from the main visuals. But yes, the whole thing does make for a rather striking look, doesn't it? This configuration is something that audiences are going to see more frequently from me now. I'm more interested in theatrical extensions of the concert format. That's one of the reasons that *Koyannisqatsi* was very interesting for me, because it allowed me to get past the concert situation and into a larger audience kind of experience. Now, what that means is that I'm starting to write works that will be more dramatic theatrically, works that include the ensemble below the screen. So I'm working on a piece now, the working title is "Visitors" which I have to change by the way because I found out there was a TV show by that name. It's a piece about encounters with extraterrestrials. It uses one actor and a script by David Hwang. So imagine what you saw last night, then replace the screen with a three-dimensional screen, and add an actor.

With all this happening, does it seem a long time ago that you were driving taxis and working on people's plumbing?
You're darn right, it does! But it's still all about keeping your family, while trying not to get trapped into a day job that interferes with your touring. That's why I can never really work in an academic job.

Epilogue

In June 2016 Philip Glass appeared at the Bergen International Festival of the Arts, where he conducted several concerts and participated in a few Q&A sessions with the public. I sat down with him the morning following his performance of *Powaqqatsi* and seized the opportunity to talk with him about what was really on my mind, his opera, *The Perfect American*, his controversial imagining of the last days of Walt Disney.[2] My question grew out of my own background, growing up in Walt's home town, Kansas City; I've

---

[2]*The Perfect American* was composed in 2011–2012. The story imagines the last months of Walt Disney's life as he languishes in a hospital bed. And it reviews the circumstances of his life and work, from Marceline, Missouri, to Hollywood.

taught courses on Disney at the University of Kansas; and I've visited many of Disney's haunts, including the farming community of Marceline, Missouri, where he spent his idyllic boyhood.

GLASS: You could have been my consultant on the opera. It's on my mind right now. I'm looking forward to its American premiere at the Long Beach Opera this winter [it premiered there on 12 March 2017]. I've been to Marceline, too. It's in the opera! I have him yearning to return there, to the magic of his youth. Where would people like Andy Warhol be without Walt Disney? He invented the "factory studio," and Warhol perfected it. They're together in the opera, by the way. I have Warhol talking about why Walt was a great innovator and why he is following in his footsteps. Of course, that didn't really happen, but most of the opera did happen.

Some think I am trashing Disney, but it's too hard to write an opera to go in for that sort of thing. No, it's an important American story, and I really wanted to do it. Sure, he had his problems. He had problems with race. In the opera I imagined him arguing about the progress of the black race with the robot Abraham Lincoln. He was probably a misogynist. He cooperated with the Communist witch hunts in Hollywood. And his last years were pretty frightening, you know? He was afraid of death, obsessed with it, and feared that his empire was collapsing.

John McGlinn: "It's All to the Good that *Show Boat* Does Keep Stirring Things up"

John C. Tibbetts
June 1993 and May 1994, New York City

Show Boat, **with music by Jerome Kern and book and lyrics by Oscar Hammerstein II (1895–1960), has remained an iconic and controversial work since its high-profile Broadway opening on 27 December 1927. Based on Edna Ferber's popular novel of the same name, the multi-generational story of love, loss, and reconciliation highlights the ill-fated effects of racial discrimination, alcoholism, and gambling on its principal characters. Several historians date the beginning of "modern Broadway" to Show Boat's influence, felt in the work of such renowned composer-lyricist teams as Rodgers and Hammerstein, Alan Jay Lerner and Frederick Loewe (1901–1988), and John Kander and Fred Ebb** (Fig. 2).

In addition to his work with the New York City Opera and other ensembles, John McGlinn supervised complete cast recordings of shows such as *Anything Goes, Annie Get Your Gun,* **and** *Kiss Me Kate.* **In 1983 he worked with veteran orchestrator Hans Spialek on the Broadway revival of** *On Your Toes.* **In 1987 McGlinn used Richard Russell Bennett's original orchestrations**

Fig. 2 John McGlinn

for his landmark recording for EMI of *Show Boat*, featuring Frederica von Stade, Jerry Hadley, Teresa Stratas, and Bruce Hubbard.

JOHN C. TIBBETTS: Tell me about your early musical interests.
JOHN McGLINN: From the start I never thought of musical theater and classical music as being different, somehow. I would play *Die Walküre* and *Mame* interchangeably as a kid, with little sense of division. In my teens my two greatest musical joys were the operettas of [W. S.] Gilbert [1836–1911] and [Sir Arthur]

Sullivan [1842–1900] and the *Ring* cycle of Richard Wagner. My mother had the old Malcolm Sargent 78s of *Pirates* and *Iolanthe*. I could hear a tune once and remember it. But at the theater the lyrics flew by so fast I couldn't remember them. I remember walking down to the orchestra pit where I saw on the podium a book of the vocal score. I leaned over and opened it and saw the music and the words. I decided then and there to find a vocal score. I lived near the Theodore Presser Company and bought a score to *The Mikado*. At the same time, while hunting for another G&S score, I ran into references to something called *Das Rheingold*. I was so young, I thought—an opera about beer? (Most people forget that American beer is indigenous to Philadelphia.) I had three dollars burning a hole in my pocket, so I asked for *Das Rheingold* and they brought out the Schirmer edition with the green cover and gold lettering. I bought it and took it home, went into my father's study, and opened it up. There were the stage directions: "At the bottom of the river Rhine. Light haze above, dark haze below. Movement of the water on the rocks." Now, I didn't know who Alberich was or who the Nibelungen were, etc. I was just a kid going to the Episcopal Academy Country Day School for Boys. But here [in Wagner] were magic swords, giants, dragons, and the like ... *what is this*??? I felt my heart starting to race. Even though I couldn't read music at this point, just the words were enough. But the ending seemed rather inconclusive to me. I looked back at the cover. There *must* be a Part Two! A few weeks later at Presser's I asked about that. And they told me there were *four* parts. I saved up and bought *Valkyrie*. This was where the gods on Mount Olympus went zap!

One time I went into my sister's room and borrowed her record player. I took out the score to *Das Rheingold*, put on the first side of the record, and that's when I heard the opening measures. I was gone. For two and a half hours I just followed along as the music swept over me. It just floored me. What was it about that E-flat horn arpeggio, the opening of nature that reached down and ripped out my guts? It was like a stroke of lightning. I knew my life would never be the same again!

When did you first become aware that there was a lack of scholarship about American musical theater?
Yes, that was in college at Northwestern, when I became aware of the gaps in our knowledge of America's own musical theater. I happened to have a vocal score of *Show Boat*, already a favorite of mine, and it didn't match any of the recordings I knew. I got very interested in the notion that composers' works had been altered by other hands. Then came musical theater historian Miles Kreuger's ground-breaking history of *Show Boat*. It was absolutely the thing that sent me over the edge. Without his book, I wouldn't have pursued my dream of mounting an original, "authentic" *Show Boat*. I've told him that often. That was in 1977. Two years later, after coming to New York with a degree in theory and composition, I was very intrigued to know what "Ol' Man River" sounded like in its original form. I went out to the library at Rodgers and Hammerstein's and saw the original parts. I had always thought the song was too heavy and pompous. What I found was quite simple by contrast. Flash forward a few more years. On a whim, I called

John DeMain, the music director at the Houston Grand Opera, and talked with him about the upcoming revival of *Show Boat*. He had done the complete *Porgy and Bess* [1935] in the mid-1970s. He came to New York to hire me to work as music editor. I had found some of the original 1927 [*Show Boat*] orchestral parts. We worked from a script provided by Miles Kreuger. I think it must have been the first attempt to restore the original script and orchestrations. Still, there were many cuts and changes to account for. No matter that I had hardly any credentials. That was my first real job in the musical theater. I really owe John a tremendous debt of gratitude.

Please talk about your landmark EMI project.
EMI asked me to record a musical show. What would I like to do? I said, "*Show Boat*, please!" When I told them I didn't want to do just one 75-minute CD but a *complete* version, which would probably take three CDs and no less than eighteen recording sessions, they exploded, like Frank Morgan in *The Wizard of Oz* [1939 on film]. I laid it out and their jaws dropped. Of course they said no. But then they realized that if they didn't do it, somebody else would!

The estate of Jerome Kern granted you its blessing, correct? And ten years' worth of research was about to be fulfilled.
It was the summer of 1987. We had to record it over a two-month period. We did half of it in July and half in August. A glorious year for me. The most beautiful high English summer you've ever seen. Not a day of rain. People flew in from all over the world. That recording changed my life.

Please explain your approach to the most controversial aspect of Show Boat*: namely, its portrayals of race and racism.*
I was determined to keep that original text, or I never would have made the recording. I doubt I'd be so brave now.

What did you want to know about those first stage performances in November 1927?
I had already met people that had been connected with it, like Norma Terris, who sang Magnolia, and Phil Sheridan, who had been in the chorus. What would I want to verify? Well, we do have the recordings and stuff from the 1929 film with Tess Gardella (there she is, doing "Hey, Feller"). A lot of stuff we did we lifted from Tess, like the way she said "hot feet" during "Can't Help Lovin' Dat Man." I think that if somebody today could go back to that time, he would find the performance incredibly stilted. People who listen to acoustic recordings from that period find it tight. But nothing Kern and Hammerstein wrote makes you wince—even the most 'ordinary' material in our Appendix, like "Out There in an Orchard," "A Pack of Cards," and other pastiche pieces. There's something to be said for being a completist. Nothing is going to hurt *Show Boat*. It's time to hear the cut-outs, even if they have no place in the show anymore. Every note Kern wrote is worth hearing. At least it should be there and available.

Nevertheless, controversies about the show's subject matter have dogged your own revival efforts.

It's all to the good of *Show Boat* that it does keep stirring things up. There aren't a lot of theater pieces that can do that.

I understand that, in particular, members of the black chorus objected to the restoration of Hammerstein's original words, in which the "n-word" is heard.

I wasn't there at the time of the chorus rehearsals. I was in Salzburg. But I had already met with Willard White, my Joe, at Glyndebourne and explained to him why we had to retain the words. It is hateful and shocking, but I feel Hammerstein was doing it purposefully. He did change it the following year at Paul Robeson's request. Willard at first tried to explain to the chorus about singing the original words. But after their objections, he changed his mind and said he couldn't do it. It was shameful to him. I had no idea what to do. It was two days before the "Ol' Man River" sessions. They wrote a letter to EMI and said that unless the word was changed, they were out. I had already had this problem in Houston on the first day of rehearsals. When the chorus said they wouldn't sing it, the conductor buckled and said it was out. I almost got fired for going to them the next day to try to convince them. But now, I called Bruce Hubbard, who was originally cast as Jake, to do it. He said he needed a day to think about it. He called back and told me he'd do it. You can see him in that videotape documentary singing that, and you can see his anger.

Meanwhile, EMI, to their eternal credit, allowed me to hire the Ambrosian Singers. They didn't care they were white. And Bruce got a lot of flack from his colleagues in *Porgy*. Bruce's friend, Eartha Kitt, in the meantime, went in and told them that you don't eliminate prejudice by pretending it didn't happen. You have to depict it, to show what happened. If you don't, people forget and it will happen again. That is the curse of history. Now Bruce is dead. He always felt he had made the right decision.

Can you say a bit more about the show and its racial controversy?

I think that if you view the problem in its context, you realize that the word "nigger" was not used as a racial slur. Imagine that you're sitting in 1927 New York. And we know that in 1927 miscegenation was still a crime punishable by castration in certain parts of this country. Oscar Hammerstein is the same person, after all, who wrote the lyrics to "You've Got to Be Carefully Taught" [for *South Pacific*, 1949]. In which he explains that you have to be taught to hate. Now, could this man have possibly in 1927 written something that was a racial slur and then turned around 180 degrees by the time he wrote *South Pacific*? I don't think so. In its original concept, you were supposed to hear, "Niggers all work on de Mississippi /Niggers all work while de white folks play," as the first thing. Now, can you imagine a white, upper class, New York audience sitting down today in the Ziegfeld Theatre, expecting to hear another Flo Ziegfeld extravaganza—and being hit in the face with *that*? And there's "Ol' Man River"—what more progressive, socialist song could there have possibly ever been written?

During the recording sessions, there was a chorus of African Americans who were at the Glyndebourne Festival doing *Porgy and Bess* at the time. They objected to the use of the word "nigger," and they also objected to "In Dahomey," which takes place in the Chicago World's Fair scene. In that scene a group of black people come out dressed as African natives, and they sing this chorus of nonsense syllables meant to entertain the promenaders at the World's Fair. And when all these people are scared away by these supposed African savages, they take off their African gear and sing, "In Dahomey /Let the Africans stay ... Our home ain't in Dahomey at all! /Oh, take me back today to Avenue A." And again, it was pointing up the terrible double standard and the terrible repression that black people were subjected to in this country. Well, unfortunately, it was such a knee-jerk, emotional issue, and I think for me as a white man, to say they were wrong to pull out of the project, would be ludicrous because I don't, I don't understand at my core what that kind of feeling of prejudice is. But they pulled out of the project along with Willard White, who was supposed to sing Joe. Bruce Hubbard, who eventually sang the role of Joe, was also in Glyndebourne doing that production of *Porgy and Bess*. He was approached by EMI to come in and replace Willard. Well, he was in a hell of a position; so to Bruce's credit, he took what I thought was a very reasoned approach to it and called Ben Hooks, Eartha Kitt, and Jesse Jackson. He said, "What should I do?" And Eartha put it best when she said, "Honey, this piece was not written for black people; this piece was written for white people to show them what they done to our people. Now, you're never going to change prejudicial attitudes by pretending they didn't exist. So you go there, you make that recording and you use the word, 'nigger,' because that's what they called us."

If you haven't heard *Show Boat* in its entirety, and haven't put it in context, it's unfair and it's wrong to say it was in any way a racial slur. I'll never forget when we did the miscegenation scene—which we did in one day, believe it or not!— which is a dialogue with underscoring. It's the point at which Julie LaVerne and her husband Steve are forced to leave the show boat because it is discovered that she is part black. And there is a line in there when the actor who is playing the part of the sheriff sent on board to investigate this, looks at Julie and says, "We understand that your daddy was white and your mammy was black. Is that true?" And she said, "Yep." He says, "Well, that makes you black around these parts." Remember that prior to the sheriff coming on board, Julie's husband slits his hand open and slits her hand open and presses the two hands together to mingle their blood. So, he in response to the sheriff's charge of her being black says, "Sheriff, what would you say if I told you I had black blood in me?" And he looks at him and says, "Son, in these parts, one drop of nigger blood makes a man a nigger." What a hateful, Neanderthal thing to say. And it made the whole cast shudder the day we recorded that. And we listened to the playback, and you know, if I've done nothing else in my life, I felt like I was provided with an opportunity to be a part of a project which, even though my character doesn't deal with that issue, I think it was important because it's a part of our past that we can't ignore. As the years have gone by, the issue may have waned a bit. But now that *Show Boat* has once again become the center of controversy because the Hal Prince production in Toronto comes to Broadway in October [i.e., in 1994]. Pickets rage. It's happening again. I'm sure all of it will be rehashed again in October. Jesse Jackson came out in print about six months ago decrying the street rap that's using words like that.

The Show Boat *recording project was a springboard for your future projects wasn't it?*
Fame! Television! Hero worship! Money! When you're pursuing a career and appeasing your own ego and ambition, you can sometimes forget, or be unaware, of how powerful an effect your work can have on other people. I'm terribly proud of our *Show Boat*. For the first time [i.e. in 1994] since I did the recording I'll be conducting it with the Scottish Chamber Orchestra in Edinburgh in July. The cast will include Rebecca Caine [as Magnolia], Kevin Anderson as Ravenal, Carla Burns as Queenie, Sally Burgess as Julie. It's going to be very strange to do that music again.

Now to consider some of your other work. I believe you spent two years restoring Babes in Toyland *[1903] by Victor Herbert [1859–1923], which you conducted in 1994.*
It was glorious, if I do say so myself. Much deeper and darker than we remember.

Another find was Herbert's The Magic Knight [1906], *which I believe you discovered in a box at the Tams-Witmark warehouse in Secaucus, New Jersey.*
[laughs] The box was marked "Miscellaneous Fragments, Inconsequential." The manuscript had no title page! But when I looked at the music I recognized the horn melody. I almost had a stroke! Materials to many more American musical shows are scattered to the winds. More to the point, it didn't occur to people to save these materials. So we have orchestra parts for some things, full scores for others, and others are simply lost. Maybe some piano/vocal scores only. We might have lyrics to many songs, but no music at all. These works are only fifty years old. Also some material is under copyright, or it's been sequestered by wary families. They are still business commodities, a potential source of income, rather than works of art. It's distressing to realize things are treated in this way. I know of some works by composers that are denied us because the families don't trust the music and fear they might demean their reputations.

Are there others out there tracking down these treasures?
A big problem I see is that there are not very many people out there hunting these things down. I feel this tremendous weight on my shoulders. It's a cup I would love to have passed from my lips at this point. I've been at this for ten years. How many other gems are still out there? Maybe I'll pack it all in and try to be an opera conductor. I've cleaned up enough messes. But, if I don't do this, who will? I feel like Kundry [in Wagner's *Parsifal*]: "*Muss Ich?*" [Must I?] ...[long pause] You said you were surprised at my, well, childish enthusiasm. It doesn't mean, though, that I'm in any way frivolous. I'm not. I'm much too dark and serious and

sometimes seemingly not "fun" enough. I'm profoundly serious about my work, whether it's Jerome Kern or [Richard] Wagner. Once I wore shorts to a rehearsal of the Cleveland Orchestra at the Blossom Music Festival. It was 98 degrees, but it offended the players. I have no time for that kind of pomposity. Think of the players in the pit at Bayreuth, in their underwear! On a hot day that theater is intolerable!

Tommy Tune: "I'm a Very 1920s Kind of Guy!"

John C. Tibbetts
15 October 1990, Kansas City

Many musicians more or less ignore dance. Yet dancing emerged long ago, probably in prehistoric times, and in the Western musical world it has taken many forms: the pairs of sixteenth-century Europe's pavane-galliards, the court dances of Louis XIV's Versailles, ballet (which took its final form in conjunction with nineteenth-century French grand opera), and a host of twentieth-century popular dances. Choreographers assign dance steps to particular passages or moments of music; one famous example involves Marius Petipa (1818–1910) and Lev Ivanov (1834–1901), who choreographed Tchaikovsky's *Nutcracker* ballet for its 1892 Russian premiere. Borrowing in part from vaudeville and other earlier entertainments, Broadway choreographers have employed the waltz, tap, the ragtime dance, the soft shoe, the kick line, and almost anything else they can think of.

Dancer, choreographer, director, and producer Tommy Tune has amassed ten Tony Awards as well as seven Drama Desk Awards and the National Medal of Arts. Texas-born Tune first appeared on screen in Ken Russell's *The Boy Friend* (1971) and on the Broadway stage in *Baker Street* (1965); he made his stage debut as director/choreographer in *The Best Little Whorehouse in Texas* (1978). Tune's memoir *Footnotes* was published in 1997 (Fig. 3).

This conversation transpired backstage at Kansas City's Midland Theater, as Tune prepared for a two-person stage show with musical-theater star Donna McKechnie. He also provided an advance peek at his new production, *The Will Rogers Follies*.

JOHN C. TIBBETTS: First of all, we have to talk about your name ...
TOMMY TUNE: Yes, my real name is Tommy Tune. Hard to believe!

They'll never believe it in Poughkeepsie! Really!
[laughs] I know! I was born Thomas James Tune. The family shortened it from "Tunesmith." Isn't it odd, that I end up being a song and dance man and working in the theater and my name is Tommy Tune? What's in a name!

Fig. 3   Tommy Tune

And here you are, in Kansas City, dancing with Donna McKechnie, in a show called On Broadway.
We're dancing separately, you see. I've been working on my own show for about five years. Considering it takes that long to refine it to perfection, why would you expect that just because we're in Kansas City for a Tuesday night opening, that we were going to do some spectacular number together? These things don't happen like that. It's twice as difficult to work with someone as working alone, because you have to balance each other, and these things take weeks to perfect. So, both of us being perfectionists, we wouldn't want to get out and show people in Kansas City something that was less than perfect. I don't think you can arrive at that in a couple of hours of rehearsals, although my dream has always been to dance with Donna, so maybe this will be the beginning, you know.

That's my next question: might an association like this—apparently it's on an occasional basis—develop into some sort of a program that you perform together?
Yes, nothing would please me more. Donna and I worked together many years ago on the first show that Michael Bennett choreographed. She was the star of the show and I was in the chorus. Well, you know, she's just the best dancer in the world. So someday it would be nice if we got to share the same spotlight.

Here at the Midland Theater we have a relatively shallow stage. It was often used for prologues for old movies back in the day. Can you adjust to a playing space this size?
Oh, yes, this is big for me; this is a big stage for me. I'm used to working on much smaller spaces, so I have plenty of room. I don't need more than a twelve-foot depth for my dancing.

You remind me that dancing can still be elegant, can still be supple, can still be graceful—and that height need not get in the way!
Well, good, I'm glad you believe that. I learned to dance, of course, before I got this tall. [gestures] I'm more than six and a half feet tall now. I started taking dancing when I was five, so little by little as my height increased, I learned how to dance. I don't think if I'd gotten full-grown before I started dancing, it would have worked out. Most dancers aren't built this way. I've lost count of the number of bumps on my head from hitting low-hanging pipes and doorways!

Are bodies different for different people? That is to say, do some people really have longer legs than others? Your legs always seemed longer, somehow, in proportion to the rest of your body.
I suppose so. You know, it's all a matter of proportion. Some people have a longer waist, some a shorter waist. They say that my legs go up to my armpits! It's not true!

Does the height however ever become a problem, maybe in terms of a dancing partner, or in a certain routine?
Definitely. [laughs] I think it's more on the plus side.

Think of a mismatch, like Buddy Ebsen and Shirley Temple, for example.
That was novelty. On the plus side, I have more to dance with. But control is certainly easier for a shorter dancer when it comes to staccato [quick steps or] moves; but I've moved into more lyrical things, more like the Fred Astaire-type dancing.

I guess the first time I was aware of you was in Ken Russell's The Boyfriend *[1971]. What a special movie that was! Did it point to a direction that you ever wanted to follow up more, as a movie performer?*
Twiggy got me that job, you know. After we made Ken's movie, we were asked to do a sequel. Where *The Boyfriend* was set in the 1920s, the sequel was going to take place in the 1930s. Twiggy and I did not end up together in the first one, but we were going to end up on an ocean liner in the sequel. We both were just getting out of divorces, and we found each other. We worked on it for a while, but it really never materialized. I'd say almost fifty percent of the projects that I develop do get on, but that was one that didn't. But twenty years after our movie, Twiggy and I did end up on Broadway together in a show called *My One and Only* [1983]. So, eventually, you know, these things come to fruition. Let's face it, Twiggy and I were no Adele and Fred Astaire.[3] We were Twiggy and Tommy Tune, but we had a lot of fun.

There's theatrical symmetry for you! Russell's film seems to be one of the sunnier works of a self-professedly tortured man. Did you notice a sense of serenity on the set?
Well, [Russell] had just made *The Devils* [1971] with Vanessa Redgrave and Oliver Reed, so I guess he was wanting to purify and cleanse himself. He just wanted to make a Valentine. But about three quarters of the way through, he got so bored with all the sweetness and light that he started doing lesbian scenes and all sorts of things. After dinner each night, Ken would slide under the door a new script and shooting schedule with all these darker things added—stuff about what was going on in the company. We were all appalled.

But early in your career it must have been an exciting risk to work with a wild man like that?
Oh, Ken Russell was an enormous influence on me as a performer and especially as a director. He's a mad genius, and I don't use the word "genius" often. He's

---

[3]The sibling song-and-dance team Adele (1896–1981) and Fred (1899–1987) Astaire delighted Broadway audiences in the early twentieth century in landmark shows such as *Lady, Be Good!* (1924, with songs by George and Ira Gershwin).

brilliant and he taught me so much, so much about art and, well, surrealism.[4] He explained surrealism beautifully to me. This is a long time ago, and I was very green. I just think the world of him; I really do.

That image of you in those white flannel trousers and white shoes is indelible. Perfect for Tommy Tune!
Well, I'm a very 1920s kind of guy. I've always felt I was born too late, that I should have been born in the 1920s. That music, that style—the "Oxford bags" is what they call those trousers I wore—and the saddle shoes and the raccoon coat and the pork pie hat and plus fours: it all feels right on my frame. I put it on and I go right into it; and all of that music of the 1920s and 1930s, those are my favorite songs.

This brings us to On Broadway, *your show here in Kansas City. You were quoted in the paper recently as noting that all of the songs you sing were written before you were born.*
Yeah.

What does that tell us about songwriting today?
Well, it's just personal taste. There's great music out there today, but when I started putting together this show I wanted to make it an American classic. I wanted it to be something that wouldn't date. Songs by Cole Porter, Gershwin, Irving Berlin [1888–1989], these songs from that classic golden period of the American popular song last because they are universally true; the feelings remain within us. The times have changed but the feelings remain. So I call it "contemporary nostalgia."

From performer Harry Connick to arranger and conductor John McGlinn, it seems to be a time when mere nostalgia is blossoming into a need to go back and get the old songs and shows and do them right. Does it seem like there's an awful lot about that music that we have misunderstood over the years?
I'm not trying for authenticity so much as to perform them *now*, tomorrow night, and every night, and through the week. Every night I do them I sing them *in the moment*. I don't try to ape a style from before. On the other hand, I don't jerk them around to give them some modern context. I just feel them as I sing them. I think everything old is new again. When it's really good, it lasts. I've always had a penchant for things that were created in an earlier time that have somehow survived and flourished in the present. Besides the music I'm talking about tuxedos

---

[4]The terms "surrealism" and "surreal" have several meanings. One involves "more real than real"; 3-D films might be called "surreal" in this sense. Another is associated with early and mid-twentieth-century artists, among them Salvador Dalí (1904–1989) and Max Ernst (1891–1976), who painted imaginary worlds often associated with dream images.

and Chanel No. 5 [perfume] and really fine things that last. Like the fountain pen, which is almost extinct.

When we put on a tux and go to a party, we feel very special don't we? But when you are a dancer and you put on a tux, it must have an amazing impact on how you perform.
Right away your posture changes. By the way, I wear tails in the show as opposed to the tuxedo. I wear tails because they move better and they give you a longer line. You do not slump, like I am right now; you just sit up. It requires it. That stiff front shirt and the collar that goes up—right away everything is already up a level. And the music starts and that lifts you further …

I remember reading somewhere that Fred Astaire was very self-conscious about the size of his hands. Your hands are not inordinately large for your height, but Astaire had all kinds of little tricks to minimize the size of his hands on screen. Are there things about the reach of your arms and legs that enhance your gracefulness on stage?
All you have to remember is that Fred Astaire was a movie star, and so he saw himself on the screen and studied himself to that purpose. On stage, I work in three dimensions, performing live, so what I have to go on is the mirror. All dancers use the mirror.

I guess we think that choreographers on and off screen have to get tough with performers, like Warner Baxter does in 42nd Street. *That doesn't square with the image of Tommy Tune we know. You seem to be a very gentle guy. You're soft-spoken, you're very genial, you don't seem to have a mean bone in your body. But is there a Tommy Tune that's tough and hard as nails?*
That's not my style, it doesn't come out of me that way. I feel sometimes like I'm creating a hothouse atmosphere for exotic plants to grow in, the exotic plants being the actors; so I like to make the climate right and get everybody growing to their maximum capacity. I don't think you can bark at them; it doesn't seem to work. I like the gentler touch. I've matured as a director, and I find that it's alright to use this phrase, "I don't know" if a dancer comes to me, asking, "Should I do it this way, should I do it that way …?" When you honestly say, "I don't know," you find that everybody says, "Well then would you like to see it like this?" or "How about if I did that way?" So I say, "Try it," and suddenly we're all working on same painting, working in the same style, be it pointillism or brush strokes or whatever. You get everyone onto the same wavelength by making them feel comfortable.

What about in your show, On Broadway, *any special moments that you'd like to talk about?*
I do this one tap number that is a tribute to my friend, [choreographer and dancer] Charles "Honi" Coles [1911–1992]. He is one of our great American tap dancers. I danced with him in *My One and Only* [1983] for over a thousand performances.

He was seventy-five at the time. He's quite a fabulous gentleman. He taught me a number that he did in vaudeville with his partner, and it was billed as the world's slowest soft shoe. It is probably the most difficult thing I've ever attempted as a dancer. It's deceptively simple to look at, but if I'm doing it right, you won't even think about it. I've found that sometimes dancing very, very fast is easier than dancing very, very slow; so every time I slide into that number I say, "Oh, Honi, help me through this one!" It's not just a question of balance but of the rhythms; the beats are so far apart and the tendency always in tap dancing is to rush. I really have to sit on my inner clock and say, "Calm down." I have to breathe down into it to make it work.

You're carrying a sketchbook with you. I guess even on the road, you're working on something. Let's have a scoop on this. What's going on here?
Well, since you've asked, I'm planning my next show. I'm in close, constant touch with the fabulous scenic designer Tony Walton, who I worked with on *Grand Hotel* [1989]. Our working title is *Ziegfeld Presents the Will Rogers Follies* [1991].

I see a design around the set that looks like a lariat.
[points out elements in his drawing] Yes, a lariat motif here is going around the proscenium. Here's the obligatory stairs. And I want to have a giant blowup of [comedian and actor] Will Rogers [1879–1935] that covers the proscenium as the act curtain. Then we would scrim through that and see this sort of white thunder-bird Indian showgirl.... [pauses and shrugs] It's hard to explain. And then this cowboy rises up from the stage looking up at the picture with his back to us; and then he turns around. But it's not a cowboy, it's a *cowgirl* who is dressed like Will Rogers. This just got written out this morning.... [gestures again at his draw-ing] Here's a line of showgirls. Actually, it's a showgirl, a showboy, a showgirl, a showboy—boy, girl, boy, girl—and then the curtain flies [up] ... and down the steps comes the ponies. Ponies are the girls that are not as tall as the showgirls. They're called ponies. I don't know why.

Is that a term that goes way back?
Yeah, it goes back to Ziegfeld. He had showgirls, and then he had ponies. They had to really dance, while the showgirls sort of paraded around. The ponies worked harder! [laughs].

Anyway [turns again to his drawing], then this big picture of Will Rogers will fly out. This will be the "big reveal" of Will. I'll have him on stilts. Another option is to have him walk on stage with the girl, only he'll be twice their height. I'm going to storyboard the show as I see it, and then I'm going to fax it off to Tony.

I should explain that these are thumbnail sketches, very simple, very graphic, just like a storyboard for a movie.
Well, they have to go through the fax machine so any detail is lost.

You're thinking visually here. Are these your first conceptions, or is there a script you are working with?
We've been working on this show for about three years, but the visuals are the last thing I get to. I deal with all the words and all the music first, because the visuals are the easy part for me.

Now does this mean that sometime in the future I can save this interview and play it later when the show is finished? Is it for television or Broadway?
No, it's Broadway. It's going to reopen the Palace Theater in New York around the middle of April, if all goes right. I should knock some wood.

About that title …?
Ziegfeld Presents The Will Rogers Follies? I don't know what we're really going to call it. It seems kind of flat. I think we need a new one.

Will you be in it, then?
No, no, no, no, no. We have a fabulous, fabulous man [Keith Carradine] playing Will Rogers.

As we sit here, I wonder how many things are on your mind at once?
Well, yeah, I'm casting right now, and I close here Sunday night in Kansas City and go directly back to New York. On Monday morning we start rehearsal on the national company of *Grand Hotel*, which will be touring all over America and to Japan and so on. We'll rehearse that for four weeks, and it will open in Tampa. Then I go to Berlin to do the German company, which will be played in German; and then on the way back from Germany, I'll stop off in London and cast the London company of *Grand Hotel*. Then, I'll come back and start rehearsals for this show.

Carl Davis: "Music Informs the Motion Picture!"

John C. Tibbetts
January 1997 and August 2017, London

Movie music has a checkered history. Originally denigrated even as it attracted a number of "art" composers, it rose to increasing prominence during the 1950s and 1960s with scores by Miklós Rózsa (1907–1995) for *Ben Hur* (1959); Bernard Herrmann (1911–1975) for *Psycho* (1960); Ennio Morricone for *The Godfather* (1972), *Days of Heaven* (1978), and other prestigious productions; and John Williams for *Star Wars* (1977)—to name just a few examples. In fact, movie music has become "classical" music for many twenty-first-century concert-goers, and star composers such as John Williams

Fig. 4 Carl Davis

and Hans Zimmer continue to earn fortunes composing scores for award-winning films (Fig. 4).

Born in New York City and a graduate of Bard College, Sir Carl Davis CBE belongs to a select company of classically trained composers who have scored silent films. Other members of that company include Camille Saint-Saëns for *L'Assassinat de duc de Guise* (1909), Erik Satie for *Entr'acte* (1924), Paul Hindemith (1895–1963) for *Krazy Kat at the Circus* (1927), Arthur Honegger (1892–1955) for *La Roue* (1922), Jacques Ibert (1890–1962) for *The Italian Straw Hat* (1927), and Dmitri Shostakovich for *The New Babylon* (1929). Davis has also won international renown for his scores for theatrical feature films, including Ken Russell's *The Rainbow* (1988) and Karel Reisz's *The*

French Lieutenant's Woman **(1981), and for his own concert works, including his collaboration with Paul McCartney on the** *Liverpool Oratorio* **(1991). In 2005 Davis was made a Commander of the British Empire.**

In the conversation that follows, Davis speaks in his London home about his work with film preservationist/restorer Kevin Brownlow and about his scores for the various versions of the "complete" *Napoléon.*

JOHN C. TIBBETTS: Looking around your apartment I see an incredible assortment of scores, posters, books, musical instruments, and old LPs (bless you!). In the middle of all this, what's on your mind right now?
CARL DAVIS: I'm giving myself up for a recording of source music for a huge series commissioned by [BBC] Channel Four called *A Dance to the Music of Time*, which are twelve novels written by Anthony Paul. It takes a group of characters from the 1920s through to the 1960s in London. They're cult books with a passionate number of readers. Their heyday has passed, I'm afraid, but after this [laughs] they'll come out of the woodwork next year! And I'm excited that the team that put together *The World at War* has been commissioned by Turner and the BBC to do a follow up, to be called *The Cold War*. We're in the middle of that now.

Is any of your music "source music ... "?
To define that—when you look at the screen, you see the source of the music, maybe coming from a band in a bar, or an orchestra at the Ritz, or if someone is playing a piano. Other people call it "diegetic music": music in the story. Today, I'm working on an episode set during the Second World War, so there's a band playing the Conga in what is supposed to be the Café de Paris.

You are American born?
Yes. I was born in Brooklyn. I like to say, within the same circle that bred Aaron Copland and George Gershwin!

When did movies come into your life?
I think I was four years old when I first went to the cinema. My interest in films has always been part of the broader picture. But I never thought for a minute that I would ever devote myself entirely, one hundred percent, to film. If I had done that, you wouldn't find me in London, but in L.A.

How and when did you and Kevin Brownlow team up? It was before Napoléon, *correct?*
It all starts with Thames Television and producer Jeremy Isaacs. I met Isaacs in the mid-1970s during *The World at War* [completed in 1973]. He told me he was starting to work on this *Hollywood* series, a documentary history of the silent film in Hollywood produced by Mark Brownlow. We got together with his brother Kevin, and it was an immediate success all over the world. I knew Brownlow, the producer, had made a number of feature films, very small-scale, very good, very

detailed, like *It Can Happen Here* [1965]; and that he had written this wonderful book, *The Parade's Gone By* [1968]. We finished *Hollywood* in 1980, and it was an immediate success for Thames Television. They sold it instantly to fifty countries! In the euphoria of all that, I thought, "Now that I've composed music for three-or-four hundred movie excerpts, why don't I try to score a complete silent film?"

The idea was yours?
Yes. Why not a whole one? But then, something else happened: the Coppolas were putting together a presentation of Abel Gance's *Napoléon* [1927] That was the other obsession of Kevin's, [the silent film] *Napoléon*. As a teenager, he started collecting "lost" fragments, which existed in only about an hour-and-a-half version. It had been dispersed and ruined over the years, and no one had been interested in it at all. Kevin slowly began to build up more of the print, as much as he could afford, and over the years he got various grants to help him, and so on.

Had you heard the score that [Swiss composer Arthur] Honegger composed in 1927 for Napoléon, *or Coppola's score?*
I'll say categorically that I've not heard one note of the [Francis Ford] Coppola score. We looked for the Honegger music, but couldn't find it; it did turn up later. At the point I got it, I had already worked out about three hours of music. I decided to use Honegger's setting of the *Marseillaise* in counterpoint with [Étienne] Méhul [1763–1817]'s French patriotic song *Le Chant du Départ*, during the "Beggars of Glory" section, which was the March of the invading French Army into Italy. [hums the tune] So that was my little homage to Honegger, at that point. I knew that silent film composers before me had always drawn upon the classics, so it seemed a valid thing to do. We did the premiere on 30 November 1980. The Coppola premiere was in New York in January 1981.

What orchestra did you use?
We used a London orchestra, a very odd orchestra called the Wren, as in "Christopher." They were funded by a commercial radio station called Capitol Radio. It was an uneasy relationship. But I was close to them at the time.

As I understand it, you used classical quotations from other composers of Napoleon [Bpnaparte]'s time, including Beethoven. But back to the recording session!
There we were, on a November 1980 Sunday morning at the Empire Theater in Leicester Square … and I'm conducting with my back to the audience, the orchestra and the screen in front of me. In fact, I'm conducting *to the film*, attempting to synchronize the score to the action on the screen. Nobody knew if we would be able to stay in "sync" with the film, but I was just lucky, a lot of the time. I never vamped. There were certain "escape hatches." Which means, if I came to the end of a sequence a little too soon, I would strike a fermata, something with a drum riff, maybe, just to cover the gap.

You've alerted the players for such situations?
They're written into their scores. Nothing is left to question. Anyway, the response was overwhelming on that day. It was a historic day. People were just amazed at the power and the freshness of hearing Beethoven played against some of the scenes. And my own themes run through, as well. Like motifs running throughout, themes that can be repeated, and varied, and transformed as you need them. Maybe a theme for the hero, or a love theme, or for war, etc.

Among your own thirty-odd silent-film scores, is there one that, for one reason or another, is more meaningful to you?
I think the Lillian Gish film *The Wind* [1928] is special. It's a wonderful story about a woman who goes into the desert southwest and is driven mad by the elements. I was able to "lift" the film, you know? Even if you see it silently, it has a stunning impact; but with music it became an extraordinary visual and aural experience.

Let's take a particular sequence, say, the climactic wind storm, when Gish goes mad.
I always have great respect for the period in which any film is made, or for the time period of the subject matter. In this case, 1928. I won't write anything that would "abuse" the ears of somebody living in that period. Of course, there are opportunities here to use technology to make the audience feel they "are there." When Gish is deafened and buffeted about by the sandstorm, I wanted the listener to feel as if they were in it with her. So I composed in an aleatoric way, which is actually a passage written without bar lines.

Which means …?
It's written on counts, and when we get loud enough, I shout the count numbers to the players. They are given responsibility to make their own sounds; they have a lot of leeway. Kind of a mass improvisation. It's more controlled than it seems, and I do teach it as well as conduct it. I have five percussionists, each with his own group of instruments, so that by the time the storm is at its peak, you have five gongs being battered simultaneously.

Some say that music in itself has affective properties, that certain rhythms, melodic lines, tonalities have an affinity with emotions, people, actions, etc.[5] What do you think about that?
I do think music has affective properties, as you say, although I wouldn't be too literal about it. It's a tricky issue. Stravinsky said that music in itself doesn't mean anything … [goes to the piano and demonstrates] If you play a C-major scale, it doesn't really *mean* anything; but if you play it very slowly, with feeling, *then* it

---

[5]See Lawrence Kramer, *Musical Meaning* (Berkley and Los Angeles: University of California Press, 2002).

might have something; and if you play it very fast with lots of discords, it might have something else! It elicits different responses, don't you think? Of course! Even so, ask three different people and you get three different interpretations!

Isn't this really pertinent to the film composer?
I don't think you should distinguish between ... *film* composers as opposed to just *composers*. I heard Miklós Rózsa say that he doesn't think of himself as a "film composer;" he's a composer who writes for films. So, I bring all my baggage, all my inherited or trained or developed baggage as a composer, into film. I just try to do what's right, what I feel will help the film, will bring out a character in the film, enhance a mood. Yes, music *informs* the picture. It's telling the viewers a lot, even though they might not intellectually be able to define just what that is.

It would be useful to sit in with you at work and see how you work out your film and TV scores.
I was working with Kevin [Brownlow] on a silent film called *The Chess Player* [1927]. We filmed taking one scene from it and talking over how to score it. It showed me writing a score and then going into the recording session with the players. You see me looking at the picture on the monitor while cuing the players. That sort of thing.

I assume you've heard from a lot of people and gotten a lot of publicity ...?
Not as much as you might think! I'm afraid that somebody writing soundtracks is interesting only to people who write soundtracks! I think when most people go to a movie, they don't really think much about the costumes, the lighting, much less the music. It was only when I started performing publicly, conducting my scores, making appearances that I started getting a little more attention.

You've done so much especially for silent film! Who knew that "silents" could make such a comeback! That today they could attract audiences?
There is a public out there learning about our film history, about silent films. They don't just purchase the videos we put out, but actually come to the theaters to see and hear them "live." And isn't that where it all began?

Epilogue

It is 2017 and Carl Davis speaks from his home in London.

TIBBETTS: Carl, here we are, many years later, with many more films scored, concerts performed, and new ventures into composition that include original ballets. Your new version of Napoléon *comes immediately to mind.*
DAVIS: John, I've spent the last five years preparing for the recording of my extended *Napoléon* score for DVD/Blue-ray, and CD. *Napoléon* now runs 5 ½ hours! For these recordings I'm writing a new march to replace the Honegger from 1927. It's a better "match" in the famous Triptych if I write my own music to match the shifting rhythms and locations in the imagery.

Bringing this newest version to a "live" movie audience and in concert has to be very emotionally fulfilling. You and the film and the character of "Napoléon" have grown older together, right?
Oh, conducting that "live" performance in March 2012 was a great personal triumph for me, although it exercised my mental and physical powers to their utmost. But when you ask me if I feel any personal "identification" with Napoleon [Bonaparte] himself, I have to plead—not at all. However, amongst my players, I have noticed some casualties! [laughs]

The event certainly put you into the public spotlight! I've discovered that many of the musicians in the pages of this *book* [i.e., Performing Music History] *not only enjoy direct contact with their public, but encourage it. Indeed, that's the whole point of the book! What about you?*
Well, the very *idea* of *performing* is very enticing, and you're excited and there's nervous energy everywhere. There's always a buzz. But it's never as simple as it seems. Conducting, for me, is especially a challenge, not only musically, but physically and psychologically as well. It can be a delight for all concerned, but equally a challenge. For *Napoléon* you have to have stamina. A real endurance test! If you are conducting really great music from the classics, something like a Beethoven symphony or a Mozart concerto, there is nothing better for me and my audiences!

You have been composing for the ballet stage these days. How is ballet music, like your Cyrano *and* Aladdin, *different from your work on silent films?*
Quite simply, the "silent" films we were talking about earlier had been completed by the time I begin work on them. My framework is prepared already for me. That's very different from a new ballet, which I create from scratch, with the component needing to be invented. They operate interactively: the plot (if it's a story ballet), the designs, even the lighting influence the score. This constitutes a *living* collaboration, a team I work with, all of us contributing to the whole.

I notice one of your ballets, Mermaid, *was created for your daughter, Hannah.*
Yes, Hannah and her husband, David, are attempting these days the impossible—writing, directing, sometimes acting, producing, fundraising. I love their work, which is very dark and sardonic. So, if they ask me, I do their scores.

John Kander: "When Fred Ebb and I Are Together, We Create a Third Person: Kander and Ebb"

John C. Tibbetts
January and April 1997

Fig. 5 John Kander and Fred Ebb

Kander and Ebb's *Cabaret* won eight Tonys in 1967, two years after it opened on Broadway. But that wasn't all. Among other things, *Cabaret* became part of an ongoing American exploration of 1930s German cabaret music; among other prominent performers of such music were the Germans Marlene Dietrich (1901–1992) and Lotte Lenya (1898–1981), whose careers lasted into the 1970s. Later, choreographer Bob Fosse(1927–1987)'s production of *Cabaret* (1975)—dubbed by scholar David Rodgers "perhaps the darkest satire ever to open on Broadway"—employed a musical style based on the Berlin songs of Kurt Weill (1900–1950), and "for the first time" a popular American musical comedy recreated authentic *period* music. Not all of Kander and Ebb's shows have been successful, but *Cabaret*, *Chicago*, and *Kiss of the Spider Woman* (1992 in London, 1993 on Broadway) helped establish the concept musical[6] as an important genre of dramatic-music history (Fig. 5).

---

[6]A musical comedy that emphasizes style, message, and metaphor rather than plot.

Between the mid-1940s and 1957, John Harold Kander served intermittently in America's armed forces, then completed his musical studies at Oberlin College and Columbia University; his teachers included electronic pioneer composer Otto Luening (1900–1996) and American opera composer Douglas Moore (1893–1969). Kander served as rehearsal accompanist for the original Broadway production of *West Side Story*. For almost his entire career as a Broadway, film, and pop-song composer, Kander collaborated with lyricist Fred Ebb (1928–2004), who studied English at Columbia and New York University. Iconic "Kander and Ebb" products include the title song from Martin Scorsese's film *New York, New York* (1977): the last the official song of New York City.

In the following interview, Kander talks about his Broadway career, past and present, including his work with his longtime collaborator, the late Fred Ebb.

JOHN C. TIBBETTS: You're from Kansas City. Can you talk a bit about that?
JOHN KANDER: My ties to Kansas City were, and are, very strong. My parents were both from Kansas City. I started playing piano when I was about four. You could say I *found* the piano on my own. Fortunately, my family loved music, too. My father sang and my grandmother and my aunt played piano. Soon my aunt took charge and did something marvelous that I'll always remember: she placed her hands over mine and we made a chord together. That did it. I started plucking out tunes when I was six. My teacher was a woman named Lucy Parrot. She lived about four blocks away, and she looked a little like the Wicked Witch of the West. She was eccentric, but looking back I realize she was a wonderful teacher and had great enthusiasm. She had a recording of Wagner's *Tristan und Isolde*, and if I had a good lesson, she would give me cookies and a glass of goat's milk and would play it for me. It's very hard to explain to you how exotic those moments were for me. There I was, sitting in this dark house with this hawk-like woman feeding me goat's milk … and listening to Wagner. I guess I was afraid of her, but she stirred something in me.

I kept hearing more Wagner as a kid and all through high school. There was Mabel Glenn, the head of the music department of the Kansas City Public Schools—they don't have those sorts of positions any more, because of cutbacks—who would come to school once a week and play music and talk about it; and one day she came and played something I had never heard in my life (I was about twelve or so). It was the opening of the third act of *Götterdämmerung*, the "Rhine Maidens" scene. I was fascinated by it. I remember taking a streetcar to the public library to ask her to tell me more about the music. She lent me the records, and I took them home. So you see, from Lucy Parrott and Mabel Glenn I was a confirmed Wagnerian from then on.

Can you talk a bit about your time in the Army?
I was able to make something of a living. I played at the Officers Club on Saturday nights to make money; and I played in a whorehouse in Shanghai to keep warm (it

was very cold there!). After the War I went to Oberlin College, wrote some shows, and came to Columbia to do graduate work. I got an assistantship in the opera workshop there (which meant coaching singers and playing scores). I think it was apparent by then that I was committed to music.

When did you start thinking of composing?
I was still kind of musically schizophrenic at Columbia, not sure what direction I was going. Douglas Moore was the head of the Music Department there, and he and his family became my great friends, sort of my New York family. Douglas confessed to me one time that during World War I he had written a lot of popular songs. If he had it to do all over again, he said, he'd choose instead to write for the theater, for Broadway. I've always remembered that as a kind of "legitimizing" moment for me. Sometimes with a very simple song, if it turns out well, I'll get some sort of fulfilled feeling that must be similar to somebody writing fine opera.

After leaving Columbia in 1954, I spent nine years in the trenches, coaching singers, playing for auditions and show rehearsals, conducting in stock, working as a pianist in stage productions like *The Amazing Adele* [1956] and *An Evening with Beatrice Lillie* [1952], and composing dance arrangements for Broadway and television shows. By the time I had done the dance music for *Gypsy* [1959] and *Irma La Douce* [1963] the theater community knew me. It's not a class-oriented community, by the way. I was known as a professional and had access to everything. When the time came to do a musical, Hal Prince heard a piece I had done called *Family Affair* [1962]—about the obstacles family members put between two young people who want to marry—which I had done with James and William Goldman in 1962. Hal directed it. In fact, it was the first thing he ever directed. We've worked together many times since.

When did you first meet Fred Ebb?
That was in 1962. Freddie is two years younger than me. Unlike me, he is a New Yorker through and through. He was brought up on the Lower East Side. He had been writing material for nightclub acts and the satirical television series like *That Was the Week That Was* [1962–1963]. And he had written lyrics for his first stage musical, *Morning Sun* [1962], which had recently failed after only a few performances. We liked each other almost right away. He likes to say our neuroses complemented each other! We started working together immediately. It was as if we were pregnant all the time. We wrote fast. The very first "hit" song we had was "My Coloring Book." That was one of the only times Fred came to *my* house, by God, and he had an idea for a comic song for Kaye Ballard. But because I was in a bad mood, or something, I didn't want to be funny; so I suggested we try it as a ballad. Barbra Streisand turned it into a hit.

Can you talk more about the differences between you two?
Freddie and I are very, very different people. He's a cynical New Yorker and I'm a sentimental Midwesterner. The main thing I can say is that things I'm afraid of, Fred is not; and vice versa. Our pleasures are quite different. Classical music does

not interest him at all. We have mutual friends, but not mutual close friends. But when we're in a room working together, we improvise together. We can both be very thin-skinned with other people; but together we can say anything without being upset. When we're together, we create a third person, "Kander and Ebb." If there is a "secret" to our success, it might be that third person. The best time of all with us is the writing. It's after you finish writing the score that it turns to work. Sometimes things get improved working with a director, producer, choreographer, and a cast, but you're always fighting to preserve the original dream.

Let's turn now to Cabaret.
That show did everything for us. We were accepted as professionals. We must have written sixty songs for *Cabaret*. But for the film version, we were working under contract and had no control of the thing at all. Our one stipulation was that if anything new were written for it, Fred and I would be the ones to do it. We never went to Hollywood, nor were we involved with the film that much. One thing I do remember was that Bob Fosse needed a different kind of "Money Song." The original "Money Song" was a big production number for the emcee and lots of girls. But Bob wanted a number just for Sally Bowles and the emcee. That new song is a better "moment" than the original, and we incorporated it into the 1987 revival.

What about shows that struggled?
Take *The Rink* [1984] a musical drama about the estranged relationship between a mother [Chita Rivera] and her daughter; and *70, Girls, 70* [1971], which ran for only a few weeks. *The Rink* is just a piece waiting to have its day, I think. It was our first collaboration with Terrance McNally, and it was a step forward for us. It was adventurous and emotional. It has always reminded me of that line about circus life, "I love you honey, but the season's over." When you're working together with a cast on a piece like this, it's the most intimate life possible. You're all in love with each other. You have to be, because these are the only people you're going to see for a long time; and it's all very, very emotional. And then it opens. And even though you stay friends, there's this kind of "Oh, hi" thing later. *The Rink* and *Kiss of the Spider Woman* are the two shows from our earlier years I'm closest to. They are so full out in their emotions; where people are allowed to feel, very deeply.

Can you say a bit more about 70, Girls, 70?
It's a rowdy, very lowbrow piece based on an English comedy called *Breath of Spring*, which was later filmed as *Make Mine Mink* [1960]. The critics would not let us do that. The subject of naughty old ladies who turn to a life of crime didn't work for them. The favorite for Fred, I think, would be our first staging of *Chicago* in 1975. That's because it's peppy. Fred's told me his idea of a perfect score is something without a single ballad in it. I tend to be much more drawn to things that are more lyrical and more emotional, like "The Happy Time" [1968], which also has moments I really care about. I prefer songs like "Dear One" or "You Can Never Shame Me" and "Sometimes a Day Goes By" [from *Woman of the Year*, 1981].

How important to your work are the film projects?
My first job for the movies was for Harold Prince's *Something for Everyone*
[1969]. And with Freddie, I wrote new numbers for Bob Fosse's film version of
Cabaret—although, ironically, none of the film's eight Academy Awards acknowledge our work! That was remedied by the Academy[7] in 1975 when "How Lucky
Can You Get" was sung by Barbra Streisand in *Funny Lady* and was nominated for
an Oscar.

How do you and Fred Ebb work together? Can you give any "inside" details?
After working separately on our respective musical and lyrical efforts, we gather
in Freddie's kitchen over sandwiches and coffee. At that point we're mostly concerned with "fixing" the many problems of integrating music and staging. I'll sit
at the keyboard and try out a tune or a rhythm, while Fred messes around with a
phrase or a quatrain. He can improvise in rhyme and meter the way I can with a
melody. Ninety-five percent of our output has been written in that fashion. There's
no way of predicting how fast a song will come. Once at Fred's house somebody
challenged us to write a song between dinner and dessert. "What do we write
about?" asked Fred. "I don't care much," I said. Well—that was our title, "I Don't
Care Much"! We wrote it in fifteen minutes and Streisand recorded it. By contrast,
the song "Where You Are" in *Kiss of the Spider Woman* took lots of work, at least
seven or eight versions. I think the best time for us is the writing. After the score is
finished, then it turns to work. Then you have to fight with the director, producer,
choreographer, and cast to preserve the original dream.

Epilogue: June 2017, Upstate New York

*JOHN TIBBETTS: Looks like I find you these days away from New York City. Have
you abandoned it entirely?*
JOHN KANDER: I still have my house in New York. But here in the country, I'm
two hours north of New York on the west side of the Hudson near Kingston. I see
woods outside one window and what we laughingly call mountains out the other.
I built this house in 1973. It was a sort of get-away, originally. Now I'm using it
more and more. I can work easily here, no distractions. Greg Pierce, who is my
current collaborator, and I have devised a way of working by phone when we're
apart; but since I am not in rehearsal at the moment, he's here now. We have one
more working day to go.

But Fred Ebb was a confirmed New Yorker, wasn't he?
Fred hated the country! He hated this place! He was here only once before
he passed away. When I first built it, he said he would have to come and visit.
I reminded him he *hated* the country. But he said he would come up on a weekend.
We spent three hours working on *New York, New York*, and then he went home.

---

[7]The Academy of Motion Picture Arts and Sciences. Their awards are known as "Oscars."

He didn't even stay for dinner! He said he was afraid I would take him on a picnic, or something!

The last time I saw you two together was in 2002 [17–18 April], *when you both appeared at the William Inge Festival in Independence, Kansas.*
Oh, my. They put on what they called "All That Jazz: A Celebration … etc." at the Community College. There were matinée performances with students and an evening show with professional singers. And we did a few things on stage. Fred really loved it! I'm the opposite, although I was very touched by it. I remember several years ago, we did a series of performances at the 92nd Street Y[MCA]. It went very well and Fred was very happy, but I remember leaving the theater singing, "Oh, there's not enough money in all the world to make me do this again!" [laughs] I'm not the "spotlight kid." We were so every different, but when we were together working, we created this third person we called "Kander and Ebb."

You turned ninety in March of this year [2017]. Are there times, like with all of us, when you wake up and ask yourself, "How did this *happen?"*
I still don't quite know how to deal with that. Whatever birthday I am, I think of myself six months further on to the next one. I understand the significance of ninety, but I've been ninety for most of the year now; and it's just not something I think about much. Life didn't change the next day. I'm working now more than I ever have. But all the celebrating has been really wonderful, but I'm handling it badly. I'm very private and not good at crowds and public events like that. Fred was very good at that. There was recently a party with my little "family," Susan Stroman, Tony Thompson, about six of us who work all the time, at her house. That was perfect.

And there have been other celebrations. Were any of them especially close to your heart?
There was a special birthday performance last March at the Ambassador Theatre. A lot of "alumni" from several of our shows got together, and it was quite wonderful. I remember that Joel Grey was there, and Ann Reinking and Chita Rivera. Bebe Neuwirth did a curtain call speech. They put up a plaque designating the theater as the "special home" of *Chicago*.

Would you talk about Fred Ebb? It's been thirteen years since his passing. Do you remember when you last spoke with him?
I'm sure we were on the phone a day or two before he died. [long pause] I was up here in the country at the time. I got a phone call in the afternoon telling me Fred had had a heart attack; and he died fairly quickly after that. I was in no way prepared for that. It was a shock, a very emotional moment. We were working on several projects at the time. When something is a shock like that, without any preparation, your life changes radically. It's a mixture of things, and it takes quite a while to digest it. We were together longer than any other writing partnership on record. It took me days to realize what had happened. Another thing, as the

days went on, we had about three unperformed projects that needed to be finished, *The Scottsboro Boys* [2010], *Curtains* [2007], [and] *Skin of Our Teeth*.[8] So, as I was working on that material, in a funny way I felt that our partnership was still going on. He was only partially absent, if you know what I mean. *Scottsboro* and *Curtains* are finished. *Skin of Our Teeth*, because of some contractual details, we lost the rights to it temporarily. We had several versions, and it's something I still want to get done.

You said a minute ago you are busier than ever. What can you tell us?
Yes, there are at least three things going on. There's a piece called *The Beast in the Jungle* that I'm working on with Susan Stroman and Tony Thompson.
Is that the short novel by Henry James [1843–1916]?
Yes, it's adapted from his story. There's no singing in it, just music and dance and drama. We've done a workshop on it, and we're doing another in November. It gets produced in the Vineyard Theater in, I think, January or February.

This is amazing news! Henry James loved the theater, but he could never make his plays work! And now, here you are, bringing him to the musical stage?
It's a piece that Stroman and Tony love working on. We stumbled onto it, and I had a wonderful time with it. It's all waltzes. It's a very interesting form. I do admit, however, that I'm not a big Henry James fan. Sometimes reading him is like walking through mud! [Brother] William James [1842–1910] should have been the novelist and Henry the psychologist!

But it's a story about a person to whom nothing happens!
Ah, yes. It's really about somebody who refuses to live his life. He's just *waiting*. ... But we do have a lot of action, and it's a big dance piece. Keep in touch, or watch the papers, and you can see it. And I'm working with Greg on two pieces, we have a director for one; and the other is very early in the process. I've been working with him for quite awhile now. The first thing we did for the Vineyard Theater, which is our home, so to speak, was called *The Landing*. This year we have another piece coming, called *Kid Victory*.

You showed me your computer back in New York a few years ago. Are you still composing with it?
Yeah, because I'm really lazy. There are so many ways to shortcut the pencil. Anything that makes life easier! You can improvise and the computer will "hear" it and notate it. It can be a mess, but it gives you something to work with. I've been working at the computer for a long time now. I use a Roland electronic keyboard and a computer program called Finale that allows me to notate directly into the computer. When it first arrived, it seemed like a new guest that I had to get to

---

[8]Originally titled *Over and Over* (1999), the show was revamped as *All About Us* (2006).

know, to relate to. I had to make it feel "at home," you know? I began working with it during a revival in 1987 of *Flora the Red Menace* [1965], when a computer expert friend from Yale taught me the program. A really great thing is if you have something you wrote for a show in a particular key, but somebody else comes in and asks you to transpose it, you can just push a button. When Fred and I were working separately—me in the country and him in the city—I would just finish writing out a song out in pencil, a complete arrangement, and he would call me and say he wanted to change the lyric! Which meant I would have to erase everything. I didn't like that, but now with the computer, it's easy.

Do you feel your work belongs to a vanishing tradition in Broadway show music?
There are no profound answers to that question, not from anyone who has lived in a generation before now. You hear about the Golden Age of singers, for example, which always occurred *a generation before*. That's true of my generation, too, and the one before that. Anyone who can answer that question with real objectivity is not telling the truth. We are who we are, *we are who we were*, a lot of the time. Too many people will say, "Well, in my day" or when "my generation was producing things." Fred and I, Stephen Sondheim, Jerry Bock, Sheldon Harnick, we lived at a time when the generation before us was considered the Good Old Days. But I have to say that I think a lot of things happening right now are really exciting. Lin-Manuel Miranda is a good friend, and he is just brilliant. He has managed to combine all the elements of popular theater music and distilled them into his own voice. The work he's doing is terrific. No, I just try to write what pleases me and not worry about traditions and such. I try as much as possible in my whole life to do things that I find fulfilling and, consequently, pleasurable. I don't think in an historical way. There isn't a day in my life that I don't realize how lucky I am. I'm lucky to have spent so much of my life doing something I enjoy and which I seem to be good at.

Maybe instead of talking about the "Good Old Days," we can talk about the "Good New Days."
I think I'm lucky in that I don't think about *what do I think about*. If that makes sense. I don't go to the theater to find out what my opinion is. I'm very lucky in that the world that I work in, as a writer, is not an "ageist" world. We all are just *doing*, not thinking about what is past or what is ahead.

Engaging Audiences

Introduction

Since public concerts began centuries ago, engaging audiences has been a concern. Every generation of composers, performers, and concert music-lovers seems to be concerned that theirs will be the last and that their beloved art form will soon cease to exist. Nevertheless, audiences for classical music have enjoyed longer lives than those for other musical genres.

But how does one engage today's younger generations with "classical" music? Many tried-and-true approaches remain valid: professional orchestras offering young people's concerts, public school music programs, college courses open to non-music majors, participatory community music programs, and more. Performers—especially conductors, chamber musicians, and solo pianists—are increasingly expected to speak directly to their audiences about the music they are performing. Their remarks forge connections with audience members, who then may be more responsive to the music being performed.

Today, podcasts, YouTube videos, flashmob performances of Beethoven, and other postmodern forms of expression bring historic music to new audiences. In their interviews, Eugenia Zukerman employs television as her medium for engaging audiences; 'cellist Steven Isserlis embraces making film documentaries and writing children's books. Peter Schickele, the well-known musical satirist, utilizes humor. The means and opportunities for engaging audiences remain today as wide and limitless as the tools of media and the human imagination (Fig. 1).

Michael Saffle

© The Author(s) 2018
J. C. Tibbetts et al. (eds.), *Performing Music History*,
https://doi.org/10.1007/978-3-319-92471-7_11

Eugenia Zukerman: "Audiences like to Know About the Music You're Playing, and They like to Know It from the Performer"

John C. Tibbetts
17 October 1986, Kansas City, Missouri, and 6 October 2016, New York City.

As a means of disseminating music, television has become a new kind of musical instrument. The overwhelming importance of mediated music has often been slighted, overlooked, or dismissed by critics and historians. But the media cannot be ignored. Radio, TV, and—increasingly—the Internet are the concert halls of the present *and* the future. Consider the popularity of Metropolitan Opera digital broadcasts: where once we had only sound, via radio, today we have sight, sound, and supertitles to explain it all. Consider

Fig. 1 Eugenia Zukerman in 2017

Ken Burns's *Jazz* documentaries for public television. These are but a few examples. And today, music itself is often composed with the internet in mind.

For biographical information about Eugenia Zukerman, please see her interview in "A Clutch of Instruments" earlier in this volume.

In the following conversations, Zukerman talks about her years on television and her many encounters with classical performers.

JOHN C. TIBBETTS: It seems that you've gone where no person has gone before: You've brought the arts to a mass-audience via commercial, network television. Congratulations!
EUGENIA ZUKERMAN: I am not the one to be congratulated, but thank you! But really, it wasn't me. It was a very far-seeing individual named [Robert] Shad Northshield, who's the head of *CBS Sunday Morning*, and he brought the arts to that program. In fact, Northshield accosted me and said, I have a job for you, you're gonna do it, you're gonna love it! He had seen me on several TV shows and heard me play in concert, and had read my novel that came out in 1981, called *Deceptive Cadence*, set in the world of classical music. At the same time I had not seen *Sunday Morning*, and he said, well, check it out! In fact, he and I just had our fifth anniversary lunch together [in 1986], because I really am forever grateful to him for bringing me into this world, and allowing me to be enriched by it.

Was it Charles Kuralt who had been instrumental in that, or your producer?
It was Northshield, the executive producer of the program. Of course, it's been a real pleasure to be associated with Kuralt and to work with him and to just be around him, because he's a very inspiring man. But I think CBS has to be saluted for putting the arts on a nationally broadcast, network program. The arts are *news*, the arts are part of what is a lifeblood of a country, not something extra that is tacked on at the end. And I have found that what that program does so wonderfully is allow the arts to speak for themselves. There is not a great deal of narrative gobbledy-gook that goes with it. As I travel, playing concerts, and talking with people, I hear that television made a terrific mistake in the past by not respecting the intelligence of its viewers.

Your television broadcast packages are how long, generally?
Eight minutes is the very shortest. We've gone to fifteen. We've even done half an hour.

As a broadcaster myself, I know that two minutes for a television arts package is regarded as a generous length of time. Fifteen? I can scarcely believe it!
Again, the arts are not for the elite; the arts are for the informed; and you best inform the viewers not by somehow lecturing them, or pandering to them, or spoon-feeding them. The format of *Sunday Morning* is so wonderful, because you hear the artist play, and you also get to know them, so it's kind of a double reward. Television has brought all kinds of music to the American public!

Let me guess—after some initial reserve, they must just welcome you, right? I mean, a "Come into my laboratory!" sort of thing.
Well, I think, being a musician and a performer, I know what *not* to ask.

Let's run down the list and talk about some of the people you've done profiles on. Sticking to music, of course.
Let me tell you my very first experience, which was a trial by fire. My very first interview was with Virgil Thomson, who is one of the great icons of twentieth century American music—world music, really. He's a man who is hard of hearing, and he's a little feisty—absolutely terrific, but a little feisty. I had read his books and was very well prepared, but also very much in awe of this man and his life. As a writer, he's superb. So I went into the interview, and I think the very first question was something like, "What was it like living in Paris in the 1920s with all the great writers?" And he misheard me, and he said, "You made that all up!" He had heard something totally different. We proceeded to have the strangest interview, because he didn't quite catch what I was saying. But then we got on very well and it was fine; but I thought: can it be this difficult?

Wow, where do you go from there?
I don't know! I guess you ask a different question, go at it in a different way, obliquely. Remember, Thomson was the one who gave the music world some wonderful insights, some wonderful lines, like "Hearing Heifetz play Mozart was like watching the *Queen Elizabeth* berth to the Staten Island ferry slip." Or "Hearing Wanda Landowska play the harpsichord was like experiencing a silver shower of needles."

Did the camera bother Thomson at all?
He wasn't too comfortable with it. But we got some wonderful shots. And I also got to interview Aaron Copland about his friend Thomson. Which was very interesting, because Copland's memory of the present is not very keen, but his memory of the past is absolutely—or was, five years ago—absolutely sensational. I have done pieces on people for whom I have such a reverence that I can hardly speak when I walk into the room, like Segovia, or [violinists] Nathan Milstein and Isaac Stern. In fact, my involvement in the show varies from time to time. *Sunday Morning* is just wonderful at allowing me to fit my own schedule, rather than the other way around.

How large is your crew?
Our crews are very small. We are absolutely bare-bones. We only have one camera, and I have a producer, and a soundman, and a cameraman. It's just the three of us—or four of us. How many? "She can't count, but she can play the flute!"

Typically, you're given how much time for a story. Because these are not just one-day shoots you're talking about?
That varies a lot. For example, I did a piece on pianists Mischa and Cipa Dichter, and it was one of the more fun pieces, because it came at a time when I scheduled

to be at the Aspen Festival. We had a lot of hanging-out time there, and the producer had a lot of hanging-out time, and we got some wonderful footage of informal stuff, like hiking, and things like that. Stories can be shot over a period of months. Sometimes they are brief, maybe one or two months. I just interviewed [pianist] Leon Fleischer in Boston, having begun this piece nearly a year ago (Fig. 2).

Have you kept video copies of all these interviews?
[laughs] I am not an organized human being! I was thinking the other day I should have catalogued all of this, et cetera, and I'm about to launch into trying to organize some of it. But I figure I've done somewhere between forty and fifty pieces for *Sunday Morning*.

It seems you've inspired other musicians to talk to the public, some of whom I've met and talked with, like pianist Israela Margalit, who has done some public television. And pianist Robert Guralnick, who walks onto the concert platform dressed as the Abbé Liszt, talking, playing, and performing Liszt's life.
Well, I think that we're looking for a variety of ways to inform the public. The traditional format of concert-going has been around for several hundred years, and

Fig. 2 Eugenia Zukerman on location in Cracow for a CBS broadcast

people are now exploring ways of changing it. I myself note a difference in an audience's response to me when I speak to them and when I don't. They like to know about the music you're playing, and they like to hear about it from the performer; so if I can say something interesting about the piece before I play it, it's much more interesting for an audience than reading program notes; the lights are never right for notes, the notes are distracting, etc. You have to make the music come alive! I have to admit I have an ambivalence about all this, because there's a part of me that would like the music to speak for itself. We do, however, live in the age of personality, and in fact I recently played a concert in California and didn't speak to the audience. Someone came up to me afterward and said, "You know, I thought you were very rude. You came out there, and you didn't even say 'Good evening, ladies and gentleman.'" I think about this and I wonder myself, sometimes, is this classical music business *The Tonight Show*, or is it a concert? The little voices, those of Mozart and Schubert and Bach, saying, "Do you have to do that to play my music?"

Do you have to restrain yourself from asking a musician, maybe, a question that a mass audience might consider irrelevant? Do you have to ride herd on yourself?
We don't always use the material that we have, of course, because we don't want to be arcane, or esoteric. But we do find that our listeners can be interested in technical matters. An example that comes to mind is a piece I did on the Soviet Émigré Orchestra, and I asked the leader to explain the difference between the "Russian Sound" and the "Western Sound" on the violin. He was able to give an answer that a lot of people commented on, explaining differences in the employment of vibrato, for example. I truly believe that people like to know *how a performer does things*. They want to know how it works.

Have you encountered some nay-sayers about this approach?
No. In fact—and I know this is totally, outrageously unique—*Sunday Morning* encourages interesting pieces. I go to them with ideas, they come to me with ideas, and many of my ideas get done. And I've done some very unusual pieces, like a piece on a deaf dancer. And that was very moving, very emotionally satisfying. And informative.

Do you see other networks being influenced by what CBS has been doing?
[laughs] I am not a TV watcher! I'm a grave embarrassment to *Sunday Morning*, because often I don't get a chance to watch it! The show comes on at a time when I'm with my children, or I'm on an airplane to a concert. I do know the people who watch *Sunday Morning* are a very special audience, and they get a lot from it. There are many people who say to me—and this is heretical, maybe!—but they say, "*Sunday Morning* is, for me, like going to church. I have given up going to church, but I watch that program, because it's got everything in it."

Moments ago, you mentioned a dance piece you learned from. I'm curious about other aspects of the world of arts and entertainment that you explored without

having had any prior knowledge, where it was a real learning experience, maybe a startling one.
Well, I've done some visual arts pieces. I did something on the painter Willem De Kooning [1904–1997], which was fascinating.

Are there circumstances when you become part of the story, maybe as a performer?
I've been in quite a number of pieces. I played with flutist Jean-Pierre Rampal on a piece I did about him as part of a piece I did on Bach, we put on camera something from a Bach concert of mine at the New York Public Library. But I'm not interested in having a piece done about me on *Sunday Morning*—although, now that Beverly Sills is one of our commentators, I'd like to do a piece on her. That would be fun to do.

May I assume there's material on the tape-editing floor that we will never see— that you'll make sure we never see?
I don't remember any grave moments of embarrassment. Although sometimes I help my colleagues in the cutting of musical segments, so that, you know, we select a take of a particular passage that sounds best, you know …?

Isn't that amazing, watching video editors at work?
Oh, they are brilliant! They are the ones who really make it all happen!

Finally, how you would assess your work—not as a performer, but as a broadcaster and interlocutor between the arts and a public? What do you think you do best, and what are some of the things you're still working on?
I always think about trying to do better. I feel that I have very high standards, and I feel that every once in a while, I manage to meet them. You know, there are one or two concerts in a year I think, wow, I did something special. And the same for the pieces I do for *Sunday Morning*. I am a good listener. It's my job to listen. And if something opens up that I hadn't been expecting, I have to be sharp enough to follow it, instead of just thinking about the next question. That's really tough. In a way, my training as a musician is very helpful, because I'm a good listener.

Steven Isserlis: "I Want to Bring Music to Younger People"

John C. Tibbetts
29 November 2016, London

For biographical information about Steven Isserlis, please refer to his interview in "A Clutch of Instruments" earlier in this volume.

JOHN C. TIBBETTS: In our previous conversations we've talked primarily about the 'cello—

STEPHEN ISSERLIS: —and why not?!

Right. We also talked about your relationship with György Kurtág. But how about some other issues at hand? What about how media are increasingly central to your work and your outreach?

I wouldn't say such things are increasingly central, as you say, but yes, I've done many videos and/or television programs about this and that. And more and more of my performances are filmed, of course.

Speaking of media outreach, I see you're working on a number of music festivals.

Well, I am the Artistic Director of just one festival—or actually, a seminar. It's the International Musicians Seminar at Prussia Cove, Cornwall. That's an important part of my musical life—a way for me, and for several other like-minded musicians, to pass on the musical values that we imbibed from Sándor Végh and others. As you know, Végh was a wonderful musician who emphasized the importance of playing in a free, natural way—just follow the contour of every phrase in order to bring out its character. He has certainly been a major influence on my own approach to music, although not the only one. Anyway, I try to be at Prussia Cove twice a year, every year, giving classes and playing chamber music with young people.

Steven, you answer a number of death-defying questions in Why Beethoven Threw the Stew, *such as "Why did Bach's son call him 'The Old Wig,' "How did Mozart keep his pigtails styled," and, above all, "Why in heaven's name did Beethoven throw the stew!"* Thank you!

You're welcome! I wrote the book for my son, really, when he was about nine years old. He was becoming interested in the lives of the great composers, and I couldn't find exactly the sort of book I wanted for him. So I thought I'd try to write one myself!

You have an abiding interest in children, their music, and their education.

Yes, I work fairly regularly with children. Apart from the two books you mentioned, I've also written the texts for three musical fairy stories, with music by Anne Dudley. We've written three musical stories together, pieces to be played at children's concerts. They're all based on fairy stories, as you can tell from titles like "Little Red Violin," "Goldiepegs and the Three 'Cellos"; and "Cindercella!" They all involve a narrator and, respectively, violin/'cello, violin/three 'cellos, string quartet, and either piano or string orchestra accompaniment. I've given countless concerts for children. Of course, I'm keen to bring young people into the world of music for their sakes—but I also get involved in all these activities simply because they're fun! I love interacting with children. Their responses are always fresh and genuine, and sometimes very surprising. So I'm very gratified when I'm told that child has started to learn a musical instrument because of my books—that's a lovely feeling!

You made a film that seems tailor-made as an educational tool for viewers of all ages, yes?
You're talking about *Schumann's Lost Romance* [1997]. Jan Young's husband contacted me to work with her on it. She was head of [BBC's television] Channel 4, and she was working on a film about Schumann for Rhombus Television. She told me that Steve Ruggi was director and that I would be credited as "Presenter." From the start, we were to pursue the format of interviews, fictive footage, and documentary location work. So, it ended up being part documentary, part theatrical film, part performance film. Anton Lesser and Anna Farnworth portrayed Robert and Clara in the fictive sequences. And it was a wonderful opportunity for me to perform on camera [in black-and-white sequences] with Christoph Eschenbach and Joshua Bell with the Deutsche Kammerphilharmonie.

It's rather like you're in a detective story, isn't it?
Yes, I'm searching for clues as to what happened to Schumann's last 'Cello Romances that Clara had withheld from publication. And since then, they have gone missing.

During which time, you take us on a tour of Schumann's locations.
I'm on camera all the time. The viewer follows me as I travel to Germany and visit Schumann's last house in Düsseldorf, on Bilkerstrasse, but we couldn't go in. There was a 'cellist living there at the time. At Endenich, where Schumann spent his last years in the mental institute, we went to the second floor, where we think Schumann had his room. It was horrible to see how small it was, and how he must have suffered. What an awful way for a great man to end. And that he died by himself. When you read those notes by his doctor, Dr. Richarz, you realize Schumann was crazier than the letters reveal. It is all endlessly tragic and endlessly touching, because he was such a wonderful man, a good man.

It was great to see that Clara's biographer, Nancy Reich, is included in the film.
As I recall, it was my idea to bring in Nancy Reich to talk about Clara. She and I are on camera talking about Clara. Nancy was the "opposition," you know! As you can see on camera, Nancy and I don't quite see eye-to-eye on Clara. I can't stand Clara! She was horrible about Liszt, too, even when she was trying to help Robert. Horrible woman. But Nancy put out a good case for her and why she wanted to protect Schumann's reputation against some of those last works. I know Clara had a bad time with everything, with her father, then with her husband going mad, etc.

About those fictive sequences. I was fascinated by the concluding dialogue you have with "Clara."
It was my chance, in a way, to "talk" with Clara and ask her why she so disliked those last 'cello romances. We're in a modern setting, a café, but she's dressed in a nineteenth-century gown. Anna Farnsworth's dialogue was written out, but for my part, I wanted to improvise along with her. She states her case, that Clara wanted

to protect Robert from a public's dislike of what she thought was second-rate music. But I point out that his last works are gaining a new public these days.

That scenes ends with a kind of "wink," doesn't it? I mean, she doesn't outright admit those pieces are irretrievably lost ...
That's right. She admits she burned them, but not before she *may* have made a fair copy of them.... As she gazes into the camera, the question remains unanswered.

Peter Schickele and P.D.Q. Bach: *"Missa Hilarious!"*

John C. Tibbetts
February and March 2017, Kansas City, Missouri

Among the best-known and most successful musicological parodists of all time, Peter Schickele made a name for himself through his alter ego "P.D.Q. Bach," whose name hints at C.Ph.E. (i.e., Carl Philip Emanuel) Bach, the most famous of Bach's twenty children. This last and least respectable of his offspring is credited with composing oratorios, cantatas, orchestral works, motets, and madrigals: anything and everything that traditional musicologists love to discover—in Schickele's case, in the bottoms of dust bins and other unlikely places. P.D.Q. "is the only dead composer who still accepts commissions." Recordings of this imaginary composer's music include *The Wurst of P.D.Q. Bach*, *Oedipus Tex and Other Choral Calamities*, and *WTWP Classical Talkity-talk Radio* (Fig. 3).

For his appearance at a 2016 concert presented in New York City's Town Hall, the eighty-year old Peter Schickele arrived in a wheelchair. "As Mr. Schickele surely knows and undoubtedly intends," observed *New York Times* critic James R. Oestreich, "the wheelchair will draw laughs, the audience thinking it's part of the show." It was. The son of an agricultural economist and university professor, Schickele graduated from Swarthmore College and Juilliard. He earned an early reputation as music arranger for several pop stars, including Joan Baez, and he wrote and performed the music for the 1969 revue *Oh! Calcutta!* His credits also include several TV and film scores. Between 1990 and 1993 Schickele's recorded send-ups earned four Grammy Awards for Best Comedy Albums.

This conversation transpired via email and telephone from Professor Schickele's home in New York City.

JOHN C. TIBBETTS: When you introduce yourself to folks, which persona do you start out with these days: Professor Schickele or P.D.Q Bach?
PETER SCHICKELE: I never impersonate P.D.Q. Bach. When people sometimes ask to me to sign an autograph, to sign it "P.D.Q. Bach," I point out to them that that would be forgery. That's a felony! I certainly wouldn't engage in it.

Fig. 3 Peter Schickele and P.D.Q. Bach

But forgery was something, however, that P.D.Q. seems to have been adept at.
Well, you know, the laws weren't as strict in those days. So, no, I do have a sort
of Jekyll and Hyde personality, and I spend these days pretty much mostly on the
road inflicting P.D.Q. Bach's music on people.

That's when you get away from your home base in the little town of Hoople, North Dakota?
That's right! That's about it! Then summers I sort of reserve for Peter Schickele's music.

Your colleague, [conductor] Jorge Mester, insists that we know that in actuality you are a "very serious guy," a "really great composer for orchestra." That's a quote.
I've never liked the phrase "serious music" because it implies that all those great jazz and rock and folk musicians aren't serious—but they are. I just do a whole bunch of different kinds of music and I love it all.

Yet your background is so different from P.D.Q.'s! You're Juilliard trained, have studied with Roy Harris [1898–1979] and [Vincent] Persichetti, and worked as Composer-in-Residence on a Ford Foundation Grant—
—And yes, P.D.Q. was by all means the least of Johann Sebastian Bach's twenty-odd children! And I do mean, *odd*. P.D.Q. never had formal musical training. And he never let mediocrity stand in his way. Is that where you're going with this?

And we're not even sure when he lived and died!
No, we know definitively that he was born in 1807 and died in 1742. That's on his tomb!

Oh.... Of course, we love Pete Schickele's film scores, like Silent Running, *and cycles like* Knights of the Burning Pestle—*are there other works you'd like to tell me about?*
There aren't an awful lot of recordings, but one of the best is my First String Quartet, which is called *American Dreams*, which has been recorded for RCA Red Seal by the Audubon quartet. It's got a lot of jazz, and there's even a Navajo song in it. Quite a tremendous performance, I must say. And there's also a piece for flute and piano called *Spring Serenade* that's recorded on CRI. Things like that.

Look back, if you would ... how many years, now, have you and P.D.Q. been together?
It's been twenty-five "official years," coming up on twenty-six, since the first public concert in New York City's Town Hall. That was in April 1965. But the first sort of proto-P.D.Q. Bach concert was back when I was a student at Juilliard in 1959, majoring in composition. Jorge Mester and I were both students there. We were sitting around the cafeteria one day—I've always said that I majored in "cafeteria" at Juilliard; that's the only place I remember—and we would sit around talking about the funny things we liked to do in concerts or we'd seen in concerts. And one day, the guy who organized Juilliard's in-house concerts came and said, "Look, we've got this pianist who's been sick; he's only worked up half a program. Do you guys want to do the other half of the program?" So we thought we would write a Concerto for Horn and Hardart—there was a restaurant chain then

on the East Coast called "Horn and Hardart"—and so that first concert included the Concerto for Horn and Hardart and also a quodlibet, which is a pastiche piece, combining themes of different origins. Both of them, in somewhat varied form, ended up six years later on the first P.D.Q. record. These humorous concerts went on at both Juilliard and Aspen in the summer of 1959 with both Jorge and me. They became annual affairs. And so, by the time I did the first public concert in 1965, we'd worked out the format and some of the repertoire.

What is, exactly, a "hardart"?
It's an eighteenth-century instrument that doesn't exist today. We have to work with reconstructions that use plucked strings, a bicycle horn, a few whistles, and a cooking timer.

One of many unusual instruments, yes?
My favorites are the left-handed sewer flute and the Oscar Mayer wiener whistle.

When did you begin your Tarzan-like rope swinging?
I first made that entrance years before, at the Aspen summer program for composers in 1959. Jorge and I were both students there, and we put on a humorous concert at the Wheeler Opera House. I came down from the back of the balcony and sort of rolled over the railing of the balcony and dropped to the stage. Not every entrance I did after that was dangerous, but it became a bit of a tradition. At a certain point, it was time to start phasing the really dangerous ones out. We started trying different versions, like coming in on a bicycle.

I guess some of that early repertoire, like the "Beethoven Fifth Symphony Sportscast," was popular right away?
That's probably one of the most commonly requested things from the recordings. When we do it live, we use certain elements that we don't have on the recording. We often include cheerleaders, for example; there's an injury in the bass section; and we have instant replays. It gets a little more spectacular when we do it live. One of these days, I hope I can do it in the movies or on television and really do it from a real announcer's booth! That's the way it oughta be done!

It's no secret that classical musicians have wonderful senses of humor, but have you ever run into fans, musicians, conductors, in that field, who just either don't get it or are even violently opposed to your brand of humor?
A famous music educator once said to a friend of mine, "Peter Schickele makes fun of things that some of us hold sacred." Yes, there are people who have that attitude. I think most musicians recognize that mine is actually a satire of affection, and I think what a lot of people don't stop to think about is that most satirists make fun of what they like, not what they don't like. There's [comedian] Victor Borge, for example, who studied to be a concert pianist. I certainly was a fan, but I don't think of him as an influence exactly. A big part of his whole shtick was not getting around to playing, he'd be about to play and then he'd think of something

else to say. But I certainly enjoyed his act. I think you have to have an affinity for what you're doing a takeoff on; and you're going to have the most affinity for what you like.

Should we include Spike Jones as an influence?
Spike Jones was definitely a hero. I saw him do his act twice when I was a kid, once in Washington D.C. and once in Fargo. Years later, when I was playing somewhere in the L.A. area, a few members of his band came to my show and came backstage afterwards, which was a big thrill. Spike Jones was definitely the beginning of it all for me. And we can't forget Anna Russell, who actually had classical opera training. She studied at the Royal Academy of Music, but she never let that stand in her way! Classical music is a great source for jokes. Orchestra musicians are tremendous purveyors of jokes! You know, I never play with an orchestra without going away with a new viola joke these days! For example, "What's the difference between a violin and a viola?" "A viola burns longer!" One of the best ones is, "The conductor gets up on the podium at the rehearsal, and one of the inside chair violists is crying. 'What's wrong?,' asks the conductor. And the violist says, 'The second oboe player loosened one of my tuning pegs.' And the conductor says, 'Well, that's pretty juvenile behavior, but you seem to be overreacting a bit. Why are you crying?' And the violist says, 'He won't tell me which one [sob]!'"

Now: is Peter Schickele himself still composing?
I recently had the pleasure of unearthing a new P.D.Q. Bach Piano Concerto, which is being performed in cities around the country. There are no current plans for a reissue of "Peter Schickele" compositions. You asked about *Knight of the Burning Pestle*[1] and my soundtrack score for *Silent Running* [1972]. Maybe we'll put *Knights* into the hopper. And you may or may not know that *Silent Running* has been reissued by the Intrada label. It's available at screenarchives.com. My Third Symphony has never been recorded—more for the hopper! As for my favorite compositions, that's a difficult question, just because I've been writing music for so long that I've written so much of it. It's hard to pick a favorite. I guess I would pick my First Symphony as one of my favorites. And I would be very happy if musicians of the future played my chamber music.

Finally, how do you spend your time when off the concert stage?
I split my time between a wonderful little house in the Catskills and a wonderful apartment in New York City overlooking the Hudson River. I do some writing, a little traveling from time to time. I'm a big fan of movies, so that's always a treat, I watch them at home with my wife, Susan, or we go out. I recently went to see a restored copy of *Beat the Devil*, which is a great John Huston movie from 1954. I also go to concerts pretty frequently.

---

[1]Incidental music for the five-act play (1607), the first parody dramatic work in English, by Elizabethan author Francis Beaumont (1584–1616).

Further Reading

Antokoletz, Elliott, Victoria Fischer, and Benjamin Suchoff, eds. *Bartók Perspectives: Man, Composer, and Ethnologist*. Oxford: Oxford University Press, 2000.

Auner, Joseph. *Music in the Twentieth and Twenty-First Centuries*. New York: W. W. Norton, 2013.

Barzun, Jacques. *Berlioz and the Romantic Century*, 3rd ed. New York: Columbia University Press, 1969.

Benestad, Finn, and Dag Schjulderup-egge. *Edvard Grieg: The Man and the Artist*, trans. William H. Halverson and Leland B. Sateren. Lincoln: University of Nebraska Press, 1988.

Blesh, Rudi, and Harriet Janis. *They All Played Ragtime: The True Story of an American Music*. New York: Alfred A. Knopf, 1950.

Bowers, Jane, and Judith Tick, eds. *Women Making Music: The Western Art Tradition, 1150–1950*. Urbana: University of Illinois Press, 1987.

Bukofzer, Manfred F. *Music in the Baroque Era*. New York: W. W. Norton, 1947.

Burkholder, J. Peter, Donald Jay Grout, and Claude V. Palisca. *A History of Western Music*, 9th ed. New York: W. W. Norton, 2014.

Cooke, Mervyn. *A History of Film Music*. Cambridge: Cambridge University Press, 2008.

Daverio, John. *Robert Schumann: Herald of a "New Poetic Age."* New York: Oxford University Press, 1997.

Dizikes, John. *Opera in America: A Cultural History*. New Haven: Yale University Press, 1993.

Driggs, Frank, and Chuck Haddix. *Kansas City Jazz: From Ragtime to Bebop—A History*. Oxford: Oxford University Press, 2006.

Everett, William A., and Raul R. Laird, eds. *The Cambridge Companion to the Musical*, 3rd ed. Cambridge: Cambridge University Press, 2017.

Fabbri, Paolo. *Monteverdi*, trans. Tim Carter. Cambridge: Cambridge University Press, 2007.

Fink, Robert. *Repeating Ourselves: Minimal Music as Cultural Practice*. Berkeley: University of California Press, 2005.

Fischer, Jens Malte. *Gustav Mahler*. New Haven, CT: Yale University Press, 2013.

Gardiner, John Eliot. *Music in the Castle of Heaven: A Portrait of Johann Sebastian Bach*, 4th ed. London, UK: Penguin, 2014.

Giddons, Gary. *Visions of Jazz*. New York: Oxford University Press, 1998.

Griffiths, Paul. *Modern Music and After*, 3rd ed. New York: Oxford University Press, 2011.

Haskell, Harry. *The Early Music Revival: A History*, new edition. New York: Dover, 1996.

Hitchcock, H. Wiley, with Kyle Gann. *Music in the United States: A Historical Introduction*, 4th ed. Upper Saddle River, NJ: Prentice Hall, 2000.

© The Editor(s) (if applicable) and The Author(s) 2018
J. C. Tibbetts et al. (eds.), *Performing Music History*,
https://doi.org/10.1007/978-3-319-92471-7

Johnson, Graham, and Richard Stokes. *A French Song Companion*. New York: Oxford University Press, 2002.

Jones, David Wyn. *The Life of Haydn*. Cambridge: Cambridge University Press, 2009.

Keates, Jonathan. *Handel: The Man and His Music*. London, UK: Random House, 2010.

Kramer, Lawrence. *Musical Meaning: Toward a Critical History*. Berkeley, CA: University of California Press, 2002.

Lockwood, Lewis. *Beethoven: The Music and the Life*. New York: W. W. Norton, 2005.

Loesser, Arthur. *Men, Women & Pianos: A Social History*. New York: Dover, 1954.

Longyear, Rey M. *Nineteenth-Century Romanticism in Music*, 3rd ed. Englewood Cliffs, NJ: Prentice Hall, 1988.

Millington, Barry. *Wagner*, rev. ed. Princeton: Princeton University Press, 1992.

Moore, Gerald. *The Unashamed Accompanist*, rev. ed. London: Franklin Watts, 1985.

Music in the Air—A History of Classical Music on Television. DVD, Region 1, 2012.

Newbould, Brian. *Schubert: The Music and the Man*, new ed. Berkeley and Los Angeles: University of California Press, 1997.

Nichols, Roger. *The Life of Debussy*. Cambridge: Cambridge University Press, 1998.

Palmer, Tony. *All You Need Is Love: The Story of Popular Music*. New York: Viking, 1976.

Parakilas, James. *Piano Roles: A New History of the Piano*. New Haven, CT: Yale University Press, 2002.

Reynolds, William Jenson, David W. Music, and Milburn Price. *A Survey of Christian Hymnody*, 4th ed. Carol Stream, IL: Hope Publishing, 1991.

Rooley, Anthony. *Performance: Revealing the Orpheus Within*. Shaftesbury, UK: Element Books, 1991.

Rosen, Charles. *The Classical Style: Haydn, Mozart, Beethoven*, expanded ed. New York: W. W. Norton, 1998.

Ross, Alex. *The Rest Is Noise: Listening to the Twentieth Century*. New York: Farrar, Straus, and Giroux, 2007.

Sachs, Curt. *The History of Musical Instruments*. New York: Dover, 2012.

Saulnier, Daniel. *Gregorian Chant: A Guide to the History and Liturgy*, trans. Mary Berry. Brewster, MA: Paraclete Press, 2009.

Schickele, Peter. *The Definitive Biography of P.D.Q. Bach*. New York: Random House, 1977.

Schwartz, Elliott, Barney Childs, and Jim Fox, eds. *Contemporary Composers on Contemporary Music*. Expanded ed. New York: Da Capo, 1998.

Slobin, Mark, ed. *Retuning Culture: Musical Changes in Central and Eastern Europe*. Durham, NC: Duke University Press, 1996.

Solomon, Maynard. *Mozart: A Life*. New York: Harper Perennial, 2005.

Taruskin, Richard. *Oxford History of Western Music*, 5 vols. Oxford: Oxford University Press, 2009.

Tibbetts, John C. *Composers in the Movies: Studies in Musical Biography*. New Haven: Yale University Press, 2005.

Treitler, Leo. *With Voice and Pen: Coming to Know Medieval Song and How It Was Made*. Oxford: Oxford University Press, 2003.

Watson, Derek. *Liszt*. New York: Oxford University Press, 2001.

Yang, Hon-Lun, and Michael Saffle, eds. *China and the West: Music, Representation, Reception*. Ann Arbor: University of Michigan Press, 2016.

Zamoyski, Adam. *Chopin: A New Biography*. New York: Doubleday, 1980.

Index

Doctorow, E.L., 241
dodecaphony, 240
Dohnányi, Ernst von, 217, 218
Doktor Faustus (novel), 120
Domingo, Placido, 186, 189, 191
Dowland, John, 25, 26, 28, 30, 34, 36
    First Book of Songs, 29
    "Flow my Tears", 29
Downbeat (magazine), 255
dramma per musica. See opera seria
Dresden, 58, 184
Dressler, Marie, 251
drums, 255
Dublin, 67
Dudley, Anne, 334
Dufay, Guillaume, 39
Dun, Tan, 283
Duparc, Henri, 203, 206
Dussek, Jan Ladislav, 83
Düsseldorf, 5, 187
    Schumann's last house on Bilderstrasse, 335
DVDs (digital video disks), 317
Dvořák, Antonin, 209, 213, 214, 216
    Concerto for piano and orchestra, 214
dynamics, 27, 46

E

Early Music (journal), xi
Early Music Movement (EMM), 9, 33, 37, 38
Ebb, Fred. *See* Kander, John
Ebsen, Christian Ludolf ("Buddy"), 308
Edinburgh, Scotland, 304
Edison cylinder machine, 241
editions of music, 134
Eichendorff, Joseph von, 149
Eldridge, Roy ("Little Jazz"), 256
Eleanor of Aquitaine, 15
electric keyboards, 325
electronic music, 47
eleventh chords, 203
embellishments, 38, 49
EMI and EMI Group Limited, 37, 299,
    301–303
EMM. *See* Early Music Movement (EMM)
Endenich, Germany, 335
England, 8, 15, 17, 24, 26, 34, 35, 37, 46, 52,
    60, 64, 76, 97, 105, 233, 257
English Baroque Soloists (ensemble), 58, 61,
    121, 124
English (language), 12, 65, 66, 78, 285
English Opera Group, 98
Erard (manufacturing firm), 127
Erfurt, 96
Eschenbach, Christoph, 335

ethnomusicology, 217
Europe, 7, 11, 19, 23, 24, 27, 29, 41, 50, 90,
    92, 159, 171, 180, 198, 270, 287,
    296, 305
Everett, William, 1, 5, 275, 285, 286, 290

F

Fach (voice type), 42*See also* contralto
    (voice); countertenor (voice); mez-
    zo-soprano (voice); soprano (voice),
    tenor (voice); white voice (without
    vibrato)
fantasias, 9
Fargo, North Dakota, 5, 340
Farkas, Philip, 95
Farnworth, Anna, 335
Farrell, Eileen, 56
Fauré, Gabriel, 205, 206
Ferber, Edna, 251, 298
fermata, 315
Ferris, David, 5
Fibich, Zdeněk, 216
Field, John, 137
films, 185–187, 289, 292, 294–296, 309, 313,
    314, 317, 318
film scores, 291, 316, 336, 338
Finale (computer program), 325
fingering, 48, 90
Firing Line (TV program), 52
Firkušný, Rudolf, 3, 178, 209–211
Fischer-Dieskau, Dietrich, 231, 235
Fischer, Ivan, 188
flashmobs, 327
Fleischer, Edwin, 133
Fleisher, Leon, 331
Florida, 203, 206
Florida State University, 264
Floyd, Carlisle
    Susannah, 4, 240, 264, 266
    "Ain't It a Pretty Night?", 265
    "The Trees on the Mountain", 266
    Willy Stark, 266
flute, 3, 19, 45, 54, 55, 57, 58, 69, 81–85, 99,
    142, 152, 199, 211, 231, 275, 277,
    330, 338, 339
Foley, John Miles, 11
folk song, 177, 181, 194, 196, 198, 217
Fordham University, 5
Forrester, Maureen Kathleen Stewart, 3, 178,
    196
forte and *fortissimo* (dynamic markings), 118,
    123
fortepiano, 3, 78, 107, 121, 123, 125, 126,
    135, 136

CPSIA information can be obtained
at www.ICGtesting.com
Printed in the USA
LVHW081933151118
597265LV00002B/86/P